Socio-Technical Networks

Science and Engineering Design

Socio-Technical Networks

Science and Engineering Design

Edited by
Fei Hu
Ali Mostashari
Jiang Xie

CRC Press
Taylor & Francis Group
Boca Raton London New York

CRC Press is an imprint of the
Taylor & Francis Group, an **Informa** business
AN AUERBACH BOOK

CRC Press
Taylor & Francis Group
6000 Broken Sound Parkway NW, Suite 300
Boca Raton, FL 33487-2742

© 2011 by Taylor and Francis Group, LLC
CRC Press is an imprint of Taylor & Francis Group, an Informa business

No claim to original U.S. Government works

International Standard Book Number: 978-1-4398-0980-8 (Hardback)

Library of Congress Cataloging-in-Publication Data

Socio-technical networks : science and engineering design / editors, Fei Hu, Ali Mostashari, Jiang Xie.
      p. cm.
      Summary: "While there are some sporadic journal articles on socio-technical networks, readers need an integrated resource discussing the STN design. This book provides a complete introduction to the fundamentals of socio-technical networks, including its definition, historical background, and significance. The authors provide basic network architecture from the OSI model perspective and address some challenging design issues. The text also covers all major network protocol design in a typical STN and the application of wireless networks such as sensor networks, WiMAX, etc. in STN access. The book presents STN case studies from healthcare, virtual communities"-- Provided by publisher.
      Summary: "This book provides a complete introduction to the fundamentals of socio-technical networks, including its definition, historical background, and significance. The authors provide basic network architecture from the OSI model perspective and address some challenging design issues. The text covers all major network protocol design in a typical STN and the application of wireless networks in STN access. The last part presents case studies from healthcare, virtual communities, and power plant management"-- Provided by publisher.
      Includes bibliographical references and index.
      ISBN 978-1-4398-0980-8 (hardback)
      1. Computer networks. 2. Command and control systems--Design. 3. Online social networks--Design. 4. Information networks--Design. I. Hu, Fei. II. Mostashari, Ali. III. Xie, Jiang. IV. Title: Sociotechnical networks.

TK5105.5.S6325 2010
004.6--dc22
      2010033013

Visit the Taylor & Francis Web site at
http://www.taylorandfrancis.com

and the CRC Press Web site at
http://www.crcpress.com

To Fang Yang and Gloria Yang Hu ......
To Ali's family ......
To Linda's family

Contents

vii

Preface

Needless to say, one of the hottest research fields across computer networking and social sciences is sociotechnical networks (STNs). In general when we discuss sociotechnical networks in this book, we are referring to systems such as the Internet, power grids, and transportation networks enabled by data communication networks and telecommunication networks. Thus, the focus is on the technological network and understanding the complexities of designing, managing, and operating such networks using social/organization networks. This sets the focus apart from work process design or ergonomics, and concentrates on the design and architecture of large-scale technological networks that are influenced by and in turn impact a social network of people and organizations with different goals and values.

Here, we define a sociotechnical system as a dynamic entity comprised of interdependent and interacting social/institutional and physical/technological parts, characterized by inputs, processes/actions, and outputs/products. Sociotechnical systems are usually composed of a group of related component and subsystems, for which the degree and nature of the relationships is not always clearly understood. They have large, long-lived impacts that span over a wide geographical area. Many have integrated subsystems coupled through feedback loops and are affected by social, political, and economic issues.

Examples of systems that fall within this category are transportation networks, telecommunication systems, energy systems, the World Wide Web, water allocation systems, financial networks, etc. Such systems have wide-ranging impacts, and are characterized by different types and levels of complexity, uncertainty, and risk, as well as a large number of stakeholders.

This book will mainly cover the following aspects in STNs:

1. *Fundamentals of Sociotechnical Networks:* In this part, we will introduce the basic concept of STN including its definition, historical background, and significance.
2. *STN Models:* Social Network Analysis (SNA) is a mathematical method for "connecting the dots." SNA allows us to map and measure complex, and sometimes covert, human groups and organizations.

3. *Privacy and Security:* We will cover the following topics: risk models, trust models, and privacy preserving protocols. Those topics will assist in defining the parameters and processes for reducing risk, managing security, and maintaining continuity of operations for critical infrastructure systems in vulnerable social network regions.

4. *STN applications:* We will explain the STN applications in some popular fields, such as healthcare, virtual community, and others.

This book can serve as a good technical reference for college students, researchers, and social scientists. To the best of our knowledge, up to this point this is the first book that covers the comprehensive knowledge on STNs.

About the Authors

Dr. Fei Hu is currently an associate professor in the Department of Electrical and Computer Engineering at the University of Alabama (main campus), Tuscaloosa, Alabama. His research interests are sensor networks, wireless networks, network security, and their applications in biomedicine. His research has been supported by the U.S. National Science Foundation, Cisco, Sprint, and other sources. He obtained his Ph.D. degrees at Tongji University (Shanghai) in the field of signal processing (in 1999), and at Clarkson University (New York) in the field of electrical and computer engineering (in 2002). He obtained his M.S. and B.S. degrees in telecommunication engineering from Shanghai Tiedao University in 1996 and 1993, respectively. He has published over 100 journal/conference papers and book (chapters).

Dr. Ali Mostashari is currently the director of the Center for Complex Adaptive Sociotechnological Systems (COMPASS), and an associate professor (Research) at the School of Systems and Enterprises, Stevens Institute of Technology, Hoboken, New Jersey. He obtained his Ph.D. in engineering systems/technology, and management and policy from the Massachusetts Institute of Technology in 2005. He was a Young Global Leader Nominee 2008. He was also listed as Asia 21 Young Leader by the Asia Society (2007). His research focus is complex sociotechnical network design.

Dr. Jiang (Linda) Xie received her B.E. degree from Tsinghua University, Beijing, China, in 1997, M.Phil. degree from Hong Kong University of Science and Technology in 1999, and M.S. and Ph.D. degrees from the Georgia Institute of Technology in 2002 and 2004, respectively, all in electrical engineering. She is currently an assistant professor with the Department of Electrical and Computer Engineering at the University of North Carolina at Charlotte. She was a graduate research assistant in the Broadband and Wireless Networking Laboratory (BWN-LAB) at the Georgia Institute of Technology from August 1999 to April 2004. She is also a member of the IEEE Communications Society, IEEE Women in Engineering, the Association of Computing Machinery (ACM), and Eta Kappa Nu (ECE Honor Society).

Contributors List

Todd Aycock
ECE Department
University of Alabama
Tuscaloosa, Alabama

Jian Cai
Peking University
Beijing, China

Stefan Parry Carmien
Department of NeuroEngineering
Fatronik-Tecnalia Foundation
San Sebastian, Spain

Jonathan Scott Corley
ECE Department
University of Alabama
Tuscaloosa, Alabama

Cameron Dale
School of Computing Science
Simon Fraser University
Burnaby, British Colombia,
Canada

Joshua Davenport
ECE Department
University of Alabama
Tuscaloosa, Alabama

Justin Floyd
ECE Department
University of Alabama
Tuscaloosa, Alabama

Xiaohong Guan
System Engineering Institute
Xi'an Jiaotong University
Xi'an, China

Qi Hao
ECE Department
University of Alabama
Tuscaloosa, Alabama

Justin Headley
ECE Department
University of Alabama
Tuscaloosa, Alabama

Gabriel Hillard
ECE Department
University of Alabama
Tuscaloosa, Alabama

Fei Hu
ECE Department
University of Alabama
Tuscaloosa, Alabama

Nan Jing
University of Southern California
Los Angeles, California

Keli Kohoue
ECE Department
University of Alabama
Tuscaloosa, Alabama

Jiangchuan Liu
School of Computing Science
Simon Fraser University
Burnaby, British Colombia,
Canada

Stephen C-Y. Lu
University of Southern California
Los Angeles, California

Li Ma
School of Computing Science
Simon Fraser University
Burnaby, British Colombia,
Canada

Ali Mostashari
School of Systems and Enterprises
Stevens Institute of Technology
Hoboken, New Jersey

Sadith Osseni
ECE Department
University of Alabama
Tuscaloosa, Alabama

Qindong Sun
System Engineering Institute
Xi'an Jiaotong University
Xi'an, China

Ryan Andrew Taylor
ECE Department
University of Alabama
Tuscaloosa, Alabama

Haiyang Wang
School of Computing Science
Simon Fraser University
Burnaby, British Colombia
Canada

Leting Wu
Department of Software and
  Information Systems
College of Computing and Informatics
University of North Carolina at
  Charlotte
Charlotte, North Carolina

Xintao Wu
Department of Software and
  Information Systems
College of Computing and Informatics
University of North Carolina at
  Charlotte
Charlotte, North Carolina

Yao Wu
ECE Department
University of Alabama
Tuscaloosa, Alabama

Ling Xu
ECE Department
University of Alabama
Tuscaloosa, Alabama

Xiaowei Ying
Department of Software and
  Information Systems
College of Computing and Informatics
University of North Carolina at
  Charlotte
Charlotte, North Carolina

Dong Zhang
ECE Department
University of Alabama
Tuscaloosa, Alabama

Junzhou Zhao
System Engineering Institute
Xi'an Jiaotong University
Xi'an, China

Qinghua Zheng
System Engineering Institute
Xi'an Jiaotong University
Xi'an, China

Yadong Zhou
System Engineering Institute
Xi'an Jiaotong University
Xi'an, China

Chapter 1

Sociotechnical Systems: A Conceptual Introduction

Ali Mostashari

Contents

1.1 Introduction

The term *sociotechnical systems* is generally used for systems where human beings and organizations interact with technology. However, within the literature, there are many different interpretations of what aspect of the interactions between the social and technological parts constitute a sociotechnical study. In this chapter we will explore the definitions of sociotechnical networks within the context of this book and identify the various perspectives through which they will be analyzed in subsequent chapters. In general, when we discuss sociotechnical networks in this book, we are referring to systems such as the Internet, power grids and transportation networks enabled by data communication networks, and telecommunication networks. Thus, the focus is on the technological network and understanding the complexities of designing, managing, and operating such networks using social/organization networks. This sets the focus apart from work process design or ergonomics, and concentrates on the design and architecture of large-scale technological networks that are influenced and that in turn impact a social network of people and organizations with different goals and values.

Here we define a sociotechnical system as a dynamic entity comprised of interdependent and interacting social/institutional and physical/technological parts, characterized by inputs, processes/actions, and outputs/products.

Sociotechnical systems are usually composed of a group of related component and subsystems, for which the degree and nature of the relationships are not always clearly understood. They have large, long-lived impacts that span over a wide geographical area. Many have integrated subsystems coupled through feedback loops and are affected by social, political, and economic issues (Mostashari and Sussman, 2009).

Examples of systems that fall within this category are transportation networks, telecommunication systems, energy systems, the World Wide Web, water allocation systems, financial networks, etc. Such systems have wide-ranging impacts, and are characterized by different types and levels of complexity, uncertainty, risk, as well as large number of stakeholders (Mostashari, 2005).

1.2 Tightly Coupled Social and Technological Hierarchies

A sociotechnological system/network normally consists of at least two (and sometimes three) interacting and tightly coupled networks of components. One layer includes the physical/technological components of the system, and the other layer the social/institutional components, which are usually connected through an information network (Figure 1.1). Within each of these layers the components relate to each other in a hierarchy (Figures 1.2).

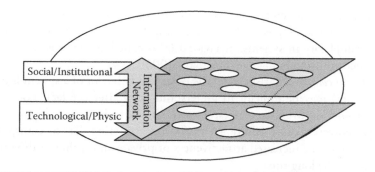

Figure 1.1   Sociotechnical system layers.

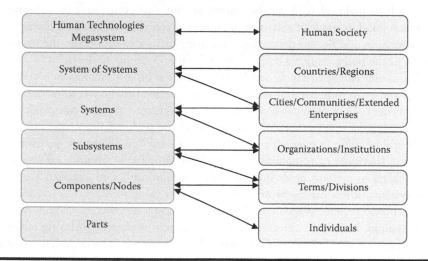

Figure 1.2   Hierarchies within the social/institutional and physical/technological layers. (Earll M. Murman and Thomas J. Allen, "Engineering systems: An Aircraft perspective." Engineering systems symposium, MIT, 2003.).

1.3 Characteristics of Sociotechnical Systems

In order to study and analyze a sociotechnical system, a deep understanding of each of these aspects is necessary. In the following paragraphs, we will look at these more closely (Mostashri, 2009).

1.3.1 Complexity

There are many definitions of complex systems, but in this context we consider a system as complex when "it is composed of a group of interrelated units (component and subsystems, to be defined), for which the degree and nature of the relationships is imperfectly known, with varying directionality, magnitude and time-scales of interactions. Its overall emergent behavior is difficult to predict, even when subsystem behavior is readily predictable." (Sussman, 2003) Sussman also defines three types of complexity in systems: behavioral (also called emergence), internal (also called structural), and evaluative (Sussman, 2003).

Behavioral complexity arises when the emergent behavior of a system is difficult to predict and may be difficult to understand even after the fact. For instance, the easiest solution to traffic congestion seems to be to build new highways. New highways, however, cause additional traffic by attracting "latent transportation demand" due to the increased attractiveness of private autos, thus leading to more congestion in the long run.

Internal or structural complexity is a measure of the interconnectedness in the structure of a complex system, where small changes made to a part of the system can result in major changes in the system output and even result in systemwide failure. A good example of this type of complexity is the side effect of chemotherapy, which, in addition to destroying cancerous cells, also suppresses the immune system of the body, resulting in death by infection in cancer patients.

Evaluative complexity is caused by the existence of stakeholders in a complex system and is an indication of the different normative beliefs that influence views on the system. Thus, even in the absence of the two former types of complexity, and even if one were able to model the outputs and the performance of the system, it would still be difficult to reach an agreement on what "good" system performance signifies. This type of complexity is one of the primary motivators for engaging stakeholders in systems modeling and policy design and is an essential aspect of such systems. There are many different criteria to value particular outcomes in a sociotechnical system. Which criteria are used to evaluate outcomes, and how they are measured, have to be determined by the consensus or overwhelming majority agreement of the stakeholders. Otherwise, the valuation can be considered that of the experts and decision makers alone. Some of the social and economic valuation approaches for outcomes include (Mostashari, 2009)

> Utilitarian: This criterion is one of neoclassic economics. Essentially, the goal here is to maximize the sum of individual cardinal utilities. ($W(x) = U1(x) + U2(x) + ... + Un(x)$). Of course, this can only function if U1 is cardinal (and if the U's are interpersonally comparable).
>
> Pareto optimality: The goal here is to reach an equilibrium that cannot be replaced by another one that would increase the welfare of some people without harming others.
>
> Pareto efficiency: This occurs when one person is made better off and no one is made worse off.
>
> Compensation principle: A better-off person can compensate the worse-off person to the extent that both of them are better off.
>
> Social welfare function: Here the state evaluates the outcome based on overall social welfare, taking into account distributional issues.

Nested complexity exhibited by sociotechnical systems, refers to the fact that a technologically complex system is often embedded or nested within in a complex institutional structure. This added dimension of complexity is what makes the design and management of a sociotechnical system a great challenge.

1.3.2 Scale

Sociotechnical systems are often large-scale systems characterized by a large number of components, often stretching over a large geographical area or virtual nodes, and across physical, jurisdictional, disciplinary, and social boundaries. Often, their impacts are considered long-lived and significant, and affect a wide range of stakeholders (Mostashari and Sussman, 2009).

1.3.3 Integration and Coupling

Subsystems within a sociotechnical system are connected to one another through feedback loops, often reacting with delays. The existence of multiple interacting feedbacks makes it harder to understand the effect of one part of the system. In such a system, an institutional decision may impact technological development, also impacting social, environmental, and economic aspects of the system.

1.3.4 Interactions with the External Environment

Systems may be characterized as either closed or open. A closed system is one that is self balancing and independent from its environment. Open systems interact with their environment in order to maintain their existence. Most sociotechnical systems are affected by the environment they operate in and, in this sense, can be considered open systems.

1.3.5 Uncertainty and Risk in Sociotechnical Systems

One of the main products of complexity in a system is uncertainty in its initial state, its short- and long-term behavior, and its outputs over time. Webster's Dictionary defines uncertainty as "the state of being uncertain." It further defines uncertain as "not established beyond doubt; still undecided or unknown." Uncertainty refers to a lack of factual knowledge or understanding of a subject matter and, in this case, to the inability to fully characterize the structure and behavior of a system now or in the future. In analyzing complex systems, uncertainty can apply to the current state of a system and its components, as well as uncertainties on its future state and outcomes of changes to the system. Essentially, there are two categories of uncertainty: Reducible, and irreducible. Reducible uncertainty can be reduced over time with extended observation, better tools, better measurement, etc., until it reaches a level when it can no longer be reduced. Irreducible uncertainties are inherent uncertainties due to the natural complexity of the subject matter. We can distinguish the following types of uncertainty (Walker, 2003):

Causal Uncertainty: When scientists draw causal links between different parts of the system, or between a specific input and an output, there is an uncertainty in the causal link. For instance, the relationship between air pollution concentration and respiratory problems is associated with causal uncertainty, given that the same air pollution concentrations can result in different levels of respiratory problems. This occurs because other, sometimes unknown, factors can influence the causal link. There is also the important difference between correlation and causation, in that an existing correlation does not necessarily indicate causation. Another source of causal uncertainty is the existence of feedback loops in a system. Causal uncertainty is strongly dependent on the "mental map" of the person drawing the linkages.

Measurement Uncertainty: When measuring physical or social phenomena, there are two types of measurement uncertainty that can arise. The first is the reliability of the measurement, and the second is its validity. Reliability refers to the repeatability of the process of measurement, or its "precision," whereas validity refers to the consistency of the measurement with other sources of data obtained in a different ways or its "accuracy." The acceptable imprecision and inaccuracy in the case of different subject matters can be very different. For instance, the acceptable inaccuracy for a weather forecast is different from the inaccuracy of measurements for the leakage rate of a nuclear waste containment casket, given the different levels of risk involved. Therefore, defining the acceptable uncertainty in measurements is a rather subjective decision.

Sampling Uncertainty: It is practically impossible to measure all parts of a given system. Measurements are usually made for a limited sample and generalized over the entire system. Such generalization beyond the sample gives rise to sampling uncertainty. Making an inference from sample data to a conclusion about the entire system creates the possibility that error will be introduced because the sample does not adequately represent that system.

Future Uncertainty: The future can unfold in unpredictable ways, and future developments can impact the external environment of a system or its internal structure in ways that cannot be anticipated. This type of uncertainty is probably one of the most challenging, given that there is little control over the future. However, it is possible to anticipate a wide range of future developments and simulate the effect of particular decisions or developments in a system across these potential futures. In sociotechnical systems, the effects of new technologies often cannot be adequately determined *a priori*. Collingridge (1980) indicates that, historically, as technologies have developed and matured, negative effects have often become evident that could not have been anticipated initially (automobile emissions or nuclear power accidents and waste disposal). Despite this ignorance, a decision has to be made today.

Experts use models to predict values of some variables based on values of other variables. A model is based on assumptions about the initial state of a system (data), its structure, the processes that govern it, and its output. Any of these assumptions has inherent uncertainties that can affect the results that the model produces. The parameters and initial conditions of a model can often be more important than the relationships that govern the model in terms of the impact on the output. The "Limits to Growth" Models of the 1970s show how long-range models are not capable of characterizing long-term interactions between the economy, society, and the environment in a sociotechnical system. Additionally, individual and institutional choices can make socioeconomic models inherently unpredictable (Land and Schneider 1987).

In real life, uncertainties cannot be reduced indefinitely, and the reduction of uncertainty is associated with costs. Therefore, an acceptable level of uncertainty for decision making has to be determined subjectively. The subjective nature of such a determination is one of the main rationales for stakeholder participation in decision making.

Risk is the combination of the concepts probability (the likelihood of an outcome) and severity (the impact of an outcome). In fact, acceptable levels of uncertainty in the analysis of a system depend on acceptable levels of risk associated with that system. The concept of acceptable risk is essentially a subjective, value-based decision. While there are methodologies, such as probabilistic risk assessment, that try to provide an objective assessment of risk, it is the perception of the risk-bearing individuals, organizations, or communities that determine how much risk is acceptable. While many experts focus on providing the public with probabilities of possible outcomes for a system, Sjöberg (1994) indicates that the public is more concerned with the severity than with the probability. Allan Mazur (1981) emphasizes the role of the media in affecting risk perceptions for people. He argues that the more people see or hear about the risks of a technology, for example, the more concerned they will become. This effect could occur both for negative coverage as well as positive coverage.

1.4 Dimensions of Sociotechnical Systems

A sociotechnical system is defined through four main aspects: Its (manmade) structure and artifacts (technology, architecture, protocols, components, links, boundaries, internal complexity), its dynamics and behavior (emergence, nonlinear interactions, feedback loops), and its actors/agents (conscious entities that affect or are affected by the system's intended or unintended effects on its environment). Finally, the environment it operates in also defines a sociotechnical system. Here, environment refers to the social, cultural, political, economic, and legal context within which the system is operating (Mostashari, 2009).

A proposed taxonomy of sociotechnical systems studies can therefore consist of the following:

■ *Structural Studies*: Research on architecture, technological artifacts, protocols and standards, networks, hierarchies, optimization and structural "ilities," etc.
■ *Behavioral Studies*: Research on nonlinearity, dynamic or behavioral complexity, dynamic "ilities," material/energy/information flows, dynamic programming, emergence, etc.
■ *Agent/Actor System Studies*: Research on decision making under uncertainty, agent-based modeling, enterprise architecture, human–technology interactions, labor–management relations, organizational theory, lean enterprise, etc.
■ *Policy Studies*: Research on the interactions of the sociotechnical system with its environment, including institutional context and political economy, stakeholder involvement, labor relations, and social goals of sociotechnical systems, as well as ecosystem and sustainability research.

1.5 Sociotechnical Networks

One major type of sociotechnical system is sociotechnical networks. These are normally networked physical/technological systems used and managed by a network of people, organizations, and enterprises. The Internet is a good example of such a system, as is the power grid. Sociotechnical networks are important because they can span across nations and impact millions of individuals. They are often critical in the effective functioning of societies and economies. Because of their networked nature, sociotechnical networks face major challenges with regard to security, resilience, reliability, multiobjective multilayer optimization, and tensions between local and global control and optimization. Additionally, there are organizational/institutional challenges in regulation, standards, management, and governance of these networks. We will look at each of these issues briefly in subsequent sections.

1.5.1 Security

The networked nature of sociotechnical systems makes them vulnerable to major security breaches that can endanger the operations of the network and compromise critical information and data. Due to the large number of access points in larger sociotechnical networks, developing a "secure" network is a highly challenging notion. The security aspect of sociotechnical networks has been primarily explored at the data network level. Many sociotechncial data network layers are heterogeneous in nature and can include a TCP/IP backbone, sensor networks, WiMax, wireless local area networks, and cellular networks, all of which are vulnerable to security breaches. There have been extensive studies on network security for different sociotechnical systems, including risk and vulnerability assessment for sociotechnical power grids (Byres and Lowe, 2005), and security technology and practice assessments (Byres and Franz, 2006). In this book we will devote a key chapter to sociotechnical network security.

1.5.2 Resilience

Resilience is defined as the ability of a system to maintain or recover its service delivery in the face of major external disruptions. Given the criticality of socio-techncial networks such as the power grid, the Internet, transportation networks, telecommunication networks, etc., in the proper functioning of society, the resilience of such systems in the face of various kinds of external shocks is critical. The resilience of sociotechnical networks is a function of their vulnerability as well as adaptive capacity (Omer et al., 2009). The less the vulnerability, the lower the possibility that sociotechnical network performance will be compromised. The more the adaptive capacity of the system, the faster will the system jump back to its initial performance levels after being affected by a shock. Sociotechnical network resilience can increase when diversity, redundancy, modularity, and cognition/ autonomy are designed into the system.

1.5.3 Reliability

Network reliability refers to the reliability of the overall network to provide communication in the event of failure of a component or a set of components in the network (*Wiley Encyclopedia of Electrical and Electronics Engineering*, 1999). For sociotechnical networks, the reliability expands to all three layers, namely, the physical/technological network layer, the data communication layer, and the social/institutional layer. The main challenge is to define the holistic reliability of the sociotechnical network, given that the reliability of each network layer cannot be easily combined with that of the other layers. This is due to the differences in the fault modes and the asynchronous nature of failures within the components within each layer (physical, data, social).

1.5.4 Distributed versus Centralized Control

In sociotechnical networks the physical or virtual connections are controlled either through a single network controller or through several controllers. The former is called centralized control, and the latter is known as decentralized control. In a sociotechnical network, distributed control systems are more common, as different parts of the system will have different types of control actions and would be distributed over jurisdictional and geographical boundaries. Issues of local versus global optimization for larger-scale sociotechnical networks are fundamental systems-level decisions that need to depend on the organization and structure of the social network layer and on the economic optimization of locally managed networks as well as other system attributes and properties such as reliability, resilience, and security.

1.6 Sociotechnical Networks and Cognition

The ability of a sociotechnical network to autonomously sense changes in its environment and respond to those changes relatively autonomously based on its prior experiences demonstrates its level of cognition. The higher the autonomy, the higher the cognitive ability of the network. One can define a Cognitioncentric System as having the following capabilities (Mitola, 2006):

1. *Sensing* individual internal and external changes
2. *Perceiving* the overall picture that these changes represent
3. *Associating* the new situation with past experienced situations and acting accordingly if similar
4. *Planning* various alternatives in response to the change within a given response timeline
5. *Choosing* course of action that seems best suited to the situation
6. *Taking action* by adjusting resources and outcomes to meet new needs and requirements
7. *Monitoring and learning* from the impact of capabilities 1–6

From the definition it follows that every system could exhibit these capabilities in different degrees. Each of these capabilities is used in a systems process that directly corresponds to it. The chain of the seven resulting processes constitutes the full cognitive process cycle for the system for any given set of changes. Chapter 10 will look at cognitioncentric sociotechnical systems in more detail.

1.7 Analyzing Sociotechnical Networks: CLIOS Analysis and the STIN Heuristics

There are two main analysis methodologies for sociotechnical networks. The CLIOS (Complex, Large-scale, integrated, open systems) process (Mostashari and Sussman, 2009, Sussman, 2003) and the sociotechnical interaction network (STIN) concept (Kling et al., 2003). We will discuss the CLIOS process in detail in the sociotechnical systems modeling chapter. STIN is based on earlier work by Kling and Scacchi (1982) and identifies the following broad analysis activities for sociotechnical networks (Kling et al., 2003):

1. Stakeholder/Actor Analysis
2. Network Relationship Analysis
3. Network Trajectory Analysis

In the first, the relevant population of system interactors is identified, the core interactor groups are mapped, and incentives within the network are characterized. In the second, excluded actors and undesired interactions are identified, and existing communication forums and resource flows are mapped. In the third, the architectural choice points are identified and mapped to the sociotechnical characteristics of the system (Kling, 2003). This approach is similar to the CLIOS process described in later chapters, although the CLIOS process identifies relevant models and methods within a step-by-step analysis framework.

In the following chapters of this book we will look at many of these issues in more detail.

References

Byres, E. and Franz, M. Uncovering Cyber Flaws, http://www.isa.org/InTechTemplate. cfm?Section=Article_Index1&tContentID=50583, January 1, 2006, accessed October 2009.

Byres, E. and Lowe, J. Insidious threat to control systems, *InTech*, vol. 52, no.1, 2005, p. 28.

David Collingridge (1980), "The social control of Technology", New York: St. Martin's Press; London: Pinter.

Encyclopedia of Electrical and Electronics Engineering 1999, ISBN: 978-0-471-13946-1. Hardcover. 17616 pages. Wiley: March 1999.

Kling, R., McKim, G., and King, A. 2003. A bit more to IT: scholarly communication forums as socio-technical interaction networks. *Journal of the American Society for Information Science and Technology*, 54(1), 46–67.

Kling, R. and Scacchi, W. 1982. The web of computing: computer technology as social organization. *Advances in Computers*, Vol. 21, 3–87.

Land, K.C. and Schneider, S.H. 1987. Forecasting in the Social and Natural Sciences: An Overview and Statement of Isomorphisms. In K.C. Land and S. H. Schneider, eds., *Forecasting in the Social and Natural Sciences*. Boston: D. Reidel.

Mazur, A. 1981. Media Coverage and Public Opinion on Scientific Controversies. 31 *J. COMM.*, 106 (1981).

Mitola, J. 2006. *Cognitive Radio Architecture: The Engineering Foundations of Radio XML*. Wiley: Hoboken, NJ.

Mostashari, A. and Sussman, J. 2009. A framework for analysis, design and operation of complex large-scale sociotechnological systems. *International Journal for Decision Support Systems and Technologies*, 1(2), 52–68, April–June.

Omer, M., Nilchiani, R., and Mostashari, A. 2009. Assessing the Resiliency of the Global Internet Fiber-Optics Network, Proceedings of the International Symposium of Systems Engineering (INCOSE), July 2009, Singapore.

Sjöberg, L. and. Drottz-Sjöberg, B.M. 1994. Risk Perception of Nuclear Waste: Experts and the Public Center for Risk Research, Stockholm School of Economics, Rhizikon: Risk Research Report 16.

Sussman, J. 2003. Collected Views on Complexity in Systems. Massachusetts Institute of Technology, Engineering Systems Division Working Paper Series ESD-WP-2003-01.06-ESD Internal Symposium.

Vincent Hogan and Ian Walker, (2003) "Education choice under uncertainty: Implications for public policy," Labour Economics, Vol 14, 2007, Issue 6, Pages 894–912.

Wall, M.B. 1996. A Genetic Algorithm for Resource-Constrained Scheduling, Doctoral Dissertation for Mechanical Engineering at the Massachusetts Institute of Technology, 1996.

Chapter 2

Systems-Level Modeling of Sociotechnical Systems

Ali Mostashari

Contents

2.1 Introduction

In addition to network models of sociotechnical networks, there are many other ways to model sociotechnical systems, taking into account the interactions between social and technological components. When analyzing a sociotechnical system, it is necessary to look at the entire system in a holistic fashion. One of the major milestones favoring this type of systemic approach in the analysis of complex systems is *systems theory*. It was first proposed as an alternative to reductionism in the 1940s by the biologist Ludwig von Bertalanffy, who published his General Systems Theory (Bertalanffy, 1968). He emphasized that real systems were open and that they exhibited behavioral complexity or emergence. Rather than analyzing the individual behaviors of system components in isolation, systems theory focuses on the relationship among these components as a whole and within the context of the system boundaries. According to Bertalanffy, a system can be defined by the system-environment boundary, inputs, outputs, processes, state, hierarchy, goal directedness, and its information content (Bertalanffy, 1968).

2.2 Systems Analysis

While systems theory provides the fundamental concepts for understanding a complex sociotechnical system, it does not provide a common methodology for how to analyze such a system. In the 1960s and 1970s, systems analysis evolved as an approach to analyzing complex systems. The American Cybernetics Society defines systems analysis as "an approach that applies systems principles to aid a decision-maker with problems of identifying, reconstructing, optimizing, and managing a system, while taking into account multiple objectives, constraints and resources. Systems analysis usually has some combination of the following: identification and re-identification of objectives, constraints, and alternative courses of action; examination of the probable consequences of the options in terms of costs, benefits, and risks; presentation of the results in a comparative framework so that the decision maker can make an informed choice from among the options."*

Many systems analysis tools and processes have been proposed for analyzing different aspects of complex systems. Here we will look at Systems Engineering, Systems Dynamics, and the CLIOS Process as important ways to analyze CLIOS. In the following sections, we will take a look at each of these approaches.

2.2.1 Systems Engineering

Systems engineering is a discipline that develops and exploits structured, efficient approaches to analysis and design to solve complex engineering problems. Jenkins

---

* *Web Dictionary of Cybernetics and Systems*, American Cybernetics Society, http://pespmc1.vub. ac.be/ASC/indexASC.html.

(1971) defines the following stages for a systems engineering approach to solving complex systems: Systems Analysis, System Design, and Implementation and Operation.

For each of these stages, a different number of systems engineering tools and methods exist that can help analyze different aspects of the system. The methods include such elements as trade-off analysis, optimization (operations research), sensitivity analysis, utility theory, benefit–cost analysis, real-options analysis, game theory, and diverse simulation methods such as genetic algorithms or agent-based modeling.* At any stage of a systems engineering analysis of a complex system, a combination of these tools and methods can be used. In the following paragraphs, we will consider each of these tools and methods and comment on their strengths and weaknesses.

2.2.1.1 Trade-Off Analysis

When dealing with a complex system, there are multiple values that we would like to maximize. Often, these goals and objectives can be in direct conflict with one another, and maximizing one can adversely affect the other. Trade-off analysis allows us to find those outcomes in the systems that have combinations of values that are acceptable to us, and which maximize the overall value of the system as a way to deal with evaluative complexity. Multiattribute trade-off analysis can be used for cases where there are multiple objectives in a given system. The drawback with trade-off analysis is that many benefits are not continuous in nature. For instance, in the case of a sociotechnical power grid, there is a trade-off between local and global optimization: either the grid parameters are optimized for a local area or for the global grid as a whole. Trade-off is thus not a continuous curve and cannot be well represented using trade-off analysis.

2.2.1.2 Optimization

Optimization is the maximization or minimization of an output function from a system in the presence of various kinds of constraints. It is a way to allocate system resources such that a specific system goal is obtained in the most efficient way. Optimization uses mathematical programming (MP) techniques and simulation to achieve its goals. The most widely used MP method is linear programming, which was made into an instant success when George B. Dantzig developed the simplex method for solving linear-programming problems in 1947. Other widely used MP methods are integer and mixed-integer programming, dynamic programming, and different types of stochastic modeling. The choice of methodology depends mainly on the size of the problem and the degree of uncertainty. Table 2.1 shows what

---

* The Institute for Systems Research, What is Systems Engineering, http://www.isr.umd.edu/ISR/about/definese.html#what.

Table 2.1   A Systems Engineering Approach for Dealing with Complex Sociotechnical Systems

Stages	*Methods*
• System Analysis	1. Recognition and formulation of the problem
	2. Organization of the project
	3. Definition of the system
	4. Definition of the wider system
	5. Definition of the objectives of the wider system
	6. Definition of the objectives of the system
	7. Definition of the overall economic criterion
	8. Information and data collection
• System Design	1. Forecasting
	2. Model building and simulation
	3. Optimization
	4. Control
• Implementation	1. Documentation and sanction approval
	2. Construction
• Operation	1. Initial operation
	2. Retrospective appraisal of the project

Source: Jenkins, 1971.

methods are used for certain and uncertain conditions in the strategy evaluation and generation stages of systems analysis.

Another type of optimization method is *Genetic Algorithm* (GA). A genetic algorithm is an optimization algorithm based on Darwinian evolutionary mechanisms and uses a combination of random mutation and crossover and selection procedures to breed better models or solutions from an originally random starting population or sample (Wall, 1996).

Optimization methods are tools that are suitable for analyzing large-scale networks and allocation processes, but may not fit all purposes. Often when social considerations exist, the goal is not optimization but satisfaction of all stakeholder groups involved. Also, when optimization occurs, there is no room for flexibility in the system, making the system vulnerable to changes that happen in its environment over time.

Table 2.2 Mathematical Programming and Simulation Modeling Methods for Sociotechnical Systems

	Solution Evaluation	*Solution Generation*
Certainty	– Deterministic Simulation	– Linear Programming
	– Econometric Models	– Network Models
	– System of ODEs	– Integer and mixed-integer programming
	– Input–Output Models	– Nonlinear programming
		– Control Theory
Uncertainty	– Monte Carlo Simulation	– Decision Theory
	– Econometric Models	– Dynamic Programming
	– Stochastic Processes	– Inventory Theory
	– Queuing Theory	– Stochastic Programming
	– Reliability Theory	– Stochastic Control Theory

Source: Applied Mathematical Programming. Bradley, Hax, and Magnanti. Addison-Wesley, 1977.

2.2.1.3 Game Theory

Game theory is a branch of mathematics first developed by John von Neumann and Oskar Morgenstern in the 1940s, and advanced by John Nash in the 1950s. It uses models to predict interactions between decision-making agents in a given set of conditions. Game theory has been applied to a variety of fields such as economics, market analysis, and military strategy. It can be used in a complex system where multiple agents (conscious decision-making entities) interact noncooperatively to maximize their own benefit. The underlying assumption for game theory is that agents know and understand the benefits they can derive from a course of action, and that they are rational.

2.2.1.4 Agent-Based Modeling

Agent-based modeling is a bottom-up system modeling approach for predicting and understanding the behavior of nonlinear, multiagent systems. An agent is a conscious decision-making element of the system that tries to maximize its local benefit. The interaction of agents in a system is a key feature of agent-based systems. It assumes that agents communicate with each other and learn from each other. The proponents of this approach argue that human behavior in swarms (or society) within a CLIOS can only be predicted if individual behavior is considered a function of information exchange among individuals who are trying to maximize their profits (Cetin and Baydar, 2004). The main drawback of agent-based modeling approaches is that the initial assumptions about an individual's behavior can predetermine the aggregate systems behavior, making the outcome very sensitive to the initial assumptions of the system.

2.2.1.5 Benefit–Cost Analysis and Discounted Cash Flow

Benefit–cost analysis (also called cost–benefit analysis) is a methodology developed by the U.S. Army Corps of Engineers before World War II that allows decision makers choose projects that produce the greatest net benefit for every dollar spent. This method has been used to analyze the feasibility of complex large-scale projects by the public and private sectors. It uses the net present value (NPV) as a basis for decision making, and is used extensively to this day. The underlying assumption of this type of analysis is that benefits and costs can be converted easily to monetary benefits and can be compared across heterogeneous projects. This can be a particularly bad assumption when dealing with social systems, where benefits are less tangible in monetary terms and evaluated differently by different stakeholders. Also, the choice of the discount rate and distributional effects are hard to capture with this methodology.

2.2.1.6 Utility Theory

Utility is an economic concept that realizes that the benefits of a specific good or service are not uniform across the population. It is a measure of the satisfaction obtained from gaining goods or services by different individuals. It can complement benefit–cost analysis by including the decision-maker's preferences as a measure of comparison of large-scale projects. One of the problems with utility theory is that people's preferences can change very fast, and often there are conflicting utilities among the different decision makers and stakeholders, making it difficult to use a single utility for a course of action or a system outcome.

2.2.1.7 Real-Options Analysis

Real-options analysis is the application of financial option pricing to real assets. Instead of the now-or-never investment options that are used in a traditional NPV (Net Present Value) analysis, real-options analysis provides an opportunity but not an obligation for the decision maker to make use of opportunities that arise under uncertain conditions. Similar to stock options, the decision maker spends an initial investment that provides them with an opportunity to act under certain conditions to improve the value of the system they manage (Amram and Kulatlaika, 1998). A drawback of the real options analysis is that it depends on a known volatility profile for any given system, something that is a far stretch for most complex systems where historical data is not necessarily predictive of future behavior.

2.2.2 System Dynamics

System dynamics is a tool for modeling complex systems with feedback that was developed by Jay Forrester at the Massachusetts Institute of Technology in the 1960s. He developed the initial ideas by applying the concepts from feedback control theory to the study of industrial systems (Forrester, 1961). One of the best-known and most controversial applications of the 1960s was Urban Dynamics (Forrester, 1969). It tried to explain the patterns of rapid population growth and subsequent decline that had been observed in American cities such as New York, Detroit, St. Louis, Chicago, Boston, and Newark. Forrester's simulation model portrayed the city as a system of interacting industries, housing, and people, and was one of the first systems models for a sociotechnical system. Another widely known application of system dynamics was the "Limits to Growth" study (Meadows et al., 1972), which looked at the prospects for human population growth and industrial production in the global system over the next century. Using computer simulations, resource production and food supply changes in a system with growing population and consumption rates were modeled. The model predicted that societies could not grow indefinitely and that such growth would bring the downfall of the social structure and result in catastrophic short-ages of food for the world population. Given that the results of the model were highly dependent on initial assumptions as well as the designed structure, most of the predictions were not confirmed by observation in the years since, and many in the academic community have used this as evidence to discredit the value of system dynamics in modeling large-scale sociotechnical systems. Therefore, system dynamics has in recent years shifted mostly toward solving specific prob-lems rather than modeling entire large-scale systems. While system dynamics has made substantial progress in the past four decades, those academics not in the field still consider its merits limited, mainly because of the early large-scale experiments by Forrester and Meadows.

System dynamics uses causal loop diagrams to represent relationships and causal links between different components in a system.

In addition to qualitative representations, system dynamics also uses control theory for quantification. It uses stocks and flows along with feedback loops and delays, which can explain how the different elements of a complex system are linked together. Its qualitative representation, combined with its quantitative output, make it a suitable tool for modeling sociotechnical systems. In terms of quantitative capa-bilities, system dynamics has the ability of performing extensive multivariable sen-sitivity analysis. This means that, if we are not certain of the inputs into the model, we can provide a range for each, and the system dynamics model will calculate all the possible combinations and provide a range of values as the output.

One of the major strengths of system dynamics is in simulating effects that are delayed in time. This helps us model how an event or series of events five years ago might have contributed to the status of things today, or how current policies might start to pay off in a couple of years and not immediately. System dynamics emphasizes quantification of a systems model as the only way to gain insights from its behavior. The CLIOS process, which uses a similar concept for representing complex systems, emphasizes both qualitative and quantitative insights. We will look at the CLIOS process in more detail in the upcoming section.

2.2.3 The CLIOS Process

The CLIOS process (Mostashari and Sussman, 2009) is an approach to fostering understanding of complex sociotechnical systems by using diagrams to highlight the interconnections of the subsystems in a complex system and their potential feedback structures. The motivation for the causal loop representation is to convey the structural relationships and direction of influence between the components within a system. In this manner, the diagram is an organizing mechanism for exploring the system's underlying structure and behavior and then identifying options and strategies for improving the system's performance.

2.2.3.1 Physical Domain and Institutional Sphere

A CLIOS system can be thought of as consisting of a physical *domain*—with interconnected physical *subsystems*—nested in an institutional *sphere* (i.e., nested complexity). This is illustrated in Figure 2.1. Therefore, when we speak of a CLIOS system, we refer both to the physical and the institutional aspects of the system in which we are interested. The choice of system boundary (for both the physical domain and the institutional sphere) within the CLIOS process depends on the problem we are trying to address and the extent of our leverage over the system.

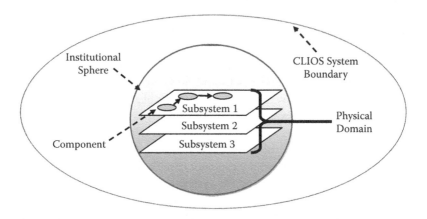

Figure 2.1   A CLIOS system consists of a physical domain (made up of subsystems), nested within an institutional sphere.

However, the choice of systems boundary for the physical domain will affect our choice of boundary for the institutional sphere, and vice versa.

Recently, there have been important attempts at looking at complex CLIOS-type systems from a holistic, enterprise perspective (Swartz and DeRosa, 2006). There has been a recognition on behalf of systems engineering practitioners that standard processes need to be adapted based on insights from complexity science, and various principles for incorporating complexity as a consideration within such processes have been proposed (Sheard and Mostashari, 2009). One of the most important developments in this area was the definition of a research agenda for *Complex Engineered, Organizational and Natural Systems* by over 50 thought leaders in complexity (Rouse, 2007). In particular, with regard to particular CLIOS Systems, there have been important studies looking at the analysis and design of urban and regional transportation systems (Sussman, Sgoruidis and ward, 2004), air combat systems (Kometer, 2005), maritime surveillance systems (Martin, 2004), lean manufacturing systems, aerospace systems design (McConnell, 2007), regional energy systems design (Mostashari, 2005), nuclear waste transportation and storage systems (Sussman, 2000), municipal electric utilities (Osorio Urzua, 2007), public–private partnerships in infrastructure development (Ward, 2005), and environmental systems (Mostashari and Sussman, 2005) among others.

2.2.3.2 The CLIOS Process as a Conceptual Methodology

As an alternative systems design process for CLIOS Systems, this chapter proposes the CLIOS process, a highly iterative and modular 12-step *conceptual* process for concurrent analysis, design, and management of coupled complex technological and institutional systems in the face of uncertainty. An overview of the CLIOS process is presented, followed by papers exploring detailed applications in complex large-scale engineering systems. As an engineering systems design, analysis, and management process, the CLIOS process does not rely on a particular analysis methodology or modeling tool. Rather similar to ANSI/EIA 632, it is a conceptual process that can serve as an organizing framework for the design, analysis, and management process of CLIOS systems.

2.2.3.3 Relationship to Other Quantitative and Qualitative Systems Methodologies and Tools

As indicated, the CLIOS process is a conceptual framework and does not limit the user to a particular methodology. As such, it allows for a variety of computational (quantitative) or qualitative tools to be utilized for analyzing the physical domain and the institutional sphere. Table 2.4 represents the variety of quantitative and qualitative methodologies and tools that can be applied in the different steps of the CLIOS process. This is not an exhaustive list but provides a starting point for the user depending on the type of CLIOS system at hand.

2.2.3.4 Overview of the CLIOS Process

The CLIOS process is composed of twelve steps divided into three stages (see Figure 2.2). The three stages are Representation; Design, Evaluation, and Selection; and Implementation and Adaptation (Table 2.3). In stage one—Representation— the CLIOS system representation is created and considered in terms of both its

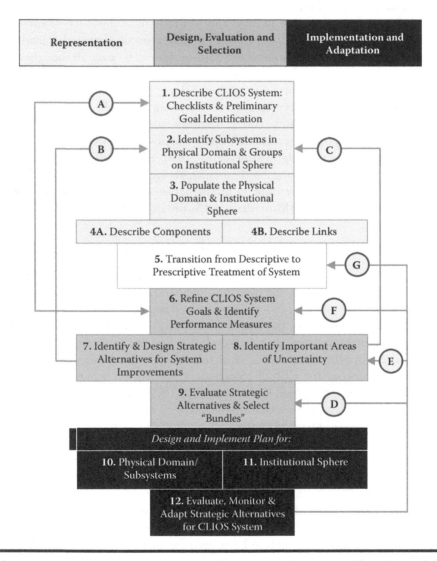

Figure 2.2 The twelve steps of the CLIOS process with suggested iteration points. (From Mostashari A. and Sussman J. 2009. A framework for analysis, design and operation of complex large-scale sociotechnological systems. *International Journal for Decision Support Systems and Technologies*, 1(2), 52–68, April–June 2009.)

Table 2.3 Summary of Three Stages of CLIOS

Stage	Key ideas	Outputs
1. Representation	• Understanding and visualizing system structure and behavior • Establishing preliminary system objectives	System description, issue identification, goal identification, and structural representation
2. Design, Evaluation, and Selection	• Refining system objectives while cognizant of complexity and uncertainty • Developing bundles of strategic design alternatives	Identification of performance measures, identification and design of strategic alternatives, evaluation of bundles of strategic alternatives, and selection of the best performing bundles
3. Implementation and Adaptation	• Implementing bundles of strategic alternatives • Following-through—changing and monitoring the performance of the CLIOS System	Implementation strategy for strategic alternatives in the physical domain and the institutional sphere, actual implementation of alternatives, and postimplementation evaluation

structure and behavior. In this stage, we also establish preliminary goals for the system—that is, in what ways do we want to improve its performance? In stage two—Design, Evaluation, and Selection—strategic alternatives for performance improvements to the physical domain and institutional sphere are designed, evaluated, and, finally, some are selected. In stage three—Implementation and Adaptation—implementation plans for the physical domain and the institutional sphere are designed and refined. The strategies are then adapted to new needs and observations. An overview of the three stages is shown in Figure 2.2. The twelve steps are coded by the shading of the boxes to indicate whether they are part of the representation; design, evaluation, and selection; or implementation stage.

2.2.3.5 Iterative Nature of CLIOS

While the CLIOS process is constructed as a set of ordered steps, it constitutes an iterative process, and not a rigid, once-through process. Indeed, as shown in Figure 2.2, there are several important points where iteration can occur. In the following sections, we will outline each of the steps in more detail.

Table 2.4 Selected Quantitative and Qualitative Methodologies for the CLIOS Process

CLIOS Process Step	Methodology	Quantitative or Qualitative	Description
CLIOS Step 1: Describe CLIOS system	**Data collection and stakeholder surveys and interviews**	Qualitative	Interactive and written interviews with people with knowledge, expertise, and critical interest in the system, and data collection from existing published info on system
	Delphi process	Qualitative	Structured process for stakeholder knowledge collection and distillation with controlled opinion feedback (Adler and Ziglio, 1996)
	Requirements Elicitation and Analysis	Qualitative	Process that identifies and extracts the necessary attributes, capabilities, characteristics, or quality of systems from stakeholders (Young, 2001)
	Mutually Exclusive, Collectively Exhaustive (MECE) analysis	Qualitative	Information grouping process dividing information into subgroups that are collectively comprehensive and that do not overlap (Rasiel, 1999)
CLIOS Steps 2, 3, 4, and 5: Identify subsystems, populate them, and identify components and links within each	**Causal Loop Diagramming (Systems Mapping)**	Qualitative	Systems diagramming process visualizing how interrelated variables within a system affect one another (Sterman, 2000)
	Stakeholder-Assisted Modeling and Policy Design (SAM-PD) process	Qualitative	Collaborative stakeholder process using insights from systems thinking, conflict assessment, and linguistics to extract stakeholder knowledge for systems representation (Mostashari, 2005)

CLIOS Steps 6, 7, and 8: Refine system objectives, identify system design and improvement strategies, and identify uncertainties	Delphi process	Qualitative	Described earlier
	SAM-PD process	Qualitative	Described earlier
	Scenario Analysis	Qualitative	Process of analyzing possible futures for a system (Schwartz, 1996)
	Risk Management	Qualitative/ quantitative	Process for analyzing threats to a system and identifying ways to mitigate them
CLIOS Step 9: Evaluate strategic alternatives (Systems Modeling)	Systems Dynamics Modeling	Quantitative	Control-theory-based stock and flow modeling methodology addressing feedback loops and time delays that affect the behavior of the entire system (Sterman, 2000)
	Social Network Analysis	Quantitative	Analysis methodology for modeling the interactions and connections on the institutional sphere and among social actors interacting with the physical domain (Mullins, 1973)
	Agent-Based Modeling	Quantitative	Computational model for simulating the actions and interactions of actors (individuals or organizations) in a network (Holland, 1995)

(Continued)

Table 2.4 (Continued)   Selected Quantitative and Qualitative Methodologies for the Clios Process

CLIOS Process Step	Methodology	Quantitative or Qualitative	Description
	Flow Network Analysis methodologies	Quantitative	A mathematical methodology for analyzing flows within a network consisting of nodes (edges) and links (arcs). Applicable to most CLIOS systems that can be modeled as networked systems (Ahuja et al., 1993)
	Statistical and Economic Analysis methodologies	Quantitative	Methods for analyzing relationships between different variables based on existing data sets; Useful for systems in which ample long-term data exist
	Operations Research (OR) methods	Quantitative	An interdisciplinary field that uses mathematical modeling and statistics to arrive at optimal or near-optimal solutions based on constraints and objective functions
CLIOS Steps 10, 11, and 12: Implement, monitor, and improve system	**Project Management**	Qualitative	Structured process for implementing a product, service, or system with quality assurance in a limited time
	Adaptive Management	Qualitative	A structured, iterative process of optimal decision making in the face of uncertainty, accruing information needed to improve future systems management (Holling, 1978)

Source: Mostashari, A. and Sussman, J. 2009. A framework for analysis, design and operation of complex large-scale sociotechnological systems. *International Journal for Decision Support Systems and Technologies*, 1(2), 52–68, April–June 2009.

2.2.3.5.1 CLIOS Stage 1: Representation

The representation stage aids in the understanding of the complete CLIOS system by examining the structures and behaviors of the physical subsystems and institutional sphere and the interactions between them. The CLIOS process usually uses a combination of diagrams and text to capture the critical aspects of the CLIOS system and present them in an easy-to-comprehend format. When the CLIOS process is carried out jointly by a group of analysts, decision makers, and stakeholders, the representation stage is used to create a common understanding of the system among these actors (Mostashari and Sussman, 2005).

2.2.3.5.1.1 CLIOS Step 1: Describe CLIOS System: Checklists and Preliminary Goal Identification — In defining the system that pertains to the problem, we first create several checklists to serve as a high-level examination of the CLIOS system. The lists should address the question "What is it about the system that makes it interesting, and what major systems issues/goals are we interested in?" (Puccia and Levins, 1985).

The first of the checklists is the characteristics checklist that may relate to (a) the temporal and geographic scale of the system, (b) the core technologies and systems, (c) the natural physical conditions that affect or are affected by the system, (d) the key economic and market factors, (e) important social or political factors or controversies related to the system, and (f) the historical development and context of the CLIOS system. The second checklist, essentially a SWOT Strengths, Weaknesses, Opportunites, and Threats analysis, captures opportunities, issues, and challenges—those aspects of the CLIOS System for which we may seek constructive improvements through strategic alternatives in Stage 2. Finally, in the third checklist, we identify preliminary system goals and requirements that often relate to the opportunities, issues, and challenges found in the second checklist. To compile the lists, one can draw upon a wide range of sources: academic articles and books, popular press, reports published by the government, business, nongovernmental organizations (NGOs), discussions/interviews with stakeholders, or personal expertise or experience with the system, etc.

2.2.3.5.1.2 CLIOS Step 2: Identify Subsystems in the Physical Domain and Actor Groups on the Institutional Sphere — To outline the general structure of the CLIOS system, we determine (a) which major subsystems make up the physical domain of the CLIOS System, (b) who the main actor groups are on the institutional sphere, and (c) how they relate to one another on a macro level (Mostashari and Sussman, 2009).

For the Physical Domain: Here we parse the physical domain (or system) into subsystems, map out the structure of those subsystems (which can be envisioned as layers), and finally identify the key linkages between the subsystems. This is a difficult process but worthwhile in that many of the insights into the structure and behavior of the CLIOS system will come through while thinking about how it can be subdivided into the different layers.

For the Institutional Sphere: We then identify the major actor groups on the institutional sphere. The general categories may include government agencies, private sector firms, citizen groups, as well as independent expert/advisory entities and so forth. This can be derived from the checklists in terms of who manages the system, who is affected by it, who attempts to influence, it, and, in general, who worries about it.

2.2.3.5.1.3 CLIOS Step 3: Populate the Physical Domain and the Institutional Sphere — *Populating the Physical Domain*: In this step we employ the type of basic subsystem diagram common in systems sciences, "defined as having components and relations that may be represented (at least in principle) as a network-type diagram with nodes representing components and lines representing the relationships" (Flood and Carson, 1993). Initial CLIOS subsystem diagrams are created by detailing each subsystem and identifying the major components in each and the links indicating the influence of the components on each other. Sometimes a component can be common to more than one subsystem (Mostashari and Sussman, 2009).

Figure 2.3 shows the populated subsystems and the concept of the *common driver* linking them.

This type of representation is similar to causal loop diagrams (CLDs) used in System Dynamics, and system dynamics software provides a good platform for developing computer-aided CLIOS systems representations. One technique that can be used for increasing the resolution of the system representation without creating overcrowded diagrams is *expanding*. Expanding focuses on critical components and magnifies their functions into separate diagrams for more detailed study. This is shown in Figure 2.4.

Populating the Institutional Sphere: Parallel to populating the subsystems of the physical domain with components, we populate the institutional sphere with

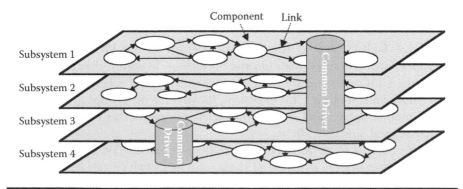

Figure 2.3 Populating the subsystem diagrams.

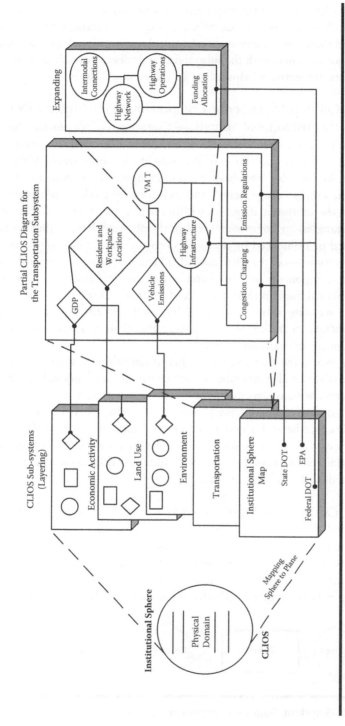

Figure 2.4 Illustration of Step 3 for a sociotechnical transportation network example. (From Mostashari, A. and Sussman, J. 2009. A framework for analysis, design and operation of complex large-scale sociotechnological systems. *International Journal for Decision Support Systems and Technologies,* **1(2), 52–68, April–June 2009.)**

individual actors within each of the major actor groups and show the links between them. Figure 2.4 illustrates the tasks described in Step 3 for a transportation system example. It shows the various subsystems selected, the institutional sphere mapped onto a plane for convenience, with the subsystems and sphere populated with components and actors, respectively (Mostashari and Sussman, 2009).

2.2.3.5.1.4 CLIOS Step 4A: Describe Components in the Physical Domain and Actors on the Institutional Sphere — *Components of the physical domain:* Up to this point, the components have been considered as generic. In this step we more carefully characterize the nature of the individual components. Within the physical domain, we consider three basic types of components. *Regular components* (or from now on, simply "components" and indicated by circles) are usually the most common in the subsystem diagrams within the physical domain. *Policy Levers* (indicated by rectangles) are components within the physical domain that are most directly controlled or influenced by decisions taken by the actors—often institutions and organizations—on the institutional sphere. *Common Drivers* (indicated by diamonds) are components that are shared across multiple and possibly all subsystems of the physical domain (Mostashari and Sussman, 2009).

In Figure 2.5 we show three shapes used for different CLIOS system components. External factors are indicated by shading, rather than by shape, and can still be either a component or a common driver.

Actors on the institutional sphere: In parallel to describing the components in the physical domain, we also describe the actors on the institutional sphere. In describing the actors, we can identify important characteristics, such as their power or mandate over different parts of the physical subsystems, their interests in the subsystems, their expertise and resources, and their positions with regard to different potential strategic alternatives. Much of this information can be derived from the actor's formal mandate, as well as interviews and other information sources that shed light on the described characteristics.

2.2.3.5.1.5 CLIOS Step 4B: Describe Links — As the components are characterized and divided into different types, we also, in parallel, need to characterize the nature of the several kinds of links. Link notation needs to be consistent; if they represent different things, one should use different diagrammatic components (Flood and Carson, 1993). In the diagrams used in the CLIOS system representation, these links will be largely qualitative. Generally, the links should indicate

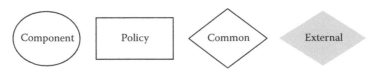

Figure 2.5   CLIOS system diagram component shapes.

directionality of influence and feedback loops, as well as the magnitude of influence (big/important or small/marginal impacts on the adjoining components) (Mostashari and Sussman, 2009).

In thinking about the linkages, a key aspect of the CLIOS system representation is to develop a framework for thinking about and describing the links in the system. We identify here three classes of links:

- Class 1: Links between components in a subsystem
- Class 2: Links between components in a subsystem and actors on the institutional sphere (also called "projections")
- Class 3: Links between actors on the institutional sphere

There are different approaches appropriate to each class of links. Generally, the links within the physical domain (Class 1) can be analyzed using engineering- and microeconomics-based methods, and will often be quantifiable. Regarding the links from the institutional sphere to the physical subsystems (Class 2 or projections), quantitative analysis is less useful since human agency and organizational and stakeholders' interests come into play as they attempt to induce changes in the physical domain. Finally, there are the interactions that take place within the institutional sphere itself (Class 3). Understanding this class of links requires methods drawing upon theories of organizations, institutions, politics, and policy. According to Karl Popper (1972), "obviously what we want is to understand how such non-physical things as *purposes, deliberations, plans, decisions, theories, intentions* and *values*, can play a part in bringing about physical changes in the physical world" (cited in Almond and Genco (1977), emphasis in original).

2.2.3.5.1.6 CLIOS Step 5: Transition from Descriptive to Prescriptive Treatment of System — Once the general structure of the CLIOS system has been established, and the behavior of individual components, actors, and links has been relatively well characterized, we can use this information to gain a better understanding of the overall system behavior and, where possible, counterintuitive or emergent system behavior by asking the following types of leading questions (Mostashari and Sussman, 2009).

First, with respect to the physical layers (Class 1 links), are there strong interactions within or between subsystems? Are there chains of links with fast-moving, high-influence interactions? Are some of the paths of links strongly nonlinear and/ or irreversible in their impact? Finally, can strong positive or negative feedback loops be identified?

Second, looking at the links between the institutional sphere and the physical subsystems (Class 2 links or projections), can we identify components within the physical domains that are influenced by many different organizations in the institutional sphere? If so, are the organizations pushing the system in the same direction, or is there competition among organizations in the direction of influence?

Alternatively, do some organizations on the institutional sphere have an influence on many components within the physical domain?

Finally, within the institutional sphere itself (Class 3 links), are the relationships between organizations characterized by conflict or cooperation? Are there any high-influence interactions, or particularly strong organizations, that have direct impacts on many other organizations within the institutional sphere? What is the hierarchical structure of the institutional sphere, and are there strong command and control relations among the organizations, and/or are they more loosely coupled? What is the nature of interaction between several organizations that all influence the same subsystems within the physical domain?

2.2.3.5.2 CLIOS Stage 2: Design, Evaluation, and Selection

Having considered the CLIOS system from the standpoint of its structure and behavior during the Representation stage, the next stage focuses on the design, evaluation, and selection of strategic alternatives for the system. This culminates in the development of a robust bundle of strategic alternatives. Among these strategic alternatives may be organizational and institutional changes that may be necessary to meet the CLIOS system goals (defined in Step 1, and to be reconsidered in Step 6).

2.2.3.5.2.1 CLIOS Step 6: Refine CLIOS System Goals and Identify Performance Measures — Entering the second stage of the CLIOS process, it is necessary to refine the preliminary goals developed in Step 1 to reflect the knowledge and insight gained at this point in the process. The concrete vision of the desired *future state* of the system, as prescribed by the *refined goals*, can then be used to identify *performance measures* that mark the progress from the current to the desired future state.

2.2.3.5.2.2 CLIOS Step 7: Identify and Design Strategic Alternatives for CLIOS System Improvement — The establishment of refined goals and performance measures naturally leads to questions about *how* CLIOS system performance can be improved through strategic alternatives. This is a creative step in the CLIOS process where imagination in developing strategic alternatives is to be valued, and out-of-the-box thinking and brainstorming is often a key to success. Performance improvements through strategic alternatives can take three forms. Thinking about nested complexity, we can characterize strategic alternatives as

■ Physical changes involving direct modification of components in the physical domain
■ Policy-driven changes involving the policy lever projections from the institutional sphere on the physical domain
■ Actor-based—architectural changes of the institutional sphere either within actors or between actors

In many cases, in order to achieve changes in the physical domain, policy-driven strategic alternatives need to be considered. These strategic alternatives may rely on incentives or disincentives such as taxes, subsidies, voluntary agreements, and restrictions on certain behaviors. Implicit in these types of alternatives is usually an assumption about how a policy change, initiated by actors on the institutional sphere, will cascade through the physical domain, and what changes in the performance measure will occur. Following this process can also reveal where strategic alternatives of this kind are counterproductive, diminishing the performance in other parts of the system.

2.2.3.5.2.3 CLIOS Step 8: Flag Important Areas of Uncertainty — A parallel activity to the identification of strategic alternatives for CLIOS system performance improvements is uncertainty analysis. In addition to internal and external risks that can be identified in a risk-management framework, there are additional uncertainties that deal with our lack of understanding of the system due to its emergent behaviors. In identifying key uncertainties, one can rely on the insights gained in Stage 1 and Step 6, in which we looked for chains of strong interactions, areas of conflict between stakeholders, or emergent behavior resulting from feedback loops. A promising qualitative methodology for identifying key uncertainties and understanding their impact on the CLIOS system is Scenario Planning as developed by Royal Dutch/Shell in the years leading up to the oil shocks of the 1970s (Schwartz, 1996). Quantitative approaches such as probabilistic risk assessment and event tree analysis are of value as well in this step of the CLIOS process. Another way of approaching uncertainty is exemplified by real options used to value flexibility and flexible strategic alternatives. McConnell (2007) describes ways that life-cycle flexibility can be integrated into the CLIOS Process.

2.2.3.5.2.4 CLIOS Step 9: Evaluate Strategic Alternatives and "Bundles" — In this step, the individual strategic alternatives that were generated in Step 7 are evaluated using the models developed in Step 6 or additional models if need be. Also, we can return here to the insights gained in Stage 1. Usually, each alternative is examined with regard to how it impacts the CLIOS system, especially for the performance areas that it was designed for. The use of *trade-off analysis* is an alternative approach that allows comparison of strategic alternatives across difference performance measures. A large number of alternatives can be compared in this manner, and there is no need to reduce performance measures to a single measure.

Given system complexity, it would be unusual if a single strategic alternative could be deployed and meet CLIOS system goals. However, by combining strategic alternatives into bundles or packages, the analyst may accomplish two objectives. First, one can mitigate and/or compensate for negative impacts. Given the interconnectedness of the CLIOS system, improvements along one dimension of performance may degrade performance in other areas of the system.

Second, different combinations of strategic alternatives can improve the robustness of the overall bundle. Here we define robustness as the ability of *bundles of strategic alternatives* to perform reasonably well under different future conditions. For example, combinations of alternatives can provide insurance against extreme changes or shocks to the system, such as major shifts in the common drivers. Seeking a robust bundle is a different approach than that of identifying a so-called "optimal" bundle, which may only perform optimally under a constrained set of conditions.

2.2.3.5.3 CLIOS Stage 3: Implementation and Adaptation

Many systems analyses approaches come to an end at Step 9 with a list of recommendations but with little guidance as to what obstacles might arise in the implementation of the recommended actions, or how the political realities will affect the actual deployment. Steps 10 and 11 (shown as parallel steps) are meant to address this common shortcoming. Step 10 focuses on how to implement those that are related to the physical domain, while Step 11 focuses on how to implement those on the institutional sphere. Akin to project management, but at a higher level, the implementation plans developed in Steps 10 and 11 would often include deployment budget/financial requirements, actor champion, and contingency planning in case some strategic alternatives fail or are not implemented on time. While we separate the two steps to emphasize the need to consider both areas, ideally, the two steps will create a common implementation plan where the strategic alternatives for the physical domain and those for the institutional sphere are mutually supportive (Mostashari and Sussman, 2009).

2.2.3.5.3.1 CLIOS Step 10: Design and Implement Plan for Physical Domain/Subsystems — As mentioned, this part of the plan for implementation concentrates on the physical and policy-driven types of strategic alternatives in the physical domain. In developing the plan, it is important to consider how each strategic alternative fits with the others. Are they independent, or are some prerequired for the success of the others? Are there enough resources to proceed with all strategic alternatives, or do additional fund-raising mechanisms need to be considered? Is the projected time horizon for achieving the CLIOS system goals reasonable, based on the ability to implement each alternative? How is implementation affected by failures in meeting the targets of specific strategic alternatives?

An additional consideration when we create a plan is focusing on all of the performance measures and the trade-offs among them. Neglecting certain performance measures, especially those that are highly valued by certain actors on the institutional sphere, can make the bundle deployment vulnerable to strong resistance from groups that feel that their interests are threatened (Mostashari, 2005).

This highlights another key task in developing a strategy for implementation, which is the use of the CLIOS system representation to identify which actor is going to implement, monitor, and enforce what strategic alternative (i.e., who will be the champion for each strategic alternative), as well as who has the potential to impede its implementation (Mostashari and Sussman, 2009). These considerations will inform the parallel Step 11.

2.2.3.5.3.2 CLIOS Step 11: Design and Implement Plan for Institutional

Sphere — Strategic alternatives developed earlier in Step 9 include needed changes to the structure of individual actors (e.g., organizations) and the relationships among them. In Step 11, we design a plan for implementation of these actor-based changes. Designing a plan for implementation requires a comprehensive understanding of the characteristics of the institutional sphere. We consider Step 11 to be a parallel activity to Step 10, with a plan for implementing actor-based changes explicitly being a central part of the overarching implementation plan (Mostashari and Sussman, 2009).

When creating a plan for how the institutional architecture can be modified along the lines drawn from the actor-based strategic alternatives of the chosen bundle, due consideration should be given to the actors' individual and collective goals. By studying actors on the institutional sphere to assess how each strategic alternative affects their interests, one can try to identify both the proponents and opponents of various strategic alternatives. This consideration is central to Step 11 by returning to the issue of mitigation or compensation; one can consider the building of coalitions that will overcome resistance created from the opponents (Mostashari and Sussman, 2009).

A well-crafted implementation plan for the institutional sphere notwithstanding, institutional changes may work against the goals of some organizations and generate not only external conflict among organizations but also internal conflict as organizations attempt to adapt to new institutional interactions. While organizations must "change internally as well as in their institutional interactions with other organizations," it is also true that "organizations, by their very nature, change slowly" (Sussman, 2000), and we need to be realistic in our time frames for improving our CLIOS system when changes to the institutional sphere are among our strategic alternatives.

2.2.3.5.3.3 CLIOS Step 12: Evaluate, Monitor, and Adapt Strategic

Alternatives — Finally, once bundles of strategic alternatives have been implemented, the next step is to monitor and observe outcomes, both in the short and long run. In particular, one should be careful to identify any unanticipated "side effects" such as degradation in the performance of one subsystem due to strategic alternatives targeted at improving a different subsystem. Indeed, creating the capability to monitor key aspects of the CLIOS system, its subsystems, and their components can and should be included as part of the plan for implementation in Steps 10 and 11 (Mostashari and Sussman, 2009).

2.3 Conclusion

In analyzing, designing, and managing complex large-scale sociotechnical systems, the tightly coupled and complex interactions between the institutional and technological systems are both a challenge and an opportunity. The concurrent consideration of the physical domain and the institutional sphere in the CLIOS process is a fundamental shift from other systems analysis and design processes for complex sociotechnical systems and allows for an improved understanding of the interactions between these two critical aspects of the problem. Thus it, allows for crafting interconnected and potentially synergetic technological and institutional strategies that would otherwise not be possible. The CLIOS process also allows for the design of flexible and robust strategic alternatives for systems design and management, taking into account the key uncertainties that the system faces throughout its life cycle. Additionally, the visual systems representation of CLIOS systems allows the engagement of a wide range of stakeholders in the pertinent analysis and decision-making processes.

References

Adler, M. and Ziglio, E. (Eds.) (1996). *Gazing into the Oracle: The. Delphi Method and its Application to Social Policy and Public Health.* London: Jessica Kingsley Publishers.

Ahuja, R., Magnanti, T.L, Orlin, J.B. (1993). *Network Flows: Theory, Algorithms and Applications.* Upper Saddle River, NJ: Prentice Hall.

Almond, G.A. and Genco, S.J. (1977). Clocks, clocks, and the study of politics, *World Politics* 29(4) pp. 489–522.

Donella H. Meadows, "To Grow or not to grow." Newsweek, March 1972.

Ferguson, E.S. (1992). *Engineering and the Mind's Eye.* Cambridge, MA: MIT Press.

Flood, R.L. and Carson, E.R. (1993). *Dealing with Complexity: An Introduction to the Theory and Application of Systems Science.*

Holland, J.H. (1995). *Hidden Order: How Adaptation Builds Complexity*, Reading, MA: Addison-Wesley.

Holland, J.H. (1998). *Emergence: From Chaos to Order.*

Holling, C.S. (Ed.) (1978). *Adaptive Environmental Assessment and Management.* Chichester, England: Wiley.

Jay Forrester, "Industrial Dynamics." Waltham, MA: Pagasus Communications, 1961.

Jay Forrester "Urban Dynamics" Pagasus Communications, 1969.

Lloyd, S. (2002). Complex Systems: A Review. *Proceedings of the ESD Internal Symposium.* May 29–30, Cambridge, MA.

Ludwigvon Bertalanffy, "General System theory: Foundations, Development, Applications," New York: George Braziller. 1968.

Lockheed Martin, Maritime surveillance system, see http://www.lockheedmartin.com/. 2004.

Kometer, M. (2005). Command in air war: centralized vs. decentralized control of combat airpower. Ph.D. Thesis, Massachusetts Institute of Technology, Engineering Systems Division, Technology, Management, and Policy Program.

Magee, C. and de Weck, L. (2002). An Attempt at Complex System Classification. *Proceedings of the ESD Internal Symposium.* May 29–30, Cambridge, MA.

Marks, D. (2002). The Evolving Role of Systems Analysis in Process and Methods in Large-Scale Public Socio-Technical Systems. *Proceedings of the ESD Internal Symposium.* May 29–30, Cambridge, MA.

McConnell, J. (2007). A Life-Cycle Flexibility Framework for Designing, Evaluating, and Managing "Complex" Real Options: Case Studies in Urban Transportation and Aircraft Systems. Doctoral Thesis, Massachusetts Institute of Technology. Cambridge, MA.

Moses, J. (2006). Foundational Issues in Engineering Systems: A Framing Paper. *Engineering Systems Division Monograph.*

Mostashari, A. and Sussman, J. (2009). A framework for analysis, design and operation of complex large-scale sociotechnological systems. *International Journal for Decision Support Systems and Technologies,* 1(2), 52–68, April–June 2009.

Mostashari, A. (2005). *Stakeholder Participation in Sociotechnological Systems Decision-making,* 258 pp.

Mostashari, A. and Sussman, J. (2005). Stakeholder-assisted modeling and policy design. *Journal of Environmental Assessment and Management,* September 2005.

Mullins, N. (1973). *Theories and Theory Groups in Contemporary American Sociology.* New York: Harper and Row.

Matthew Bartschi Wall, "A Genetic Algorithm for resource-constrained scheduling, "Ph.D. Dissertation, MIT. 1996.

Martha Amram, Nalin Kulatilaka, "Real Options" Managing strategic Investment in an uncertain world, Oxford University Press, 1998.

Osorio-Urzúa, C. (2007). Architectural Innovations, Functional Emergence and Diversification in Engineering Systems. Ph.D. Thesis, Technology, Management and Policy Program, Massachusetts Institute of Technology, Cambridge, MA.

Popper, K. (1972). *Objective Knowledge: An Evolutionary Approach,* 1972, Rev. ed. 1979.

Puccia, C.J. and Levins, R. (1985). *Qualitative Modeling of Complex Systems.* Cambridge, MA: Harvard University Press.

Rasiel, E. (1999). *The McKinsey Way,* New York: McGraw-Hill.

Rouse, W. (2007). Complex engineered, organizational and natural systems, *Systems Engineering,* Vol. 10, No. 3, 2007, pp. 260–271.

Schwartz, P. (1996). *The Art of the Long View: Planning for the Future in an Uncertain World.* New York: Currency Doubleday.

Sheard, S. and Mostashari, A. (2009). Principles of complex systems for systems engineering, *Systems Engineering,* the Journal of INCOSE, Vol. 12, No. 1, January 2009.

Sterman, D. (2000). *Business Dynamics: Systems Thinking and Modeling for a Complex world.* Irwin/McGraw-Hill.

Sussman, J. (2002). Collected Views on Complexity in Systems. *Proceedings of the ESD Internal Symposium.* May 29–30, Cambridge, MA.

Sussman, J. (2000). Toward Engineering Systems as a Discipline. MIT Engineering Systems Division Working Paper Series. ESD-WP-2000-01.

Sussman, J. and Dodder, R. (2002). The Concept of a "CLIOS Analysis" Illustrated by the Mexico City Case. *Proceedings of the ESD Internal Symposium.* May 29–30, Cambridge, MA.

Sussman, J., Sgouridis, S., and Ward, J. (2004). An Engineering Systems Approach to Transportation Planning: Regional Strategic Transportation Planning as a CLIOS. *Proceedings of the 84th Transportation Research Board Annual Meeting.* January 2005, Washington, D.C.

Swartz, R.S. and DeRosa, J.K. (2006). Framework for enterprise systems engineering processes. *Proceedings of the 19th International Conference Software & Systems. Engineering and Their Applications,* December 2006.

Ward, J. (2004). Toll Road Public–Private Partnerships in Malaysia: Using the CLIOS Process for Policy Improvements. Master's Thesis in Transportation, Massachusetts Institute of Technology, Cambridge, MA.

Young, R. (2001). *Effective Requirements Practices.* Boston: Addison-Wesley.

Zuckerman, B. (2002). Defining Engineering Systems: Investigating National Missile Defense. *Proceedings of the ESD Internal Symposium.*, May 29–30, Cambridge, MA.

Chapter 3

Dynamic Models and Analysis for Information Propagation in Online Social Networks

Xiaohong Guan, Yadong Zhou, Qinghua Zheng, Qindong Sun, and Junzhou Zhao

Contents

As one of the most important media, Internet provides various communication platforms for information propagation. Especially on a blog site, BBS (Bulletin Board System), and a forum, users can post and spread their ideas and thoughts through an online social network, which composes of groups of users with particular patterns of communication between them [1]. Analyzing and predicting the dynamic characteristics of information propagation is obviously helpful in designing propaganda strategy and testing the performance of an advertisement, mining some latent business opportunities for corporations, and recommending the content of growing hot topics to improve users' experiences for obtaining popular information for Social Networking Sites (SNS), etc.

This chapter is designed to introduce the related work on dynamic models and analyze results for information propagation in online social networks. First we give the description of the traditional epidemic model and rumor model and introduce recent works on modeling and predicting briefly the propagation scale of information based on them. Second, we introduce the analysis of relationship among users and models of user behavior, such as reading and posting behavior. Finally, analysis of information flow pathway and models of innovation diffusion are introduced.

3.1 Models of Information Propagation Based on the Epidemic Model and the Rumor Model

The traditional epidemic model is based on compartmental models, in which individuals in the population are divided into a set of different groups. Related theory has been used in planning, implementing, and evaluating various prevention, therapy, and control programs. Based on the analogy between the spread of disease and the spread of information in networks, the rumor model has been investigated to describe the dynamics of the rumor propagation process. However, it is different from disease spreading in that the rumor dynamics is driven by direct contacts between individuals of different classes. Prior research supports a valuable basis for modeling and analyzing the information propagation process in online social networks.

3.1.1 Epidemic Models

The study of epidemic models has attracted the attention of epidemiologists and grown exponentially since the middle of the 20th Century, so that a tremendous variety of models has now been formulated, mathematically analyzed, and applied [2–6]. Epidemic models have been used in planning, implementing, and evaluating various prevention, therapy, and control programs.

Here, we introduce a traditional model that describes disease spreading through a population by contacts between infected and healthy individuals: the *susceptible infected removed* (SIR) model. Other models and generalizations can be found in References 3–7.

The theoretical approach to epidemic spreading is based on compartmental models, that is, models in which the individuals in the population are divided into a set of different groups [3, 4]. The SIR model describes diseases resulting in the immunization or death of infected individuals, and assumes that each individual can be in one of three possible states: *susceptible* (denoted by S), *infected* (I), or *removed* (R). Susceptible individuals are healthy persons who can catch the disease if exposed to infected individuals. Once an individual catches the infection, he or she moves into the infected (and infective) class, and then, after some time, into the removed class. The model is based on two parameters: the transmission rate λ, and the recovery rate μ. The following model is based on the homogeneous mixing hypothesis, meaning that individuals with whom a susceptible individual has contact are chosen at random from the whole population.

$$\frac{ds(t)}{dt} = -\lambda \bar{k} \rho(t) s(t),$$

$$\frac{d\rho(t)}{dt} = -\mu \rho(t) + \lambda \bar{k} \rho(t) s(t), \tag{3.1}$$

$$\frac{dr(t)}{dt} = \mu \rho(t)$$

where $s(t)$, $\rho(t)$, and $r(t)$ are, respectively, the density (i.e., the fraction) of susceptible, infected, and removed individuals at time t, and $\bar{k}$ is the number of contacts per unit time that is supposed to be constant for the whole population.

More recently, starting with the works by Pastor–Satorras and Vespignani [8], there has been a burst of activity on understanding the effects of complex network topology on the rate and patterns of disease spread. They [8] analyzed real data from computer virus infections and defined a dynamical model for the spreading of infections on scale-free networks that could help in the understanding of other spreading phenomena on communication and social networks. Yamir Moreno et al. [9] exploited the mean-field-like rate equations describing the system and studied the susceptible–infected–removed epidemiological model on assortative networks, providing numerical evidence of the absence of epidemic thresholds. J. G′omez-Gardenes et al. [10] studied an immunization strategy that could be used for designing and deploying a digital immune system.

3.1.2 Rumor Models

Based on the epidemic model, Daley and Kendal [11] proposed the basic rumor model (also called the DK model). The basic DK rumor model is defined as follows. Each of the N elements of the network can be in one of three possible states. Following the original terminology [12], these three classes correspond to *ignorant* (denoted by *I*), *spreader* (*S*), and *stifler* (*R*) nodes. Ignorants are those individuals who have not heard the rumor and hence are susceptible to being informed. Spreaders comprise active individuals who are spreading the rumor. Finally, stiflers are those who have heard the rumor but are no longer spreading it.

In the homogeneous mixing hypothesis, the DK model can be described in terms of the densities of ignorants, spreaders, and stiflers, that is, $i(t)$, $s(t)$, and $r(t)$, respectively, as a function of time:

$$\frac{di(t)}{dt} = -\lambda \bar{k} i(t) s(t),$$

$$\frac{ds(t)}{dt} = \lambda \bar{k} i(t) s(t) - \alpha \bar{k} s(t)[s(t) + r(t)], \tag{3.2}$$

$$\frac{dr(t)}{dt} = \alpha \bar{k} s(t)[s(t) + r(t)]$$

where $\bar{k}$ is the number of contacts per unit time that is supposed to be constant for the whole population; and when an ignorant meets a spreader, it turns itself into a new spreader at rate λ; spreaders become stiflers with probability α if they are in contact with another spreader or a stifler. The decay of spreading may be due to a process of "forgetting" or because spreaders learn that the rumor has lost its "news value."

Recently, several investigators [13–16] have explored this model on top of complex network topology. The heterogeneity of the connectivity distribution inherent to scale-free networks makes it necessary to take into account that nodes could not only be in three different states but they also belong to different connectivity classes *k*. Denoting by $ik(t)$, $sk(t)$, and $rk(t)$, respectively, the densities of ignorants, spreaders, and stiflers and then connectivity k, with $ik(t)+ sk(t)+ rk(t) = 1$, respectively, the rumor model can be formed as

$$\frac{di_k(t)}{dt} = -\lambda k i_k(t) \sum_{k'} \frac{k' P(k') s_{k'}(t)}{\bar{k}},$$

$$\frac{ds_k(t)}{dt} = \lambda k i_k(t) \sum_{k'} \frac{k' P(k') s_{k'}(t)}{\bar{k}} - \alpha k s_k(t) \sum_{k'} \frac{k' P(k')[s_{k'}(t) + r_{k'}(t)]}{\bar{k}}, \quad (3.3)$$

$$\frac{dr_k(t)}{dt} = \alpha k s_k(t) \sum_{k'} \frac{k' P(k')[s_{k'}(t) + r_{k'}(t)]}{\bar{k}}$$

where $P(k)$ is the connectivity distribution of the nodes, and $\sum_{k'} k' P(k') s_{k'}(t) / \bar{k}$ is the probability that any given node points to a spreader. Furthermore, D.H. Zanette [13] found that the rumor model exhibits critical behavior at a finite randomness of the underlying small-world network and studied the transition occurring between regimes where the rumor "dies" in a small neighborhood of its origin. He [17] studied the dynamics of an epidemic-like model for the spread of a rumor on a small-world network and found that this model exhibits a transition between regimes of localization and propagation at a finite value of the network randomness. Zonghua Liu et al. [14] investigated infection dynamics by using a three-state epidemiological model that does not involve the mechanism of self-recovery, and found that there is a substantial fraction of nodes that can never be infected, and heterogeneous networks are relatively more robust against spreads of infection as compared to homogeneous networks. Yamir Moreno et al. [15] studied the dynamics of the epidemic spreading processes aimed at spontaneous dissemination of information updates in populations with complex connectivity patterns, and analyzed the behavior of several global parameters, such as reliability, efficiency, and load. Yamir Moreno et al. [16] studied the spreading process in detail for random scale-free networks, and the result shows that the model could be applied in replicated database maintenance, peer-to-peer communication networks, and social spreading phenomena.

3.2 User Behaviors in the Information Propagation Process

User behaviors in the information propagation process in online social networks usually include posting a blog article or picture; reading, commenting on, and recommending other users' posts, etc. These multiple user behaviors describe the details of how the information appears and spreads among online social networks [43]. Besides, through modeling and analyzing user behaviors and relationship between users, we can discover the important users [27–30] who play key roles in the information propagation process, design an effective propaganda strategy to maximize the spread of information through a social network [65, 68], mine some latent business opportunities for corporations [39], and an effective information-recommending mechanism to supply suitable information to each type of users [52, 63]. In this section, we focus on the recent research progress on the analysis and models of user behaviors in the information propagation process.

3.2.1 Relationship between Users

As one of the most significant characteristics of online social networks, the relationships between users mainly include blogroll link [18, 19, 22, 25], information interaction [20, 23, 24], and the connection between social networks and outside information networks [21, 23], etc. To analyze the information propagation process, we should understand the relationship between users and find out how the relationship influences the process.

Blogroll links are usually located in the blog's sidebar and point to other blogs that the author may read or that may simply be the author's friends' blog. Blogroll links are the most simple and common relationship between users. Prior works have investigated the quantitative features of blogroll links, such as overlap, distance, reciprocity, in-degree and out-degree, density and centralization, community structure, etc.

3.2.1.1 Overlap

Overlap is defined as the intersection between the sets of nodes that are reachable from each starting point. Considering all the paths having three hops for blog *a*, blog *b*, and blog *c*, and four hops for blog *d*, then classifying all the nodes reached into sets that were reached by *a*, *b*, *c*, or *d* individually, or in any combination, the members of these sets were classified as A-list [19] or not and counted. A chi-square test for independence was conducted. The test is significant (chi-sq = 194.2, 3 df, $p < .0001$), suggesting a strong association between a blog's membership in the A-list and how reachable it is from the four starting blogs. The largest deviance (177.2) came from A-list nodes reachable from all four starting points, suggesting that A-list blogs tend to be reachable from any starting point, whereas the same is not true for non-A-list blogs. This result indicates that A-list blogs are more central in the network than other blogs.

3.2.1.2 Distance

Distance is defined as the shortest paths between users. Mislove Alan et al. [25] analyzed the data of four online social networks (Flickr, LiveJournal, Orkut, and

Youtube). Table 3.1 shows the average path lengths, diameters, and radius for the four social networks. In absolute terms, the path lengths and diameters for all four are remarkably short. Interestingly, despite being comparable in size to the Web graph we considered, the social networks have significantly shorter average path lengths and diameters. This property may again result from the high degree of reciprocity within them. Incidentally, Broder et al. [26] noted that if the Web were treated as an undirected graph, the average path length would drop from 16.12 to 7.

3.2.1.3 Reciprocity

Ali-Hasan and Adamic [19] analyzed the reciprocity of three types of link (blogroll links, citation links, and comment links) based on the data of three blog communities (Kuwait, UAE, DFW), and the results in Table 3.2 show a high degree of reciprocity in all three communities, but the level varied by the type of link. In all three communities, a greater fraction of blogroll links are reciprocated than post citations, possibly because blogroll links are more numerous in our data set, and bloggers sometimes reciprocate blogroll links merely as a courtesy. Furthermore, reciprocal blogroll links indicate possibly only a mutual awareness, whereas reciprocal post citations imply a greater level of interaction, both blogs actively discussing or linking to one another in their posts rather than one blog simply finding

Table 3.1 Average Path Length, Radius, and Diameter of the Studied Networks

Network	Avg. Path Length	Radius	Diameter
Web	16.12	475	905
Flickr	5.67	13	27
LiveJournal	5.88	12	20
Orkut	4.25	6	9
Youtube	5.10	13	21

Table 3.2 Percentage of Links That Are Reciprocated

	Kuwait	UAE	DFW
Post citations	19%	16%	26%
Blogroll links	32%	43%	27%
Comments	43%	N/A	N/A

another's post interesting enough to cite. Finally, it is interesting to observe that, for the Kuwait blogs, it is the comments that are most often reciprocated, making commenting the most conversational and mutual activity in that community.

3.2.1.4 In-Degree and Out-Degree

To measure the in- and out-linkage of the blogs, Herring et al. [18] excluded blogs that were at the ends of the paths in the sample, and that had not occurred elsewhere in the sample, as their out-degree is unknown. Log-linear regressions of in-degree against out-degree show out-degree to be a significant predictor of in-degree, but less strongly so for A-list blogs than non-A-list ones. The slope of the regression line is steeper for the non-A-list blogs (0.446 log in-degrees per log out-degree), explaining 35.8% of the variance, while that for the A-list is flatter (0.179 log in-degrees per log out-degree), explaining 27.3% of the variance. Hence, linking to other blogs on one's blog is likely to earn more links pointing back, but more so among non-A-list blogs that have a lower in-degree to begin with than among the A-list blogs.

The investigating of overlap, distance, reciprocity, in-degree, and out-degree in online social networks has been introduced. Further, Ali-Hasan and Adamic [19] investigated the density and centralization, community structure, and online and offline relationships between users, Adar et al. [22] studied the link structure created by automated trackbacks in blog networks, and Mislove Alan et al. [25] measured and analyzed the correlation of in-degree and out-degree, link degree correlations, and densely connected core in online social networks.

Except for the obvious link relationship between users, some latent relationships are also important, such as users having the same interest in some topic chatting with each other via IM (instant messaging) tool or e-mail, which can be called information interaction relationship.

Shen et al. [20] studied the method of mining the latent friend from blog data. Latent friends are defined as people who share similar topic distribution in their blogs. The method is two-level similarity based, which is conducted in two stages. In the first stage, an existing topic hierarchy is exploited to build a topic distribution for a blogger. Then, in the second stage, a detailed similarity comparison is conducted for bloggers that are close in interest to each other that are discovered in the first stage.

Singla and Richardson [23] analyzed the IM social networks and the search engine data, and exploited the relation between who talks to whom on the IM network and what they search for. The investigation result shows that there exists a correlation between users' chatting behaviors and the category of their searches, ages, locations, and genders (that is, users who talk to each other are more likely to be of opposite gender than would be expected). They also found that these correlations strengthen with the total amount of time the two users spend talking. Interestingly, the correlation decreases with the amount of time spent per message; users who send very brief messages (perhaps indicating that they are closer friends and thus need less formality in their communication) are more likely to be similar to each other. They also found that the more time a user spends per message, the more likely it is that he or she is talking to someone of the opposite gender.

As already introduced, Reference 23 investigated the relation between social networks and other outside information networks (that is, search engine in the reference). Some other investigators have also studied this situation. Bhagat et al. [21] used the blogs as a starting point to pull in data about other multiple information networks and studied how these multiple networks interact with each other. They exploited three types of cross-information networks, which are blog–blog (two different blog sites), blog–web, and blog–messaging networks. Some interesting results were concluded, such as bloggers using the same blogging service cite each other significantly more than those using other services in the blog–blog situation, and the percentage of users that share any IM contact decreases with their age. Adamic and Glance [24] analyzed the posts of 40 "A-list" blogs over a period of 2 months preceding the U.S. Presidential Election of 2004 across multiple blog sites to study how often they referred to one another and to quantify the overlap in the topics they discussed, both within the liberal and conservative communities, and also across communities. The results show that liberals and conservatives link primarily within their separate communities, with far fewer crosslinks exchanged between them. An interesting pattern that emerged was that conservative bloggers were more likely to link to other blogs: primarily other conservative blogs, but also some liberal ones.

3.2.2 Analysis of User Behaviors

Throughout the information propagation process in online social networks, user behaviors [42] could be divided into two types: reading and posting. Reading behavior means that users read the articles, pictures, or videos they are interested in. This type of behavior is the prior step of users' posting behaviors, which are posting comments and articles about what they have read. However, studying reading behaviors is quite difficult because most SNS did not support the data about who had read the article or picture. We find that just one research team has investigated it based on the SNS's log data [31, 38]. The studying on posting behaviors is more popular. Investigators have analyzed the behavior based on the social network structure, users' content interests, and time factors [32, 33, 36, 37, 44, 47]. Note that there is a significant relative research focus: mining the users' interests [34, 35, 50], which is obviously helpful to analyzing and modeling posting and reading behaviors.

3.2.2.1 Reading Behavior

Furukawa et al. [31, 38] studied the various aspects of blog reading behavior by analyzed user log data obtained from Doblog (a Japanese weblog hosting service), and found a regular reading relation (RR relation) between social relations and readership relations. They defined the weblog regular reading relation as follows:

Regular Reading (RR): Blogger *A* has an RR relation with blog *B* if blogger *A* reads blog *B* more frequently than every *m* times the blogger logs in.

The experiment results show that if *m* = 5, half of the blogs that are read more than three times. Moreover, they use five attributes to predict the creating and holding of reading links between two weblogs (*x* and *y*) based on a machine-learning approach:

- Adamic/Adar: $\sum_{z \in \Gamma(x) \cap \Gamma(y)} 1 / \log |\Gamma(z)|$
- Gragh distance: Length of shortest path between *x* and *y*
- Common neighbors: $|\Gamma(x) \cap \Gamma(y)|$
- Jaccard's coefficient: $|\Gamma(x) \cap \Gamma(y)| / |\Gamma(x) \cup \Gamma(y)|$
- Preferential attachment: $|\Gamma(x)| \cdot |\Gamma(y)|$

where $\Gamma(x)$ is the set of neighbors of *x* in the network. These attributes are built based on four social networks: citation, blogroll, comment, and trackback networks. The detail description and testing of these attributes are given in References 45 and 46.

3.2.2.2 Predicting the Posting Behavior Using a Dynamic Probability Model

This is different from the read behaviors in that the user writing about something will be influenced by more factors. Generally, the users' posting behavior is influenced by their interests [37], social network link [44], group behavior [47], time factor, outside news source, etc. Some of these factors are difficult to obtain and analyze. For instance, we cannot understand the newspapers, news site pages, or other news source that one user would read, unless we can track the user's life. However, investigators have analyzed and modeled posting behavior by factors that can be obtained from some open data sources.

Zhou et al. [47] studied the factors that influence the user's posting—behavior—whether one user will post something about one specific topic or not and proposed a dynamic probability model that could predict the tendency of the user's posting behavior in the online social network. In the topic discussion process, a user's posting behavior would be mostly affected by three factors: individual interest, group behavior, and time lapse. The relative hypotheses are proposed as follows:

> **Hypothesis 1:** Individual interest factor. Assuming that the more times one user attends the discussion on topic *T* at present and has attended in the past, the more probably it is that he or she will attend the discussion the next time.

Hypothesis 2: Group behavior factor. Assuming that the larger the number of users who attend the discussion on the topic at present and have attended in the past, T increases, the more probable that they will attend the discussion the next time.

Hypothesis 3: Time lapse factor. Assuming that the longer the interval between the present and peak time, the less probable that users will attend the discussion the next time.

Based on Hypothesis 1, the behavior tendency function $f(x)$ is given for user a at time n ($1 < n < N$), from which the tendency probability of the user's posting behavior can be calculated as follows:

$$f(\vec{x}) = \prod_{i=1}^{s} k_i^{[2-(x_n-x_{n-i})^2]} \cdot e^{-k_i}, k_i > 1 \tag{3.4}$$

where x_n is the behavior state of user a regarding posting on a topic at time n. When x_n is 1, the value of the function is in direct proportion to the probability of user a attending the discussion at time n, and contrarily when x_n is 0. K_i is a parameter to be estimated, e is the base of the Napierian logarithm, and s is the available duration of the individual interest factor, which means user behavior at time n only associates with the behavior from time $n - s$ to time $n - 1$ and can be evaluated by experience. The more frequently x_{n-i} equals x_n, the larger the value of the function. That is, the more frequently the predicted behavior of user a at time n is the same as the previous behavior, the larger the probability of the predicted behavior happening, and contrarily, the lesser the probability.

Based on Hypothesis 2, the behavior tendency function $h(x)$ is given for user a at time n ($1 < n < N$), from which the probability of the group behavior trend of can be calculated.

$$h(\vec{x}) = \prod_{j=1}^{s'} l_j^{1+r(2x_n-1)} \cdot e^{-l_j}, l_j > 1 \tag{3.5}$$

$$r = \frac{\|G(n-j)\| + \|G(n-j-1)\| + \|G(n-j-2)\| + 1}{\|G(n-j-1)\| + \|G(n-j-2)\| + \|G(n-j-3)\| + 1} \tag{3.6}$$

where $\|G(n-j)\|$ is the total number of users who attend the discussion at time $n - j$, and r is the changing ratio of the number of users that is calculated by dividing the total number of users who are involved from time $n - j$ to $n - j - 2$ with the total number of users from time $n - j - 1$ to $n - j - 3$. If the total number decreases in the duration, r is less than 1. s' is the available duration of group behavior factor, which means the user behavior at time n only associates with the group behavior from time $n - s'$ to time $n - 1$, and can be evaluated by experience. L_j is a parameter to be estimated. *e* is the base of the Napierian logarithms. x_n is the predicting behavior state of user *a* at time *n*; if x_n is equal to 1, then $(2x_n - 1)$ is 1, so the more the frequencies in which *r* is larger than 1, the larger the value of the behavior tendency function, which shows that the more the total number of users who discuss the topic, the larger the probability of one user attending the discussion, and contrarily, the lesser the probability.

Based on Hypothesis 3, the behavior tendency function *g(x)* is given for user *a* at time *n* $(1 < n < N)$, from which the probability of behavior trend by the time lapse factor can be calculated.

$$g(x) = \frac{1}{(n - t_p)^{\lambda \cdot x_n}}, \lambda > 0 \tag{3.7}$$

where *n* is the time point to be predicted, t_p is the peak time when the number of participators is the largest from initial time to time *n*, λ is the lapse exponential coefficient (usually is 0.5–1) to be evaluated by experience, and x_n is the predicting behavior state of user *a* at time *n*. In formula 3.9, if x_n is equal to 1, then the value of the function is larger than 1, and the larger *n* is, the less the value of the behavior tendency function will be. This demonstrates that the longer the interval from peak time to predicting time, the less the probability of user behavior in attending the discussion; if x_n is equal to 0, the value of the behavior tendency function is 1.

Considering all the three hypothesis factors, the behavior tendency function $\chi(x)$ is given for user *a* at predicting time *n*.

$$P(x_n) \sim \chi(\vec{x}) = f(\vec{x}) \cdot h(\vec{x}) \cdot g(\vec{x}) = \frac{\{\prod_{i=1}^{s} k_i^{[2-(x_n - x_{n-i})^2]} \cdot e^{-k_i}\} \cdot \{\prod_{j=1}^{s'} l_j^{1+(r+1)(2x_n - 1)} \cdot e^{-l_j}\}}{(n - t_p)^{\lambda \cdot x_n}}$$

and

$$k_i > 1, l_j > 1, \lambda > 0 \tag{3.8}$$

where $P(x_n)$ is the probability of the tendency to attend the discussion or not. $P(x_n)$ has positive correlation with $\chi(x)$.

All of the *q* user behavior in the universal set *A* can be expressed as

$$a_1 : \vec{x}_{a1}, a_2 : \vec{x}_{a2}, ..., a_q : \vec{x}_{aq} \tag{3.9}$$

They have estimated the parameters in formula 8 by the Maximum Likelihood Estimate (MLE) method. The results are as follows:

$$\ln L(q) = \ln[\chi(\vec{x}_{a1}) \cdot \chi(\vec{x}_{a2}) \cdots \chi(\vec{x}_{aq})]$$

$$= \sum_A \{\sum_{i=1}^{s} \{[2 - (x_n - x_{n-i})^2] \cdot \ln k_i - k_i\} + \sum_{j=1}^{s'} \{\{1 + r^{(2x_n - 1)}\} \cdot \ln l_j - l_j\} \tag{3.10}$$

$$\frac{d \ln L(q)}{dk_i} = \sum_A \{\frac{2-(x_n-x_{n-i})^2}{k_i} - 1\} = 0 \Rightarrow k_i = \frac{\sum_A [2-(x_n-x_{n-i})^2}{q} \qquad (3.11)$$

$$\frac{d \ln L(q)}{dl_j} = \sum_A \{\frac{1+r^{(2x_n-1)}}{l_j} - 1\} = 0 \Rightarrow l_j = \frac{\sum_A \{1+r^{(2x_n-1)}}{q} \qquad (3.12)$$

According to formulas 11 and 12, the parameters in formula 8 can be estimated by sample data, and the value of the behavior tendency function $\chi(X)$ can be calculated by setting x_n as 1 and 0. If x_n is 1, $\chi(X)$ has positive correlation with $P(x_n = 1)$; if x_n is 0, $\chi(X)$ has positive correlation with $P(x_n = 0)$. After normalizing $\chi(X)$, the values of $P(x_n = 1)$ and $P(x_n = 0)$ are obtained.

Figure 3.1 shows the comparison between real data and the predicting results about two topics; and x axis is time whose unit is day, y axis is the number of participators whose unit is user; blue line with diamond figure corresponds to the real data, while black line with cross figure corresponds to the predicting result. The values of s, s' and λ are 7, 3 and 0.5 respectively; and the other parameters are calculated by MLE which has been mentioned in formula 11 and 12.

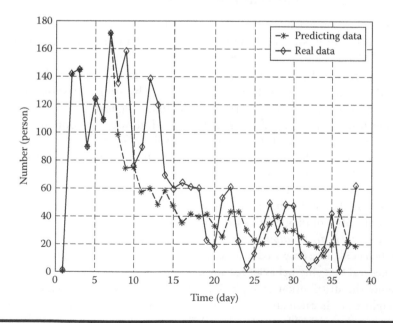

Figure 3.1   Comparison between real data and the predicted results.

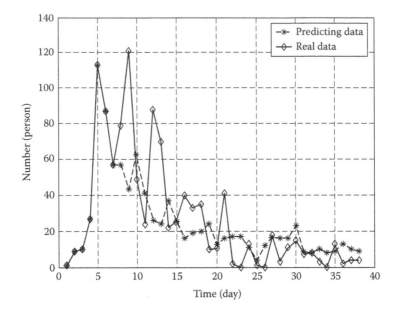

Figure 3.1 **(Continued) Comparison between real data and the predicted results.**

3.2.2.3 Predicting the Posting Behavior Based on a Machine-Learning Approach

Besides the foregoing, Chen et al. [37] also built a social network and profile-based blogging-behavior model to predict the posting behavior. Based on social-network and profile-based blogging behavior features $< \vec{T}_z, \vec{T}_p(j)_z, \vec{C}_p(j)_z, \vec{S}(j)_z >$ for blogger j, they trained the social network and profile-based blogging-behavior model and predicted future blogging behaviors of blogger j by using regression techniques. The details of the features are described in the following text.

Topic distribution vector $\vec{T}_z$: For each time window z, the content of the blog entries is represented as a topic distribution vector $\vec{T}_z = < t_1, t_2, t_3, ..., t_n >_z$ that represents the distributions of blog entries with respect to the list of topics, where n is the number of topics, and t_i represents the weight of the i-th topic within time window z. The i-th component of a topic distribution vector can be calculated as the total number of blog entries belonging to i-th topic divided by the total number of blog entries in time window z.

Personal topic distribution vector $(\vec{T}_p(j)_z)$: For the profile-based topic distribution, Chen et al. have proposed to add the personal topic distribution vector $T_p(j)_z$ to the general blogging-behavior features, $\vec{T}_p(j)_z = < t_{1j}, t_{2j}, t_{3j}, ..., t_{nj} >_z$, where t_{1j} represents the distribution of topic 1 for blogger j within time window z. Here the weight of t_{1j} is calculated as the percentage of blog entries posted by blogger j belonging to topic *1* (denoted as $| t_{1j} |$) against the total number of blog entries posted by blogger j (denoted as $|tj|$) in the time window z.

Comment distribution vector $\vec{C}_p(j)_z$: This vector can be represented as $\vec{C}_p(j)_z = \vec{C}_p(j)_z = <c_{1j}, c_{2j}, c_{3j}, ..., c_{nj}>_z$, where c_{1j} represents the distribution of comment on topic 1 for blogger j within time window z. Here the weight of c_{1j} is calculated as the percentage of comments belonging to topic 1 (denoted as $|c_{1j}|$) posted by blogger j against the total number of comments posted by blogger j (denoted as $|cj|$) in the time window z.

Social network vector $(\vec{S}(j)_z)$: The social network features of blogger j in time window z are represented as a vector $S(j)_z = <s_{1j}, s_{2j}, s_{3j}, ..., s_{nj}>_z$ in

$$\vec{S}(j)_z = \sum_{x=1}^{m} \frac{C_{j \to x}}{TC_j} \cdot \vec{T}_p(x)_z, TC_j = \sum_{x=1}^{m} C_{j \to x} \tag{3.13}$$

where m is the total number of social neighbors of blogger j in the network, $C_{j \to x}$ represents the number of comments written by blogger j to blog entries posted by blogger x in a certain time window, and TC_j represents the total number of comments written by blogger j in the same time window.

Based on the social-network and profile-based blogging behavior features $<\vec{T}_z, \vec{T}_p(j)_z, \vec{C}_p(j)_z, \vec{S}(j)_z>$ for blogger j, we can train the social-network and profile-based blogging-behavior model and predict the future blogging behaviors of blogger j by using regression techniques. We take the previous k combined vectors $<\vec{T}_z, \vec{T}_p(j)_z, \vec{C}_p(j)_z, \vec{S}(j)_z>$ from the $(z - k + 1)$-th time window to the i-th time window as the input vectors, and the combined vector $<\vec{T}_z, \vec{T}_p(j)_z, \vec{C}_p(j)_z, \vec{S}(j)_z>$ in the $(z + 1)$-th time window as the target vector to train the model. Then, by using the trained regression model, the future blogging behavior of blogger j can be predicted based on the historical general blogging behavior, the blogger's own historical blogging behavior, and his or her neighbors' historical blogging behavior.

3.2.2.4 Modeling the Posting Behavior Based on the Cascade Model

In the traditional research on modeling, the spread of an idea or innovation throughout a social network G can be represented as a direct graph. There are two basic models: the independent cascade model [48] and the linear threshold model [49]. In the innovation-spreading process, one user's states can be divided into active (an adopter of the innovation) or inactive. Therefore, the aim of modeling the innovation-spreading process can be transferred to predicting the user node's tendency to become active, which increases monotonically as more of its neighbors become active. Thus, the process will look roughly as follows from the perspective of an initially inactive node u: as time unfolds, more and more of u's neighbors become active; at some point, this may cause u to become active, and u's decision may in turn trigger further decisions by nodes to which u is connected.

Independent Cascade Model: Whenever a social contact $v \in \Gamma(u)$ ($\Gamma(u)$ is the set of the neighbors of node u) of a node u adopts an innovation, it does so with a probability $P_{v,u}$. The process of the independent cascade model can be described as follows. Starting with an initial set of active nodes A_0, the process unfolds in discrete steps according to the following randomized rule. When node v first becomes active in step t, it is given a single chance to activate each currently inactive neighbor u; it succeeds with a probability $P_{v,u}$ (a parameter of the system) independently of the history thus far. (If u has multiple newly activated neighbors, their attempts are sequenced in an arbitrary order.) If v succeeds, then u will become active in step $t + 1$; but whether or not v succeeds, it cannot make any further attempts to activate u in subsequent rounds. Again, the process runs until no more activation is possible.

Linear Threshold Model: Each node u in the network chooses a threshold $\theta_u \in [0,1]$, typically drawn from a probability distribution. Every neighbor v of u has a nonnegative connection weight $w_{u,v}$ so that $\sum_{v \in \Gamma(u)} w_{u,v} \leq 1$, and u adopts a threshold if and only if $\sum_{adopters\, v \in \Gamma(u)} w_{u,v} \geq \theta_u$. Given a random choice of thresholds and an initial set of active nodes A_0 (with all other nodes inactive), the diffusion process unfolds deterministically in discrete steps: in step t, all nodes that were active in step $t - 1$ remain active, and we activate any node u for which the total weight of its active neighbors is at least θ_u.

Based on the independent cascade model, Gruhl et al. [44] proposed a model to predict the tendency of users' posting behaviors in a blogosphere, on an assumption that users do not write multiple postings on the topic. Given a set of N nodes, at the initial state of each episode a possibly empty set of nodes has written about the topic. At each successive state, a possibly empty set of authors write about the topic. The process will end when no new articles appear for a number of time steps.

Under the independent cascade model, users are connected by a directed graph where each edge (v,w) is labeled with a copy probability $k_{v,w}$. When author v writes an article at time t, each node w that has an arc from v to w writes an article about the topic at time $t + 1$ with probability $k_{v,w}$. This influence is independent of the history of whether any other neighbors of w have written on the topic.

Note that a user may visit certain blogs frequently and other blogs infrequently. Therefore, an additional edge parameter $r_{u,v}$ is added to denote the probability that u reads v's blog on any given day. Formally, propagation in the model occurs as follows. If a topic exists at vertex v on a given day, then the model computes the probability that the topic will propagate from v to a neighboring vertex u, which occurs as follows. Node u reads the topic from node v on any given day with reading probability $r_{u,v}$, so a delay is chosen from an exponential distribution with parameter $r_{u,v}$. Then, with probability $k_{u,v}$, the author of u will choose to write about it. If u reads the topic and chooses not to copy it, then u will never copy that topic from v; there is only a single opportunity for a topic to propagate along any given edge. Alternatively, one may imagine that once v is infected, node u will become infected with probability $k_{u,v}r_{u,v}$ on any given day, but once the $r_{u,v}$ coin comes up heads, no further trials are made.

Thus, given the transmission graph (and, in particular, each edge's reading frequency r and copy probability k), the distribution of propagation patterns is now fully established. Given a community and a timeout interval, the goal is therefore to learn the arcs and associated probabilities from a set of episodes. Using these probabilities, given the initial fragment of a new episode, it is able to predict the propagation pattern of the episode.

In the following text, a closed-world assumption is made that all occurrences of a topic except the first are the result of communication via edges in the network. A topic in the following is a URL, phrase, name, or any other representation of a meme that can be tracked from page to page. All blog entries can be gathered that contain a particular topic into a list $[(u_1,t_1),(u_2,t_2),...,(u_k,t_k)]$ sorted by the publication date of the blog, where u_i is the universal identifier for blog user i, and t_i is the first time at which user u_i contained a reference to the topic. This list can be referred to as the *traversal sequence* for the topic. The following observation is critically used: the fact that user a appears in a traversal sequence, and user b does not appear later in the same sequence, gives us evidence about the (a, b) edge—that is, if b were a regular reader of a's blog with a reasonable copy probability, then sometimes memes discussed by a should appear in b's blog.

An EM-like algorithm is presented to induce the parameters of the transmission graph [51], in which the model first computes a "soft assignment" of each new infection to the edges that may have caused it, and then updates the edge parameters to increase the likelihood of the assigned infections. Take an initial guess at the value of r and k for each edge and improve the estimate of these values. A two-stage process is adopted:

Soft-Assignment Step: Using the current version of the transmission graph, compute for each topic and each pair (u, v) the probability that the topic traversed the (u, v) edge. Given the traversal sequence and the delay between u and v for a particular topic j as input, for each v in the sequence, consider all previous vertices u in the sequence and compute the probability $P_{u,v}$ that topic j would have been copied from u to v. Then normalize by the sum of these probabilities to compute the posteriors of the probability that each node u was v's source of inspiration. That is, setting $r = r_{u,v}$, $k = k_{u,v}$, and δ is to be the delay in days between u and v in topic j:

$$P_{u,v} := \frac{r(1-r)^{\delta}k}{\displaystyle\sum_{w<v} r_{w,v}(1-r_{w,v})^{\delta_{w,v}}k_{w,v}} \tag{3.14}$$

Parameter-Update Step: For fixed u and v, recompute $r_{u,v}$ and $k_{u,v}$ based on the posterior probabilities just computed. Perform the following operation for each fixed u and v. Let S_1 denote the set of topics j such that topic j appeared first at node u and subsequently at node v, and let S_2 denote the set of topics j such that u was infected with topic j but v was never infected with the topic. For each topic $j \in S_1$, require as input the pair (p_j, δ_j), where p_j is the posterior probability computed earlier, and δ_j is the delay in days between the appearance of the topic in u and in v. For every topic $j \in S_2$, require as input the value δ_j, where δ_j days elapsed between the appearance of topic j at node u and the end of the snapshot. Then estimate an updated version of r and k as follows:

$$r := \frac{\sum\limits_{j \in S_1} p_j}{\sum\limits_{j \in S_1} p_j \delta_j} \quad k := \frac{\sum\limits_{j \in S_1} p_j}{\sum\limits_{j \in S_1 \cup S_2} \Pr[r \le \delta_j]} \tag{3.15}$$

where $P_r[a \le b] = (1-a)(1-(1-a)^b)$ is the probability that a geometric distribution with parameter a has value $\le b$.

Now take an improved guess at the transmission graph, so return to the soft-assignment step and recompute the posteriors, iterating until convergence. In the first step, use the model of the graph to guess how data traveled; in the second, use the guess about how data traveled to improve the model of the graph.

Some investigators have improved the work we have just described. Leskovec et al. [32] find that the popularity of posts drops with a power law, and the size distribution of cascades follows a perfect Zipfian distribution; based on these, they present a simple model that mimics the spread of information on the blogosphere and produces information cascades very similar to those in real life. Kleinberg [33] considers a collection of probabilistic and game-theoretic models for information cascades through the network and investigates the cascading behavior in a number of online settings, including word-of-mouth effects in the success of new products and the influence of social networks in the growth of online communities.

3.2.2.5 Analysis of Users' Interests

As described in the initial part of section 2.2 in chapter 2, mining users' interests can be the basis of analysis and modeling of their reading and posting behavior, and supply more inspiration for this work. Generally, mining users' interests is to discover which type of topics can raise one user's interest, or how to display the information that may attract more users.

Teng and Chen [34] proposed a method to detect bloggers' interest from three kinds of important features (textual features, temporal features, and interactive features) contained in blogs. The analysis of textual features comprises three aspects. First, examine the interest words relative to the all words used in a weblog. Then observe the number of interest documents relative to the overall entries in a weblog.

Last, identify the particular weight change of interest words caused by the used patterns of bloggers.

Interest words are defined as words related to a blogger's interest. For example, if a blogger's interest is computer, the interest words are "computer," "hardware," etc. To compare the differences between interest words, use the interest word ratio as an indicator. Interest word ratio is defined as the ratio of the number of interest words to the number of words in all weblogs. Similarly, an interest post is defined by the weblog entry related to a blogger's interest, and interest post ratio indicates the percentage of the number of interest posts to all posts. Tf-idf is adopted as the term-weighting scheme. The weight change, that is, the change of term weight, or the ratio of the new term weight to the average term weight, is an indicator of the interest words used by interested bloggers compared to the average bloggers.

Observing the relationship between the interest word (post) and time based on real data, two phenomena were found: (1) interested bloggers post interest posts/words more frequently than uninterested bloggers, and (2) the frequency of interest posts/words posted by interested bloggers does not change significantly with time. That is, the result implies that interested bloggers post more regularly than uninterested bloggers. Two metrics are used to measure these two phenomena: average time period between two interest posts (formula 3.16), and variance of the time period between two interest posts.

$$Period \ per \ post = \frac{\sum Period \ between \ post}{Number \ of \ post} \tag{3.16}$$

Interactive features represent the degree of interactivity at which a blogger acts in the blogosphere. Interactive features consist of response time (formula 3.17), length of the comments, and the frequency of interest-related comments. The higher the degree of interactivity, the higher the probability that the blogger may have this interest.

$$Response \ time = comment \ time - post \ time \tag{3.17}$$

A machine-learning approach can be applied to detect users' interests using these three features.

Besides detecting users' interests, let us also investigate the influence factors of users' interests and proposed models to predict the tendency of users' interests. Santos-Neto et al. [40] analyzed whether usage patterns can be harnessed to improve navigability in a growing knowledge space. The author studied collaborative tagging social networks with CiteULike and Bibsonomy, including presenting a formal definition of tagging communities, characterizing tagging activity distribution among users, and investigating the structure of users' shared interests. From this they could define the interest-sharing graph and investigate several definitions of interest similarity, with which users' activities could be predicted. Cheng et al. [35] proposed a bloggers' interests modeling approach based on the forgetting mechanism. Short-Term Interest Models (STIM) and Long-Term Interest Models (LTIM) are constructed to describe bloggers' short-term and long-term interests. Experiments show that both models can identify bloggers' preferences well.

3.3 Models and Analysis of Information Flow

In this section we introduce prior research on models and analysis of information flow in online social networks, including analysis of the information flow pathway [53, 55, 57] and models of innovation diffusion [54, 56, 58–62, 64]. It is different from the research on user behaviors in that this research focuses on the dynamic propagation process on a larger scale.

3.3.1 Discovering and Analyzing the Information Flow Pathway

In blogspace, each information flow pathway indicates a sequence of blog users who post articles related to the same topic sequentially. The pathway can identify the users who discussed the same topic and the sequence of these users.

Based on a closed-world assumption (that in a given blog community all posts on a topic except the first one are the result of communication within the community), Stewart et al. [53] defined the problem of discovering the information propagation pathway from blogspace as a frequent pattern mining problem. The following are a few necessary definitions:

Definition 1. [Blog community] A blog community collected in a given time period $[t_s, t_e]$ is a set of n blog $\Omega = \{b_1, b_2, ..., b_n\}$. Each blog $b = (p_1, p_2, ..., p_m)$ contains a set of published posts, where each post is associated with a publishing time point, $T(p_i)$ such that $t_s \leq T(p_i) \leq t_e$.

Definition 2. [Topic blog sequence] Given a particular topic c, a topic blog sequence $Q(c) = < (b_1, t_1), (b_2, t_2), ... (b_k, t_k) >$ is a list of blog-time pairs such that each blog b_i publishes a post on the topic c at time t_i. Moreover, $\forall_i \in [1, k), t_i \leq t_{i+1}$.

Definition 3. [Blog sequence database] Given a blog community collected in time period $[t_s, t_e]$, which contains a set of blogs $\Omega = \{b_1, b_2, ..., b_n\}$ and a set of posts on k topics $\Gamma = \{c_1, c_2, ..., c_k\}$, it can be modeled as a blog sequence database D in the form of $(i, Q(c_i))$, where $i(1 \leq i \leq k)$ is the identity of a topic and $Q(c_i) = < (b_1, t_1), (b_2, t_2), ... (b_m, t_m) > (c_i \in \Gamma, b_i \in \Omega, t_s \leq t_i \leq t_e)$ is a topic blog sequence.

Definition 4. [Support] Given a blog sequence database D and a blog sequence S, the support of S with respect to D, denoted as *SuppD*, is the fraction of the topic blog sequences in D that support S.

$$Supp_D(S) = \frac{|\{Q(c_i) \mid S \subseteq Q(c_i) \,\&\, Q(c_i) \in D\}}{|D|} \qquad (3.18)$$

where $|D|$ is the total number of topic blog sequences in the database. The support measure takes on values from 0 through 1. The more the topic blog sequences supporting a blog sequence, the higher the support value of the blog sequence.

Definition 5. [Strength] Given a blog sequence database D, a latency threshold δ, and a blog sequence $S = \{b_1, b_2, ..., b_m\}$, the strength of the sequence, denoted as $StregD,\delta(S)$, is

$$Streg_{D,\delta}(S) = \frac{\{Q \mid Lat(M(Q,S)) \le \delta, S \subseteq Q, Q \in D}{\{Q \mid S \subseteq Q, Q \in D\}} \qquad (3.19)$$

That is, the strength of a blog sequence is the fraction of supporting topic blog sequences that have the latency of their matched topic blog subsequences less than or equal to the given latency threshold.

Given a blog sequence database, we are interested in blog sequences that are not only supported frequently by the database but also by topic blog sequences that propagate information quickly. Thus, we define an Information Diffusion Path (IDP) as a blog sequence satisfying constraints specified as follows.

Definition 6. [IDP] Given a blog sequence database D, a support threshold α, a latency threshold δ, and a strength threshold β, a blog sequence S is an IDP if (1) $Supp_D(S) \ge \alpha$, and (2) $Streg_D(S) \ge \beta$.

For instance, given the support threshold $\alpha = 0.4$, the latency threshold $\delta = 3$ and the strength threshold $\beta = 0.6$, the blog sequence $S = <b_1 b_2>$ is an IDP since $Supp_D(S) = 0.6 \ge \alpha$ and $Streg_D(S) = 0.67 \ge \beta$.

Then, the problem of information diffusion path mining can be formally stated as follows. Given a blog sequence database D, a support threshold α, a latency threshold δ, and a strength threshold β, the problem of information diffusion path mining is to discover the set $\{S \mid Supp_D(S) \ge \alpha \,\&\, Streg_{D,\delta}(S) \ge \beta\}$.

Furthermore, Kossinets et al. [57] analyzed the temporal dynamics of the information flow pathway using online data, including e-mail communication among the faculty and staff of a large university over a 2-year period. The authors proposed a framework for analyzing this kind of systemic communication as shown in Figure 3.2. In the figure, a complete communication history for a group of five people over three days is shown. (Edges are annotated with the one or more times at which directed communication took place.) Based on a long period data, the latency, speed, and frequency of communication can be analyzed using this framework. Although this framework is constructed for e-mail communication, it can be also used to analyze the information propagation pathway for IM social network and blogosphere. While analyzing the information flow pathway in blogosphere is

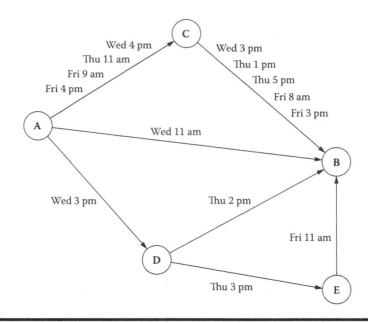

Figure 3.2 Systemic communications in faculty/staff's email systems. [57]

more complicated, we need to consider different types of communications, including commenting, posting, and citing.

3.3.2 *Models of Innovation Diffusion*

Investigators have proposed a few models to describe the information flow in social networks, although it is quite difficult to solve this problem because the flow is derived by humans' psychology and can be affected by multiple complex factors. Some investigators [54, 56, 58–62, 64] formalize the information propagation as diffusion of innovation, that is, an innovation is communicated through certain channels over time among the members of a population, and the perceived novelty of the innovation by an individual determines his or her reaction to it. A typical example of this type of information propagation is word-of-mouth communication [48], and other related works have been applied to improve the performance of virtual marketing [58], such as designing the strategy to maximize the spread of product information through a social network [68]. Modeling the diffusion of innovation ignores the particular information communication pattern and classifies adopters of innovations into five categories based on the fact that certain individuals are inevitably more open to adoption than others in a population. The five adopter categories—innovators, early adopters, early majority, late majority, and laggards—follow a standard deviation curve. The aim of modeling the diffusion of innovation can be simply described as two problems: When will one user receive the innovation? What's the probability that the user will adopt the innovation?

To solve this problem, Song et al. [73] proposed a rate-based information flow model based on the foundation of Continuous-Time Markov Chain (CTMC). The model can identify where information should flow to, and who will most quickly receive the information.

The definition of CTMC is

Definition 1: A Continuous-Time Markov Chain is a continuous-time stochastic process $\{X(t), t \leq 0\}$ s.t. $\forall s, t \geq 0$, and $\forall i, j, x(h)$.

$$P\{X(t+s) = j \mid X(t) = i, X(h) = x(h), 0 \leq h \leq t\}$$
$$= P\{X(t+s) = j \mid X(t) = i\} \tag{3.20}$$

A CTMC satisfies the Markov property and takes value from a discrete state space. Assume that the transition probabilities are independent from the initial time t, which means the chain is time homogeneous and denotes $P_{ij}(s)$ as the transition probability from i to j over s time period.

Definition 2: Define the transition rate matrix as

$$Q = \begin{pmatrix} q_{0,0} & q_{0,1} & \cdots \\ q_{1,0} & q_{1,1} & \cdots \\ \vdots & \vdots & \ddots \end{pmatrix} \tag{3.21}$$

where

$$q_{ij} = \lim_{\Delta t \to 0} \frac{P\{X_{t+\Delta t} = j \mid X_t = i\}}{\Delta t} = \lim_{\Delta t \to 0} \frac{P_{ij}(\Delta t)}{\Delta t} \ (i \neq j) \tag{3.22}$$

as the probability per time unit that the CTMC makes a transition from state i to state j or the transition rate. Thus, the total transition rate out of state i is

$$Q = \begin{pmatrix} q_{0,0} & q_{0,1} & \cdots \\ q_{1,0} & q_{1,1} & \cdots \\ \vdots & \vdots & \ddots \end{pmatrix} = \begin{pmatrix} -q_0 & q_{0,1} & \cdots \\ q_{1,0} & -q_1 & \cdots \\ \vdots & \vdots & \ddots \end{pmatrix} \tag{3.23}$$

Definition 3: Define the time until the CTMC makes a transition and leaves state i, given that the CTMC is currently in state i, as the state-staying time of the chain in state i, T_i.

$$T_i = \inf\{t : X_t \neq i \mid X_0 = i\} \tag{3.24}$$

where *inf* denotes the inferior limit. T_i is exponentially distributed with rate q_i. When the stochastic process leaves state i, it will next enter state j with probability P_{ij}, which is independent of the time spent at state i and satisfies

$$\begin{cases} \displaystyle\sum_{j\neq i} P_{ij} = 1 \\ P_{ii} = 0 \end{cases} \tag{3.25}$$

Also we have

$$P_{ij} = \frac{q_{ij}}{q_i} \ (i \neq j) \tag{3.26}$$

In this subsection, we propose a rate-based information flow model on a network $G(n,w,\tau)$ based on the CTMC, in which each node is a state, the weight is represented as the transition probability, and the delay is represented as the staying time in each state. Figure 3.3 illustrates an example of our model. We assume that the information stays in a node i for a certain time period T_i before making a transition to others. Then the information flows to other nodes j, k, and l according to transition probabilities P_{ij}, P_{ik}, and P_{il}.

3.3.2.1 Out-State Rate Estimation

Assume that the staying time at node i follows an exponential distribution with the out-state rate q_i. According to the property of the exponential distribution, the expected value of an exponentially distributed random variable X_i with rate q_i is given by

$$E(X_i) = \frac{1}{q_i} = T_i \tag{3.27}$$

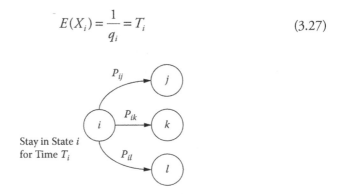

Figure 3.3   Rate-based information flow model.

3.3.2.2 Transition Probability

Estimate the transition probability based on the instances on the interstate transition and the time delay on each transition. Given the out-state rate, we estimate the transition probability from user i to user j as

$$P_{ij} = \sum_{c} q_i \exp(-q_i t_{ij(c)})$$ (3.28)

where $t_{ij}(c)$ is defined as the interstate diffusion time from node i to node j on c instances.

According to Equation 28, we have

$$q_{ij} = q_i P_{ij} \quad (i \neq j)$$ (3.29)

which we define as the interpersonal diffusion rate from user i to user j. Thus, we have all the elements in the **Q** matrix ready for use.

3.3.2.3 Recommendation Algorithm

For the recommendation problem, given at time $t = 0$, the user i adopts an item, and then the information starts to flow from this user to others in the network. We predict users' preferences of information by estimating who will most likely adopt the item by time $t = \tau$; in other words, information will flow to them. To predict users' preferences by time $t = \tau$, we estimate the probability that the information flows from user i to others as the probability that transition $i \rightarrow j$ ($j \neq i$) is enabled in $[0, \tau]$ as $L(j|i, \tau)$, which is the (i,j)-th element in $L(\tau)$, with

$$L(\tau) = \int_0^{\tau} P(t) dt$$ (3.30)

where $P(t)$ is the transition probability matrix with (i, j)-th entry $P_{ij}(t)$.

Formally, when the state space is finite, we can estimate the transition probability by solving

$$\begin{cases} P'(t) = P(t)Q \\ P(0) = I \end{cases}$$ (3.31)

where I is the identity matrix. The solution is

$$P(t) = e^{tQ} = \sum_{m=0}^{\infty} \frac{(tQ)^m}{m!} \qquad (3.32)$$

If $\mathbf{Q}$ can be diagonalized by $\mathbf{Q} = \mathbf{MDM}^{-1}$, then

$$P(t) = \sum_{m=0}^{\infty} \frac{M(tD)^m M^{-1}}{m!} = Me^{tD}M^{-1} \qquad (3.33)$$

For large $\mathbf{Q}$, the Taylor approximation can also be used:

$$P(t) \approx \lim_{m \to \infty} \left(I + Q\frac{t}{m} \right)^m \qquad (3.34)$$

3.3.2.4 Ranking Algorithm

Similarly, we assume that we are given the user adoption data as described in Section 4.3. For the ranking problem, we pose the problem that, if an arbitrary user $j (j \neq i)$ adopts an item at $t = 0$, when will be the average time in which user i adopts it? In CTMC, this question can be answered by the mean first-passage time.

Let $\mathbf{M}$ be the first-passage time matrix of the CTMC with the (i,j)-th element as m_{ij}. The mean first passage time m_{ij} from i to j is defined as the expected time taken until first arrival at node j, starting at node i.

Let v be any constant such that $v \geq \max i(q_i)$. Divide the off-diagonal components of $\mathbf{Q}$ $(q_i P_{ij}\ (i \neq j)\ )$ by v and replace its diagonal components $-q_i$ by $1 - q_i/v$. We then have a uniformized chain (discrete time) whose transition matrix P_v can be related to $\mathbf{Q}$ though v as follows:

$$P_v = I + \frac{1}{v}Q \qquad (3.35)$$

Let $\mathbf{M}\lambda$ denote the matrix of the first-passage time of the uniformized chain (discrete time). The mean first-passage time matrix of DTMC is given by

$$M_v = \left(I - Z_v + E(Z_v)_{dg} \right)D \qquad (3.36)$$

where $\mathbf{I}$ is the identity matrix, E is a matrix containing all ones, and $\mathbf{D}$ is the diagonal matrix with elements $d_{ii} = 1 / \pi(i)$, where $\pi(i)$ is the steady-state distribution of node $\mathbf{I}$ in this DTMC, and $\mathbf{Z}_v$ is its fundamental matrix, with

$$Z_v = \left(I - P_v + P_v^{\infty} \right)^{-1} \qquad (3.37)$$

$(\mathbf{Z}_v)_{dg}$ results from $\mathbf{Z}_v$ by setting off-diagonal entries to zero, and $\mathbf{P}_v^\infty$ is the limiting matrix of $\mathbf{P}_v$ with each row of $\mathbf{P}_v^\infty$ as π^T, or $\mathbf{P}_v^\infty = \mathbf{e}\pi^T$, where $\mathbf{e}$ is a column vector with all ones. The matrix of the first-passage time of the original CTMC $\mathbf{M}$ is

$$M = \frac{1}{v}(M_v)_{of} + \Lambda(M_v)_{dg}$$

(3.38)

where $\Lambda = diag(q_i^{-1})$, $(\mathbf{M}_v)_{dg}$ results from $\mathbf{M}_v$ by setting off-diagonal entries to zero, and $(\mathbf{M}_v)_{of}$ results from $\mathbf{M}_v$ by setting diagonal entries to zero. Thus, the rank score for each user j is estimated as

$$R(j) = \frac{1}{\frac{1}{|N-1|}\sum_{i \neq j} m_{ij}}$$

(3.39)

As introduced in Section 2.2.4, the cascade model describes the probability of user behavior, whether a user adopts an innovation from his neighbors or not. This model can be also employed in predicting the diffusion of innovation. If we predict each user behavior at each time point, then we can predict the whole process of innovation propagation. Kimura and Saito [69] considered the problem of finding influential nodes for innovation propagation in a large-scale social network and proposed two natural special cases of the Independent Cascade Model (ICM) such that a good estimate of the expected number of nodes influenced by a given set of nodes can be efficiently computed. Saito et al. [70] focused on the independent cascade model and defined the likelihood for information diffusion episodes where an episode means a sequence of newly active nodes. Then Neal and Hinton [51] presented a method for predicting diffusion probabilities by using the EM algorithm.

Besides considering the linking relationship and previous behavior of the users, investigators also studied other influence factors of information propagation. Choudhury et al. [66, 67] developed a computational framework for predicting communication flow in social networks based on several contextual features. The authors determined the intent to communicate and communication delay between users based on three contextual features in a social network, corresponding to the neighborhood context, topic context, and recipient context. The intent to communicate and communication delay are modeled as regression problems, which are efficiently estimated using Support Vector Regression.

References

1. J. Scott. 2000. *Social Network Analysis: A Handbook*. Sage Publications, London, 2nd ed.
2. N.T.J. Bailey. *The Mathematical Theory of Infectious Diseases and Its Applications*, Hafner Press, New York, 1975.

3. R.M. Anderson., R.M. May. *Infectious Diseases in Humans*, Oxford University Press, Oxford, England, 1992.
4. J.D. Murray. *Mathematical Biology: Spatial Models and Biomedical Applications*, Published by Springer, New York, 2003.
5. O. Diekmann, J. Heesterbeek. *Mathematical Epidemiology of Infectious Diseases: Model Building, Analysis, and Interpretation*, Wiley, New York, 2000.
6. Herbert W. Hethcote. The mathematics of infectious diseases. *SIAM Review.*, Vol. 42, No. 4, pp: 599–653. 2000.
7. H.J. Herrmann. Geometrical cluster growth models and kinetic gelation. *Physics Reports*, Volume 136, Issue 3, pp. 153–224, 1986.
8. Romualdo Pastor-Satorras, Alessandro Vespignani. Epidemic spreading in scale-free networks. *Physical Review Letters*, Vol. 86, No. 14, April 2, 2001.
9. Yamir Moreno, Javier B. Go´mez, Amalio F. Pacheco. Epidemic incidence in correlated complex networks. *Physical Review E.*, 68, 035103(R), September 2003.
10. J. G´omez-Gardenes, P. Echenique, Y. Moreno. Immunization of real complex communication networks. *The European Physical Journal B*, 49, 259–264 (2006).
11. D.J. Daley, D.G. Kendall. Epidemics and rumours, *Nature*, 204, 1118 (12 December 1964).
12. D.J. Daley, Joe Gani. *Epidemic Modelling*, Cambridge University Press, Cambridge, England, 2001.
13. Damián H. Zanette. Critical behavior of propagation on small-world networks. *Physical Review E*, 64, 050901 (2001).
14. Zonghua Liu, Ying-Cheng Lai, and Nong Ye. Propagation and immunization of infection on general networks with both homogeneous and heterogeneous components. *Physical Review E*, 67, 031911 (2003).
15. Yamir Moreno, Maziar Nekovee, Alessandro Vespignani. Efficiency and reliability of epidemic data dissemination in complex networks. *Physical Review E*, 69, 055101 (2004).
16. Yamir Moreno, Maziar Nekovee, Amalio F. Pacheco.1. Dynamics of rumor spreading in complex networks. *Physical Review E*, 69, 066130 (2004).
17. Damián H. Zanette. Dynamics of rumor propagation on small-world networks. *Physical Review E*, Vol. 65, 041908, March 28, 2002.
18. S.C. Herring, I. Kouper, J.C. Paolillo et al. Conversations in the blogosphere: An analysis from the bottom up. Proceedings of the 38th Annual Hawaii International Conference on System Sciences, 2005.
19. Noor F. Ali-Hasan, Lada A. Adamic. Expressing social relationships on the blog through links and comments. *ICWSM'2007*, Boulder, CO.
20. Dou Shen, Jian-Tao Sun, Qiang Yang, Zheng Chen. Latent friend mining from blog data. Sixth International Conference on Data Mining (ICDM '06). pp. 552–561. 2006.
21. Smriti Bhagat, Irina Rozenbaum, Graham Cormode et al. No blog is an island—analyzing connections across information networks. *ICWSM'2007*, Boulder, CO.
22. E. Adar, L Zhang, L.A. Adamic, R.M. Lukose. Implicit structure and the dynamics of blogspace. Workshop on the Weblogging Ecosystem, WWW2004 (2004).
23. Parag Singla, Matthew Richardson. Yes, there is a correlation—from social networks to personal behavior on the web. Proceeding of the 17th International Conference on World Wide Web (WWW'08, 2008), pp. 655–664.
24. Lada Adamic, Natalie Glance. The political blogosphere and the 2004 U.S. election: divided they blog. Proceedings of the 3rd International Workshop on Link Discovery (LinkKDD '05, 2005), pp. 36–43.

25. Mislove Alan, Marcon Massimiliano, P. Gummadi Krishna et al. Measurement and analysis of online social networks. Internet Measurement Conference: Proceedings of the 7th ACM SIGCOMM Conference on Internet Measurement, 24–26 October, 2007.

26. A. Broder, R. Kumar, F. Maghoul, P. Raghavan, S. Rajagopalan, R. Stata, A. Tomkins, J. Wiener. Graph structure in the Web: experiments and models. Proceedings of the 9th International World Wide Web Conference (WWW'00), Amsterdam, May 2000.

27. S. Nakajima, J. Tatemura, Y. Hino et al. Discovering important bloggers based on analyzing blog threads. Proceedings of WWW 2005 2nd Annual Workshop on the Weblogging Ecosystem (2005).

28. Nitin Agarwal, Huan Liu, Lei Tang, Philip S. Yu. Identifying the influential bloggers in a community. Proceedings of the International Conference on Web Search and Web Data Mining (WSDM'08, 2008), pp. 207–218.

29. Xiaodan Song, Yun Chi, Koji Hino, Belle Tseng. Identifying the influentials in blogosphere. Proceedings of the 16th ACM Conference on Information and Knowledge Management (CIKM '07, 2007), pp. 971–974.

30. Habiba, Yintao Yu, Tanya Y. Berger-Wolf, Jared Saia. Finding Spread Blockers in Dynamic Networks. The 2nd SNA-KDD Workshop '08 (SNA-KDD'08), August 24, 2008, Las Vegas, Nevada.

31. Tadanobu Furukawa, Yutaka Matsuo, Ikki Ohmukai et al. Analyzing reading behavior by blog mining. Proceedings of AAAI 2007, pp. 1353–1358.

32. Jure Leskovec, Mary Mcglohon, Christos Faloutsos et al. Cascading behavior in large blog graphs. SIAM International Conference on Data Mining (SDM), 2007.

33. Jon Kleinberg. Cascading Behavior in Networks: Algorithmic and Economic Issues. Chapter 24 of *Algorithmic Game Theory*, Cambridge University Press, Cambridge, England, 2007.

34. Chun-Yuan Teng, Hsin-Hsi Chen. Detection of bloggers' interests: using textual, temporal, and interactive features. Proceedings of the 2006 IEEE/WIC/ACM International Conference on Web Intelligence (WI'062006), pp. 366–369.

35. Y. Cheng, G. Qiu, J. Bu. Model bloggers' interests based on forgetting mechanism. Proceeding of the 17th International Conference on World Wide Web, 2008, pp. 1129–1130.

36. A. Vazquez, Gama J. Oliveira, Z. Dezso et al. Modeling bursts and heavy tails in human dynamics. *Physical Reviews E*, Vol. 73 (2006).

37. Bi Chen, Qiankun Zhao, Bingjun Sun et al. Predicting blogging behavior using temporal and social networks. Seventh IEEE International Conference on Data Mining (2007).

38. Tadanobu Furukawa, Yutaka Matsuo, Ikki Ohmukai et al. Social networks and reading behavior in the blogosphere. Proceedings of ICWSM 2007, Boulder, Co. pp. 51–58.

39. Daniel Gruhl, R. Guha, Ravi Kumar et al. The predictive power of online chatter. Proceeding of the 11th ACM SIGKDD International Conference on Knowledge Discovery in Data Mining (KDD '05, 2005), pp. 78–87.

40. Elizeu Santos-Neto, Matei Ripeanu, Adriana Iamnitchi et al. Tracking user attention in collaborative tagging communities. Proceedings of the International ACM/IEEE Workshop on Contextualized Attention Metadata: Personalized Access to Digital Resources (June 7, 2007). Vancouver, BC, Canada

41. Fernando Duarte, Bernardo Mattos, Azer Bestavros et al. Traffic Characteristics and Communication Patterns in Blogosphere. Boston University Technical Report. 2006.

42. Tadanobu Furukawa, Tomofumi Matsuzawa, Masayuki Takeda. Users' behavioral analysis on weblogs. American Association for Artificial Intelligence. 2006.

43. Munmun De Choudhury, Hari Sundaram, Ajita John et al. What makes conversations interesting? Themes, participants and consequences of conversations in online social media. Proceedings of the 18th International World Wide Web Conference (WWW 2009) Madrid, Spain.
44. Daniel Gruhl, R. Guha, David Liben-Nowell et al. Information diffusion through blogspace. *SIGKDD Explorations Newsletter*, Vol. 6, No. 2 (December 2004), pp. 43–52.
45. D. Liben-Nowell, J. Kleinberg. The 12th Annual ACM International conference on information and knowledge management (CIKM '03). The link prediction problem for social networks. Proceedings of CIKM, pp. 556–559, 2003.
46. L. Getoor, C.P. Diehl. Link mining: A survey. *SIGKDD Explorations Newsletter*, 2(7), 2005.
47. Y. Zhou, X. Guan, Z. Zhang, B. Zhang. Predicting the tendency of topic discussion on the online social networks using a dynamic probability model. Proceedings of the Hypertext 2008 Workshop on Collaboration and Collective Intelligence, pp. 7–11 Pittsburgh, PA USA.
48. Jacob Goldenberg, Barak Libai, Eitan Muller. Talk of the network: a complex systems look at the underlying process of word-of-mouth. *Marketing Letters*, 12(3):211–223, 2001.
49. Mark Granovetter. Threshold models of collective behavior. *American Journal of Sociology*, 83(6):1420–1443, 1987.
50. Xiaochuan Ni et al. Automatic Identification of Chinese Weblogger interests based on text classification. WI'2006. Proceedings of the 2006 IEEI/WIC/ACM International conference on web intelligence, pages 247–253, 2006. Hong Kong.
51. Radford Neal, Geoffrey E. Hinton. A view of the em algorithm that justifies incremental, sparse, and other variants. *Learning in Graphical Models*, MIT Press, Cambridge, MA, 1999.
52. K. S. Emaili, M. Neshati, M. Jamali, H. Abolhassani. 2006. Comparing performance of recommendation techniques in the blogsphere. ECAI'06 Workshop on Recommender Systems, Riva del Garda, Italy.
53. Avaré Stewart, Ling Chen, Raluca Paiu et al. Discovering Information Diffusion Paths from Blogosphere for Online Advertising. Proceedings of the 1st International Workshop on Data Mining and Audience Intelligence for Advertising, San Jose, CA, pp. 46–54.
54. Raquel Recuero. Information Flows and Social Capital in Weblogs: A Case Study in the Brazilian Blogosphere. Proceedings of the 19 ACM Conference on Hypertext and Hypermedia (HT'08, 2008), pp. 97–106.
55. Mary McGlohon, Jure Leskovec, Christos Faloutsos. Information Propagation and Network Evolution on the Web. DA Project, Machine Learning Department, Carnegie Mellon University.
56. Mike Thelwall, Liz Price. Language evolution and the spread of ideas on the Web: a procedure for identifying emergent hybrid. *Journal of the American Society for Information Science and Technology*, Vol. 57, No. 10, pp. 1326–1337 (August 2006).
57. Gueorgi Kossinets, Jon Kleinberg, Duncan Watts. The structure of information Pathways in a social communication network. Proceeding of the 14th ACM SIGKDD International Conference on Knowledge Discovery and Data Mining, Las Vegas, NV, pp. 435–443. August 2008.

58. D., Liben-Nowell, J. Kleinberg., Tracing information flow on a global Scale Using Internet chain-letter data. Proceedings of the National Academy of Sciences USA. 2008, Vol 105; No. 12, pp. 4633–4638.
59. E. Adar, L.A. Adamic. Tracking information epidemics in blogspace. Proceedings of the IEEE/WIC/ACM International Conference on Web Intelligence (2005), pp. 207–214.
60. Jennifer Wortman. Viral Marketing and the Diffusion of Trends on Social Networks. Department of Computer & Information Science Technical Reports (CIS). University of Pennsylvania, PA, 2008.
61. Xiaojun Wan, Jianwu Yang. Learning information diffusion process on the Web. Proceedings of the 16th International Conference on World Wide Web, Banff, Alberta, Canada, pp. 1173–1174.
62. Jure Leskovec, Ajit Singh, Jon Kleinberg. Patterns of influence in a recommendation network. *Advances in Knowledge Discovery and Data Mining* (2006), pp. 380–389.
63. Xiaodan Song, Belle L. Tseng, Ching-Yung Lin et al. Personalized recommendation driven by Information flow. Proceedings of the 29th Annual International ACM SIGIR Conference on Research and development in Information Retrieval (SIGIR '06), pp. 509–516.
64. J. Kleinberg. Temporal dynamics of on-line information streams. In *Data Stream Management: Processing High-Speed Data Streams* (2005).
65. Kimura Masahiro, Saito Kazuini. Approximate solutions for the influence maximization problem in a social network. Lecture Notes in Computer Science, 2006, No. 4252, pp. 937–944.
66. Munmun De Choudhury, Hari Sundaram, Ajita John et al. Contextual prediction of communication flow in social networks. Proceedings of the IEEE/WIC/ACM International Conference on Web Intelligence (2007), pp. 57–65.
67. Munmun De Choudhury, Hari Sundaram, Ajita John et al. Dynamic prediction of communication flow using social context. Proceedings of the 19th ACM Conference on Hypertext and Hypermedia. Pittsburgh, PA, pp. 49–54.
68. D. Kempe, J. Kleinberg, E. Tardos. Maximizing the spread of influence through a social network. Proceedings of the 9th ACM SIGKDD International Conference on Knowledge Discovery and Data Mining, pp. 137–146. Washington, D.C.
69. M. Kimura, K. Saito. Tractable Models for Information Diffusion in Social Networks. Lecture Notes in Computer Science, 2006, No. 4213, pp. 259–271.
70. Kazumi Saito, Ryohei Nakano, Masahiro Kimura. Prediction of information diffusion probabilities for independent cascade model. Proceedings of the 12th International Conference on Knowledge-Based Intelligent Information and Engineering Systems, 2008, pp. 67–75. Zagreb, Croatia.
71. Akshay Java, Pranam Kolari, Tim Finin. Modeling the spread of influence on the blogosphere. Technical Report TR-CS-06-03 (March 2006).
72. Marti A. Hearst, Matthew Hurst, Susan T. Dumais. Modeling trust and influence on blogosphere using link polarity. Proceeding of the 2008 ACM Workshop on Search in Social Media, Napa Valley, CA, pp. 95–98.
73. Xiaodan Song, Yun Chi, Koji Hino. Information flow modeling based on diffusion rate for prediction and ranking. Proceedings of the 16th International Conference on World Wide Web (2007, WWW '07), pp. 191–200.

Chapter 4

Analyzing Sociotechnical Networks: A Spectrum Perspective

Xintao Wu, Xiaowei Ying, and Leting Wu

Contents

4.1 Introduction

Many natural and social systems develop complex networks; for example, the Internet, the World Wide Web, networks of collaborating movie actors and those of collaborating authors, etc. The management and analysis of these networks have attracted increasing interest in the sociology, database, data mining, and theory communities. Most previous studies are focused on revealing interesting properties (e.g., degree sequences, shortest connecting paths, power-law degree distributions, small-world phenomenon, and clustering coefficients) of networks and discovering efficient and effective analysis methods [2–4, 9, 13, 15, 19, 21, 22, 24, 30, 33, 34, 36, 39].

In this chapter we analyze social networks from a spectrum point of view. Graph spectral analysis deals with the analysis of the spectra (eigenvalues and eigenvector components) of the graph's adjacency matrix or other derived matrices. The spectrum of a graph is usually defined as the set of eigenvalues of the graph. It has been shown that there is an intimate relationship between the combinatorial characteristics of a graph and the algebraic properties of its adjacency matrix [30]. Our graph spectral analysis centers on two applications: graph randomness analysis and graph perturbation.

Social networks tend to contain some amount of randomness and some amount of nonrandomness. Consider an online social network where each node denotes an individual, and an edge between two nodes denotes a social interaction between the two individuals. An individual's social network tends to consist of members of the same ethnic group, race, or social class. Intuitively, two friends of a given individual are more likely to be friends with each other than they are with other randomly chosen members. The edge connecting one individual's two friends contains less randomness. However, an individual also tends to have some number of random friends from other groups, and those edges between this individual and his random friends contain more randomness. The amount of randomness versus nonrandomness at node/edge levels can clearly affect various properties of a social network. Although randomness plays an important role in understanding the geometry and topology of social networks, very few studies have formally investigated this issue. In this paper, we theoretically analyze graph randomness and present a framework that provides a series of nonrandomness measures at levels of edge, node, and the overall graph. We show that graph nonrandomness can be obtained mathematically from the spectra of the adjacency matrix of the network. We conduct both theoretical and empirical studies in spectral geometries of social networks and show that our proposed nonrandomness measures can better characterize and capture graph randomness than previous measures.

Many applications of networks such as anonymous Web browsing require relationship anonymity due to the sensitive, stigmatizing, or confidential nature of relationships. The privacy concerns associated with data analysis over social networks have been addressed by recent research works [1, 5, 16, 17, 26, 40–42, 44, 45]. Naturally, graph randomization techniques can be applied in addition to graph anonymization to protect the identity and relationship privacy of individuals. For example, we can remove some true edges and/or add some false edges. After randomization, the randomized graph is expected to be different from the original one. As a result, the true sensitive or confidential relationship will not be disclosed. On the other hand, the released randomized graph should also keep some properties not much changed or, at least, some properties should be enabled to be reconstructed from the randomized graph. Since there are numerous characteristics related to networks, it is tedious to evaluate how those characteristics are affected by the randomization process. In this chapter we investigate this problem by focusing on the change of graph spectrum since the spectrum has close relation with the many graph characteristics and can provide global measures for network properties. A spectrum-preserving graph randomization method, which can better preserve network properties while protecting link anonymity, is then presented and empirically evaluated.

4.1.1 Contribution

Our contributions are summarized as follows:

- We discover spectral geometry properties in social networks that can determine the graph's nonrandomness at all granularity levels. We present a framework that can quantify graph nonrandomness at and the edge, node, overall graph levels. We show that all graph nonrandomness measures can be obtained mathematically from the spectra of the adjacency matrix of the network. We present a relative nonrandomness measure of the overall graph, which allows quantitative comparisons between various social networks with different sizes and densities, or between different snapshots of a dynamic social network.
- We show theoretically and empirically how the real characteristics of graphs are related with spectral characteristics and how the two edge-based pure randomization strategies affect both real and spectral characteristics. We develop spectrum-preserving randomization methods, *Spctr Add/Del* and *Spctr Switch*, which can better preserve graph characteristics without sacrificing much privacy protection during randomization.

4.1.2 Organization

The rest of this chapter is organized as follows. In Section 4.2 we revisit the relationship between the real characteristics and the spectral characteristics of graphs. In Section 4.3 we theoretically analyze how coordinates of node points are distributed in the k-dimensional spectral space and why they can be used to measure graph nonrandomness. We then present our framework and analyze in detail how to derive edge nonrandomness, node nonrandomness, and the overall graph non-randomness from graph spectrum. In Section 4.4 we show how randomization affects spectral characteristics, and present our spectrum-preserving edge-randomization approach. We offer our concluding remarks and discuss future work in Section 4.5.

4.2 Spectral versus Real Characteristics

A network or graph, $G(V, E)$, is a set of n nodes, V, connected by a set of m links, E. The network considered here is binary, symmetric, connected, and without self-loops. Let $A = (a_{ij})_{n \times n}$ be its adjacency matrix, $a_{ij} = 1$ if node i and j are connected, and $a_{ij} = 0$ otherwise. Associated with A is the degree distribution $D_{n \times n}$, a diagonal matrix with row-sums of A along the diagonal, and 0's elsewhere. Recall that the degree of a node in a network is the number of edges connected to that node.

Let λ_i be the eigenvalues of A, and x_i the corresponding eigenvectors, and $\lambda_i \in \{\lambda_1 \ \lambda_2 \ ... \ \lambda_n\}$. The spectral decomposition of A is $A = \Sigma_i \lambda_i x_i x_i^T$. We call λ_i the index of G, and call $x_1 = (x_{11}, ..., x_{1n})^T$ the principal eigenvector of the graph G where x_{1i} is the i-th component of the principal eigenvector.

Another matrix related to A is the Laplacian matrix defined as $L = D - A$.* Similarly, let μi be the eigenvalues of L, and $\mathbf{u}_i$ the corresponding eigenvectors. We have $0 = \mu_1 Y \mu_2 Y ... Y \mu n Y n$. Since the degree $Dii = \Sigma j Aij$, all rows and columns of the Laplacian sum to zero. Hence, there exists one eigenvalue zero with eigenvector $\mathbf{1} = (1, 1, ..., 1)$. μ_2 is an important eigenvalue of the Laplacian matrix and can be used to show how good the communities separate, with smaller values corresponding to better community structures. Let $\mathbf{u}_2 = (y_{21}, ... , y_{2n})^T$ where $y_2 i$ is the i-th component of the eigenvector $\mathbf{u}_2$.

To understand and utilize the information in a network, researches have developed various measures to indicate the structure and characteristics of the network from different perspectives [9]. In this chapter, we use four real-space characteristics of a graph. The first one is the harmonic mean of the shortest distance, h, which is defined in Reference 25 as $h = \{\frac{1}{n(n-1)} \Sigma_{i \neq j} \frac{1}{d_{ij}}\}^{-1}$. The inverse of the harmonic mean of the shortest distance, also known as the global efficiency, varies between 0 and 1, with $h^{-1} = 0$ when all vertices are isolated, and $h^{-1} = 1$ when the graph is complete.

The second measure is the modularity measure, Q, which indicates the goodness of the community structure [9]. It is defined as the fraction of all edges that lie within communities minus the expected value of the same quantity in a graph in which the vertices have the same degrees but the edges are placed at random without regard for the communities. A value $Q = 0$ indicates that the community structure is no stronger than would be expected by random chance, and values other than zero represent deviations from randomness.

---

* The third matrix is the normal matrix defined as $N = D^{-1/2} A D^{-1/2}$.

The third measure is the transitivity measure, C, which is one type of clustering coefficient measure and which characterizes the presence of local loops near a vertex. It is formally defined as $C = 3N_\Delta/N_3$, where N_Δ is the number of triangles and N_3 is the number of connected triples.

The fourth measure is subgraph centrality, SC, which is used to quantify the centrality of the subgraphs based on the vertex i [12]. It is formally defined as $SC = \frac{1}{n}\Sigma_{i=1}^n SC_i = \frac{1}{n}\Sigma_{i=1}^n \Sigma_{k=0}^\infty \frac{P_i^k}{k!}$, where P_i^k is the number of paths that start with i and end in i with length k.

Throughout this chapter, we focus on two important eigenvalues of the graph spectrum. The first one is the largest eigenvalue (λ_1) of the adjacency matrix A. The eigenvalues of A encode information about the cycles of a network as well as its diameter. Since A contains no self-loops, the sum over all eigenvalues ($\Sigma_{i=1}^n \lambda_i$) is zero. The sum of product pairs ($\Sigma_{i=1} \lambda_i\lambda_j$) is equal to minus the number of edges, and $\Sigma_{i\neq j\neq k} \lambda_i\lambda_j\lambda_k$ is twice the number of triangles in G. The maximum degree, chromatic number, clique number, and extent of branching in a connected graph are all related to λ_1. In Reference 37, the authors studied how a virus propagates in a real work and proved that the epidemic threshold for a network is closely related to λ_1.

The second one is the second eigenvalue (μ_2) of the Laplacian matrix L, which is also called the algebraic connectivity of the graph. The eigenvalues of L encode information about the tree structure of G. The spectrum of L contains a 0 for every connected component. The multiplicity of 0 as an eigenvalue is equal to the number of components in G $\frac{1}{n}\Pi_{i=2}^n \mu_i$ and equals the number of spanning trees of G. When μ_2 is close to zero, the graph is almost disconnected. Its diameter is small if the eigenvalue gap is large (i.e., $\mu_2 \gg \mu_1$).

Many graph topological features can be expressed as an explicit function of spectrum and eigenvectors. For example, the authors in Reference 12 show that the subgraph centrality SC, which characterizes the participation of each node in all subgraphs in a network, can be calculated mathematically from the spectra of the adjacency matrix of the network, $SC = \frac{1}{n}\Sigma_{i=1}^n e^{\lambda_i}$. The diameter of a general graph is related to μ_n and μ_2 and bounded by

$$Diam(G) \leq \left\lceil \frac{cosh^{-1}(n-1)}{cosh^{-1}\left(\frac{\mu_n+\mu_2}{\mu_n-\mu_2}\right)} \right\rceil.$$

Another example is the commute time [27] based on random walks on a graph G, which can be calculated using the eigenvalues and eigenvectors of the normal matrix N. Refer to Reference 30 for more relationships between the spectral and real characteristics of graphs.

Many social network mining methods have been developed based on the spectral characteristics. For example, the HITS algorithm [20], which detects the authoritative/important individuals in the network, is based on eigenvectors of the adjacency matrix; the maximal-cliques-finding algorithm developed in Reference

29 is based on the L_1-constrained eigenvectors of the adjacency matrix; various community/cluster partition algorithms [30] have been developed based on the spectrum of Laplacian or normal matrix.

4.3 Spectrum-Based Graph Randomness Analysis

In this section we analyze graph randomness at all granularity levels, from edge node to the whole graph. We show that all our nonrandomness measures can be determined by spectral coordinates of nodes in the first k-dimensional spectral space, where k corresponds to the number of communities in the graph. We then present a framework that provides a series of nonrandomness measures at different levels. Nonrandomness specified at the edge level can help users quantify how different a given interaction is from random interactions. Similarly, nonrandomness specified at the node level can help users quantify how different a given individual is from random nodes (those individuals actually not belonging to this social network). In our framework, we first examine how much nonrandomness a given edge (social interaction) has, then measure a node's nonrandomness by examining the nonrandomness values of edges connecting to this node. Finally, we derive the nonrandomness measure of the whole graph by incorporating the nonrandomness values of all edges within the whole graph.

Throughout this section, we use the politics book network [23] as an example to illustrate how we define and calculate graph nonrandomness at various levels. The politics book network contains 105 nodes and 441 edges as shown in Figure 4.1. In this network, nodes represent books about U.S. politics sold by the online bookseller Amazon.com, while edges represent frequent copurchasing of books by the same buyers on Amazon. Each node is labeled "liberal" (blue), "neutral" (white), or "conservative" (red). These alignments were assigned separately by Mark Newman based on a reading of the descriptions and reviews of the books posted on Amazon.

4.3.1 Graph Spectral Geometry

Let xi be the unit eigenvector of λ_i, and let x_{ij} denote the j-th entry of x_i.

$$
\alpha_u \rightarrow
\begin{array}{cccc}
x_1 & x_i & x_k & x_n \\
& \downarrow & & \\
\end{array}
\begin{pmatrix}
x_{11}\cdots & x_{i1} & \cdots x_{k1} & \cdots & x_{n1} \\
\vdots & \vdots & \vdots & & \vdots \\
x_{1u}\cdots & x_{iu} & \cdots x_{ku} & \cdots & x_{nu} \\
\vdots & \vdots & \vdots & & \vdots \\
x_{1n}\cdots & x_{in} & \cdots x_{kn} & \cdots & x_{nn}
\end{pmatrix}
\tag{4.1}
$$

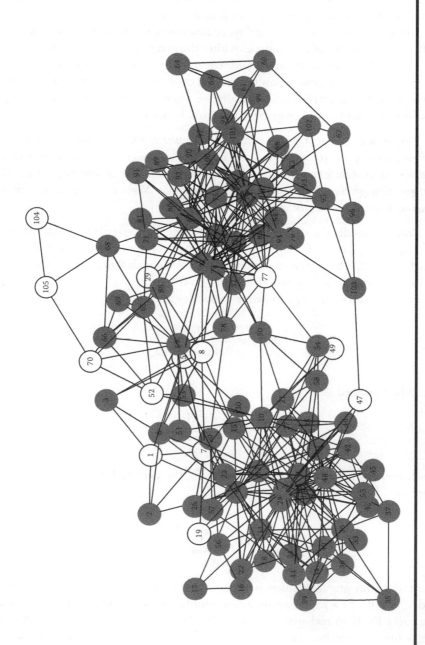

Figure 4.1   The politics book social network.

We can see from Formula (4.1) that the eigenvector *xi* is represented as a column vector. The row vector $(x_1u, x_2u, ..., xnu)$ represents the coordinates of node *u* in the *n*-dimensional spectral space. Next, we shall show that only the coordinates of node *u* in the first *k*-dimensional spectral space determine the randomness of *u* where *k* indicates the number of communities within the graph. Hence, we define $\alpha u = (x_{1u}, x_{2u}, ..., x_{ku})$ Î $R^{1\#k}$ as the spectral coordinate of node *u* in the *k*-dimensional space.

In this section we explore how the spectral coordinate (α) of a node point locates in the projected spectral space. Especially, we show that node points locate along *k* quasi-orthogonal lines when graph *G* contains *k* communities.*

Proposition 1. *For a graph with k communities, the coordinate of node u in k-dimensional space,* $\alpha_u = (x_{1u}, x_{2u}, ..., x_{ku})$ *Î* $R^{1\#k}$, *denotes the likelihood of node u's attachment to these k communities. Node points within one community form a line that goes through the origin in the k-dimensional space. Nodes in k communities form k quasi-orthogonal lines in the spectral space.*

Proof. Consider the division of a graph *G* into *k* nonoverlapping communities $G_1, G_2, ..., G_k$. Let $si = (s_{i1}, s_{i2}, ..., s_{in})$ be the index vector of community G_i, and s_{ij} equals 1 if node *j* belongs to community G_i, and it equals 0 otherwise. Note that s_i and s_j are mutually orthogonal, that is, $s_i^T s_j = 0$.

For community *Gi*, we can define its density as

$$D(G_i) := \frac{\# \text{ of edges in } G_i}{\# \text{ of nodes in } G_i}.$$

It can be expressed as

$$D(G_i) = \frac{s_i^T A s_i}{s_i^T s_i}$$

where *A* is the adjacency matrix of graph *G*. The density for this division of the graph is

$$\sum_{i=1}^{k} D(G_i) = \sum_{i=1}^{k} \frac{s_i^T A s_i}{s_i^T s_i}. \qquad (4.2)$$

The task of our graph partition is to maximize Equation 4.2 subject to *sij* Î {0, 1} and $s_i^T s_j = 0$, if $i \neq j$. This optimization problem is NP-complete. However, if we relax *sij* Î {0, 1} to real space, based on Wielandt's theory [35], we have that the target function reaches the maximum $\Sigma_{i=1}^{k} \lambda_i$ when taking *si* to be *xi*. Hence we

---

* Communities are loosely defined as collections of individuals who interact unusually frequently.

can conclude that x_{ij} reflects the degree of node j's attachment to the community Gi."□"

Property 1. A node u belongs to one community Gt if the t-th entry of αu, x_{tu}, is much greater than the rest of the entries and $x_{iu} \approx 0$ for $i \neq t$. A node u does not belong to any community if all the entries of αu are close to 0, or equivalently, $\|\alpha\|2 \approx 0$. We call such nodes noise nodes.

Property 2. If nodes u and v belong to the same community, then $|cos(\alpha u, \alpha v)| \approx 1$. If nodes u and v belong to two different communities, respectively, then $|cos(\alpha u, \alpha v)| \approx 0$. Otherwise, if node u belongs to one community G_v, and bridging node v locates in the overlap of two communities Gt and Gw, then $|cos(\alpha u, \alpha v)|$ is not close to either 0 or 1.
   Explanation. Notice that

$$\cos(\alpha_u, \alpha_v) = \frac{\alpha_u \alpha_v^T}{\|\alpha_u\|_2 \|\alpha_v\|_2}.$$

When nodes u and v are in the same community G_t, x_{tu}, we have that x_{tv} is much greater than the rest of entries in α_u and α_v. Hence

$$\frac{\alpha_u \alpha_v^T}{\|\alpha_u\|_2 \|\alpha_v\|_2} = \frac{\sum_{i=1}^{k} x_{iu} x_{iv}}{\left(\sum_{i=1}^{k} x_{iu}^2\right)^{\frac{1}{2}} \left(\sum_{i=1}^{k} x_{iv}^2\right)^{\frac{1}{2}}} \approx \frac{x_{tu} x_{tv}}{|x_{tu}| |x_{tv}|} = \pm 1.$$

In other words, points α_u and α_v approximately locate along a straight line that goes through the origin.
   Similarly, when node u and v are in two different communities G_t and G_w, respectively, with $x_{wu} \approx 0$ and $x_{tv} \approx 0$, we have

$$\frac{\alpha_u \alpha_v^T}{\|\alpha_u\|_2 \|\alpha_v\|_2} \approx \frac{x_{tu} x_{tv} + x_{wu} x_{wv}}{|x_{tu}| |x_{wv}|} \approx 0,$$

which means that α_u and α_v are approximately orthogonal.
   If a bridging node v is in the overlap of two communities St and Sw, both t-th and w-th entries in α_v are not negligible. Hence, $\|\alpha_v\|_2 \approx (x_{tv}^2 + x_{wv}^2)^{\frac{1}{2}}$. For a node u from Gt, we have

$$\frac{|\alpha_u \alpha_v^T|}{\|\alpha_u\|_2 \|\alpha_v\|_2} \approx \frac{|x_{tu} x_{tv}|}{|x_{tu}|(x_{tv}^2 + x_{wv}^2)^{\frac{1}{2}}} = \frac{|x_{tv}|}{(x_{tv}^2 + x_{wv}^2)^{\frac{1}{2}}}.$$

Since neither xtv nor xwv is close to 0, $|cos(u, v)|$ is not close to either 1 or 0, which indicates that bridging nodes locate between the quasi-orthogonal lines formed by communities, and are also away from the origin. "□"

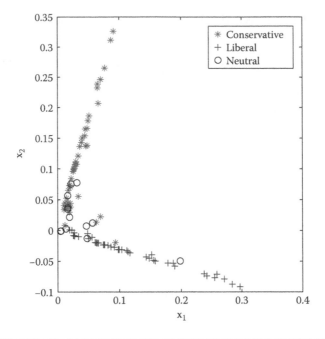

Figure 4.2 The 2-D spectral geometries of the politics book social network.

Figure 4.2 shows the 2-D spectral geometries of the politics book network data. We can observe from Figure 4.2 that the majority of vertices projected in the 2-D spectral space distribute along two straight and quasi-orthogonal lines. It indicates that there exist two communities with sparse edges connecting them. The first uptrend line consists of most nodes in red color, while the second downtrend line consists of most nodes in blue color. White nodes distribute either around the origin or between two quasi-orthogonal lines in the projected space.

4.3.2 Spectrum-Based Randomness Framework

In this section we present our framework that can quantify randomness at all granularity levels from edge node to the overall graph. We begin with a study of edge nonrandomness by spectral coordinates of its two connected nodes in the spectral space. We then define the node nonrandomness as the sum of nonrandomness values of all edges that connect to it. Similarly, we define the overall graph nonrandomness as the sum of nonrandomness values of all edges within the the whole graph. The formal definition is as follows:

Definition 1. *Denote* $\alpha u = (x_{1u}, x_{2u}, \ldots, x_{ku})$ Î R^k *as the spectral coordinate of node u, and* $\alpha v = (x_{1v}, x_{2v}, \ldots, x_{kv})$ Î R^k *as the spectral coordinate of node v.*

1. *The edge nonrandomness $R(u, v)$ is defined as $R(u,v) = \alpha_u \alpha_v^T = \sum_{i=1}^{k} x_{iu} x_{iv}$.*
2. *The node nonrandomness $R(u)$ is defined as $R(u) = \sum v \hat{I}_{\Gamma(u)} R(u, v)$, where $\Gamma(u)$ denotes the neighbor set of node u.*
3. *The graph nonrandomness R_G is defined as $R_G = \sum_{(u, v)} \hat{I}E R(u, v)$.*

4.3.2.1 Edge Nonrandomness: R(u, v)

The spectral coordinates of a node reflect its relative attachment to different communities in G. When it comes to the measure of nonrandomness of an edge that connects two nodes, intuitively, we need to incorporate the relationship of two nodes' spectral vectors.

The edge nonrandomness measure $R(u, v)$ in Definition 1 can be rewritten as

$$R(u,v) = \| \alpha_u \|_2 \| \alpha_v \|_2 \cos(\alpha_u, \alpha_u),$$

which is determined by the product of $\|\alpha_u\|_2\|\alpha_v\|_2$ and the cosine of the angle between αu and αu. Generally, $R(u, v)$ tends to be large when u and v clearly belong to the same community (since $\cos(\alpha_u, \alpha_u) \approx 1$). $R(u, v)$ tends to be small when (1) u and v are from two different communities (since $\cos(\alpha_u, \alpha_u) \approx 0$); (2) or either node is (or both nodes are) noisy (since $\|\alpha_u\|_2\|\alpha_v\| 2 \approx 0$). This intuitively reflects the formation of real-world social networks: two individuals within the same community have relatively higher probability to be connected than those in different communities.

Figure 4.3(a) plots the distribution of edge nonrandomness values, where the x-axis is the cosine value between α_u and α_v, while the y-axis denotes the product of the two vector lengths. Figure 4.3(b) shows a snapshot of different types of 441 edges characterized by edge nonrandomness values of the politics book network. We can observe that distributions of edge nonrandomness values characterized by different regions reflect different types of edges in the original graph: edges with large cosine value (plotted along the vertex line $x = 1$ and denoted by the blue "+") mostly connect two nodes within the same community; edges with small vector length product (green "+" and plotted along the line $y = 0$) mostly connect to noncentral nodes; edges plotted in other areas form bridging edges between the two communities. All this is consistent with our previous explanations.

4.3.2.2 Node Nonrandomness: R(u)

A node's nonrandomness is characterized by the nonrandomness of edges connected to this node. This is well understood since edges in social networks often exhibit patterns that indicate properties of the nodes such as the importance, rank, or category of the corresponding individuals. Result 1 shows how to calculate node nonrandomness using the spectral coordinates as well as the first k eigenvalues of the adjacency matrix.

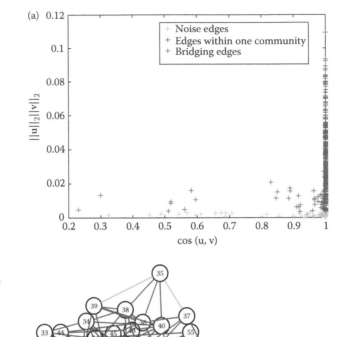

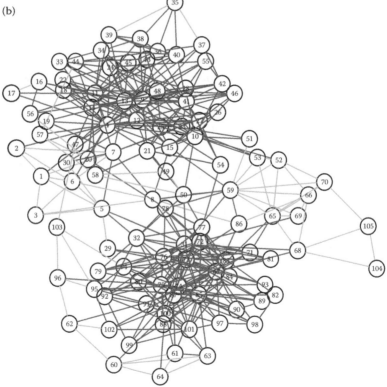

Figure 4.3 **(a) Distribution of edge nonrandomness values. (b) Snapshot of different types of edges characterized by edge nonrandomness of the politics book network.**

Result 1. *The nonrandomness of node u is the length of its spectral vector with eigen-values weighted on corresponding dimensions:*

$$R(u) = \sum_{i=1}^{k} \lambda_i x_{iu}^2 = \alpha_u \Lambda_k \alpha_u^T, \qquad (4.3)$$

where $\Lambda_k = diag\ \{\lambda_1, \lambda_2, \ldots, \lambda_k\}$.

Proof. Let $\boldsymbol{a}_u$ denote the *u*-th row of the adjacency matrix *A*. Since $\boldsymbol{x}_i$ satisfies $A\boldsymbol{x}_i = \lambda_i\boldsymbol{x}_i$ and *A* is symmetric,

$$\begin{pmatrix} a_1 \\ \vdots \\ a_n \end{pmatrix} x_i = A x_i = \lambda_i \begin{pmatrix} x_{i1} \\ \vdots \\ x_{in} \end{pmatrix}.$$

Hence, $\boldsymbol{a}_u\boldsymbol{x}_i = \lambda_i x_{iu}$, and we have

$$R(u) = \sum_{v \in \Gamma(u)} R(u,v) = \sum_{v=1}^{n} \sum_{i=1}^{k} a_{uv} x_{iu} x_{iv} = \sum_{i=1}^{k} \left(x_{iu} \sum_{v=1}^{n} a_{uv} x_{iv} \right)$$

$$= \sum_{i=1}^{k} x_{iu} a_u x_i = \sum_{i=1}^{k} \lambda_i x_{iu}^2 = \alpha_u \Lambda_k \alpha_u^T.$$

We can see that the result is elegant since node nonrandomness is actually determined by its vector length weighted by eigenvalues of the adjacency matrix.

Using the node nonrandomness measure, we can easily separate singleton nodes* and noise nodes (with small $R(u)$ values) from those nodes strongly attached to some community (with large $R(u)$ values). We can also identify those nodes bridging across several groups by examining its relative positions to orthogonal lines corresponding to different communities.

4.3.2.3 Graph Nonrandomness RG and Relative Nonrandomness R_G^*

In our framework, graph nonrandomness *RG* is defined as the sum of nonrandomness values of all edges within the graph. Result 2 shows that *RG* can be directly calculated using the first *k* eigenvalues.

Result 2. The graph nonrandomness of the overall graph G can be calculated as

---

* The singletons are degree-zero nodes who joined the network but have never made an interaction with another user in the social network.

$$R_G = \sum_{(u,v)\in E} R(u,v) = \frac{1}{2}\sum_{u\in G} R(u) = \sum_{i=1}^{k} \lambda_i. \qquad (4.4)$$

Proof. The second equation is straightforward since every edge is counted twice in the sum of node nonrandomness. For the third equation, denote X as $(x_1, x_2, \ldots, x_k)$ where each column is an eigenvector of A: $Ax_i = \lambda_i x_i$, and hence we have

$$\sum_{(u,v)\in E} R(u,v) = \sum_{u,v} a_{uv}\alpha_u\alpha_v^T = trace(X^T A X) = \sum_{i=1}^{k} \lambda_i. \text{"}\square\text{"}$$

The foregoing result is elegant since we can use the sum of the first k eigenvalues to determine the nonrandomness of the overall graph. Recall that k indicates the number of communities in the graph. In this chapter we assume that the value of k is either specified by domain users or discovered by those graph partition methods. There are many studies on how to partition a graph into k communities (refer to a survey paper [6]).

All real networks lie somewhere between the extremes of complete order and complete randomness. While the absolute nonrandomness measure RG can indicate how random a graph G is, it is more desirable to give a relative measure so that graphs with different size and density can be compared. One intuitive approach is comparing the graph's nonrandomness value with the expectation of the nonrandomness value of all random graphs generated by the ER model [11]. We can use the standardized measure defined as

$$R_G^* = \frac{R_G - E(R_G)}{\sigma(R_G)}$$

where $E(RG)$ and $\sigma(RG)$ denote the expectation and standard deviation of the graph nonrandomness under the ER model. Our Theorem 1 shows the distribution of RG.

Theorem 1. For a graph G with k(>n) communities where each community is generated by the ER model with parameter n/k and p, R_G has an asymptotically normal distribution with mean $(n - 2k)p + k$ and variance $2kp(1 - p)$ where $p = 2km/n(n-k)$.

Proof: In G, each community has n/k nodes, and hence,

$$p = \frac{2m}{k\frac{n}{k}(\frac{n}{k}-1)} = \frac{2km}{n(n-k)}.$$

Let λ_i be the largest eigenvalue of the i-th community (i = 1, 2, ..., k). Then $R_G = \Sigma_{i=1}^{k} \lambda_i$. Since λi has the asymptotical normal distribution with mean ($n/k{-}2$) p + 1 and variance $2p(1{-}p)$ [14], then R_G also has the asymptotical normal distribution with mean and variance as in the theorem,"□"

With Theorem 1, we directly have the following result.

Result 3. The relative nonrandomness of the overall graph G(n, m) can be calculated as

$$R_G^* = \frac{R_G - [(n-2k)p + k]}{\sqrt{2kp(1-p)}}, \tag{4.5}$$

where $p = \frac{2km}{n(n-k)}$.

For any two graphs, G_1 and G_2, if $|R_{G_1}^*| < |R_{G_2}^*|$, we can conclude that G_1 is more random than G_2. Since the relative nonrandomness measure R_G^* of the ER graph approximately follows the standard normal distribution with mean 0 and standard variance 1, we can use $1 - \Phi(R_G^*)$ to indicate the similarity between this graph and a random graph, where F(x) denotes the cumulative distribution function of the standard normal distribution. Strictly speaking, $1 - \Phi(R_G^*)$ is the probability of how less likely it is that graph G is actually generated by the ER model.

The relative measure indicates to what extent one real-world graph is different from random graphs in terms of probability. When R_G^* is close to 0, the graph G tends to be more likely generated by the ER model. From the statistical hypothesis testing point of view, we cannot reject the null hypothesis that G is generated by the ER model. On the contrary, when R_G^* is far away from 0, it indicates that graph G leans toward being an extreme ordered graph. We can safely reject the null hypothesis since $1 - \Phi(R_G^*)$ is significantly small.

Another interesting property is that R_G^* of any graph is lower (upper) bounded by that of r-regular (l-complete) graph, respectively. For graphs $G(n, m)$ with k communities, we define the r-regular graph as a graph with each node having r neighbors, and define l-complete graph as a graph where each community is a clique of l nodes. Refer to [40] for details.

We used several network data sets in our evaluation. All data sets (except synthetic and Enron data), together with descriptions, can be found at http://www-personal.umich.edu/˜mejn/netdata/. The Enron network was bulit from the email corpus of a real organization over the course covering a 3-year period. We used a preprocessed version of the data set provided by Shetty and Adibi [31]. This data set contains 252,759 emails from 151 Enron employees, mainly senior managers. In this chapter we have focused on emails sent *from* and *to* these 151 people. An email graph is an undirected and unweighted graph with edges connecting senders and recipients of emails during the corresponding time periods. The semantics of an edge (u, v) in such a graph is that there has been at least five e-mail communications between u and v. The synthetic data was generated using the ER model with parameters $n = 1000$ and $p = 0.2$.

Table 4.1 shows graph statistics and graph nonrandomness values (calculated using RG and R_G^*) of various social networks. We can observe that the relative nonrandomness measures (R_G^*) of real-world social networks are significantly greater than zero, while that of the synthetic random graph is very close to zero. Using R_G^*, we can relatively compare the randomness of graphs with different sizes and densities. For example, we can observe that the network of the dolphins contains less randomness than the karate data since R_G^* of the dolphins (1.61) is greater than that of the karate data (1.22). Furthermore, R_G^* also indicates to what extent the graph is different from random graphs. For the karate graph, we have $R_G^* = 1.22$ and $1 - \Phi(R_G^*) = 0.11$, which indicates how less likely the karate graph is generated by the ER model. Similarly, for the dolphins data, we have $R_G^* = 1.61$ and $1 - \Phi(R_G^*) = 0.054$.

The graph spectrum has been well investigated in the graph analysis field. Chung and Graham indicated the use of the largest eigenvalue λ_1 as an index of the nonrandomness of the overall graph since the first eigenvalue of random graphs characterizes the frequency of subgraphs [7]. Our analysis shows that λ_1 may not be an appropriate measure to quantify the graph nonrandomness for real-world social networks since they usually contain more than one community. Actually, we can see that the index of graph nonrandomness using λ_1 is a special case of our proposed measure RG with $k = 1$.

It has been shown that the eigenvectors of the Laplacian matrix and the normal matrix are good indicators of community clusters [10, 28, 32, 38]. The difference between our nonrandomness framework and those traditional spectral clustering

Table 4.1 Graph Nonrandomness and Characteristics of Various Social Networks

Network	n	m	RG	R_G^*
Synthetic	1000	99820	200	0.02
Karate	34	78	11.7	1.22
Dolphins	62	159	13.1	1.61
Polbooks	105	441	23.5	6.87
Enron	151	869	41.2	4.18
Netsci	1589	2742	38.5	128
Polblogs	1222	16714	134	187

methods is two-folded. First, spectral clustering methods aim to minimize the cut between communities, while our randomness framework is based on maximizing the densities of communities. Second, in traditional spectral clustering methods, communities are represented by dense clusters in the spectral space of Laplacian or normal matrix, whereas communities in our framework are represented by quasi-orthogonal lines in the spectral space of the adjacency matrix. Our proposed framework can quantify randomness at all edge, node, and overall graph levels using the spectra of the adjacency matrix. It is interesting to explore whether similar frameworks can also be derived using the spectra of the Laplacian or normal matrix. We will study this issue in our future work.

4.4 Spectral Analysis of Graph Perturbation

Two natural edge-based graph perturbation strategies are often applied to protect link privacy in privacy-preserving social-network analysis.

- *Rand Add/Del*: We randomly add one edge followed by deleting another edge and repeat this process k times. This strategy preserves the total number of edges in the original graph.
- *Rand Switch*: We randomly switch a pair of existing edges (t, w) and (u, v) (satisfying that edge (t, v) and (u, w) does not exist in G) to (t, v) and (u, w) and repeat it k times. This strategy preserves the degree of each vertex.

Edge randomization may significantly affect the utility of the released randomized graph. To preserve utility, we expect certain aggregate characteristics of the original graph to remain basically unchanged or, at least, for them to be able to be reconstructed from the randomized graph. Since there are so many graph characteristics, we focus on how randomization affects the spectrum of a graph and give bounds of the spectrum change. We first empirically show how the spectrum of a graph and some real-space characteristics are affected by the random perturbation strategies and then give the bounds of the spectrum changes. Lastly, we present our advanced spectrum-preserving randomization strategies that can better preserve structural properties.

4.4.1 Graph Characteristics versus Perturbation: An Illustrating Example

In this section we empirically show how the graph characteristics (including two spectral $[\lambda_1, \mu_2]$ and four real [harmonic mean of the geodesic path, modularity, transitivity, and subgraph centrality]) vary when *Rand Add/Del* and *Rand Switch* perturbation strategies are applied. This experiment was conducted on the U.S. politics book data.

We can observe from Figure 4.4 that the changes of spectral measures display similar trends as those of real graph characteristics while applying the two perturbation strategies. Especially, as shown in Figures 4.4(b–e), the μ_2 of the Laplacian matrix displays a very similar pattern as the harmonic mean of the geodesic path, modularity, and transitivity. Similarly, as shown in Figures 4.4(a)(f), the λ_1 of the adjacency matrix displays a similar pattern as the subgraph centrality measure for both *Rand Add/Del* and *Rand Switch* strategies. Networks with community structures are not resilient to the random perturbation strategy. This is intuitively reasonable, as shown in Figure 4.4(d). Average vertex–vertex distance may change sharply when edges across communities are switched with edges within communities.

We can also observe that neither *Rand Add/Del* nor *Rand Switch* can well preserve the graph characteristics when we increase k to more than 100. Since we have 441 edges in this graph, even medium randomization (k = 100) significantly decreases the utility of the released graph. Generally, more perturbation can lead to stronger privacy protection, but it also greatly changes many features of the network, decreasing information utility. For example, network resilience and community structure are of particular importance in epidemiology where removal of vertices or edges in a contact network may correspond to vaccination of individuals against a disease. Then, the epidemiological solution developed from the randomly perturbed graph may not be applicable to the real graph. In Section 4.4.3 we shall investigate how to perturb graphs without changing much network structural features such as resilience and community structure.

4.4.2 Theoretical Analysis of Spectral Perturbation

The graph perturbation theory is concerned primarily with changes in eigenvalues that result from local modifications of a graph such as adding or deleting an edge. In the following, we let A and $\tilde{A}$ be the adjacency matrices of the original graph G and the perturbed graph G' with spectra $\lambda_1 \geq \lambda_2 \geq \ldots \geq \lambda_n$ and $\tilde{\lambda}_1 \geq \tilde{\lambda}_2 \geq \ldots \geq \tilde{\lambda}_n$, respectively.

Lemma 1: [8] Spectra $\tilde{\lambda}_1 < \lambda_1$ *whenever G' is obtained from G by deleting an edge or vertex. Similarly,* $\tilde{\lambda}_1 < \lambda_1$ *whenever G' is obtained from G by adding an edge or a nonisolated vertex.*

Lemma 1 shows that any proper subgraph of G has smaller index value λ_1, and any supgraph of G has larger index value λ_1. This is also one reason why we only focus on the perturbation strategies that keep the number of edges unchanged. Otherwise, the index of the graph λ_1 may be significantly changed, which will affect many real-space graph characteristics.

Theorem 2: Weyl's Theorem [18]. Given two $n \times n$ symmetric matrices A and E, assume that $\lambda 1 \geq \lambda 2 \geq \ldots \geq \lambda n$ and $\Sigma 1 \geq \Sigma 2 \geq \ldots \geq \Sigma n$ are their eigenvalues, respectively. Let $\tilde{A} = A + E$ and $\tilde{\lambda}_1 \geq \tilde{\lambda}_2 \geq \ldots \geq \tilde{\lambda}_n$ be its eigenvalues. Then Weyl's inequalities are

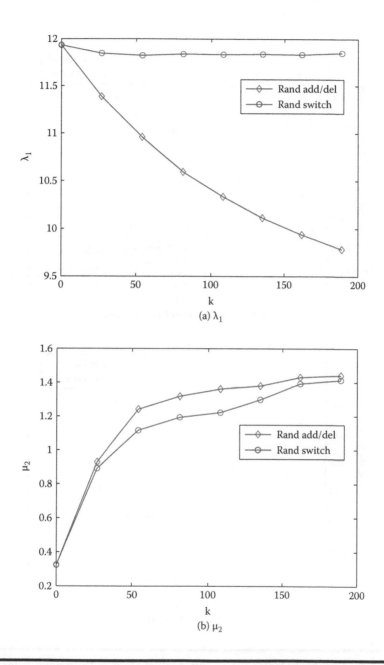

Figure 4.4 Graph characteristic versus perturbation with varying k for Rand Add/Del and Rand Switch.

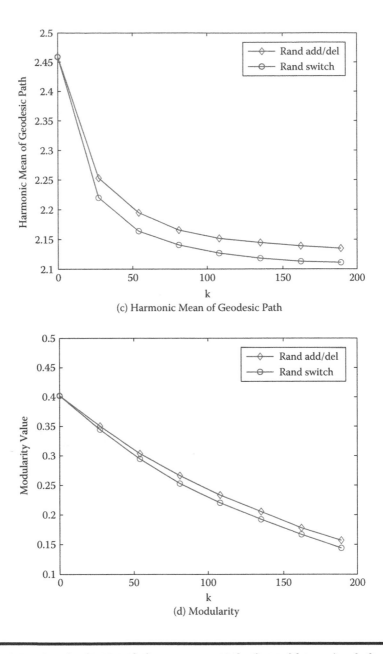

(c) Harmonic Mean of Geodesic Path

(d) Modularity

Figure 4.4 Graph characteristic versus perturbation with varying k for Rand Add/Del and Rand Switch. (Continued)

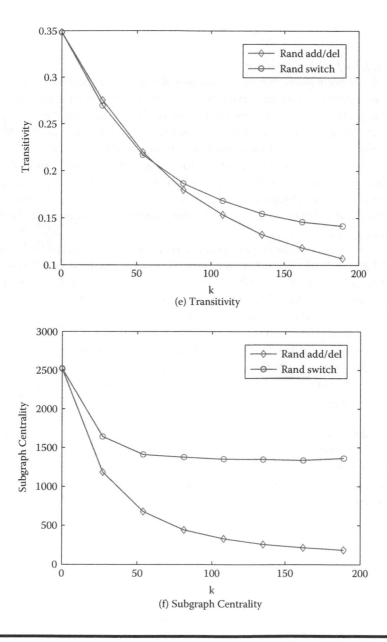

(e) Transitivity

(f) Subgraph Centrality

Figure 4.4   Graph characteristic versus perturbation with varying k for Rand Add/Del and Rand Switch. (Continued)

$$\tilde{\lambda}_{i+j-1} \leq \lambda_i + \varepsilon_j \leq \tilde{\lambda}_{i+j-n} \qquad (4.6)$$

for $1 \text{ Y } i, j, i+j-1, i+j-n \text{ Y } n.$

Weyl's theorem states that the eigenvalues of a matrix are perfectly conditioned, that is, no eigenvalue can move more than the range specified by Equation 4.6.

Some graph features (e.g., the number of vertices n, the number of edges m) remain unchanged after randomization and are assumed to be available. We also assume the number of perturbations k is available to data miners. The reason is that k denotes the magnitude of perturbation that may be needed to analyze the perturbed graph by data miners. In this section we present to what extent the graph spectrum may change with respect to those graph invariants, specifically, k and n for *Rand Add/Del*, and k, n, and d_i for *Rand Switch*, where d_i is the degree of vertex i.

When $k = 1$, we call the perturbation matrix the elementary perturbation matrix (EPM). Obviously, the perturbation matrix E when $k > 1$ is the sum of EPMs along the perturbation. For *Rand Add/Del*, we have two different cases. One is that we add the edge (i, p) and delete an existing edge (i, q). Specifically, $eip = epi = 1$, and $eiq = eqi = -1$, where eij denotes the component of E. We can derive $\varepsilon_1 = \sqrt{2}$, $\varepsilon_n = -\sqrt{2}$, and $oi = 0$ $(2 \text{ Y } i \text{ Y } n-1)$. The other case is that we add the edge (i, j) and then remove one existing edge (p, q) where i, j, p, q are distinct. Specifically, $eij = eji = 1$, and $epq = eqp = -1$. In this case, we have $o_1 = o_2 = 1$, $on = on_{-1} = -1$, and $oi = 0$ $(3 \text{ Y } i \text{ Y } n-2)$. For *Rand Switch*, when we switch one pair of edges, $(t, w), (u, v)$ to (t, v) and (u, w), $etw = ewt = euv = evu = -1$, and $etv = evt = euw = ewu = 1$. We can also derive $o_1 = 2$, $on = -2$, and $oi = 0$ $(2 \text{ Y } i \text{ Y } n-1)$. However, when $k > 1$, it is hard to derive directly the eigenvalues of E based on the released k. In the following, we show our result based on the Gershgorin Circle Theorem [18].

Theorem 3: Gershgorin Circle Theorem. For an $n \times n$ matrix A, define $R_i = \sum_{j=1, j \neq i}^{n} |a_{ij}|$. Then each eigenvalue of A must be in at least one of the disks in the complex plane:

$$C_i(A) = \left\{ z : |z - a_{ii}| \leq R_i \right\}.$$

Result 4: Let $0_1 \varepsilon_1 \geq \varepsilon_2 \geq \ldots \geq \varepsilon_n$ on be the eigenvalues of E. For all $i(1 \leq i \leq n)$, we have

$$\varepsilon_n \leq |\lambda_i - \tilde{\lambda}_i| \leq \varepsilon_1 \qquad (4.7)$$

or more loosely,

$$|\lambda_i - \tilde{\lambda}_i| \leq \|E\|_2, \qquad (4.8)$$

where for Rand Add/Del,

$$\| E \|_2 \leq \min\{2k, n-1\} \tag{4.9}$$

and for Rand Switch,

$$\| E \|_2 \leq 2 \min \left\{ k, \max_i \left(\min\{d_i, n-1-d_i\} \right) \right\}. \tag{4.10}$$

Proof. Equation 4.7 and Equation 4.8 can be easily derived from Weyl's Theorem. Notice that the diagonal elements of E are always 0. Hence,

$$C_i(E) = \left\{ z : |z - e_{ii}| \leq R_i \right\} = \left\{ z : |z| \leq R_i \right\}.$$

All these circles are concentric, and all the eigenvalues of A are thus in the circle of the largest radius: $\|E\|_2$ Y $\max_i\{R_i\}$, and $R_i = \Sigma_{j \neq i} |e_{ij}|$ is actually the total number of added and deleted edges of vertex i.

Hence, for *Rand Add/Del*, when $k < n/2$, the worst case is that all the perturbations involve the same vertex; when $k < n/210490\_\chi o\mu\mu X004\xi 015.\rho\tau\phi$ $n/2$, the worst case happens when a certain vertex is removed from all original edges to its neighbors and adds new edges to all the rest of the vertices. In this case, $\max_i\{R_i\}$ Y $\min\{2k, n - 1\}$, and Equation 4.10 follows.

For *Rand Switch*, if one edge is deleted, there must be an edge added to the same vertex. Therefore, $1/2\ R_i \leq \min\{d_i, n-1-d_i\}$, through which we immediately get

$$\max_i R_i \leq 2 \min \left\{ k, \max_i \left(\min\{d_i, n-1-d_i\} \right) \right\}$$

and Equation 4.10 follows. "□"

The graph spectrum has been well investigated in the graph analysis field. It has been shown that the eigenvectors of the Laplacian matrix and the normal matrix are good indicators of community clusters [10, 28, 32, 38]. The difference between our nonrandomness framework and those traditional spectral clustering methods is two-folded. First, spectral clustering methods aim to minimize the cut between communities, while our randomness framework is based on maximizing the densities of communities. Second, in traditional spectral clustering methods, communities are represented by dense clusters in the spectral space of the Laplacian or normal matrix, while communities in our framework are represented by quasi-orthogonal lines in the spectral space of the adjacency matrix. Our proposed framework can quantify randomness at all edge, node, and overall graph levels using the spectra of the adjacency matrix. It is interesting to explore whether similar frameworks can also be derived using the spectra of the Laplacian or normal matrix. We will study this issue in our future work.

Actually, the bound given in Equation 4.11 is the loose bound in the worst case. It may not accurately reflect the magnitude of spectrum change. In Section 4.4 we develop our spectrum-preserving randomization approach that can control the change of spectrum during the randomization process. Note that all the foregoing results can be easily extended to the Laplacian matrix with some simple adjustment since $\tilde{L} - L = A - \tilde{A} = -E$.

4.4.3 Spectrum-Preserving Randomization

Since many graph structures are shown to have strong association with the spectrum, a very mature idea is whether we can figure out a perturbation strategy such that one or some particular eigenvalues will not significantly change. Hence the new strategy is more probable to better preserve structural characteristics without sacrificing much of the privacy protection aspect.

From the matrix perturbation community, researchers have achieved results on the intermediate eigenvalue problem of the second type, that is, how to determine E such that the eigenvalue λ_1 of $A + E$ can be greater or less than that of A. Specifically, Cvetkovic et al. [8] gave results on how to increase or decrease λ_1 of the adjacency matrix by constructing the noise matrix E based on the principal eigenvector values of the adjacency matrix. We list their results in the first two rows of Tables 4.2 and 4.3. For example, according to row 1 in Table 4.2, if we add edge (i, j) and delete edge (p, q), and $x_1 i x_1 j - x_1 p x_1 q > 0$ stands, λ_1 necessarily increases. Note that $x_1 i$ denotes the i-th component in the principal eigenvector of λ_1.

Table 4.2 Conditions on Adjusting λ_1 and μ_2 for *Spctr Add/Del*

Condition	Action
$x_1 i x_1 j - x_1 p x_1 q > 0$	$\tilde{\lambda}_1 > \lambda_1$
$x_1 i x_1 j - x_1 p x_1 q < 0$ and $\lambda_1 - \lambda_2 > \frac{x_{1i}^2 + x_{1j}^2 + x_{1p}^2 + x_{1q}^2}{2(x_{1p}x_{1q} - x_{1i}x_{1j})}$	$\tilde{\lambda}_1 < \lambda_1$
$y_2 i y_2 j - y_2 p y_2 q > 0$	$\tilde{\mu}_2 < \mu_2$
$y_2 i y_2 j - y_2 p y_2 q < 0$, and $\mu_3 - \mu_2 > \frac{y_{2i}^2 + y_{2j}^2 + y_{2p}^2 + y_{2q}^2}{2(y_{2p}y_{2q} - y_{2i}y_{2j})}$	$\tilde{\mu}_2 > \mu_2$

In this chapter, we also need to know whether the eigenvalue μ_2 of the Laplacian matrix L of a particular graph G increases or decreases when an edge is relocated. We derive sufficient conditions on how to adjust μ_2 of the Laplacian matrix for two randomization strategies, *Rand Add/Del* and *Rand Switch*. We summarize our results in the last two rows of Tables 4.2 and 4.3 (the detailed proof can be found in the Appendix of Reference 40). Note that μ_2 is the important eigenvalue of the Laplacian matrix L. We use μ_i and $\tilde{\mu}_i$ to denote the i-th smallest eigenvalue of L and $\tilde{L}$, respectively, and $\mathbf{u}_2$ denotes the eigenvector of μ_2. Spectrum $y_2 i$ is the i-th component of $\mathbf{u}_2$.

Based on the derived conditions, we give our spectrum-preserving approach, which can improve simple edge randomization by considering the change of spectrum in the randomization process. Here we can determine which edges we should add/remove or switch so that we can control the move of target eigenvalues. As a result, real graph characteristics (or graph utility) are expected to be better preserved. Our *Spctr Switch* algorithm follows.

In Row 2 of the algorithm, we only calculate the first one or two eigenvalues of the corresponding graph matrices. It is not necessary or desirable to calculate the entire eigen decomposition. Note that calculation of the eigenvectors of an $n \times n$ matrix takes in general a number of operations $O(n^3)$. Rows 6 to 11 present how to switch based on the sufficient conditions listed in Table 4.3. The algorithm can be modified to *Spctr Add/Del* with some minor changes: replacing the switch process with the *Add/Del* process in Rows 8 and 11; and finally, in Rows 7 and 10, referring to Table 4.2 for the conditions under which the eigenvalues increase or decrease.

Table 4.3   Conditions on Adjusting λ_1 and μ_2 for *Spctr Switch*

Condition	Action
$(x_1 t - x_1 u)(x_1 v - x_1 w) > 0$	$\tilde{\lambda}_1 > \lambda_1$
$(x_1 t - x_1 u)(x_1 v - x_1 w) < 0$, and $\lambda_1 - \lambda_2 > \frac{y_{1t} - y_{1u}}{y_{1w} - y_{1v}} + \frac{y_{1w} - y_{1v}}{y_{1t} - y_{1u}}$	$\tilde{\lambda}_1 < \lambda_1$
$(y_2 t - y_2 u)(y_2 v - y_2 w) > 0$	$\tilde{\mu}_2 < \mu_2$
$(y_2 t - y_2 u)(y_2 v - y_2 w) < 0$, and $\mu_3 - \mu_2 > \frac{y_{2t} - y_{2u}}{y_{2w} - y_{2v}} + \frac{y_{2w} - y_{2v}}{y_{2t} - y_{2u}}$	$\tilde{\mu}_2 > \mu_2$

Algorithm 4.1 Spectrum-preserving graph randomization through edge switch	
Input: graph data G, perturbation magnitude k	
1.	Derive the adjacency matrix A and the Laplacian matrix L.
2.	Calculate the eigenvalues and eigenvectors $(\lambda_1, \lambda_2, \mathbf{e}_1)$ of A and $(\mu_2, \mu_3, \mathbf{u}_2)$ of L, respectively.
3.	$l = 0$
4.	While $l < k$
5.	From graph G, randomly pick one edge (t, w);
6.	If $l/2 = =0$
7.	Find all the edge combinations such that $\tilde{\lambda}_1 < \lambda_1$ and $\tilde{\mu}_2 > \mu_2$;
8.	Randomly pick one (u, v), switch (t, w) and (u, v) to (t, v) and (u, w);
9.	Otherwise
10.	Find all the edge combinations such that $\tilde{\lambda}_1 < \lambda_1$ and $\tilde{\mu}_2 > \mu_2$;
11.	Randomly pick one (u, v), switch (t, w) and (u, v) to (t, v) and (u, w);
12.	$l = l + 1$

It is ideal to derive sufficient conditions regarding how much one or some particular eigenvalues will change. This is the issue of estimating changes in eigenvalues under a wide range of perturbations. The eigenvalues of the perturbed graph can be determined as implicit functions of algebraic and geometric invariants of the original graph. However, this problem has not been solved in the matrix perturbation field.

Figure 4.5 shows that spectral randomization can significantly better preserve both graph spectrum and real-space characteristics of the political book graph data set than the previous random perturbation that does not consider spectrum preserving during the perturbation process. Due to space limitations, we only include the comparison between *Spctr Switch* and *Rand Switch*. We can see that *Spctr Switch* can significantly better keep both spectral characteristics and real characteristics close to those computed from the original graph even when we increase the number of switches k to 180. Note that the spectrum-preserving approach adjusts both λ_1 and μ_2. The intuition here is that the more eigenvalues we control in perturbation, the more real-space characteristics we can preserve in the randomized graph.

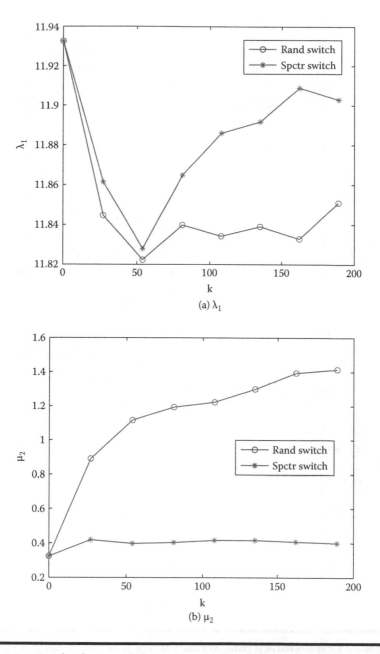

Figure 4.5 **Graph characteristic versus varying k between *Spctr Switch* and *Rand Switch*.**

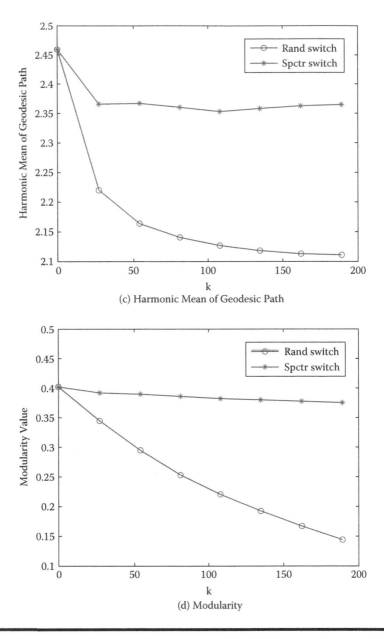

(c) Harmonic Mean of Geodesic Path

(d) Modularity

Figure 4.5 **Graph characteristic versus varying k between *Spctr Switch* and *Rand Switch*.**

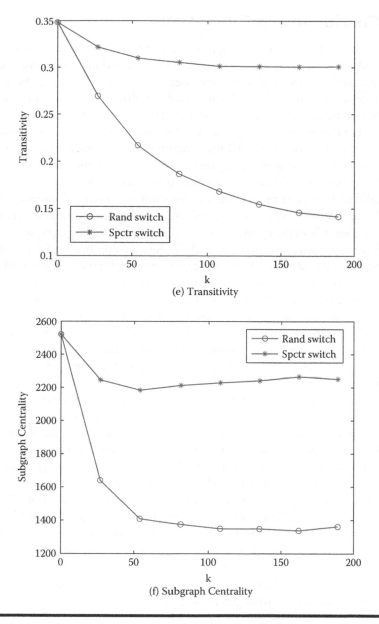

(e) Transitivity

(f) Subgraph Centrality

Figure 4.5 **Graph characteristic versus varying k between** *Spctr Switch* **and** *Rand Switch.*

4.5 Conclusion and Future Work

The focus of the first part of our paper was the development of a spectrum-based framework characterizing graph nonrandomness at various levels. We first proposed a novel measure to characterize edge nonrandomness using the spectral coordinates of two connected nodes projected in k-dimensional spectral space. We then characterized node nonrandomness based on the nonrandomness of edges connected to this node, and graph nonrandomness based on the nonrandomness of all edges within the graph. All nonrandomness measures are simple numerical indices that can be derived elegantly from the graph spectrum. We studied several real-world social networks for which our nonrandomness measures display useful and desirable properties. We also show that nonrandomness measures have different distributions between real-world networks and random graphs. In the future, we will explore how different choices of k affect graph nonrandomness. Second, we will investigate in full the relationship between our proposed nonrandomness measures (especially graph nonrandomness) with traditional measures. Traditional measures such as modularity can also be used to measure community structural property. It is interesting to compare our measures with traditional ones and explore how to apply the proposed nonrandomness framework to solve practical problems such as graph partition. We will consider computational complexity issues when extremely large networks are available. Finally, we will explore how to extend our framework to directed and weighted graphs.

In the second part of this paper, we have developed one spectrum-preserving randomization approach that can significantly improve edge-based graph randomization methods (*Rand Add/Del* and *Rand Switch*) by increasing the utility of the perturbed graph. We have also given a loose bound of the graph spectrum changes for pure randomization strategies (i.e., reallocating or switching edges randomly). Since the graph spectrum is closely related to many real-graph characteristics, this bound provides a perspective on the extent to which edge randomization affects the graph structure. In the future, we are interested in deriving some (tight) bound of graph spectrum changes for spectrum-preserving randomization strategies. We will also investigate the intermediate eigenvalue problem, aiming to derive conditions to adjust any eigenvalue (in addition to λ_1 and μ_2) that may indicate a certain structure character of the graph. Finally, we will investigate thoroughly how spectrum-preserving randomization strategies protect link privacy.

Acknowledgments

This work was supported in part by U.S. National Science Foundation IIS-0546027 and CNS-0831204. Partial results have been published in two papers [40, 43].

References

1. L. Backstrom, C. Dwork, and Jon Kleinberg. Wherefore art thou r3579x?: Anonymized social networks, hidden patterns, and structural steganography. In *Proceedings of the 16th International Conference on World Wide Web (WWW '07)*, New York, pp. 181–190, 2007, ACM Press.

2. Lars Backstrom, Dan Huttenlocher, Jon Kleinberg, and Xiangyang Lan. Group formation in large social networks: membership, growth, and evolution. In *Proceedings of the 12th ACM SIGKDD International Conference on Knowledge Discovery and Data Mining (KDD '06)*, New York, pp. 44–54, 2006, ACM Press.

3. Jeffrey Baumes, Mark K. Goldberg, Malik Magdon-Ismail, and William A. Wallace. Discovering hidden groups in communication networks. In *ISI*, pp. 378–389, 2004.

4. Tanya Y. Berger-Wolf and Jared Saia. A framework for analysis of dynamic social networks. In *KDD'06*, pp. 523–528, 2006.

5. Alina Campan and Traian Marius Truta. A clustering approach for data and structural anonymity in social networks. In *PinKDD'08*, 2008.

6. Deepayan Chakrabarti and Christos Faloutsos. Graph mining: laws, generators, and algorithms. *ACM Comput. Surv.*, 38(1):2, 2006.

7. Fan Chung and Ronald Graham. Sparse quasi-random graphs. *Combinatorica*, 22(2):217–244, 2002.

8. D. Cvetkovic, P. Rowlinson, and S. Simic. *Eigenspaces of Graphs*. Cambridge University Press, Cambridge, England, 1997.

9. Luciano da F. Costa, Francisco A. Rodrigues, Gonzalo Travieso, and P. R. Villas Boas. Characterization of complex networks: A survey of measurements. *Adv. Phys.*, 56:167, 2007.

10. Chris H. Q. Ding, Xiaofeng He, Hongyuan Zha, Ming Gu, and Horst D. Simon. A minmax cut algorithm for graph partitioning and data clustering. In Proceedings of the 2001 IEEE International conference on Data Mining. pp. 107–114, 2001.

11. P. Erdos and A. Renyi. On random graphs i. *Publicationes Mathematicae*, 6:290–297, 1959.

12. Ernesto Estrada and Juan A. Rodríguez-Velázquez. Subgraph centrality in complex networks. *Phys. Rev. E*, 71(056103), 2005.

13. Andrew Fast, David Jensen, and Brian Neil Levine. Creating social networks to improve peer-to-peer networking. In *KDD'05*, pp. 568–573, 2005.

14. Z. Furedi and J. Komlos. The eigenvalues of random symmetric matrices. *Combinatorica*, 1 (3):233–241, 1981.

15. M. Girvan and M. E. Newman. Community structure in social and biological networks. *Proc. Natl. Acad. Sci. USA*, 99(12):7821–7826, June 2002.

16. M. Hay, G. Miklau, D. Jensen, P. Weis, and S. Srivastava. Anonymizing social networks. *University of Massachusetts Technical Report*, 07-19, 2007.

17. Michael Hay, Gerome Miklau, David Jensen, Don Towsely, and Philipp Weis. Resisting structural re-identification in anonymized social networks. In *VLDB*, 2008.

18. R. Horn and C. R. Johnson. *Matrix Analysis*. Cambridge University Press, Cambridge, England, 1985.

19. David Kempe, Jon M. Kleinberg, and Éva Tardos. Maximizing the spread of influence through a social network. In *KDD'03*, pp. 137–146, 2003.

20. Jon M. Kleinberg. Authoritative sources in a hyperlinked environment. *J. ACM*, 46(5):604–632, 1999.
21. Jon M. Kleinberg. Challenges in mining social network data: processes, privacy, and paradoxes. In *KDD'07*, pp. 4–5, 2007.
22. Yehuda Koren, Stephen C. North, and Chris Volinsky. Measuring and extracting proximity in networks. In *KDD'06*, pp. 245–255, 2006.
23. V. Krebs. http://www.orgnet.com/. 2006.
24. Ravi Kumar, Jasmine Novak, and Andrew Tomkins. Structure and evolution of online social networks. In *KDD*, pages 611–617, 2006.
25. Vito Latora and Massimo Marchiori. Efficient behavior of small-world networks. *Phys. Rev. Lett.*, 87, 2001.
26. K. Liu and E Terzi. Towards identity anonymization on graphs. In *Proceedings of the ACM SIGMOD Conference*, Vancouver, Canada, 2008, ACM Press.
27. L. Lovasz. Random walks on graphs. *Combinatorics*, 2:1–46, 1993.
28. M. Newman. Detecting community structure in networks. *Eur. Phys. J. B—Condensed Matter*, 38(2):321–330, March 2004.
29. Marcello Pelillo, Kaleem Siddiqi, and Steven W. Zucker. Matching hierarchical structures using association graphs. *IEEE Trans. Pattern Anal. Mach. Intell.*, 21(11):1105–1120, 1999.
30. A.J. Seary and W.D. Richards. Spectral methods for analyzing and visualizing networks: an introduction. *National Research Council, Dynamic Social Network Modelling and Analysis: Workshop Summary and Papers*, pp. 209–228, 2003.
31. J. Shetty and J. Adibi. The Enron email dataset database schema and brief statistical report. *Information Sciences Institute Technical Report*, University of Southern California, 2004.
32. Jianbo Shi and Jitendra Malik. Normalized cuts and image segmentation. In *Proceedings of the 1997 Conference on Computer Vision and Pattern Recognition (CVPR '97)*. Washington, DC, p. 731, IEEE Computer Society, 1997.
33. Motoki Shiga, Ichigaku Takigawa, and Hiroshi Mamitsuka. A spectral clustering approach to optimally combining numerical vectors with a modular network. In *KDD'07*, pp. 647–656, 2007.
34. Ellen Spertus, Mehran Sahami, and Orkut Buyukkokten. Evaluating similarity measures: a large-scale study in the orkut social network. In *KDD'05*, pp. 678–684, 2005.
35. G. W. Stewart and Ji guang Sun. *Matrix Perturbation Theory*. Academic Press, San Diego, CA, 1990.
36. Chayant Tantipathananandh, Tanya Y. Berger-Wolf, and David Kempe. A framework for community identification in dynamic social networks. In *KDD'07*, pp. 717–726, 2007.
37. Y. Wang, D. Chakrabarti, C. Wang, and C. Faloutsos. Epidemic spreading in real networks: an eigenvalue viewpoint. *Proceedings of the 22nd International Symposium on Reliable Distributed Systems*, 2003. Florence, Italy.
38. Y. Weiss. Segmentation using eigenvectors: a unifying view. In *Proceedings of the IEEE International Conference on Computer Vision*, pp. 975–982, 1999. Corfu, Greece.
39. Scott White and Padhraic Smyth. Algorithms for estimating relative importance in networks. In *KDD'03*, pp. 266–275, 2003. 9th ACM Conference on knowledge discovery and data mining.
40. X. Ying and X. Wu. Randomizing social networks: a spectrum preserving approach. In *Proceedings of the 8th SIAM Conference on Data Mining*, April 2008. Atlanta, Georgia.

41. Xiaowei Ying and Xintao Wu. Graph generation with prescribed feature constraints. In *Proceedings of the 9th SIAM Conference on Data Mining*, 2009. Sparks, Nevada.
42. Xiaowei Ying and Xintao Wu. On link privacy in randomizing social networks. In *PAKDD'09*, 2009. 13th Pacific-Asia Conference on Advances in knowledge Discovery and data mining. Bangkok, Thailand pages 28–39, 2009.
43. Xiaowei Ying and Xintao Wu. On randomness measures for social networks. In *SDM 2009*. 2009 SIAM International conference on data mining, Sparks, Nevada, April 2009.
44. Elena Zheleva and Lise Getoor. Preserving the privacy of sensitive relationships in graph data. In *PinKDD'07*, pp. 153–171, 2007.
45. B. Zhou and J. Pei. preserving privacy in social networks against neighborhood attacks. *IEEE 24th International Conference on Data Engineering*, pp. 506–515, April 2008. Cancun, Mexico.

Chapter 5

Sociotechnical Network Models: A Review

Todd Aycock, Justin Headley, Justin Floyd, and Fei Hu

Contents

5.1 Introduction

Social networks are described as a social structure made of individuals called "nodes" that are tied by one or more specific types of interdependency, such as friendship, kinship, financial exchange, dislike, or relationships of beliefs, knowledge, or prestige. Nodes are the individual actors within the networks, and ties are the relationships between the actors. There can be many kinds of ties between the nodes. Network analysis focuses on relations among actors, and not individual actors and their attributes.

This chapter will explain in details on probabilistic models, dynamic social networks, small-world models, and large-scale models.

A probabilistic model is a statistical analysis tool that estimates, on the basis of past (historical) data, the probability of an event occurring again using a stochastic process, which is a statistical process involving a number of random variables depending on a variable parameter (which is usually time). The probabilistic model typically uses different hypotheses such as the individual interest factor, the group behavior factor, and the time lapse factor.

A dynamic social network can handle large dynamic multinode, multilink networks with different levels of uncertainty. A meta-group is used to define the main concept of a dynamic network. Using the hypotheses from the probabilistic model, a more accurate model can be created. Dynamic modeling is important to get an accurate representation of a network.

The small-world model uses the hypothesis that the chain of social acquaintances required to connect on arbitrary person anywhere in the world is generally short. We will explain the small-world phenomenon experiments by Stanley Milgram. We will also examine the two theorems that Kleinberg uses to study the ability of decentralized network control.

Large-scale models (better known as sociotechnical systems) are an approach to complex organizational work design that recognizes the interaction between people and technology in work places. The term also refers to the interaction between complex society infrastructure and human behavior.

5.2 Probabilistic Models [2]

Social network models can benefit from a probabilistic approach. Using probability, a network can predict the parameters, actors, and actions of these actors in the future. This prediction can be very advantageous to the stability and efficiency of the network, and it can be performed in a variety of different ways.

In one example, a learned function can be implemented as a stochastic process. In this scenario, the test will be a realization of the stochastic process, and a multistep prediction will be used to test the data. Considering a social group structure, the actions of the actors or the actors' paths into the future can be predicted. Based on these paths into the future, an evolving social group structure can be constructed. These predicted groups can be compared with the observed groups via the test data. The distribution of group sizes can be used to measure performance.

This example shows how prediction models can be integrated with learning models. However, the learning process is time consuming since there are so many possible combinations of actors that can be used to establish groups. Adding a prediction model to this will only increase the time needed. Considering that there are N actors and K groups, at each time step there are $2^{NK}/K!$ possible actors' combinations that can be used to create and set up groups. Therefore, for T time steps, the complexity of finding the optimal group path is $O(T \times 2^{NK}/K)$ or $O(T \times 2^{K(N-\log K)})$. Based on the time complexity shown here, it is easy to see how the learning process is very time consuming.

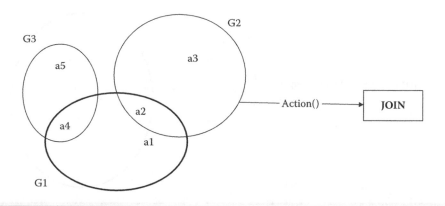

Figure 5.1 A probabilistic social group evolution model; before JOIN action. (From H.-C. Chen et al., Personalization inferring agent dynamics from social communication networks, in *International Conference on Knowledge Discovery and Data Mining*, 2007, pp. 36–45.)

Theories of probability can be used with evolution models as well. In the example shown in Figure 5.1, there are five actors and three social groups involved with the model. This probabilistic social group evolution model shows that, based on the properties of itself and other actors, α_1 decides to join a new group through the stochastic process shown as *Action*() in Figure 5.1. This stochastic process depends on a set of parameters θ_{action}, with other possible actions including leaving a group and doing nothing.

To find the information on which group to join, α_1 must gather information through its neighbors α_2 and α_4. This information includes which groups the neighbors belong to. Based on these references, α_1 can infer that the possible groups to join are G_2 and G_3 in the case shown in Figure 5.1. Based on its own actor qualifications, α_1 then decides which group to apply to. This decision weighs the actor's qualifications as measured by the average rank (by all groups) and qualification thresholds and sizes of the potential joining groups.

Once α_1 decides to join a group, it must apply to the specific group it has decided to join. This can be accomplished through a stochastic handshaking process. First, α_1 decides to "apply" to group G_2. At this point, G_2 decides whether or not to accept α_1 as a part of its group. This process is governed by a set of parameters θ_{group} and is depicted in Figure 5.2 as *Group*(). This process is similar to the one used to decide which group the actor wants to join, and the same actor qualifications are used in the group's decision.

Another example of using a probabilistic approach to describing social network models is presented in Reference 2. In considering an online social network, a dynamic probability model can be used, and this model is stated in three hypotheses.

The first hypothesis states that, through the individual interest factor, it can be assumed that the more times one user attends a discussion about a topic T, the

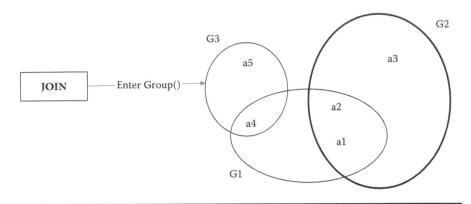

Figure 5.2 A probabilistic social group evolution model; after JOIN action. (From H.-C. Chen et al., Personalization inferring agent dynamics from social communication networks, in *International Conference on Knowledge Discovery and Data Mining*, 2007, pp. 36–45.)

higher the probability that the user will attend the same discussion in the future. Based on the assumption that each user has his or her own unique interest in a particular discussion topic contents, if one user has attended the same discussion often in over a period of time in the past, then that user would be much more interested in that particular topic. Therefore, the user would be much more likely to discuss the topic again in the future and attend that same discussion in the future.

The second hypothesis states that, through the group behavior factor, it can be assumed that if the group of users that attend a discussion about topic T increases, then there will be a higher probability that one of the users will attend the discussion again in the future. This hypothesis is similar to the first in many respects and, in some ways, is simply an addition to it with different characteristics. It also can be stated similarly that if the group of users develop their own unique interests and that group grows larger, then the group will be much more likely to revisit the discussion and continue it in the future.

The third and final hypothesis states that, through the time lapse factor, it can be assumed that the longer the interval between the present and peak time becomes, the lower the probability that users will attend the discussion in the future. This hypothesis continues with the concepts of interest in topics and expands to include the whole-time factor. Sensibly, the more the time between topic discussions attended, the less memorable the topic will become to the user and, therefore, the less interest will be shown in it. As interest lowers for a topic, the probability of the user attending a discussion on this same topic grows smaller, as stated in the hypothesis.

Based on the first hypothesis, a behavior tendency function can be developed, $f(\bar{x})$. This function takes input variables of a and time n. The function calculates the tendency probability of a user's behavior based on the user's individual interest in a topic.

$$f(\overline{x}) = \prod_{i=1}^{s} k^{2-(x_n-x_{n-i})^2} * e^{-ki}, k_i > 1 \qquad (5.1)$$

The function $f(\overline{x})$ also interprets the input variables x_n, which is the behavior state of user a about discussing the topic at time n. When the variable x_n is 1, the function value is directly proportional to user a's probability of attending a discussion on the topic at time n. When the variable x_n is 0, the function value is not directly proportional to the probability of user a attending a discussion on the topic at time n. The variable k_i is a parameter that must be estimated, while s is the available duration of the individual interest factor. This individual interest factor is when the user's behavior at time n only associates with the behavior from time $n - s$ to time $n - 1$. This value can be evaluated by experience.

The more frequent x_{n-i} equals x_n, the larger the output of the function will be and, therefore, the larger the probability. This can be stated as, the more frequently that the predicted behavior of a user a at time n is the same as the previous behavior at time $n - i$, the more probable that the predicted behavior will happen. Conversely, the less frequently the behavior of user a at time n is the same as the previous behavior, then it will be less probable that the predicted behavior will happen in the future.

Next, considering the second hypothesis, another formula can be derived. This formula is determined on the premise that, as more users attend a group discussion, the attending users will attract other users to join, causing more users to attend and, therefore, increasing any user's probability. The original users that influence other users will also be more likely to attend after attracting a larger group. Based on this concept, the behavior tendency function $h(\overline{x})$ is given for a user a at time n. The function calculates the probability of the behavior trend by the group behavior. This behavior tendency function is as follows:

$$h(\overline{x}) = \prod_{i=1}^{s'} l_j^{1+r^{2 x_{n-1}}} * e^{-l_j}, l_j > 1 \qquad (5.2)$$

This function requires the derivation of r from another formula, the changing ratio of the number of users, which is as follows:

$$r = \frac{\|G(n-j)\| + \|G(n-j-1)\| + \|G(n-j-2)\| + 1}{\|G(n-j-1)\| + \|G(n-j-2)\| + \|G(n-j-3)\| + 1} \qquad (5.3)$$

In the changing ratio of the number of users function $\|G(n-j)\|$ represents the total number of users who attend the discussion at time $n - j$. The output, r, is derived by dividing the total number of users who are involved from time $n - j$ to $n - j - 2$ with the total number of users involved from time $n - j - 1$ to $n - j - 3$. If this total number decreases as time goes on, r will turn out to be less than 1.

In the original function, the behavior tendency function s' is the available duration of the group behavior factor, meaning that user a's behavior at time n only associates with the group behavior during the timeframe $(n - s', n - 1)$. The variable l_j is a parameter that must be estimated, much like the variable k_i from the behavior tendency function from the first hypothesis. The variable x_n is the predicting behavior state of user a at time n. If this variable is equal to 1, then r will be larger than 1 more frequently than if x_n does not equal 1. This shows that, as the total number of users who attend the topic discussion increases, the higher the probability that one of the user's behavior in the future will be to attend the same discussion on the same topic.

Finally, based on the third and final hypothesis, a final formula can be derived. This final formula is based on the premise that a given user will no longer be interested in a specific topic after a long-enough period of time has passed since the last topic discussion was attended by the user. Also, the total number of participators will decrease after the peak time, the time when the largest numbers of users attend. This decline rate will increase with the augmentation of the interval form from the peak time. Based on these statements, the following formula is given:

$$g(\bar{x}) = \frac{1}{(n - t_p)^{\lambda * x_n}}, \lambda > 0 \tag{5.4}$$

This final behavior tendency function, $g(\bar{x})$, is given for a specific user a at a given time n. This formula calculates the probability of behavior trend by the time lapse factor. The value n is actually the time point that will be predicted, and t_p is the peak time or the time between the time interval $(0, n)$ when the number of participators was the largest. The value λ is the lapse exponential coefficient, which is typically between 0.5 and 1, and this value must be evaluated by experience. The value xn represents the predicting behavior state of user a at time n.

In this particular behavior tendency function, $g(\bar{x})$, if x_n is equal to 1, then $g(\bar{x})$ will be greater than 1, whereas the larger n becomes, the smaller $g(\bar{x})$ will be. This shows that the longer the interval from the peak time to the predicted time, the lower the probability of the user attending the discussion on the same topic again in the future. Also, when x_n is equal to 0, the output will be 1.

Given these three hypotheses, the final behavior tendency function $\chi(\bar{x})$ is given as follows for user a at time n:

$$P(x_n) \sim \chi(\bar{x}) = f(\bar{x}) * h(\bar{x}) * g(\bar{x}) \tag{5.5}$$

The value $P(x_n)$ represents the probability of the tendency of attending the discussion. This probability positively correlates with $\chi(\bar{x})$ as shown in the formula.

Combining the variables of the original three formulas and simplifying, the following final formula is given:

$$P(x_n) \sim \frac{\left\{ \prod_{i=1}^{s} k^{2-(x_n - x_{n-i})^2} * B^{-k_i} \right\} * \left\{ \prod_{j=1}^{s'} l_j^{(1+r^2)^{x_{n-1}}} * B^{-l_j} \right\}}{(B - t_p)^{\lambda * x_n}}, k_i > 1 l_j > 1, \lambda > 0 \quad (5.6)$$

The final step is to estimate the parameters k_i and l_j. Using the maximum likelihood estimation (MLE) method, the following formulas could be determined:

$$k_i = \frac{\sum_A [2 - (x_n - x_{n-i})^2]}{q} \quad (5.7)$$

$$l_j = \frac{\sum_A [1 + r^{(2x_{n-1})}]}{q} \quad (5.8)$$

The variables are the same as in the previous equations, except for the addition of new variables q and A. The variable q represents a total number of users in the model, and the variable A represents the universal set of behaviors and users. If x_n is set as 1, then the value of $\chi(\overline{x})$ will have a positive correlation with $P(x_n)$.

The results from testing this probability model are shown as follows:

It can be observed from Figures 5.3–5.5 that the predicted and actual results are very similar and, in fact, are relatively correlated. Figure 5.4 represents the best

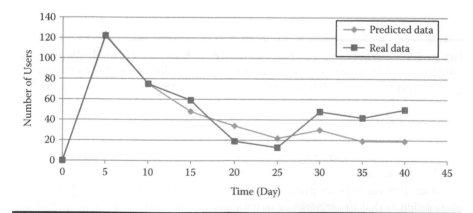

Figure 5.3 Predicted and actual results from topic 1. (From Y. Zhou et al., Predicting the tendency of topic discussion on the online social networks using a dynamic probability model, in *Conference on Hypertext and Hypermedia*, 2008, pp. 7–11.)

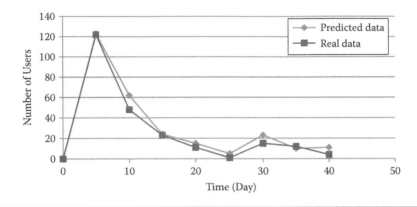

Figure 5.4 Predicted and actual results from topic 2. (From Y. Zhou et al., Predicting the tendency of topic discussion on the online social networks using a dynamic probability model, in *Conference on Hypertext and Hypermedia*, 2008, pp. 7–11.)

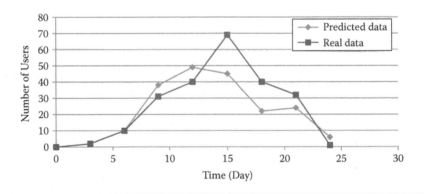

Figure 5.5 Predicted and actual results from topic 3. (From Y. Zhou et al., Predicting the tendency of topic discussion on the online social networks using a dynamic probability model, in *Conference on Hypertext and Hypermedia*, 2008, pp. 7–11.)

possible match between predicted and actual results, while Figures 5.3 and 5.5 show similar matches for most times, except for small periods of time where the number of users diverges.

Since Figures 5.3–5.5 prove the validity of the probability model, the final observation is that the experience parameters notably influence the output of the function. These three experience parameters are s, s', and λ. For parameter s, a larger value will cause the predicting result to properly coincide with the mean value of the real data [1]. The proper value of s can be set according to the individual aim of the model's application. Parameter s' determines the time constraints that the user's behavior will associate with the group's behavior. Values of 3, 4, and 5 are appropriate but, typically, value 3 is used due to its appeal at reducing algorithm complexity. The final experience parameter, λ, correlates the decay rate of the user's interest with the elapsed time. This value can be changed between 0.3, 0.6, and 0.9, with 0.3 projecting the curve above the real data, 0.6 coinciding with the real data, and 0.9 projecting the curve under the real data. This is useful in finding the lower and upper bounds of the equation data.

In conclusion, probability models are very useful in the modeling of social networks. Using probability, predictions can be made accurately, and entire network structures can be defined simply by one or two equations. Since there is a need for predictability in network modeling, probabilistic models are highly advantageous to the development of an experimental social network model design.

5.3 Dynamic Social Networks [3]

Social networks are highly different from other types of networks in that they are extremely dynamic. A social network structure is constantly changing and updating due to the human and social element involved. Most analyses of social networks have involved static computations, but adapting mathematical and computational frameworks that involve dynamic aspects are becoming more popular.

In the standard static network models, time is essentially discarded. This static nature can introduce inaccuracies and inexact data regarding data patterns [2]. This is because many patterns of dynamic data can be used to form the same static results, which is inconclusive and incorrect. Static models also prevent information about cause and effect and consequences from being recorded and analyzed.

The main concept defined to represent a dynamic network model is a meta-group. An individual user is a member of a given meta-group if the number of groups to which that user belongs is at least an *a priori* chosen membership threshold function. The following two rules must be adhered to:

■ No two groups in the meta-group can be in the same partition, and the groups are ordered by partition time steps.
■ The consecutive groups in the meta-group are similar due to a certain function and parameters.

Three values, α (persistence), β (turnover), and γ (membership), give the meaning of a group. The framework is independent of the definitions and capable of providing significant information and data. Using a weighted multipartite directed acyclic graph, the conceptual representation is made. The graph is acyclic since all edges move forward to another point in time and never backward or sideways. The graph is called a meta-group β-graph.

Metagroup statistics can be calculated quickly and efficiently using standard dynamic programming algorithms. Three example algorithms, total number of meta-groups, average meta-group length, and maximal meta-group length, are as follows [3].

■ $P(g,l) = \begin{cases} 1 & \text{if } g \text{ is minimal and } l = 0 \\ 0 & \text{if } g \text{ is minimal and } l > 0 \\ \sum_{(h,g) \in E} P(h, l-1) & \text{otherwise} \end{cases}$

■ Total number of meta-groups: $N(MG) = \sum_{\substack{maximal \ g \\ l \geq \alpha}} P(g,l)$

■ Average meta-group length: $AL(MG) = \dfrac{\sum_{\substack{maximal \ g \\ l \geq \alpha}} P(g,l) *}{N(MG)}$

■ Maximal meta-group length: $MaxL(MG) = \max_{\substack{maximal \ g \\ l \geq \alpha, P(g,l) > 0}} \{l\}$

Most of the algorithms would involve simple loops and minimal computations. Other meta-group characteristics that can be calculated are the most persistent meta-group, the most stable meta-group, and the largest meta-group. To find the most persistent meta-group, one must simply find a meta-group that maximizes the number of groups associated with it. This is equivalent to finding the longest path of DAG. To find the most stable (least turnover) meta-group, one must find the meta-group with maximum sum of edge weights divided by the length of the path. Once again, this is equivalent to a path found using dynamic programming on a DAG. Finally, to find the largest meta-group, one must find the meta-group that maximizes the number of members of the meta-group.

Combining aspects from dynamic modeling and probabilistic models, a more accurate model can be described. The main factors of this model are individual interest, group behavior, and time lapse. Using these factors, a dynamic probability model can be used to predict the user's behavior. It is important to realize the major distinctions involving dynamic modeling theories that allow the model to predict the future accurately.

The main idea is the concept of using time as a factor in the model. A static model will represent a single point in time, which obviously leads to smaller equations and less complexity in general. However, dynamic models provide a new aspect to look at internally. Using discrete time steps, new features can be added to the equations, allowing us to observe patterns in change. This observation of patterns is important in the creation of a probabilistic model. Probability itself can be implemented statically, but to use probability in this particular case, time must be used as a factor.

The concept of dynamic network modeling can also be seen in large-scale networks. In Reference 4, using a simulation-based approach to understand large-scale social networks is discussed. Important to this simulation approach are the formal mathematical and computational theories combined with the novel methods of designing and analyzing large dynamic networks.

In this model design, the problem of detecting breaks in the network is given. A simple static analysis of this network would not provide the adequate results one would desire. However, through dynamic modeling, an optimal design of an ad hoc network could be produced. To effectively model an ad hoc network, dynamic analysis would need to be used in order to understand the reaction of the nodes of the network.

Finally, dynamic modeling can be used to determine groups. Group membership is important in the modeling of social networks, and it is not hard to see that groups will likely change to dynamical, and not remain static. This concept of dynamical groups can be best explained using a dynamic group layout view. A group layout view focuses more on the shared patterns of group membership instead of specific actors involved in the groups. As opposed to a fixed-entity layout view, the dynamic group layout view uses shared regions and time windows. This time window is important to the concept of dynamic group modeling. As time changes, both the region a group belongs to and the group membership changes. This feature alone is what causes this model to correctly represent a dynamic environment.

Dynamic modeling is important in obtaining an accurate representation of a network, whether it be social or infrastructure. The equations and concepts involved with a dynamic-modeled network are considerably more complicated, and the computation time is much greater. However, to correctly assess a social network, dynamic modeling is the most reliable method. In addition, dynamic modeling is important to the development of probabilistic models, which are also very important to the accurate definition of a social network. Combining these two types of models can provide a robust description of a network, which can be used in simulations to correctly predict future events.

5.4 Small-World Models [5]

Another type of social network model is the small-world model. This type of model is based on the principle that we are all linked by a short chain of acquaintances. The common theory is that any two people in the United States are connected by at most six degrees of separation. Since the birth of experimental study in this area in the 1960s, several network models have been proposed to study the phenomena analytically.

While these models have been useful in the development of the field, they have all fallen short of explaining how individuals using local information are very good at building short paths between two points in a social network. Kleinberg [5], has formulated a new model that accounts for this issue. He defines an infinite family of network models and shows that, for one of these models, there is a decentralized algorithm capable of finding short paths with high probability.

Some of the compelling experiments done on the small-world phenomenon were those conducted by Stanley Milgram and his coworkers in the 1960s. The objective was to find links between any two people in the United States that did not know each other. In the experiment, a source person would be given a letter to send to a target person, with only their name and address being given. The source would then be instructed to give the letter to someone they knew on a first-name basis in order to transmit the letter. This next person would be given the same instructions. This would continue until the letter was received by the target. The results of the experiment showed that the average number of people between each source and target was between five and six, and hence the "six degrees of separation."

Models of this phenomenon have focused on the question of why there exists this chain of acquaintances between two random strangers. An early theory was that uniformly random social networks have a low diameter. This means that two people grouped together in a random network with symmetric acquaintanceship would be linked by a short chain with high probability. However, the low diameter in Milgram's experiments would not be achieved if the network was too clustered.

The results of Milgram's experiments really had two amazing features. The first was that these links between two people actually exist, and the second was that people could actually find these connections while knowing so little about their target person. While other models focused on the first of these, Kleinberg's paper chooses to study the question of how people are able to find these links.

While it is easy to picture networks in which short chains exist, no mechanism based solely on local information can find them. The fact that it is possible for people to find them suggests that there are latent navigational hints embedded in the network by which messages can be guided quickly from source to target. Kleinberg's work studies decentralized algorithms in which individuals attempt to transmit a message along a short path knowing only the locations of their acquaintances.

To design this model, Kleinberg chooses a two-dimensional grid with directed edges (Figure 5.6). The nodes of the grid represent individuals. The local contacts of each node are the nodes that are within a lattice distance p. Long-range contacts are represented by directed edges from u to q, and other nodes are constructed using the universal constants $q \geq 0$ and $r \geq 0$. The i-th directed edge from u has endpoint v with probability to $[d(u,v)]^{-r}$.

This model is easy to visualize: the nodes represent people on a grid who know their neighbors for a number of steps in all directions and have a few long-distance acquaintances. If p and q are constants, then different families of network models can be obtained by varying r. Increasing r increases the clustering of a node's long-range contacts near its vicinity. In this way, r is a basic parameter representing how widely networked the underlying society of nodes is.

Selecting two arbitrary nodes in the network, s and t, we try to transmit a message from s to t in as few steps as possible. As in the Milgram study, the message is passed from the current holder to one of its local or long-range contacts using only

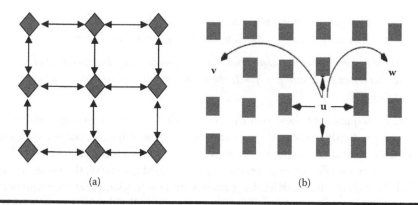

(a)   (b)

Figure 5.6 **(A) A two-dimensional grid network with n = 6, p = 1, and q = 0. (B) The contacts of a node u with p = 1 and q = 2. v and w are the two long-range contacts. (From J. Kleinberg, The small-world phenomenon: An algorithm perspective,** *Annual ACM Symposium on Theory of Computing,* **2000, pp. 163–170.)**

local information. Mechanisms guiding this are what institute decentralized algorithms. The local information available to each holder, u, is as follows [5]:

1. Neighboring contacts among all nodes (i.e., the grid structure)
2. The location of the target t
3. The locations of long-distance contacts of all nodes

With this, u must pass the message on to one of its contacts, v, without knowing which of its long-range contacts have not touched the message. It is of interest to find the number of steps taken by the algorithm to deliver the message over a network generated according to an inverse r-th-power distribution, from a source to a target chosen uniformly at random from the set of nodes. This number is called the expected delivery time. If u had any global knowledge of the nodes in the network, the shortest path could be found with a simple search.

Kleinberg then moves on to study how the ability of a decentralized algorithm to construct a short path is affected by the structure of the network. Noting that $r = 0$ results in the uniform distribution over long-range contacts, Kleinberg states his first theorem regarding the notion that there is no way for a decentralized algorithm to find short chains in the network. His *Theorem 1* states [5]:

There is a constant α_0, depending on p and q but independent of n, so that when r = 0, the expected delivery time of any decentralized algorithm is at least $\alpha_0 n^{2/3}$. (Hence exponential in the expected minimum path length.)

As r increases, the long-range contacts will be closer to u and can be used more frequently since they have a higher chance of being able to move the message in a certain direction. On the other hand, they will not be as useful in moving the message over longer distances. Kleinberg states that the value of r that best balances this trade-off algorithmically is $r = 2$, which brings us to his *Theorem 2* [5]:

> *There is a decentralized algorithm A and a constant α_2, independent of n, so that when $r = 2$ and $p = q = 1$, the expected delivery time of A is at most $\alpha_2 (\log n)^2$.*

The consequence of these two theorems is that, when long-range contacts are made independently of the grid geometry, short chains will exist, but the nodes will not be able to find them using only local information. However, when the long-range contacts are affected in a certain way by the grid geometry, the nodes are able to find these short chains. Kleinberg notes this as a fundamental consequence of his model. The representations of inverse r-th power distributions can be seen in Figures 5.7, 5.8, and 5.9.

In order to achieve the bound of Theorem 2, a decentralized algorithm must follow a simple rule: in each step, the current message holder u chooses a contact that is as close to the target t as possible, in the sense of lattice distance. One can see how this rule benefits from having long-range contacts in relatively close vicinity. With this rule, u does not even need to know anything about the previous message holders.

A strong characterization theorem can be shown for this family of models: $r = 2$ is the only value for which there is a decentralized algorithm capable of producing

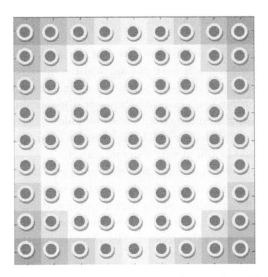

Figure 5.7 **The inverse r-th power distribution with r = 1 and n = 9. (From J. Kleinberg, The small-world phenomenon: An algorithm perspective, *Annual ACM Symposium on Theory of Computing*, 2000, pp. 163–170.)**

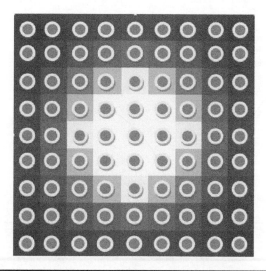

Figure 5.8 The inverse r-th power distribution with r = 2 and n = 9. (From J. Kleinberg, The small-world phenomenon: An algorithm perspective, *Annual ACM Symposium on Theory of Computing*, 2000, pp. 163–170.)

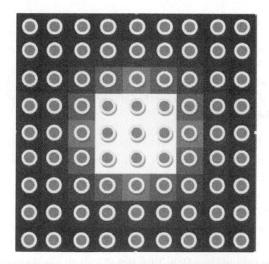

Figure 5.9 The inverse r-th power distribution with r = 3 and n = 9. (From J. Kleinberg, The small-world phenomenon: An algorithm perspective, *Annual ACM Symposium on Theory of Computing*, 2000, pp. 163–170.)

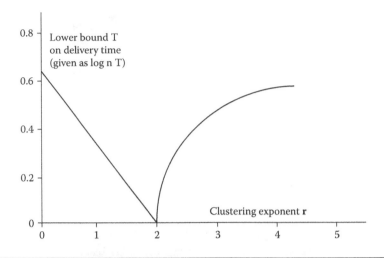

Figure 5.10 The lower bound implied by Theorem 3. The X-axis is the value of r; the Y-axis is the resulting exponent on n. (From J. Kleinberg, The small-world phenomenon: An algorithm perspective, *Annual ACM Symposium on Theory of Computing,* **2000, pp. 163–170.)**

chains whose length is a polynomial in log n. This leads to Kleinberg's *Theorem 3* [5] (see Figure 10):

> *a. Let $0 \leq r < 2$. There is a constant α_r, depending on p, q, r but independent of n, so that the expected delivery time of any decentralized algorithm is at least $\alpha_r n^{(2-r)/3}$.*
>
> *b. Let $r > 2$. There is a constant α_r, depending on p, q, r but independent of n, so that the expected delivery time of any decentralized algorithm is at least $\alpha_r n^{(r-2)/(r-1)}$.*

These results can be extended beyond two dimensions to an arbitrary k dimensions with constant k as well as other graphs with similar scaling properties. In the k-dimensional case, a decentralized algorithm can construct paths of length polynomial in log n if and only if $r = k$. The proof of these theorems uncovers a general structural property that brings to light the optimality of the $r = 2$ case for two-dimensional grids: it is the single exponent at which a node's long-range contacts are close to being uniformly distributed over all "distance scales." The rest of the paper [5] goes into detail explaining the proofs of these theorems. The proofs are not covered in [5] since we are focusing on the overall explanation of the algorithm along with the results and how they contribute to social networking models as a whole.

In conclusion, Kleinberg reiterates how these results are quite different from the results of previous studies, while sharing the general goal of identifying the qualitative characteristics of networks that make routing with local data governable, and providing a model for reasoning about effective routing schemes in those networks. He believes that a more general conclusion can be drawn about the small-world network, which is that "correlation between local structure and long-range connections provides fundamental cues for finding paths through the network." When this correlation is near a certain threshold, a gradient is formed along the long-range connections that helps individuals send the message quickly toward the target. As the correlation drops below the threshold, these hidden clues begin to die away until the long-range contacts become uniformly distributed and the individuals become disoriented. The short paths still exist, but the individuals are not able to find them.

5.5 Large-Scale Models [4, 6]

A different type of social networking model focuses on large-scale networks. These large networks can be found in transportation systems, electric power grids, public health, and even the Internet. A rising common name for these networks are "sociotechnical systems," where one or more social networks interact with one or more physical networks. In Barret et al. [4], the authors discuss the simulation and modeling approaches of the Basic and Applied Simulation Science group at Los Alamos National Laboratory.

The extremely detailed simulations that they have developed (see Figure 5.11) allow individual agents to interact among themselves as well as the network environment and infrastructure. They also state that their results show that simulation-based methods are both necessary and sufficient for understanding the dynamics of such complex systems. These systems must be studied with the knowledge that, unlike physical systems, sociotechnical systems are affected not only by physical laws but also by human behavior, regulatory agencies, and government and private enterprise (Figure 5.11).

An example of why it is important to be able to model these systems is the recent failure of the electric power grid in northeastern United States. This failure affected Internet traffic, closed down financial institutions, and threw transportation systems out of control. A simulation model can show how all of these systems are related in a network. The simulation proposed by the authors covers transportation, urban population mobility, public health, telecommunication, and commodity markets.

These simulations are based on a formal mathematical and computational theory of sociotechnical simulations, along with unique methods for the design and analysis of large dynamic networks, and efficient data compression and regeneration techniques. The networks studied are extremely large, consisting of millions of agents and paths. These simulations are able to represent the interactions of these agents in great detail.

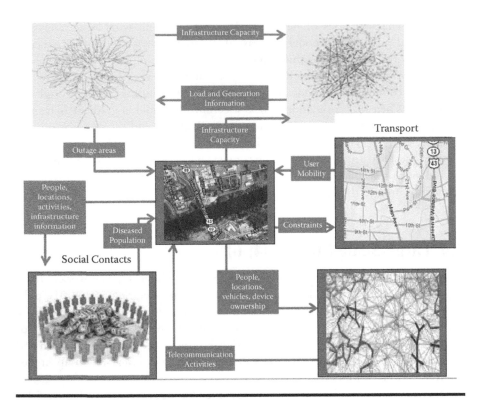

Figure 5.11 Architecture and components of the interdependent suite of infrastructure simulations developed at Los Alamos National Laboratory. The social-contacts network at the lower left is a fragment of the complete network and is obtained by looking at a single node (center) and tracing their contacts up to distance 3, which involves considering all nodes in the graph within distance 3. The wireless ad hoc network at the lower right is obtained by placing radio transceivers along city streets. The bilateral-contracts network at the upper right shows contacts between supplier and consumer pairs in the city. (From C. Barrett et al., Understanding large-scale social and infrastructure networks: A simulation-based approach, *SIAM News*, Vol. 37, No. 4, pp. 1–4, May 2004.)

Usually, boorish-grained static structural analysis of sociotechnical networks is combined with more complicated simulation-based dynamic analysis. The authors believe that, together, these analyses provide useful insights for scientists, planning personnel, and policy makers who need to incorporate specific operational goals into their systems. The static structural analysis of sociotechnical networks shows both interesting similarities and differences that arise from the way these networks form and the functions they present.

To gain a clearer perception of the differences between these networks and the applicability of different random graph models to such networks, one must closely examine their properties. Table 5.1 presents a summary of some prominent

Table 5.1 Qualitative Comparison of Structural Parameters for Some Real Social and Infrastructure Networks and Random Networks

Network	Average degree	Average clustering coefficient	Diameter	Robustness
Paper network	Very low	Very low	Medium	Easy to shatter
Wireless ad hoc network	Medium	High	Medium	Hard to shatter
Social network	High	High	Low	Very hard to shatter
Erdös–Rényi random network	Variable	Variable	Low	Hard to shatter
Random geometric graph	Medium	High	Large	Hard to shatter

Note: The Erdös–Rényi random graph is obtained by placing each edge between a pair of vertices independently with a given probability. The random geometric graph is obtained by placing points in a unit square uniformly at random and adding edges between points that are within a chosen threshold value of distance [4].

properties. In the table, the degree of a node is the number of neighbors connected directly to it. The "clustering coefficient" of node i is given as $c_i = 2n_i/[k_i\,(k_i - 1)]$, where n_i is the number of edges between the neighbors of i, and k_i is the degree of i. The "diameter" of the network is the maximum, over all pairs of nodes u and v, of the shortest-path distance between u and v. Some observations that follow from the results are

■ Social and infrastructure networks are not necessarily scale-free or small-world networks.
■ Structural measures for real infrastructure and social networks are often different from similar measures for classic random networks.
■ Social networks are characterized by high levels of local clustering. In contrast, many physical networks, such as power and transport networks, have very low clustering coefficients.

An informal definition of robustness is whether or not the deletion of a few edges or nodes breaks the network up into smaller components. The work of Barret et al. [4] shows that robustness and reliability generally differ for social and infrastructure networks. They found the most robust class of networks to be social networks, followed by mobile ad hoc networks. The least robust are transportation and electric power networks. A graph showing how different networks shatter

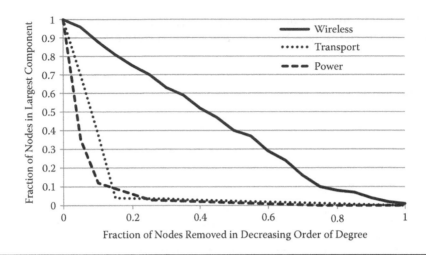

Figure 5.12 **Size of the largest component in a network as a function of the fraction of nodes deleted. Nodes were deleted in decreasing order of residual degree. The panel depicts transportation, power, and wireless radio networks. (From C. Barrett et al., Understanding large-scale social and infrastructure networks: A simulation-based approach,** *SIAM News,* **Vol. 37, No. 4, pp. 1–4, May 2004.)**

at different levels can be seen in Figure 5.12. As you can see, these graphs support the theory that social networks are more robust against node deletions than infrastructural networks. One explanation for this could be due to the underlying social contacts such as those found in the small-world social-network models. The authors suggest that it is due to the similarity between social networks and "expander graphs." This is in contrast to the similarity between ad hoc networks and random geometric graphs.

Expander graphs are graphs with high vertex expansion. In other words, any two vertices on the graph are connected by a number of disjoint paths. Infrastructural graphs such as power and transportation have low expansion, which in turn makes attacks on high degree nodes more effective than random attacks. This robustness of social networks can have some dangerous effects such as making it difficult to contain an infectious disease or even a harmful rumor.

In Bergman et al. [6], the authors focus on a different method for modeling large-scale social networks, namely, transitions. An example transition model would be the transition of horse-drawn carriages to cars, or sailing ships to steamships. Studying these historical transition models can help predict how current models are transitioning and how they can be adapted for future models. The model in Bergman et al. [6] combines agent-based modeling techniques and system dynamics, and includes interactions of individual agents and subsystems, as well as cumulative effects on system structures. To get a grasp of a transition model, focus must be on understanding radical, systematic sociotechnical change; in other words, change that goes beyond the ordering of the current system. This kind of change usually happens over decades.

Transition theory highlights the interdependency of institutions and infrastructures constituting societal systems and subsystems [6]. These societal systems are made up of interlocking economic, social, cultural, infrastructural, and regulative subsystems, which are coupled with various social groups. The stability and structure of societal systems is established and reinforced through cognitive, normative, and regulative institutions, which are signified by the concept of a regime. A regime is a particular set of practices, rules, and shared assumptions that govern the system and its actors. It is important to note that these regimes typically focus on optimization of a system rather than innovation. This is due to habits, existing competencies, past investment, regulation, prevailing norms, worldviews, and so on, acting to lock in patterns of behavior, and result in path dependencies for sociotechnical development.

In contrast to these regimes, transitions require system-exceeding innovations that change the entire structure of the network. To account for this, researchers have singled out niches as the center of radical innovations. These niches are simply actors or individual technologies outside or bordering the regimes. The stability of a regime may be compromised due to these niches, or from misalignment of actors within a regime. Once a threat is recognized, regime actors will mobilize resources from within the regime, and in some cases from within niches, to respond to it. A transition occurs either when a regime is transformed, or through regime change. In a transformation, the regime responds to the systemic and landscape changes by changing some of its practices and rules, and possibly replacing some institutions and actors. However, if a regime cannot adjust, it is overthrown and replaced by a regime better suited to the dynamics of the system, and hence the regime change. Interestingly, this model can be applied to radically different systems such as a transportation system or a governmental system.

5.6 Conclusion

Social networks have been used to examine how organizations interact with each other, characterizing the many informal connections that link them together, as well as associations and connections between individuals at different organizations. Social network analysis is important because it has been used to help understand patterns of human contact. It is also important because it may also be an effective tool for mass surveillance. Furthermore, after studying the effectiveness of the probabilistic model, the dynamic social networks, the small world model, and the large-scale model, we can conclude that social network models are great tools of measurement.

The probabilistic model and its different hypotheses have been discussed. We now know that the individual interest factor, the group behavior factor, and the time lapse factor intercorrelate with the dynamic social network because those factors create a dynamic probability model that could be used to predict a user's behavior.

After discussing dynamic social networks and how they relate to the probabilistic model, we have learned that large-scale networks go hand in hand with dynamic networks as well. This is because dynamic social networks measure on a rather large scale. Formal mathematical and computational theories were needed in conjunction with methods of designing from an analytical viewpoint of large dynamic networks.

By systematically understanding small-world models, one could evaluate the simplicity of the short chain between acquaintances. We also derived two positive outcomes from Milgram's experiments. The first was that these links between two people actually exist, and the second that people could actually find the connection while not knowing a lot about their target person.

While studying large-scale models and how they relate to dynamic social networks, we have found that simulation-based methods are both necessary and sufficient for understanding the dynamics of complex systems. From this model we have successfully studied transition theory and how it helps the large-scale model to be applied to different systems.

References

1. H.-C. Chen, M. Magdon-Ismail, M. Goldberg, W. Wallace, Personalization inferring agent dynamics from social communication networks, in *International Conference on Knowledge Discovery and Data Mining*, 2007, pp. 36–45.
2. Y. Zhou, X. Guan, Z. Zhang, B. Zhang, Predicting the tendency of topic discussion on the online social networks using a dynamic probability model, in *Conference on Hypertext and Hypermedia*, 2008, pp. 7–11.
3. T. Berger-Wolf, J. Saia, A framework for analysis of dynamic social networks, in *International Conference on Knowledge Discovery and Data Mining*, 2006, pp. 523–528.
4. C. Barrett, S. Eubank, V.S. Kumar, M. Marathe, Understanding large-scale social and infrastructure networks: A simulation-based approach, *SIAM News*, Vol. 37, No. 4, pp. 1–4, May 2004.
5. J. Kleinberg, The small-world phenomenon: An algorithm perspective, *Annual ACM Symposium on Theory of Computing*, 2000, pp. 163–170.
6. N. Bergman, A. Haxeltine, L. Whitmarsh, J. Köhler, M. Schilperoord, J. Rotmans, Modeling sociotechnical transition patterns and pathways, *Journal of Artificial Societies and Social Simulation*, Vol. 11, No. 37, pp. 1–32, June 2008.

Chapter 6

Understanding Interactions among BitTorrent Peers

Haiyang Wang, Li Ma, Cameron
Dale, and Jiangchuan Liu

Contents

Peer-to-peer content delivery has become one of the most popular Internet applications in recent years. Unlike conventional client/server systems, contents in a peer-to-peer system are not only downloaded and consumed by users, but also generated and relayed by them; therefore, interactions among the users play an important role toward achieving efficient sharing in such systems. In this chapter, we present a systematic measurement study to understand the peer interactions in BitTorrent, which is one of the most successful file sharing systems to date. Our measurement consists of a series of experiments, covering microscope piece-level interactions, to intra-torrent network topologies, and also inter-torrent localities. Our investigation provides abundant evidence that explains the success of BitTorrent, but also reveals significant limitations in its current design, thus opening possible avenues toward enhancing its performance.

6.1 An Overview of BitTorrent

Among all the peer-to-peer Internet applications available, BitTorrent [17] has become the most popular for the sharing of large files. Recent reports have indicated that half of all the current Internet traffic is due to BitTorrent [1]. This popularity can be greatly attributed to the efficiency with which BitTorrent can distribute these large files.

This efficiency is partly obtained by breaking up each large file into hundreds or thousands of segments, or *pieces*, which, once downloaded by a peer, can be shared with others while the downloading continues. The sharing of pieces of the download has been shown to be very efficient [28], allowing downloads to scale well with the size of the downloading population. Another aspect of BitTorrent's efficiency comes from its resilience to peer departures, peer failures, and misbehaving peers. Many of these properties have been confirmed through both theoretical and experimental studies; however, one aspect yet to be fully explored is the topology of the network of peers formed during a download.

We start with an overview of BitTorrent and the terminology used to describe it in Section 1.1.1. BitTorrent is well described in the literature, so more details can be found in any of the references from Section 1.2. We then discuss specific areas of BitTorrent that are relevant to our work, including the networks of peers formed by BitTorrent in Section 1.1.4.

6.1.1 Basic Operations of BitTorrent

As mentioned previously, BitTorrent breaks up each large file into hundreds or thousands of segments, or *pieces*, which, once downloaded by a peer, can be shared with others while the downloading continues. The *torrent* is the set of all peers currently downloading and uploading pieces to and from each other. It is made up of two types of peers: those who have the complete file (*uploaders* or *seeders*) and those who are still downloading it (*downloaders* or *leechers*). The influx or departure of peers from a torrent is called *churn*.

The BitTorrent system coordinates file sharing through the use of a centralized *tracker*. Upon receiving a request from a downloading peer's client, the tracker will provide a random list of peers for the client to contact. The client will then contact each of the peers and gather information about which pieces the peers have available for download. These *connected* peers are the immediate neighbors of the client, and all the information client has of the system comes from knowledge of its neighbors. There is a user-configurable limit on the maximum number of neighbors a client can have, which defaults to a value of 80 in most clients. There is also a limit on the number of connections a peer can initiate, after which it will only receive new connections from other peers, which defaults to a value of 40 in most clients.

Throughout the lifetime of a torrent, three stages are evident. The first is a *startup stage* occurring at the very beginning of the torrent, at which time only the initial seed has all the pieces of the file. Once a single copy of all pieces is uploaded to the torrent, the startup stage comes to an end and a *transient stage* begins. The transient stage is usually characterized by the rapid influx of downloaders to the torrent, which leads to a system with proportionally many more leechers than seeders. Once this influx slows, the torrent will move towards a *steady stage*, characterized by an unchanging number of seeders and leechers, so that the arrival rate of leechers must be the same as (or near to) the rate of change of leechers to seeders and the departure rate of seeds from the system. The amount of time spent in the startup stage is determined solely by the upload rate of the initial seed and the size of the file, while the time spent in the transient stage is determined by the popularity of the torrent.

6.1.2 The Rarest-First Policy

There are many policies at work in a BitTorrent client that govern how it downloads pieces. One of the most important is the *rarest-first* policy, which is responsible for choosing pieces to download with the goal of ensuring that copies of pieces are uniformly distributed throughout the system. The client constantly updates a list of the pieces each of its connected peers (neighbors) has available. Using this information, the client can determine which set of pieces it believes to be the rarest in the torrent.

These rarest pieces will be selected first to download from the connected peers. Due to the limitations of the local knowledge each peer has, the pieces chosen to download may not be the rarest in the entire torrent.

A simple alternative to the rarest-first policy is to use a random piece selection policy for downloading. This policy was used by the original BitTorrent client when it was first released, but due to the superiority of the rarest-first policy it is not in use by any clients today.

6.1.3 The Incentive Mechanism

There are many policies at work in a BitTorrent client that govern how peers connect to other peers. One of the most important is the incentive mechanism, or *tit-for-tat* policy. It is responsible for choosing peers to upload to, with the goal of ensuring that peers who upload (contribute) to the system are more likely to be able to download. This game-theoretic method of encouraging sharing and fairness is built into the system to discourage free-riding peers from not uploading.

Each client notifies other peers that have pieces the client needs of the client's *interest* in downloading from the peer. A downloading client also monitors the download rates it receives from its neighboring peers. The client then allows uploads to the peers that are interested in downloading, and that it is receiving the highest download rates from. This is referred to as *unchoking* the peer. There are a limited number of unchoke slots available, so a downloading peer's neighbors will compete for its unchoke slots by uploading to it. In addition, in order to explore the connected peers and find better peers to upload to, the client will periodically choose one peer at random to unchoke, which is known as *optimistic unchoking*.

Each peer will have to make these decisions based only on the limited local knowledge it has of the system, specifically the peers it is connected to and their current uploading rates to it. A poor policy for making this decision could lead to networks that are inefficient in distributing pieces throughout the system, or are easily susceptible to disconnection due to departing or failing peers. Either of these problems would lead to a system which makes inefficient use of the uploading bandwidth available to replicate the file.

6.1.4 Networks in the Torrents

Given the complex relations among peers, BitTorrent actually maintains four networks within a torrent. Previous studies have focused on only one or two of the following networks, but we will investigate the properties and evolution of all four networks.

Connection Network. This is the network of neighbors that each peer maintains. These neighbors are chosen randomly by the tracker from the list of peers in the torrent. Each peer creates connections to the peers returned by the tracker (up to its limit on initiating connections) and also makes return connections to other peers that connect to it (up to its maximum neighbor limit). All neighbor connections are bi-directional, so the Connection network is undirected.

Interest Network. This network represents the interest that peers have in other peers. Each peer maintains a list of the pieces stored by its neighboring peers. A peer is interested in any neighboring peer that has a piece it does not have, and so this network is a subset of the Connection network. Since interest can be uni-directional, the Interest network is directed.

Unchoked Network. This network is formed by the incentive mechanism present in BitTorrent. Each uploading peer assigns its limited number of unchoke slots to certain neighboring peers in an effort to maximize the downloads that it receives from them. Only peers that are interested in receiving an upload are unchoked, so this network's transpose is a subset of the Interest network. Since unchoking can be uni-directional, the Unchoked network is directed.

Download Network. This network is formed by the peers that are downloading from other peers. Since a peer has to be unchoked before it can download, this network is a subset of the Unchoked network's transpose. Since downloading can be uni-directional, the Download network is directed.

We emphasize that the Connection and Unchoked networks are the most important of these four networks. The Connection network forms the neighbor set for all of the peers in the system, and is a superset of the other three networks. The Unchoked network is necessary for the uploading and downloading of data from other peers, and so it is very important for the scalability and efficiency of BitTorrent.

6.2 Data Exchange among Peers: The Piece-Level Examination

We start our examination from the microscope piece selection, which decides the order of pieces to download and plays an important role in achieving high-efficient downloading. Each peer will have to make this decision based only on the local knowledge it has of the system. An inadequate policy could lead to some pieces becoming poorly replicated, and therefore almost unavailable, while others are overly replicated, leading to starvation in areas of the system where new pieces are needed. To understand how the policy for choosing pieces in BitTorrent affects the system, it is necessary to examine the system-wide population of pieces available. This microscopic information would help to understand the dynamics and evolution of the torrent, and especially the effectiveness of the policy used by BitTorrent to ensure an even distribution of pieces.

We present a systematic measurement study on the distribution and evolution of the piece population in BitTorrent. Our measurement is based on real BitTorrent data gathered from both regular Internet and controlled PlanetLab torrents. The data is collected by multiple administered clients distributed in different parts of the network, which collectively offer a global view of the piece distribution.

We examine snapshots of the population of pieces in torrents, and the evolution of the piece population over several days, mostly during the early phases of a torrent's lifetime. We find that the piece distributions are generally very narrow, and progress to more narrow distributions quickly in response to changing conditions. This shows that the downloading policy of BitTorrent is effective from a piece distribution and evolution perspective, though we do find that some enhancements are possible to achieve an ideal piece distribution, especially for larger torrent.

Very little previous work has explored microscopic piece-level measurements of BitTorrent. Niu and Li [27] attempted a theoretical evaluation of the *block variation* resulting from using network coding in a peer-to-peer system. Though focused on network coding, their results should be applicable by setting the size of network coding segments to 1, but they are only theoretical and do not match with our experimental results.

The closest work to ours is from Legout et al. [23], who administrated a single client and connected separately to 26 torrents of differing characteristics. Their results thus reflect the piece availability only in peers their single client connected to during the experiment, which may not be representative of the entire torrent, nor does it offer global knowledge of the piece population. In contrast, our work focuses on the global piece population by examining the number of copies of each piece present in *every* peer in the torrent. We also follow the piece population over time, to see how it evolves with the torrent. Some of this work has been previously published [15].

6.2.1 Distribution of Piece Population

We now present and analyze our measurement results for the piece populations of the torrents shown in Table 6.1. The results of some snapshots we took of the piece population in some real Internet torrents are shown in section "Snapshots." The evolution of two real Internet torrents over long periods of time is shown in the section "Evolution." Finally, we ran several simulated torrents on PlanetLab, the results of which are in section "Simulated PlanetLab Torrents."

In order to make visual comparisons between different torrents, some normalization of the data is needed. For all data, we normalize the number of copies (x-axis) by the total number of downloaders, so that it varies from 0 to 1. If the populations are all from the same torrent, the population size data (y-axis) will be normalized by the number of pieces, so it will also vary from 0 to 1. However, this normalization does not make sense when comparing different torrents' populations, as it leads to a much smaller population when the number of pieces is larger. Therefore, to facilitate the comparison of multiple torrents, they will be normalized so that the area under their population distribution is 1. Since we are only interested in the width of these distributions, this normalization should have no effect.

Table 6.1   The Torrents Used for the Piece Population Experiments.

Torrent Name	Pieces	Size (MB)	Leechers	Clients[a]
KNOPPIX[b]	4125	4325	169	10
FreeBSD[b]	5699	1494	34	10
mandriva[b]	2803	735	89	9
openSUSE[b]	14805	3881	398	9
feisty[c]	1387	727	65-120	20
openSUSE-2[c]	14977	3926	100-150	18
PlanetLab-1[c]	1497	784	0-340	340
PlanetLab-2[c]	1497	784	0-390	390

[a] Number of administered clients used to connect to the torrent. All peers are administrated clients in PlanetLab experiment.
[b] Snapshots of population taken.
[c] Evolution of population monitored.

Figure 6.1 shows the snapshots of the piece populations for various real torrents. All four appear to be normally distributed with mean values slightly less than half the downloaders, indicating that they are in the transient stage. The least normally distributed populations are Knoppix and openSUSE, which correspond to their being the largest torrents. This larger torrent size results in peers having a limited local view of which pieces are rarest, which leads to a distortion of the normal curve towards some pieces having extra copies (the tails evident in Figure 6.1). The other two populations are small enough that a peer's local view is nearly complete, resulting in a near perfect normal distribution.

Table 6.2 confirms our visual analysis of the width of the distributions. The largest torrent (openSUSE) has a block variation that is an order of magnitude larger than the others. The smallest block variation is for the FreeBSD torrent, which also has the fewest number of peers.

6.2.1.1 Evolution of Piece Population

To further understand the dynamics of piece population in the different stages of the torrent, we have also monitored torrents throughout their lifetime. It is worth noting that such experiments can be difficult to conduct for real Internet torrents because, in general, we do not know the exact start time of a torrent unless it is launched by ourselves. Torrents launched by ourselves, however, are not necessarily representative and the measurement results can be biased. Through constant online

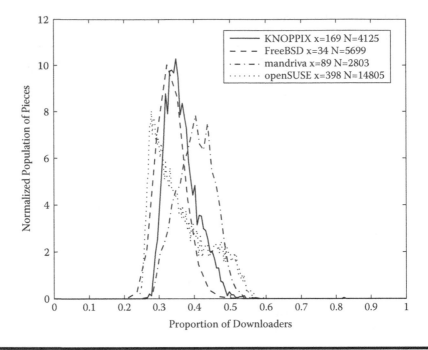

Figure 6.1 The piece population snapshots of four real Internet torrents (x = number of downloaders, N = number of pieces).

Table 6.2   The Block Variation for the Snapshot Measurements of Real Internet Torrents

Torrent Name	Pieces	Leechers	Block Variation
KNOPPIX	4125	169	5.4×10^{-4}
FreeBSD	5699	34	1.0×10^{-4}
mandriva	2803	89	4.4×10^{-4}
openSUSE	14805	398	2.0×10^{-3}

tracking, we did find several torrents that we began monitoring very early, and we now show only one of them.

6.2.1.2 The Feisty Torrents

Figure 6.2 shows the evolution of the feisty torrent over a period of 17 hours. The monitoring began soon after the torrent was launched, and though the number of leechers has already peaked, a peak is clear in the number of seeders near the middle of the experiment. This leads to the conclusion that this torrent was in a

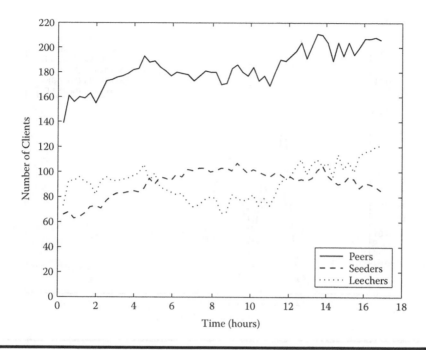

Figure 6.2   The number of peers in the feisty torrents.

transition from the transient stage to the steady stage as the experiment progressed. However, there was a large influx of peers near the 12-hour mark, probably due to a news posting.

Figure 6.3 shows three representative plots of the piece population in the feisty torrent, as well as fitted normal distributions. The piece population is seen to be progressing towards a more normal distribution early in the experiment, although it does increase in width towards the end of the experiment, as noted below by the block variation.

The mean is progressing towards a value of 0.5. This can be clearly seen in Figure 6.4, though somewhat noisy. Figure 6.5 shows the progression of the block variation towards a more narrow distribution, reaching a minimum block variation of 2×10^{-4}. However, the width does increase by an order of magnitude near the end of the experiment after the large influx of peers occurs.

6.2.1.3 Observation from Simulated PlanetLab Torrents

The controlled PlanetLab environment enables us to closely investigate the piece population of a torrent in any period throughout its lifetime, and to introduce interesting factors that it may be hard to find in real Internet torrents. We ran several torrents on PlanetLab to investigate these possibilities. Now we show one

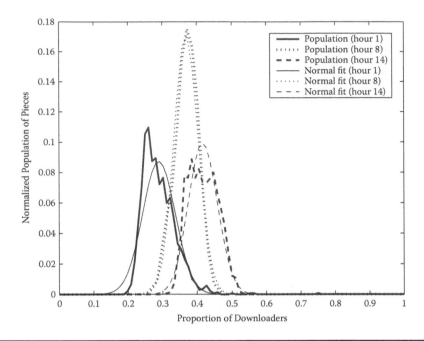

Figure 6.3   Selected piece populations from the feisty torrent.

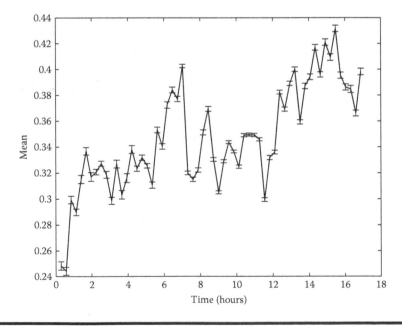

Figure 6.4   The mean of the piece population in the feisty torrent (error bars are 95% confidence intervals).

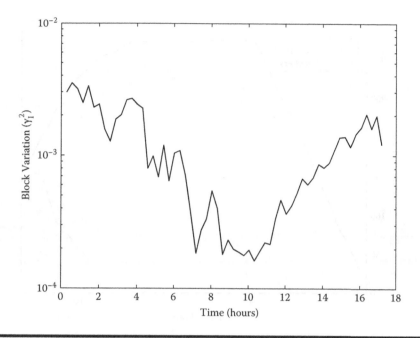

Figure 6.5   The block variation of the piece population in the feisty torrent.

of them, which is a short-lived torrent, for which the results are in section "The PlanetLab-1 Torrent."

6.2.1.4 The PlanetLab-1 Torrent

Figure 6.6 shows the evolution of the PlanetLab-1 torrent over the period of 12 hours that we simulated it. This system is in the startup stage (as seen by the single seed that is available) through most of the experiment, transitioning to the transient stage after approximately 9 hours. The system then moves quickly to an end stage not seen in the other real torrents, as no new clients join the system but many are completing their download, and many are leaving the system.

Figure 6.7 shows three representative plots of the piece population in the PlanetLab-1 torrent, as well as fitted normal distributions. The normal distribution does not match the first two plots at all, as most pieces suffer from a low replication rate, while peaks higher in the population show some pieces have a much higher replication rate. This is due to the limited upload bandwidth of the original seed, and the time it takes for a single copy of the file to be present in the network (approximately 9 hours). However, the third population at 10 hours shows that the torrent takes very little time to become very narrowly distributed after the first full copy of all pieces are present in the network.

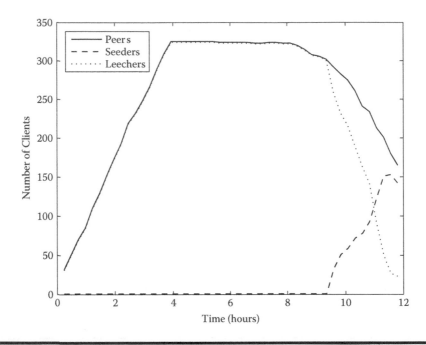

Figure 6.6   The number of peers in the PlanetLab-1 torrent.

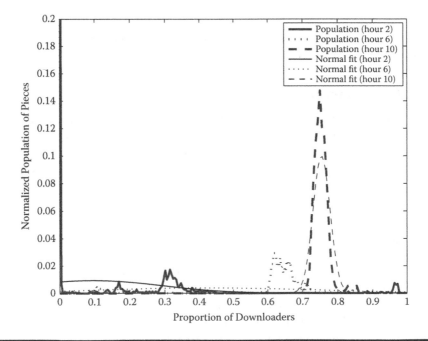

Figure 6.7   Selected piece populations from the PlanetLab-1 torrent.

The mean in this experiment, shown in Figure 6.8, progresses linearly towards a higher value, finishing very close to 1. Figure 6.9 shows the rapid progression of the block variation towards a very narrow distribution of pieces around the mean value once the first copy of the file is present in the network (at 9 hours). The large variation in the piece population in the first 6 hours is expected, as the piece population goes from an initial stage of very narrow (all pieces have no copies), to a split population (some pieces have no copies), and finally to a normal distribution of narrow size soon after all pieces enter the system. The block variation again reaches a value close to 10^{-4} by the end of the experiment.

6.3 Neighbor Selection and Network Topologies: The Intra-Torrent Level Examination

We proceed with the measurement of BitTorrent's neighbor selection algorithms along with the topology of the networks formed. In particular, the resilience to failing and misbehaving nodes suggests that the network may be *scale-free*, and the efficiency of information distribution suggests that the network may be clustered or even *small-world*. Neither of these properties has been quantitatively measured in BitTorrent, and never beyond the early stages of torrents. Since BitTorrent networks

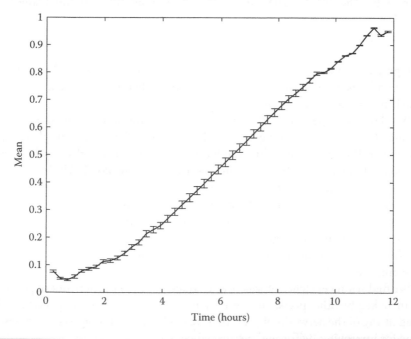

Figure 6.8 The mean of the piece population in the PlanetLab-1 torrent (error bars are 95% confidence intervals).

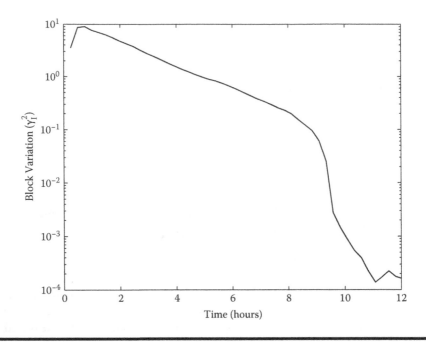

Figure 6.9 The block variation of the piece population in the PlanetLab-1 torrent.

are highly dynamic, a clear understanding of the characteristics and evolution of the networks as peers arrive and depart, and during their entire lifespans, is critical to their performance optimization.

We describe experiments that closely examine the underlying topologies of torrents. These experiments capture the intricacies of forming multiple complex networks in BitTorrent, including the formation of four networks in a BitTorrent download: Connection, Interest, Unchoked, and Download. Unlike previous work, which was confined to the startup stage, we look at all four networks' characteristics and dynamics throughout the entire lifespan of torrents. Our results demonstrate that the networks exhibit fundamental differences over time. This suggests that the initial stage of a torrent is not sufficient to predict the overall performance of the system, and in order to fully examine a torrent long-term measurements are needed.

We find strong evidence of scale-free characteristics in the network of peers that are unchoked by other peers. However, we find no clear evidence of persistent clustering in any of the networks of peers that we studied, which suggests an interesting venue for improving BitTorrent's performance.

Recently, several authors have examined the network topologies formed by BitTorrent's neighbor selection algorithm. Urvoy-Keller and Michiardi [29] used a simulated BitTorrent overlay to look at the distance of peers from the initial seed and the matrix of peer connections. Their results were based on a homogeneous collection of peers, and were limited to the startup stage of a torrent. Al-Hamra et al. [4] expanded on those results through simulation with some experimental confirmation. They also examined the diameter of the overlay created, and the robustness of the overlay to the presence of churn and attacks. Legout et al. [22] performed an experimental evaluation with around 40 heterogeneous peers, finding interesting evidence of clustering in the network of peer unchokings.

Our results differ from these earlier results in several ways. We have focused on experimental evaluation, which captures the intricacies of the formation of multiple complex networks in BitTorrent. We use over 400 peers and explore the entire lifespans of the torrents, from the initialization stage to a steady stage. This enables us to quantitatively evaluate both time-invariant characteristics and those that evolve in different stages.

We will first look at the characteristics of the networks formed in our experiment. The connectivity matrix of the peers in the experiment is presented and analyzed in Section 1.3.3. Finally, we will present the differing results of another experiment with increased churn.

6.3.1 *Background of Random Graphs*

A network may be presented by a graph $G = \{P,E\}$, where P is the set of N nodes and E is the set of edges, or links, that each connects two nodes in P.

Random graphs were first defined by Paul Erdős and Alfréd Rényi [16]. A random graph is obtained by starting with a set of n vertices and adding edges between them randomly. Different random graph models produce different probability distributions on graphs. Most commonly studied is the Erdős-Rényi model, denoted $G(n,p)$, in which every possible edge occurs independently with probability p. A closely related model, denoted $G(n,M)$, assigns equal probability to all graphs with exactly M edges. The latter model can be viewed as a snapshot at a particular time (M) of the random graph process $\tilde{G}_n$, which is a stochastic process that starts with n vertices and no edges and at each step adds one new edge chosen uniformly from the set of missing edges.

If instead we start with an infinite set of vertices, and again let every possible edge occur independently with probability p, then we get an object G called an *infinite random graph*. Except in the trivial cases when p is 0 or 1, such a G almost surely has the following property:

Given any n + m elements $a_1, \ldots, an, b_1, \ldots, bm$ Î V, there is a vertex cÎ V that is adjacent to each of $a_1, \ldots, an$ and is not adjacent to any of $b_1, \ldots, bm$.

If the vertex set is countable then there is, up to isomorphism, only a single graph with this property, namely the Rado graph. Thus any countably infinite random graph is almost surely the Rado graph, which for this reason is sometimes called simply the *random graph*.

Another model, which generalizes the Erdős-Rényi graphs, is the random dot-product model. A random dot-product graph associates with each vertex a real vector. The probability of an edge uv between any vertices u and v is some function of the dot product $\mathbf{u} \cdot \mathbf{v}$ of their respective vectors.

The network probability matrix models random graphs through edge probabilities, which represent the probability $p_{i,j}$ that a given edge $e_{i,j}$ exists for a specified time period. This model is extensible to directed and undirected; weighted and unweighted; and static or dynamic graphs. Random regular graphs form a special case, with properties that may differ from random graphs in general [16].

6.3.2 Existence of Scale-Free Networks

The existence of scale-free graphs in many real-world networks was first introduced by Albert and Barabási [7]. They found that in many real networks, such as the network of actor collaboration in Hollywood, the U.S. airline system, or the World Wide Web, the distribution of node degrees follows a power-law. These seemingly randomly-formed networks thus exhibit a complex topology not accounted for in random graph theory. More specifically, independent of the system and the identity of its participants, the probability $P(k)$ that a node in the network is connected to k other nodes decays as a power law, given by

$$P(k) \sim k^{-\gamma} \tag{6.1}$$

in which the power γ is usually found to be between 2 and 3 in various real networks [8]. This results in a large number of nodes having a small node degree and therefore very few neighbors, but a very small number of nodes having a large node degree and therefore becoming *hubs* in the system.

To determine if the node degrees in the network exhibit a power law distribution and to measure its exponent, we will plot the degree of each node against the rank of the node by degree on a log-log scale [6], as shown in Figure 6.10. The slope of a linear fit then yields the power law exponent, and an R^2 goodness of fit value can also be generated to indicate the accuracy of the fit, and therefore verify the presence of a power-law distribution.

The scale-free nature of many real-world networks was found to be a consequence of two mechanisms that were present in the construction of the network. The first is that the network was formed over time, and is continually evolving as new nodes join the network. The second is that nodes have distinguishing characteristics, and new nodes will attach preferentially to existing nodes that have desirable characteristics. Both of these conditions also exist in many peer-to-peer networks [33,32], including BitTorrent. A BitTorrent network is constantly evolving, as new nodes join the system over time, complete their download, remain to upload to others, and then eventually leave the system. Peers in a BitTorrent system will also have desirable characteristics, such as a large uploading bandwidth, or

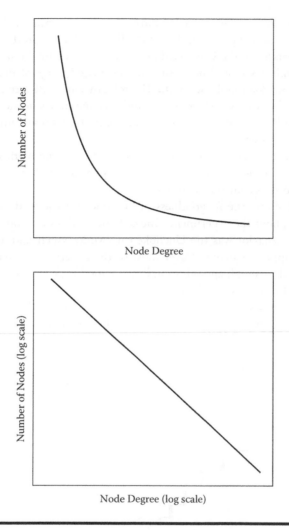

Figure 6.10 A power-law distribution of node degrees.

possession of many or all of the pieces in the system. Nodes in the BitTorrent system can then attach to these nodes and choose them for unchoking or downloading from. However, the presence of scale-free characteristics in torrents has not been previously confirmed.

The desirability of scale-free graph characteristics comes from these networks' tolerance to random node failure [5]. Due to the presence of hubs in the network, a random loss of a large percentage of the network (as much as 80%) will not result in degraded network connectivity. In a peer-to-peer system such as BitTorrent, where random node failures or departures (churn) are quite common, this resilience is necessary to maintain efficient sharing of the file by all nodes in the system. This is especially important for the Unchoked network generated by the incentive mechanism, as node failures should not result in a decreased usage of the system's total uploading or downloading bandwidth. The tolerance of scale-free graphs to node failures has also been shown to extend to misbehaving nodes in the system. This is also desirable in BitTorrent to avoid performance problems that could occur due to free-riders in the system.

As described in Section 1.3.2, we will determine if a network is scale-free by doing a linear fit to the node degree plot on a log-log scale. A sample node degree distribution and fit is shown in Figure 6.11.

Figure 6.12 shows the R^2 goodness of fit values for the in-degree of the four networks throughout the experiment. The only network of the four that exhibited this power law behavior was the Unchoked network, which had an R^2 goodness of fit value of approximately 0.9 over most of the experiment (except during the startup stage). This is high enough to indicate a good fit, while the other networks had goodness of fit values less than 0.7.

Figure 6.13 shows the power law exponent found from the fitting of the in-degree of the nodes in the Unchoked network. The power law exponent can be seen

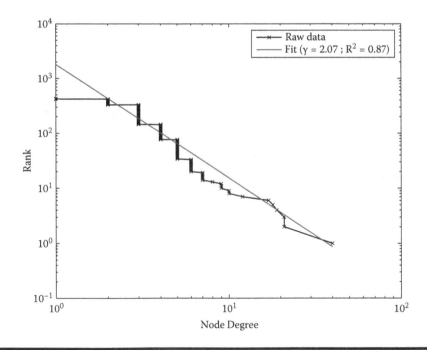

Figure 6.11 The node in-degree distribution for the Unchoked network at hour 19 of the experiments, and the resulting fit to it.

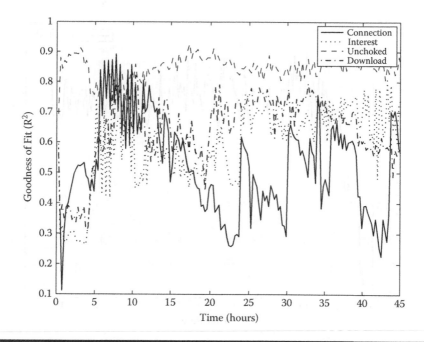

Figure 6.12 The goodness of fit (R^2) parameter measured during the experiments.

to vary quite a lot during the initial stage. However, once all the peers have joined the system the power law exponent quickly reaches its final value, and remains very steady at just over 2 through most of the transient stage and all of the steady stage.

6.3.3 Small-World Networks: Negative Results

The concept of a small-world phenomenon was first introduced by Milgram [25] to refer to the principle that people are linked to all others by short chains of acquaintances (popularly known as *six degrees of separation*). This formulation was used by Watts and Strogatz to describe networks that are neither completely random, nor completely regular, but possess characteristics of both [31,30]. They introduce a measure of one of these characteristics, the cliquishness of a typical neighborhood, as the *clustering coefficient* of the graph. They define a small-world graph as one in which the clustering coefficient is still large, as in regular graphs, but the measure of the average distance between nodes, the *characteristic path length*, is small as in random graphs.

Given a graph $G = (V, E)$, the clustering coefficient Ci of a node i Î V is the proportion of all the possible edges between neighbors of the node that actually exist in the graph. A sample graph showing a single node's neighbors and its clustering coefficient is shown in Figure 6.14. For a node i of degree k_i, the maximum

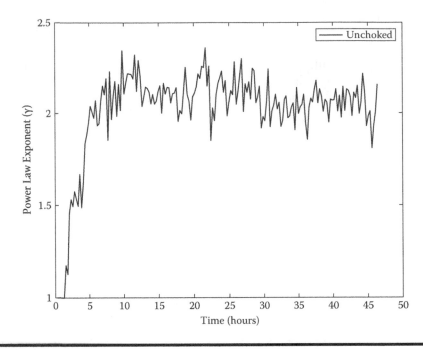

Figure 6.13 The exponent found by fitting a power law to the Unchoked graph's node degree during the experiments.

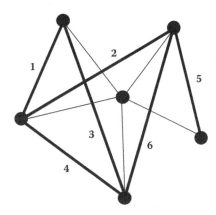

Figure 6.14 The neighborhood of a single node with a clustering coefficient of 0.6. The 6 of the 10 possible edges that exist between neighbors of the node are in bold and numbered.

possible number of undirected edges between neighbors of the node is $k_i(k_i - 1)/2$; for directed edges, this is doubled. This can be visualized as the number of triangles that exist in the graph which include the node as one of the vertices of the triangle. The clustering coefficient of the graph $C(G)$ is then the average of the clustering coefficients of all nodes. Watts and Strogatz show that many real-world networks exhibit small-world behavior [31]. They calculate the clustering coefficient for some networks to be: 1 for cliques, 0.79 for the network of collaborating actors in Hollywood, a maximum of 0.75 for circulant graphs, 0.28 for the neural network of *Caenorhabditis elegans*, and almost 0 for random networks.

Small-world networks are desirable features to have in a communication system, and especially in peer-to-peer file sharing systems, as they are expected to be efficient at delivering messages to all nodes in the system. Latora and Marchiori [21] measured the efficiency of the information exchange in small-world networks. They find that the small-world networks are both globally and locally efficient at exchanging information over the network. This was also examined by Comellas et. al. [14,13], who looked at broadcasting and the spreading of epidemics in small-world communication networks. They find that the networks are very efficient at both broadcasting and the spreading of viruses, both of which are similar to the distribution of a file in a file-sharing system such as BitTorrent.

Many existing peer-to-peer systems (e.g., Gnutella [24], Freenet [18,36], and DHT-based systems [19]) are known to be small-world. It is natural to expect that torrents would exhibit small-world characteristics, particularly since clustering has been previously observed in the early stages of torrents [22].

Figure 6.15 shows the characteristic path lengths of the four networks in our BitTorrent experiment. Note that, for the directed Interest, Unchoked, and Download graphs, the path lengths were calculated on the graphs after they were reduced to their largest strongly connected component to avoid the disconnected nature of BitTorrent graphs. The characteristic path length increases rapidly during the startup stage, though all but the Unchoked network slow their increase even before the startup stage is complete. The Unchoked graph reaches its final value early in the transient stage, after which none of the networks vary much at all.

The characteristic path lengths for the Connection, Interest, and Download networks are short, due mostly to the density of the graph (430 nodes with an average degree of 65). The Unchoked graph's characteristic path length is larger due to the reduced average degree (about 4) of nodes in this graph. Also shown are the characteristic path lengths of a randomly constructed graph [11] with the same number of nodes and edges, and with similar limits on the node degree. The random graph results are almost not visible, as the Connection, Interest, and Download graphs have nearly the same characteristic path lengths as their random graph counterparts. The only exception is the Unchoked graph, which is about 10% larger, probably due to the scale-free nature of this graph which causes it to vary slightly from being truly random.

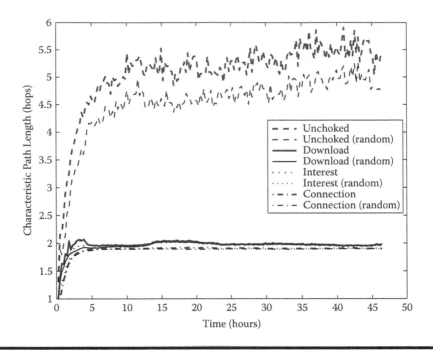

Figure 6.15 The characteristic path length during the experiments. Also shown are those of a similar-sized random graph.

Figure 6.16 shows the clustering coefficients of the four networks in the experiment. Although not shown in the figure, the coefficient starts at 1 (since it is a clique), and then has a sharp decline during the startup stage as the size of the graph increases. Once all the peers have joined the system there is some further decrease in the coefficients of all but the Unchoked graph during the transient stage. Through the end of the transient stage there are some further small oscillations in the Interest and Download graphs, until all settled into a steady stage after approximately 20 hours.

Although at first it seems that there is some clustering present in Figure 6.16, especially in the graphs of Connection, Interest, and Download peers, further investigation shows that is not the case. Figure 6.17 shows the clustering coefficients of the graphs when compared with (divided by) that of a similar sized random graph (same node and edge restrictions), which is not expected to have any clustering at all. Here we see that there is some clustering during the startup stage which begins to decrease once all the nodes have joined the system. The Unchoked graph has no clustering through the rest of the experiment, while the clustering of the other graphs reduces more slowly through the transient stage. In the steady stage, all graphs have almost no clustering. The increased noise in the comparison of the Unchoked graph with a random graph is due to its relatively tiny clustering coefficient.

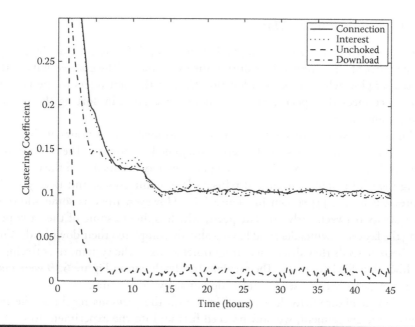

Figure 6.16 The clustering coefficient during the experiments.

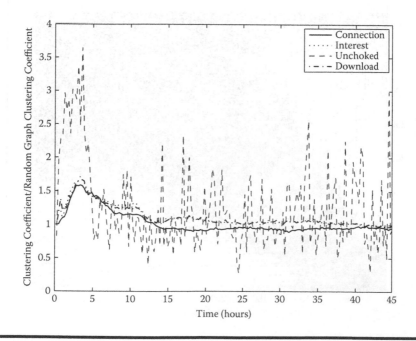

Figure 6.17 The clustering coefficient during the experiments compared with the clustering coefficient of a similar random graph.

6.3.3.1 Connectivity Matrix

To compare with the results from previous papers [29,4], we present the connectivity matrix of peer connections during the experiment. The connectivity matrix is a scatter plot, where a point at location (i, j) in the plot refers to the fact that peer i is connected to peer j. The peer index i is created by sorting the peers by their joining time.

Figure 6.18 shows the connectivity matrix formed after 4 hours at the end of the startup stage when most of the peers have joined the torrent. The fan-out shape from the lower left to upper right corner of the matrix occurs due to the early peers filling their 80-neighbor limit and refusing later connections, and is very similar to previous results [4] shown in Figure 6.19. However, there is some additional connectivity between early and late peers, which is due to some of the early peers being the fastest downloaders and having already completed their downloads. Once they become seeds they disconnect from other seeds in the system, thus freeing up neighbor slots for later peers. The previous results shown in Figure 6.19 were taken before any peers became seeds, and so do not show this feature.

Although Figure 6.18 does match well with the previous results at the early stages of the experiment, we now proceed further into the experiment to see how

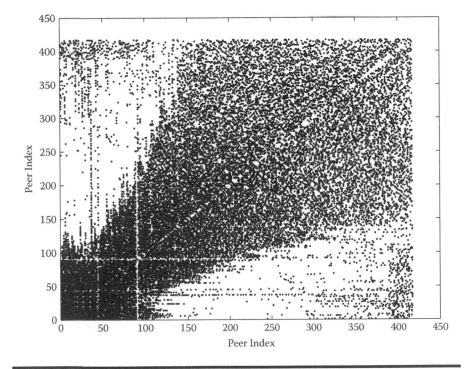

Figure 6.18   The connectivity matrix at hour 4.

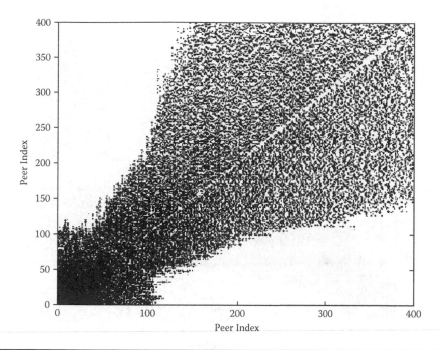

Figure 6.19 The connectivity matrix from the previous results by Al-Hamra et al.

the connectivity matrix evolves. Figure 6.20 shows the connectivity matrix 4 hours further into the experiment in the middle of the transient stage, at which point some peers have left and new peers have joined the system. The matrix is now much more random, with many early peers having lost connections to leaving peers and so allowing connections from many late peers, though the fan-out is still visible in the lower left corner. Figure 6.21 goes further to 16 hours into the experiment, where the connectivity matrix becomes an almost completely random scattering of points, and the fan-out in the lower left is almost not visible. The connectivity matrix has now reached a steady stage, as shown by the similarity of Figures 6.21 and 6.22.

The experiment we ran with no limit on the number of neighbors a peer is shown in Figure 1.23. In that experiment, the connectivity matrix throughout the entire experiment was completely random (similar to Figure 1.22), as the fan-out shape in Figure 1.18 is due only to the limit on the number of neighbors a peer can have.

6.3.3.2 Impact of Churn

To further evaluate the impact of churn on the network topology, we varied the amount of churn at certain points in the system by grouping some of the peer

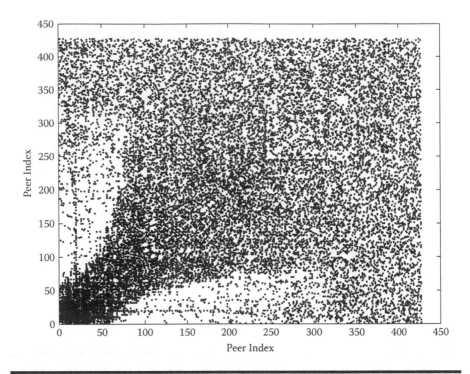

Figure 6.20 The connectivity matrix at hour 8.

departures and arrivals together.* This experiment was the same as in the previous section on the piece population in the presence of churn. As before, the increased churn occurs when the number of seeds decreases rapidly; for example, from 20 to 25 hours, 40 to 50 hours, and 60 to 70 hours. Since the number of peers is limited, the periods between these increased churn periods exhibit a state of decreased churn as compared with the previous experiment. We find that this varying churn had almost no effect on the power law exponent or the characteristic path length of the resulting graphs, which are identical to the previous results shown in Figures 6.13 and 6.15.

Figure 6.24 shows the clustering coefficient for the four networks in the experiment with varying churn. During the initial stage, it is very similar to Figure 6.16, decreasing rapidly as the peers enter the system. However, after the initial stage (i.e., after 4 hours), the effect of the varying churn can be clearly seen on the Connection, Interest, and Download networks, causing their clustering coefficients to oscillate. Interestingly, the clustering coefficient increases during the periods of light churn and decreases during the periods of heavy churn. Although the varying churn continues throughout the experiment, the oscillations in the clustering coefficients of these graphs are greatly reduced after 50 hours.

---

* The previous experiment also had churn, but the amount of churn was steady throughout the experiment.

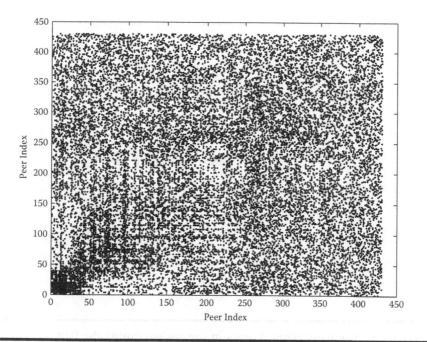

Figure 6.21   The connectivity matrix at hour 16.

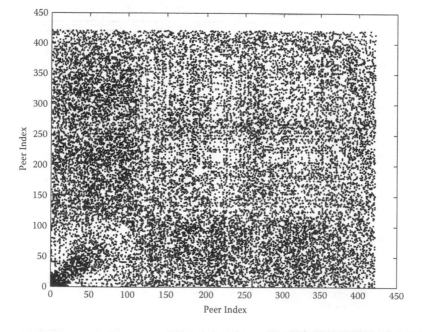

Figure 6.22   The connectivity matrix at hour 32.

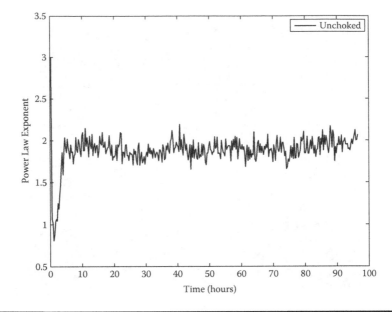

Figure 6.23   The population of peers in the system during the first 45 hours of the experiments.

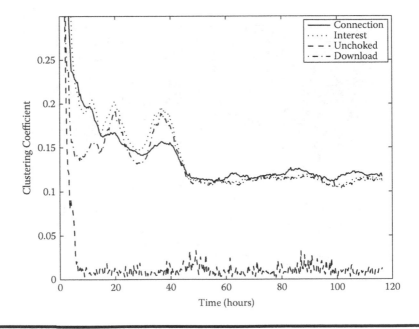

Figure 6.24   The clustering coefficient during the experiment with varying churn

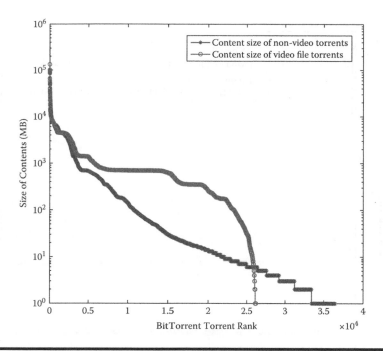

Figure 6.25   Content size of torrents (sort in descending order).

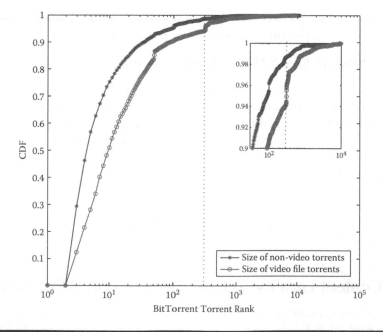

Figure 6.26   Torrent size (CDF).

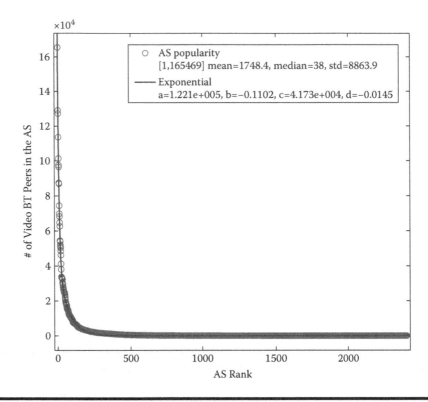

Figure 6.27   AS popularity of existing video BT torrents.

6.3.4 Possible Small-World Enhancement

In Section 1.3, we found no evidence of persistent clustering in any of the four BitTorrent networks we studied, and therefore no small-world networks are possible. It is known that small-world networks are efficient for spreading information [21,14,13]. A previous study [22] has also conjectured that BitTorrent's efficiency partly comes from the clustering of peers.

It is thus interesting to see whether BitTorrent networks can be made to cluster while maintaining a short characteristic path length, and so become small-world. We proposed a possible enhancement toward this direction through both theory and practical implementation. We also presented a theoretical attempt at increasing the small-world characteristics of BitTorrent networks.

6.4 Content Locality: The Inter-Torrent Level Examination

Finally, we move to the inter-torrent level and focus on the locality in torrents. The pioneer work of T. Karagiannis et al. [20] is the first study to address the locality issues in P2P systems. Aiming to solve the inter-ISP traffic problem, the authors

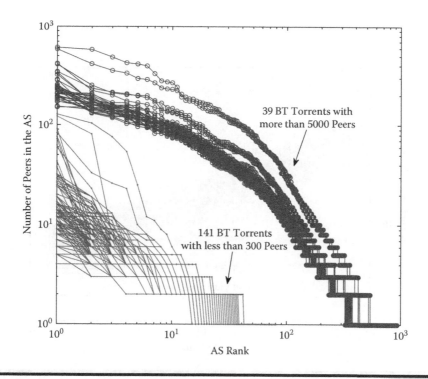

Figure 6.28 Distribution of AS cluster size.

studied both the real traces and simulation results. They evaluate the benefit of several architectures and present the concept of locality in a particular solution. Another work from H. Xie et al. [34] enables cooperation between peer-to-peer applications and ISPs by a brand new locality architecture—P4P. According to the large scale tests, P4P can reduce both the external traffic and the average downloading time. On the other hand, D. R. Choffnes et al. [12] proposed Ono—a BitTorrent extension that leverages on a CDN infrastructure. This approach is aimed to find the location of peers and group peers that are close to each other. R. Bindal et al. [9] also examined a novel approach to enhance BitTorrent traffic locality: biased neighbor selection. Using this method, a peer chooses the majority, but not all, of its neighbors from peers within the same ISP. The simulation results show that this modification can greatly reduce the inter-ISP traffic of BT networks. S. L. Blond et al. [10] performed an extensive experiment-based study on a controlled environment. The authors show that high locality values (defined by [20]) enable up to two order of magnitude saving on inter-ISP links without any significant impact on peers' download completion time.

However, most of these pervious studies are exclusively focused on a global infrastructure. The content and the peer diversities are seldom discussed. Consequently, most BT based locality approaches are processed upon every single peer in the

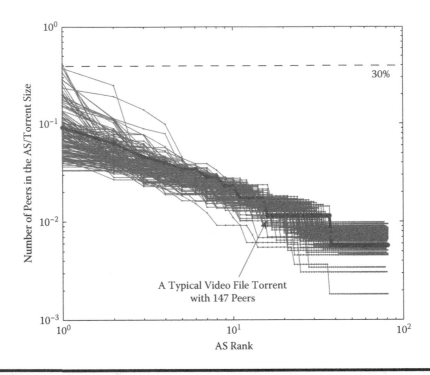

Figure 6.29 **Ratio between AS cluster size and torrent size (141 small torrents).**

torrent. These modifications will not only raise a remarkable overhead but also affect the robustness of BT networks.

6.4.1 Measurement and Analysis of AS-Level Characteristics

In this section, we for the first time examine the video torrents exclusively in BitTorrent networks in regards to the locality issues. The objective of this section is to investigate the AS-level characteristics of torrents with different contents. Such properties have the potential to address a more efficient locality scenario for the BitTorrent system.

In our study, we considered 30,415 video metainfo files and 44,317 nonvideo metainfo files. These metainfo files are manly advertised by www.btmon.com from Feb. 12, 2007 to Aug. 12, 2008. We developed a script that can automatically detect the "href" field in a given HTML file and download files ending with ".torrent."

Within the data set, there are 316 bad metainfo files, 1027 unavailable torrents due to the tracker failure, and 3340 torrents have less than two peers. None of these abnormal torrents is included in our study.

We carry out an Internet-based measurement using the PlanetLab [3] nodes. We run a modified version of CTorrent [2] (CTorrent is a very typical BitTorrent client in FreeBSD) on more than 200 PlanetLab nodes. This program was modified

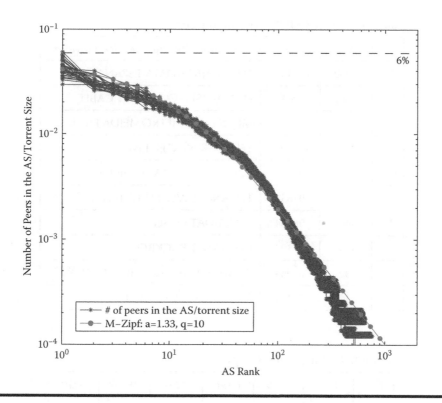

Figure 6.30   Ratio between AS cluster size and torrent size (39 big torrents).

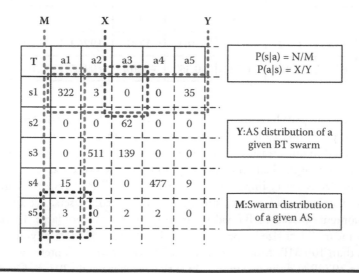

T	a1	a2	a3	a4	a5
s1	322	3	0	0	35
s2	0	0	62	0	0
s3	0	511	139	0	0
s4	15	0	0	477	9
s5	3	0	2	2	0

$$P(s|a) = N/M$$
$$P(a|s) = X/Y$$

Y:AS distribution of a given BT swarm

M:Swarm distribution of a given AS

Figure 6.31   Details of table T and different relationships.

Table 6.3 Top 10 ISPs (BT Video User)

	AS#	Peers	AS Name–Internet Service Provider
1	3352	165469	TELEFONICA-DATA-ESPANA(TDE)
2	3662	129047	DNEO-OSP7-COMCAST CABLE
3	6461	127297	MFNX MFN-METROMEIDA FIBER
4	2119	113597	TELENOR-NEXTEL T.NET
5	19262	101390	VZGNI-TRANSIT-Verizon ISP
6	3301	97658	TELIANET-SWEDEN TELIANET
7	3462	96564	HINET-DATA CBG
8	4134	87392	CHINANET-BACKBONE
9	6327	86964	SHAW-SHAW COMMUNICATION
10	174	74453	COGENT COGENT/PSI

Table 6.4 Inputs and Outputs

T	3352	2119	6461	3301	19262	3320
s_1	382	139	135	126	112	0
S_2	195	262	0	4	0	211
S_3	15	143	8	6	7	0
AS#	**3352**	**2119**	**6461**	**3301**	**19262**	**3320**
E	−1.471	−0.322	−0.353	−0.107	−0.005	−0.157

to log mainly the peer level information such as IP addresses, etc. Since the contents of many Internet torrents may involve copyright problems, no content will be downloaded in our measurement. Moreover, a preprocess is applied to filter the peer information of the PlanetLab probing nodes in the raw data.

Content size is a very important characteristic in all P2P systems. Figure 6.25 shows the distribution of content size among different data sets. We first observe that the contents shared by BT video torrents are mostly very large. In video torrents, the mean object size is approximately 1000 MB and 90% of video contents are larger than 100 MB. Moreover, there are 5% of the video contents with the size larger than 10 GB and the maximum video size reaches nearly 20 GB. On the other hand, the size of nonvideo torrents is relatively small, with only 30% of the nonvideo contents larger than 100 MB. It also worth noting that 50% of nonvideo contents are less than 20 M, whereas those small contents are very few in the video torrents.

Figure 6.26 shows the cumulative distribution of BT torrent size. This distribution is relevant to the popularity of different BT contents. We learn that although the video torrents are mostly larger than nonvideo torrents, more than 90% torrents have less than 100 peers (more than 95% torrents have less than 300 peers).

According to these basic properties, we know that the video torrents have potential to raise more inter-ISP traffic problems due to its large content size and torrent size. In particular, if the peers of a video torrents are uniformly distributed among ASes, it is more likely to generate heavy traffic through the backbone.

In order to understand such a challenge, we randomly select 8893 BT video torrents, and collect the AS information of every peer in each torrent. This probing is based on the "whois" command on Linux system and most replies are from "whois.cymru.com." From Figure 6.27, the AS popularity of video BT peers fits the exponential distribution, that is, among all 2405 ASes in our measurement, most of them have less than 10,000 peers in total. Based on our measurement results, we also present the Top-10 ISPs/ASes with the most video BT peers in Table 6.3. This result can also be regard as the challenge and the potential requirements of P2P locality in these popular ASes.

We further investigate the AS distribution of different video torrents in Figure 6.28. In this figure, 141 small video torrents and 39 big video torrent are selected. Each point in the figure indicates the number of peers in the AS, and the values are all sorted in descending order. We can learn that the AS distribution of the large torrents are more uniform than that of small ones and involves more ASes.

Figures 6.29 and 6.30 show the ratio between AS cluster size and torrent size. In Figure 6.29, we first observe that this ratio is quite high in small torrents; the largest AS cluster can even reach to 30% of the torrent size. Therefore, due to the small peer population, these torrents already have some locality features in nature. Consequently, the benefit of locality mechanism will also be limited by the total peer number.

In the case of large torrents, Figure 6.30 shows that although large AS cluster is more likely to exist in the big torrents, its ratio to the torrent size is relatively very low. In particular, the largest AS clusters only have less than 6% of peers in the AS. Moreover, we find that the distribution of this ratio can be fitted by Mandelbrot-Zipf distribution with $\alpha = 1.33$ and $q = 10$. The MZipf distribution defines the probability of accessing an object at rank i out of N available objects as: $p(i) = K/(i + q)^\alpha$, where $K = \Sigma_{i=1}^{N} 1/(i + q)^\alpha$, α is the skewness factor, and $q \geq 0$ is the plateau factor. q is so called because it is the reason behind the plateau shape near to the left part of the distribution.

These measurement results indicate that the size of most AS clusters is quite small. According to the definition of locality [20], we believe that a global locality approach may not be our best choice. On the other hand, although there are many large AS clusters in the big torrents, the locality of most peers is poor in nature. Therefore, the peers in a large AS cluster have both the potential and incentive to process the locality mechanism. The optimization of these peers is of the most important to both ISPs and individual users.

However, most existing locality approaches treat all peers in the torrent with the equal importance and changed the global peer selection mechanism. We believe that the random peer selection is the core of BitTorrent protocol. In particular, the common belief that BT is efficient, robust, and scalable, is mostly based on the random topology of such a system [4,26,35]. Therefore, a global locality mechanism will not only involve more overhead but also degrade the robustness of existing BitTorrent system. On the other hand, the challenge to design a selective locality mechanism is also sophisticated: It is well known that the locality mechanism must be processed before the form of the huge torrents. However, during the early periods, it is hard to predict whether a peer will belong to a large AS cluster in the future.

Fortunately, according to our measurements, we learned that the ASes are not independent with each other; they are highly related by sharing different peer sets of many torrents. Peers belonging to different ASes, on the other hand, will also have different features due to this relationship. Therefore, this feature has the potential to address a prediction method and help us with the design of a selective locality mechanism. Moreover, this relationship is even more useful between video torrents. This is quite intuitive because the video contents are more likely to have geographic features, which is mainly due to the language variations. For example, few people in Japan would like to download a video of Cantonese version.

6.4.2 Peer Prediction Strategy

In this section, we will discuss a peer prediction method based on the AS level relationships. The main idea of this approach is that, based on the preknowledge of AS and torrent relationship, we are trying to quantify the possible clustering features of a given AS. In particular, if we know the peers belonging to some ASes are more likely to form a big AS cluster, we can process a locality peer selection mechanism only to these peers once they are just arrive at the torrents. On the other hand, peers belonging to other ASes can be processed by the standard random peer selection to ensure the network robustness and connectivity.

We use ë to denote all ASes on the Internet, and use † to denote the set of existing video torrents. We define two random variables A and S in our framework. A is a random variable that takes on different $A \in$ ë. The probability that A takes on the value a is $P(A = a)$. S takes on values over the set of existing video torrents †. We use T to refer to the frequency table of A and S. The elements in the table, $T(a, s)$, refer to the number of peers (in torrent s) that belong to AS a.

Two relationships can be built according to the table T. (see Figure 6.31)The first one is the conditional probability $P(S|a)$. $P(S|a)$ means that for a given AS a, the frequency of torrent S belongs to a. This value can be computed by electing the column in the table T corresponding to a, and normalize it by the sum of this column.

$$P(s,a) = T(s,a) / \sum_a T(s,a) \tag{1.2}$$

On the other hand, the second relationship is the conditional probability $P(A|s)$. $P(A|s)$ means that for a given torrent s, the likelihood of ASes A being used by a given torrent s. This value can be computed by electing the row in the table T corresponding to s, and normalize it by the sum of this row. The computing detail is shown in Figure 6.27, and the elements distribution of table T are shown in Figure 6.28.

$$P(a,s) = T(s,a) / \sum_s T(s,a) \tag{1.3}$$

According to these two relationships. We can further compute the probability $P(A|a)$. $P(A|a)$ summarizes how AS a is associated with all other ASes A due to the torrent level relationship. By tally up how likely other ASes are also holding similar mount of peers from the same torrent, we sum over the contribution in proportion to how frequently torrent s is belonged to AS a.

$$P(A\,|\,a) = P(A\,|\,s_1)P(s_1\,|\,a) + P(A\,|\,s_2)P(s_2\,|\,a) + \ldots$$

$$= \sum_s P(A\,|\,s)P(s\,|\,a) \tag{1.4}$$

After the computing of $P(A|a)$, we use entropy to quantify the mount of randomness in the probability distribution. Note that this value is negative; large entropy implies AS a is weakly associated with a large number of ASes. This occurs when the Ases generally do not have large AS clusters. On the other hand, when the value of an AS is very small, the peers belonging to this AS are very likely to form a big AS cluster. Therefore, we can compute the entropy of $P(A|a)$ as follows:

$$Entropy(a) = H(P(A\,|\,a)) = \sum_{a' \in A} P(a'\,|\,a)logP(a'\,|\,a) \tag{1.5}$$

According to the entropy value of different Ases, a modified tracker protocol will carry out the following selective locality process when a BT peer has arrived (Note that the entropy of each AS is preprocessed by computing the table T according to Equations 1.1–1.4; these entropy values are already existed in the trackers before the following steps):

Step 1: When a peer x arrives, get the AS# a of this peer by sending the "whois" request.

Step 2: For a given AS# a, get the entropy of AS# a according to the results of Equation 1.5.

Step 3: If this value is smaller than a preconfigured threshold *e*, send the peer set information (the sets of neighbor peers) to peer *x* by giving high priority to the neighbors that are in the same AS with *x*; or else send the peer set information using random strategy.

We processed a simple validation of this proposed method by few AS information within three torrents. Both inputs and outputs are shown in Table 6.4, where the upper table is the table *T* and the lower table shows the entropy value of different ASes. According to the outputs, we learn that peers in AS# 3352, 2119 and 6461 are more likely to form a large AS cluster than that of others.

This is obviously not a perfect result because the data in table *T* is limited. However, it still seems somewhat reasonable because Table I can validate some of its results, where the AS# 3352, 2119, and 6461 are all very popular ASes. Note that although As popularity can provide some meaningful information for the validation, it not feasible for the peer prediction. Obviously, the variation of peer number cannot reflect the relationship between ASes; In particular, AS# 3662 and AS# 6461 have very similar popularity in Table 6.1; yet the peers inside these ASes are not necessarily having similar clustering properties.

6.4.3 Summary

In this chapter, we have discussed the interactions of BitTorrent clients, from microscope piece level to intra-torrent and inter-torrent levels. We have presented measurements on the piece populations in torrents, and investigated the effectiveness of the rarest-first policy for piece replication from a piece distribution and evolutionary perspective. We have shown that the policy is quite effective once all pieces become available in the system, and throughout the lifetime of the torrent. However, some deviations from the ideal were apparent soon after creation of the torrent, and in some of the larger torrents studied.

We have also shown experimentally the network evolutions in a torrent, which we found change significantly over time. We have quantified the scale-free nature of one of the networks in a torrent, that of peers unchoking each other. We found that this scale-free nature is independent of time and the changing parameters of the experiment. We have also gone beyond previous studies to show that, after the very early stages, most of the networks in a torrent are purely random graphs with no clustering present. Therefore, the graphs do not exhibit the small-world characteristics that have been found in many other peer-to-peer network overlays. However, the ever-present churn in a BitTorrent system may have impacted this result.

We have therefore successfully designed a tracker modification to introduce small-world networks into a torrent. The modification has been tested, both through simulation and experimentally, to have introduced a large amount of clustering, at the expense of only a small increase in the characteristic path length. Our changes are only to the tracker, yet we have introduced these small-world characteristics into all four of the BitTorrent networks we considered.

In regards to the locality issues, we have studied the existing video BT torrent. We for the first time examined the problem through a large-scale Internet-based measurement and especially focused on different peer features. According to our measurement results, a global locality approach may not be our best choice. Peers in the large AS clusters are of the most importance during the locality optimization. Based on the relationships of different ASes, a possible peer prediction approach is discussed to serve our selective locality mechanism.

A distinguishing feature of our study in comparison to previous works is the focus on real-world measurement and low-level features such as peer and content diversities. The different AS relationships are also proposed for the first time from the BitTorrent point of view. Meanwhile, one of its limitations is that a large mount of data is needed to infer such a relationship. The accuracy of this approach should also be further examined by the real-world deployment.

References

1. CacheLogic. http://www.cachelogic.com.
2. Ctorrent. http://ctorrent.sourceforge.net.
3. PlanetLab. http://www.planet-lab.org.
4. A. Al-Hamra, A. Legout, and C. Barakat. Understanding the Properties of the Bittorrent Overlay. Technical Report, INRIA, 2007.
5. R. Albert, H. Jeong, and A.L. Barabási. Error and attack tolerance of complex networks. *Nature*, 406:378–382, July 2000.
6. D. Alderson, J.C. Doyle, L. Li, and W. Willinger. Towards a theory of scale-free graphs: Definition, properties, and implications. *Internet Math*, 2(4):431–523, 2005.
7. A.L. Barabási and R. Albert. Emergence of scaling in random networks. *Science*, 286(5439):509–512, 1999.
8. A.L. Barabási and E. Bonabeau. Scale-free networks. *Scientific American Magazine*, 288(5):60–69, 2003.
9. R. Bindal, P. Cao, W. Chan, J. Medved, G. Suwala, T. Bates, and A. Zhang. Improving traffic locality in BitTorrent via biased neighbor selection. In *Proc. IEEE ICDCS 2006.*
10. S.L. Blond, A. Legout, and W. Dabbous. Pushing BitTorrent Locality to the Limit. INRIA Tech. Rep. 2008.
11. B. Bollobás. *Random Graphs.* 2nd edition, Cambridge University Press, 2001. London, England.
12. D.R. Choffnes and F.E. Bustamante. Taming the torrent: A practical approach to reducing cross-ISP traffic in peer-to-peer systems. In *Proc. ACM SIGCOMM 2008.*
13. F. Comellas, M. Mitjana, and J.G. Peters. Epidemics in Small-World Communication Networks. Technical Report SFU-CMPT-TR-2002, Simon Fraser University, October 2002.
14. F. Comellas, J. Ozon, and J.G. Peters. Deterministic small-world communication networks. *Information Processing Letters*, 76(1-2):83–90, 2000.

15. C. Dale and J. Liu. A measurement study of piece population in BitTorrent. In *GlobeCom*, Washington, DC, November 26–30 2007.

16. P. Erdős and A. Rényi. On random graphs. *Publ. Math*, pages 290–297, 1959.

17. S. Guha, N. Daswani, and R. Jain. An experimental study of the Skype peer-to-peer VoIP system. In *Proc. of the IPTPS '06*, Santa Barbara, CA, February 2006.

18. T. Hong. Performance. In Andy Oram, editor, *Peer-to-Peer: Harnessing the Power of Disruptive Technologies*, chapter 14, pp. 203–241. O'Reilly & Associates, Inc., Sebastopol, CA, 2001.

19. K.Y.K. Hui, J.C.S. Lui, and D.K.Y. Yau. Small world overlay P2P networks. *Proc. Twelfth IEEE International Workshop on Quality of Service*, pp. 201–210, 2004.

20. T. Karagiannis, P. Rodriguez, and K. Papagiannaki. Should Internet service providers fear peer-assisted content distribution? In *Proc. ACM/USENIX IMC 2005*.

21. V. Latora and M. Marchiori. Efficient behavior of small-world networks. *Phys. Rev. Lett.*, 87(19):198701, October 2001.

22. A. Legout, N. Liogkas, E. Kohler, and L. Zhang. Clustering and sharing incentives in bittorrent systems. In *SIGMETRICS*, pages 301–312, 2007.

23. A. Legout, G. Urvoy-Keller, and P. Michiardi. Rarest first and choke algorithms are enough. In *Proc. IMC'06*, Rio de Janeiro, Brazil, October 2006.

24. G. Liu, M. Hu, B. Fang, and H. Zhang. Measurement and modeling of large-scale peer-to-peer storage system. *Lecture Notes in Computer Science*, pages 270–277, 2004.

25. S. Milgram. The Small World Problem. *Psychology Today*, 2(1):60–67, 1967.

26. G. Neglia, G. Reina, H. Zhang, D. Towsley, A. Venkataramani, and J. Danaher. Availability in BitTorrent systems. In *Proc. IEEE INFOCOM 2007*.

27. D. Niu and B. Li. On the resilience-complexity tradeoff of network coding in dynamic P2P networks. *Proc. Fifteenth IEEE International Workshop on Quality of Service*, pp. 38–46, June 21–22, 2007.

28. D. Qiu and R. Srikant. Modeling and performance analysis of BitTorrent-like peer-to-peer networks. In *Proc. SIGCOMM '04*, Portland, Oregon, August 30–September 3, 2004.

29. G. Urvoy-Keller and P. Michiardi. Impact of inner parameters and overlay structure on the performance of bittorrent. In *INFOCOM*, 2006.

30. D.J. Watts. *Small Worlds: The Dynamics of Networks between Order and Randomness*. Princeton Univ. Pr., 1999.

31. D.J. Watts and S.H. Strogatz. Collective dynamics of "small-world" networks. *Nature*, 393(6684):409–10, 1998. http://www.nature.com, Nature Publishing Group.

32. S. Willmott, J.M. Pujol, and U. Cortes. On exploiting agent technology in the design of peer-to-peer applications. *Lecture Notes in Computer Science*, 3601:98, 2005.

33. R.H. Wouhaybi. Algorithms for Reliable Peer-to-Peer Networks. Ph.D. thesis, Columbia University, 2006.

34. H. Xie, R.Y. Yang, A. Krishnamurthy, Y.G. Liu, and A. Silberschatz. P4P: Provider portal for applications. In *Proc. ACM SIGCOMM 2008*.

35. X. Yang and G. de Veciana. Service capacity of peer to peer networks. In *Proc. IEEE INFOCOM 2004*.

36. H. Zhang, A. Goel, and R. Govindan. Using the small-world model to improve freenet performance. *Computer Networks*, 46(4):555–574, 2004.

Chapter 7

Sociotechnical Environments and Assistive Technology Abandonment

Stefan Parry Carmien

Contents

7.1 Introduction

This chapter will explore the use of sociotechnical analysis in design of assistive technology. We will discuss assistive technology (AT) and the various user types (roles) that are involved in its development and adoption, with particular focus on the high rate of abandonment of complex assistive technology. We will contrast the conventional approach of studying system design and adoption using a sociotechnical perspective in work environments and using the same tools in the context of voluntary use. Of course both of these environments are, in a fundamental way, voluntary; employees can always quit, but in the case of assistive technology (AT) the motivation is not so much economic and psychological (e.g., job satisfaction) as literally functional (i.e., ability to perform Activities of Daily Living (ADL)* or Instrumental Activities of Daily Living (IADL)†).

We start the discussion with defining and exploring the dimensions of assistive technology in design and use, with particular attention to the process of adoption and abandonment. Following this is a short review of the traditional process of sociotechnical systems and environments, looking at them from the perspective of typical domains studied and the evolution of the field. Within this section we present several practices or tools used in sociotechnical evaluation and design.

We illustrate the process of sociotechnical design of assistive technology by discussing MAPS (Measures of Academic Progress), a ADL task-support tool for persons with cognitive disabilities, following the process from participant designer selection and study through adoption of a prototype system and lessons learned. We then make a more formal comparison between "traditional" STE study and AT-based STE work, decomposing the elements of the MAPS system. Finally, we conclude with some suggestions for further work

7.2 Assistive Technology

Assistive technology is defined in the United States as "Any item, piece of equipment, or system, whether acquired commercially, modified, or customized, that is commonly used to increase, maintain, or improve functional capabilities of individuals with disabilities." (*Source*: The U.S. Technology-Related Assistance for Individuals With Disabilities Act of 1988, Section 3.1. Public Law 100-407, August 9, 1988; renewed in 1998 as the Clinton Assistive Technology Act.)

Assistive technology devices can be as simple as an extender for door handles to allow opening of doors by people with reduced manipulative ability or as complex as an alternative and augmentative communications device to support communications by persons with speech disabilities, like Steven Hawkins. In this chapter we will be discussing high-level computer-based AT, typically for leveraging existing abilities by persons with cognitive disabilities to perform tasks that they would not be able to do without assistance. This discussion of AT is focused on complex AT adoption because the successful adoption process for such items (1) takes a longer time (weeks or months) and involves multiple roles (e.g., end users and caregivers)

---

* ADLs refer to refers to six activities (bathing, dressing, transferring, using the toilet room, eating, and walking) that reflect the patient's capacity for self-care.
† IADLs are tasks that enable people to live independently in the community. Examples include shopping, cooking, and house cleaning. IADLs support ADLs.

and (2) since AT is designed for direct use by the end user rather than being a component in a solely technological system (e.g., a planetary gear in a transmission), studying AT in use must involve including in investigations all the direct stakeholders. These stakeholders include, besides the direct end user of the AT, professional caregivers, familial caregivers, medical personnel, and legal and governmental users, as well as those involved in the AT supply chain—from designers to sales to support. Studying the long-term adoption process must necessarily include looking at the environment of adoption (and use), as well as other parameters which we will explore in the section on deconstructing elements in an STE.

7.2.1 AT for Persons with Cognitive Disabilities

A unique aspect of software and systems for persons with cognitive disabilities is that, while the focus is on the end user, for the person with cognitive disabilities, design and evaluation must involve their caregiver; in fact, it may be taken as an axiom [3] that every system is used and must accommodate a dyad—the end user and a caregiver. Typically, the caregiver assists in the setting up and maintenance of assistive technology systems, as they often are too difficult for the person with cognitive disabilities to set up and keep up to date. Also pertinent and contributing to the success or failure of a design being adopted or abandoned are the lesser stakeholders. These include the family of the person with cognitive disabilities, the AT designers, product salesmen, and technical support, persons and organizations involved with funding the (often very expensive) AT devices, and the legal and regulatory personnel and systems designed to protect and respond to the needs of persons with cognitive disabilities. Often the motivation and goals of these different stakeholder roles can be divergent and even conflicting.

Advanced and complex AT for the cognitively disabled can take several forms, which can be classified according to the function that is being supported. Missing or deficient executive functionality and mnemonic lack is addressed by systems that support task completion [2]. Mnemonic difficulty can be alleviated using scheduling systems [25]; missing or deficient communication functionality is addressed by a wide range of augmentative and alternative communication (AAC) devices [26]. Harbingers of future AT for those with more profound cognitive disabilities are an application and environment that aides elders with Alzheimer's in properly washing hands, COACH (cognitive orthosis for assisting with activites in the home) [27] using video recognition, an instrumented bathroom, and AI to detect deviation from proper handwashing process and guided the end user back on track.

7.2.2 AT: Adoption and Abandonment

Device rejection is the fate of a large percentage of purchased assistive technology [12,13]. Caregivers report that difficulties in configuring and modifying configurations in assistive technology often lead to abandonment* [15], an especially poignant fate considering that these sorts of systems may cost thousands of dollars. Some experts estimate that as much as 70% [18, 23] of all such devices and systems are purchased and not used over the long run, particularly those designed as a cognitive *orthotic* [17]. Causes for abandonment have many dimensions; a study by Phillips and Zhao reported that a "change in needs of the user" showed the strongest association with abandonment [21]. Thus, those devices that cannot accommodate the changing requirements of the users were highly likely to be abandoned. Although this study did not address configuration issues directly, it follows logically (and is confirmed by interviews with several AT experts [2, 14]) that an obstacle to device retention is difficulty in reconfiguring the device. A survey of abandonment causes lists *"changes in consumer functional abilities or activities"* as a critical component of AT abandonment [11]. A study by Galvin and Scherer states that one of the major causes for AT mismatch (and thus abandonment) is the myth that *"a users assistive technology requirements nee to be assessed just once"* [24]; ongoing re-assessment and adjustment to changing needs is the appropriate response. A source for research on the other dimensions of AT abandonment, and the development of outcome metrics to evaluated adoption success, is the ATOMS project at the University of Milwaukee [22].

Successful AT design for this population must support, the interface requirements for users with cognitive impairments as well as view configuration and other caregiver tasks as different and equally important requirements for a second-user interface [7]. One proven approach applies techniques such as task-oriented design [16] to mitigate technology abandonment problems. Research [9] and interviews have demonstrated that complex, multifunctional systems are the most vulnerable to abandonment due to the complexity of the many possible functions. Therefore, the initial goal was a simple system that does one (or few) things very well for a large range of users/caregivers with an interface that is exceptionally easy to use initially.

7.2.2.1 Abandonment Based on the "Universe of One"

People with cognitive disabilities represent a "universe of one" problem [9] (see Figure 7.1): a solution for one person will rarely work for another. The "universe of one" conceptualization includes the empirical finding that (1) *unexpected islands of abilities* exist: clients can have unexpected skills and abilities that can be leveraged to ensure a better possibility of task accomplishment; and (2) *unexpected deficits of abilities* exist. Accessing and addressing these unexpected variations in skills and needs, particularly with respect to creating task support, requires an intimate knowledge of the client that *only caregivers* can provide [8]. Currently, a substantial portion of all assistive technology is abandoned after initial purchase and use—as

---

* There is another kind of abandonment, which is not using the system or device because the need no longer exists. This "good" abandonment of AT is not in the purview of the current study.

Islands of abilities in seas of deficits:
Unexpected abilities that can be leveraged

Islands of deficits in seas of abilities:
Causes of unexpected activity failures

Figure 7.1   Universe of one.

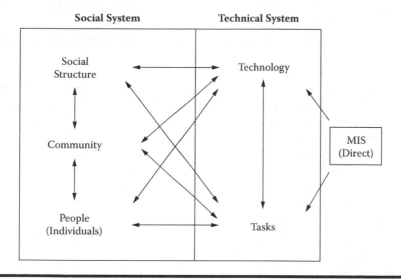

Figure 7.2   Relationship between social system and technical system.

high as 70% in some cases [21]—causing the consequence that the very population that could most benefit from technology is paying for expensive devices that end up in the back of closets after a short time.

AT for cognitive disabilities (and to a lesser degree all AT) presents unique design challenges stemming from being in the intersection of assistive technology and cognitive science. One aspect of this is that due to the distance between the experience of the designer and the end-users systems are often inappropriate or ineffetive in real context of use.

Individuals with cognitive disabilities are often unable to live independently due to their inability to perform activities of daily living, such as cooking, housework, or shopping. By being provided with *socio-technical environments* [19] (see Figure 7.2) to extend their abilities and thereby their independence, these individuals can lead lives less dependent on others. Traditionally, training has provided support for activities of daily living by utilizing prompting and task segmentation techniques. Clients were prompted through specific steps in their tasks in a rehearsal mode and were expected to use the memorized instructions later on in their daily lives.

The research that produced MAPS was driven by three related topics of interest:

- To gain a fundamental understanding of how people with moderate to severe cognitive disabilities perceive and use information in prompting systems for tasks on mobile handheld devices;
- To engage in a theoretically grounded development process of sociotechnical environments supporting mobile device customization, personalization, configuration by caregivers (meta-design), and effective use by clients (distributed intelligence); and
- To analyze and assess the process of adoption of MAPS by dyads of clients and caregivers.

MAPS was one of a number of applications and frameworks developed by the Cognitive Lever (CLever) project [4], a research group within the Center for LifeLong Learning and Design (L3D) at the University of Colorado, Boulder.

Identifying the Client Community. An individual with cognitive disabilities is defined by the Diagnostic and Statistical Manual of Mental Disorders IV (DSM-IV) [1] as a person who is *"significantly limited in at least two of the following areas: self-care, communication, home living social/interpersonal skills, self-direction, use of community resources, functional academic skills, work, leisure, health, and safety."* Four different degrees of cognitive disability are defined: mild, moderate, severe, and profound. The target populations for MAPS are individuals with cognitive disability in the mild (IQ 50–55 to 70) and upper range of moderate (IQ 35 to 55) levels.

Independence. Independence emerged as one of the critical concepts in our research. Clients have the desire to live independently without the need for help and supervision by caregivers (similar to the desire expressed by elderly people [20]). This independence from human "coaches" is achieved with the availability of innovative tools supporting a *distributed intelligence* approach [6]: the clients' limited internal scripts are complemented by powerful external scripts [5]. MAPS research has explored independence specifically in the following contexts: (1) to extend the ability to choose and do as many activities of daily living as possible; (2) to be employed, but without the constant or frequent support and supervision of a professional job coach; and (3) to prepare meals and to shop for weekly groceries. Independence is not at odds with socialization; it is the foundation of inclusion and engagement in society.

7.3 The MAPS Environment

MAPS [3] consists of two major subsystems that share the same fundamental structure but present different affordances for the two sets of users: (1) MAPS-DE, for caregivers, employs Web-based script and template repositories that allow content to be created and shared by caregivers of different abilities and experiences; and (2) MAPS-PR, for clients, provides external scripts that reduce the cognitive demands for the clients by changing the task.

7.3.1 The MAPS-Design-Environment (MAPS-DE)

The scripts needed to effectively support users are specific for particular tasks, creating the requirement that the people who know about the clients and the tasks (i.e., the local caregivers rather than a technologist far removed from the action) must be able to develop scripts. Caregivers generally have no specific professional technology training nor are they interested in becoming computer programmers. This creates the need for design environments with extensive end-user support to allow caregivers to create, store, and share scripts [10]. Figure 7.3 shows MAPS-DE for creating complex multimodal prompting sequences. The prototype allows sound, pictures, and video to be assembled by using a film-strip-based scripting metaphor.

MAPS-DE supports a multiscript version that allows caregivers to present the looping and forking behavior that is critical for numerous task support situations. MAPS-DE (see Figure 7.3) is implemented on a Microsoft OS (Windows 2000 or XP) platform connecting to and supporting PDAs that run the WIN-Compact Edition (WIN-CE) operating system.

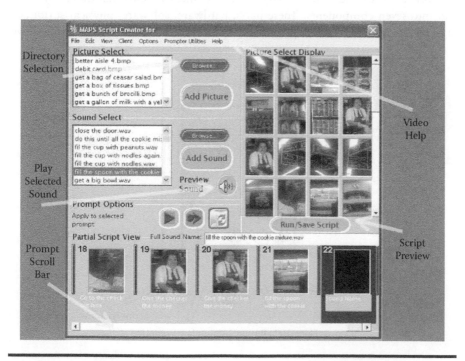

Figure 7.3   The MAPS Design Environment for Creating Scripts.

7.3.2 The MAPS-Prompter (MAPS-PR)

MAPS-PR presents to clients the multimedia scripts that support the task to be accomplished. Its function is to display the prompt and its accompanying verbal instruction. MAPS-PR has a few simple controls (see Figure 7.4): (1) the touch screen advances the script forward one prompt, and (2) the four hardware buttons on the bottom are mapped to (i) back up one prompt, (ii) replay the verbal prompt, (iii) advance one prompt, and (iv) activate panic/help status. The mapping of the buttons to functions is configurable to account for the needs of individual users and tasks.

The current platform for the MAPS-PR is an IPAQ 3850. The system was implemented for any machine that runs the WIN-CE operating system. MAPS-PR has cell phone and GPRS functionality. The prompter software was originally written in embedded Visual Basic, and then ported to the faster and more flexible C# .net environment. The prompter software supports single-task or multitask support.

The lack of support for co-evolution causes much of the *abandonment* [21] of assistive technology tools. Caregivers, who have the most intimate knowledge of the client, need to become the "programmer/end-user developer" of the application for that person by creating the needed scripts.

Frey [28] uses a schema to analyze sociotechnical systems that divides the system into seven components. These parts: hardware, software, physical surroundings, people (groups or roles), procedures, laws, and data (and data structures), give

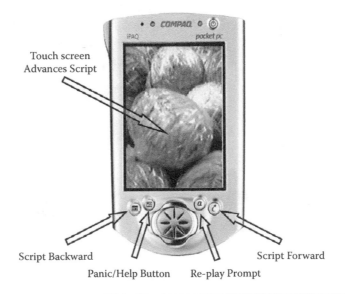

Figure 7.4   The MAPS Prompter (MAPS-PR).

a good staring point for comparing different STEs and also for clarification of the interaction between the technical and social dimensions of an STE. Table 7.1 shows the comparisons between AT and Volvo [29]. Following is the decomposition of the MAPS system:

Hardware: MAPS uses a PC for its MAPS-DE script designing tool, feeding the script composition are recorded voice prompts and images collected by a digital recorder and camera, respectively. MAPS scripts are played on by the MAPS-PR on a PDA or smart phone that runs one of the small versions of the windows operating system.

Software: The MAPS system software consists of the MAPS-PR script player and the MAPS-DE script editor. In addition to these (and in support of them) are (optionally) required an image editor for the pictures illustrating the prompt and an audio editor for the verbal prompts. Behind this would be the windows desktop and small device operating systems. Because one of the functions not disabled in the PDA was the MP3 player (to motivate retention of the PDA), the MP3 player application was also sometimes used. Additionally, some caregivers used a text editor (like MS word) for preliminary script design. The scripts themselves were stored in a Sybase database on the PC and PDA, as well in as in the MAPS script template server that held pre-outlined typical scripts.

Physical surroundings: MAPS was used in two kinds of environments. The MAPS-RP was used wherever the end user was performing tasks with the aid of the scripts prompting. In the initial trials of MAPS these ranged from in the end user's home to in a school to at employment (i.e., in a used-clothing store). As well as the MAPS-PR being used in these spaces, the caregiver would photograph them for script creation. The prompts we most often recoded were in the home, or in the case of the job coach, the office of the caregiver. Incidentally, in the case where the MAPS-PR PDA was being used as an MP3 player, the location varied with the path of the end user throughout the day.

People: The list of people includes not just individuals (roles) but also groups of people (groups). These include the designers of the MAPS system and the end-user co-designers. Central to the sociotechnical system are the end user (also referred to as the MAPS-PR user, a person with cognitive disabilities, and the client) the day-to-day caregiver, who may be a family member or a professional caregiver paid for by insurance, the family, or the state. Influencing the system at a remove are AT experts, special-ed experts and teachers (in the case of a young adult with cognitive disabilities), insurance personnel, and state funding staff. At a further remove, but still very much affecting the system, are school administrators and employers. Finally, intimate influences of the system are the end user's immediate family and friends, as well as their peer groups (either in school or employment).

Table 7.1 Comparing Industry and AT as STE

	Hardware	Software	Physical Surroundings	People (Groups and Roles)	Procedures	Laws	Data and data Structures
AT example (MAPS)	PC and PDA prompter	MAPS-DE and MAPS-PR	Caregivers home, end users world	Client Caregiver Maps developer AT special ed experts	Creating and editing a script Using prompter to do a task Segmenting a task	Privacy and copyright laws	Scripts database Folder of images Folder of recorded prompts
Industry example – Volvo from [29]	Assembly tools	Worker protocols	Automobile factory	Workers, management, line supervisors, workers families, researchers	Assembling automobiles, updating work practices, updating team practices	Worker rights, economic realities, contracts	Assembly an bills of materials, lean production artifacts

Procedures: There are several kinds of procedures in the MAPS uses several kinds of procedures in setting up the system in using it to guide task performance. Included in the tasks required to set up the system are task segmentation (i.e., breaking the task down into sections that are of the correct cognitive level), task rehearsal (i.e., performing the task yourself to ensure no implicit steps are left out), and script building. The construction of scripts (after the outlining has been done) requires collecting photographs of the task with a digital camera and recoding the verbal prompts with a computer and mike. The caregiver must master the art of using the MAPS-DE using the provided tutorial. Script assembly requires using the MAPS-DE editor and the operating system to identify and insert script steps into the script database.

Next, the caregiver has to transfer the script to the MAPS-PR from the caregiver's PC. The end user has to initially learn how to use the prompter by working with the caregiver and perhaps the MAPS designer-support personnel. The young adult with cognitive disabilities then is ready to use the script on the MAPS-PR to accomplish the task, which is embedded in a larger set of ADL and IADL tasks that he/she can do without external support.

Finally the caregiver has to review the script log to see if the script needs to have certain steps collapsed into a trigger step (collapsing scaffolding) or expended into several additional steps because the end user found performing them too difficult (expanding scaffolding).

Laws, statutes, and regulations: The MAPS system is not impacted by laws and regulations except inasmuch as its purchase is aided by state funding.

Data and data structures: MAPS stores external wave files (for the recording prompts) and jpg files (for the prompt images) in the caregiver's PC. Completed scripts are stored in a Sybase database on the caregiver's PC and scripts on the MAPS-PR are stored on a mobile lightweight version of the Sybase database. Additionally a Sybase database of template scripts is stored on a networked server, accessible through the Internet. Design documents used in creating scripts (i.e., task segmentation notes) may be stored in text documents. MAPS-PR stores a log produced by the use of a given script in a text file for later analysis.

7.4 Conculation

Good AT design is then best approached from the STE perspective. The creation of AT for persons with cognitive disabilities is particularly a STE issue due to the complexities of relationship and invasiveness of the technology. Following on this is the question of how best the STE approach can be formalized in AT design. Frameworks such as the ETHICS method [37] and the decomposition into facets as presented by

Frey [19J would be good places to start, most useful is the emphasis on etlmographic study forming the basis for understanding the potential and requirements of the situation. An explicit drawing out of stakeholders' roles and investments in the whole system is illustrated in the several ethnographic studies in Mumfords works. Illustrating a similar approach is MAPS inclusion of the caregiver's role and interface design which naturally flows out of approaching the problem from a STE perspective, a concern that is often missing in other high functioning but low adoption systems.

Developing an explicit checklist set of heuristics to incorporate STE perspective in AT design is another approach that may roll back the tremendous problem of abandonment; this chapter is an attempt to do just that. Finally STE's systemic approach of acknowledging the dynamic interaction between user, artifact, environment and tasks is critical for good AT design.

References

1. American Psychiatric Association Task Force on DSM-IV, *Diagnostic and Statistical Manual of Mental Disorders: DSM-IV-TR*. 4th text revision. ed., Washington, DC: American Psychiatric Association. xxxvii, 943. 2000.
2. Bodine, C., Personal communication, 2003.
3. Carmien, S., *Leveraging Skills into Independent Living—Distributed Cognition and Cognitive Disability*. Saarbrücken: VDM Verlag Dr. Mueller, E.K. 256. 2007.
4. Carmien, S., Dawe, M., Fischer, G., Gorman, A., Kintsch, A., and Sullivan, J.F., Socio-technical environments supporting people with cognitive disabilities using public transportation. *Transactions on Human-Computer Interaction (ToCHI)*, 12(2): 2005. pp. 233–262.
5. Carmien, S., Fischer, F., Fischer, G., and Kollar, I., *The Interplay of Internal and External Scripts—A Distributed Cognition Perspective*, in *Scripting Computer-Supported Learning—Cognitive, Computational, and Educational Perspectives*, F. Fischer et al., Eds. 2007, Springer: New York, pp. 303–326.
6. Carmien, S. and Fischer, G., Tools for living and tools for learning, in *Proceedings of the HCI International Conference (HCII)*, Las Vegas, July 2005. p. (published on a CD).
7. Cole, E., Cognitive prosthetics: An overview to a method of treatment. *NeuroRehabilitation*, 12(1): 1997. pp. 31–51.
8. Cole, E. Patient-centered design as a research strategy for cognitive prosthetics: Lessons learned from working with patients and clinicians for 2 decades. In *CHI 2006 Workshop on Designing Technology for People with Cognitive Impairments*. 2006. Montreal, Canada.
9. Fischer, G., User modeling in human-computer interaction. *User Modeling and User-Adapted Interaction (UMUAI)*, 11(1): 2001. pp. 65–86.
10. Fischer, G. and Giaccardi, E., Meta-design: A framework for the future of end user development, in *End User Development—Empowering People to Flexibly Employ Advanced Information and Communication Technology*, H. Lieberman, F. Paternò, and V. Wulf, Eds. 2006, Kluwer Academic Publishers: Dordrecht, The Netherlands. pp. 427–458.
11. Galvin, J.C. and Donnell, C.M., Educating the consumer and caretaker on assistive technology, in *Assistive Technology: Matching Device and Consumer for Successful Rehabilitation*, M.J. Scherer, Ed. 2002, American Psychological Association: Washington, DC. pp. 153–167.

12. King, T., *Assistive Technology—Essential Human Factors*. 1999, Allyn & Bacon: Boston.
13. King, T., Ten Nifty Ways to make Sure Your Clients Fail with AT and AAC! (A human Factors Perspective on Clinical Success—or Not). In *19th Annual Conference: Computer Technology in Special Education and Rehabilitation*. 2001.
14. Kintsch, A., Personal communication, 2002
15. Kintsch, A. and dePaula, R. A framework for the adoption of assistive technology, in *SWAAAC 2002: Supporting Learning Through Assistive Technology*. 2002. Winter Park, CO: Assistive Technology Partners.
16. Lewis, C. and Rieman, J., Task-Centered User Interface Design: A Practical Introduction, 1993, ftp://ftp.cs.colorado.edu/pub/cs/distribs/clewis/HCI-Design-Book.
17. LoPresti, E.F., Mihailidis, A., and Kirsch, N., Assistive technology for cognitive rehabilitation: State of the art. *Neuropsychological Rehabilitation*, 14(1–2): 2004. pp. 5–39.
18. Martin, B. and McCormack, L., Issues surrounding Assistive Technology use and abandonment in an emerging technological culture. In *Proceedings of Association for the Advancement of Assistive Technology in Europe (AAATE) Conference*. 1999.
19. Mumford, E., Sociotechnical systems design: Evolving theory and practice, in *Computers and Democracy*, G. Bjerknes, P. Ehn, and M. Kyng, Eds. 1987, Avebury: Aldershot, U.K. pp. 59–76.
20. National-Research-Council, *Technology for Adaptive Aging*. Washington, DC: National Academy Press. 2004.
21. Phillips, B. and Zhao, H., Predictors of assistive technology abandonment. *Assistive Technology*, 5(1): 1993.
22. Rehabilitation Research Design and Disability (R_2D_2) Center, Assistive Technology Outcomes Measurement System Project (ATOMS Project), 2006, http://www.uwm.edu/CHS/r2d2/atoms/.
23. Reimer-Reiss, M. Assistive technology discontinuance. In *Technology and Persons with Disabilities Conference*. 2000.
24. Scherer, M.J. and Galvin, J.C., An outcomes perspective of quality pathways to the most appropriate technology, in *Evaluating, Selecting and Using Appropriate Assistive*, M.J. Scherer and J.C. Galvin, Eds. 1996, Aspen Publishers: Gaithersburg, MD. pp. 1–26.
25. Levinson, R., PEAT: The Planning and Execution Assistant and Training System, 2003, http://www.brainaid.com.
26. Beukelman, D. and Mirenda, P., Augmentative and Alternative Communications, 2nd ed, Baltimore: Paule H. Brooks Publishing. 1998.
27. Mihailidis, A., Intelligent Supportive Environments for older Adults (Coach Project), 2007, http://www/ot/utoronto.co/iatsl/projects/intell_env.htm.
28. Frey, W., Socio-Technical Systems in Professional Decision Making, accessed May 2009. http://cnx.org/content/m14025/1.9/.
29. Mumford, E., Redesigning Human Systems, Hershey, PA: Information Science Publishing. 2003.

Chapter 8

A Sociotechnical Collaborative Negotiation Approach to Support Group Decisions for Engineering Design

Stephen C-Y. Lu, Nan Jing, and Jian Cai

Contents

8.1 Introduction and Overview

Engineering design aims to create technical solutions to engineering problems through the use of scientific methods. It is concerned with how to improve the quality and efficiency of design decisions in order to develop, test, implement, and maintain functional and purposeful engineering systems that can satisfy demanding and evolving user requirements. Traditionally, these design decisions are made by a small group of engineers in the same location and time zone. Recently, driven by market globalization, technology outsourcing, and the Internet revolution, most engineering designs are carried out by distributed teams that include engineers, architects, managers, and customers who have different backgrounds and expertise. When people from different disciplines work collaboratively across the geographical and temporal boundaries, the engineering design process becomes very complicated since such collaborative design endeavor involves numerous technical and social (namely sociotechnical) issues, such as acceptability of technical design proposals, communication of design objectives, and keeping track of designers' social interactions. In other words, the design activities are influenced not only by the technical factors but also by the social interactions among distributed, asynchronous, and yet collaborating stakeholders.

In this highly distributed and collaborative global industry, to stay competitive when dealing with the challenging design problem, engineers have to count on effective and efficient collaboration approaches that can clearly help them understand the characteristics of collaborative design activity and provide operational methods to improve design productivity. Compared with traditional individual design, collaborative design has some intrinsic characteristics. The objectives of design are not homogeneous since various persons join the design team and make group decisions on design proposals based on their own objectives and various perspectives. Organizing their objectives and integrating their perspectives is a key challenge for the engineers who collaborate with each other on technical tasks and in social interactions to make rational group decisions in engineering design. Compounded with the temporal and geographical differences, this becomes an even stronger challenge that needs to be confronted by the whole engineering research community. However, despite its importance, the current investigation of the features and characteristics of group decisions in collaborative engineering design is more limited to practiced heuristics rather than scientific principles with solid theoretical foundation. In order to establish an adequate framework to support such group decision making, it is necessary to thoroughly investigate the real-life group decision-making practices in engineering design and also study different schools of studies that contribute to this topic.

In real-life engineering design processes, engineers always need to negotiate with each other in order to reach agreement when they have conflicting opinions and competing demands. The ability to negotiate with multiple stakeholders who have different technical expertise and diverse social backgrounds (e.g., many other nontechnical factors) is just as important as the ability to analyze design parameters and build system modules in engineering design. This ability is the key to making a rational group decision in light of different objectives, criteria, and perspectives. The process through which rational decision are jointly made in collaborative engineering design is indeed a collaborative negotiation process. Traditionally, negotiation has been considered in a distributive context where the goals, values, and interests of the parties are in conflict [Sycara 1990]. However, there are many situations where integrative types of negotiation occur. In these situations, the parties have to collaboratively engage in a group problem-solving process characterized by increased cooperativeness and consensus seeking through information sharing and restructuring [Shakun 1988]. Engineering design is an example of such a collaborative negotiation process. It exemplifies situations that admit conflict needing negotiation. In other words, although the overall situation is collaborative, conflict might arise on proposing technical solutions to achieve objectives, set up evaluation criteria, integrating perspectives which choosing between, and agree upon proposals. Such situations are very common in engineering teams where, although team members have common high-level goals for the entire design process they are engaged in, conflicts also frequently arise for a specific design task. In order to effectively resolve these conflicts, especially in group decision making in a distributed and asynchronous workspace such as modern engineering design, one of the critical requirements is to structure the negotiation arguments from multiple decision makers based on their objectives and perspectives, in order to make sure that all stakeholders have a common ground for negotiation and can effectively make group decisions through the negotiation process.

Collaborative negotiation and conflict resolution have been well-researched areas for the past several decades. Although they have been examined from several perspectives including social science, economics, decision theory, engineering design, and artificial intelligence [Nash 1950, Keeney and Raiffa 1976, Raiffa 1982, Davis and Smith 1983, Sycara 1991, Bui 1987, Shakun 1992], it is only recently that frameworks for supporting collaborative negotiation and conflict resolution have emerged [Kersten 1985, Durfee and Lesser 1989, Hunks and Gasser 1989, Jelassi and Foroughi 1989, Kersten et al., 1991, Sycara 1989, Lim and Benbasat 1991, Bui 1993, Bui 1994]. Although these works have developed some theoretical approaches and systematic methods to support collaborative negotiation and conflict resolution in general, when facing the challenges of group decision-making processes in modern engineering design, none of them have either built theoretical foundations or provided practical guideline to identify and organize the objectives and preferences from decision makers and structure the negotiation arguments based on the technical propositions and these organized objectives and perspectives in order to carry out an effective collaborative negotiation process in the virtual space. A new framework for grounding these structured arguments must be established via a thorough study of the existing work and deep knowledge of real-life decision-making activities. Based on this framework, we can develop systematic models to utilize these structure arguments to support effective collaborative negotiation.

Specifically, this paper presents a sociotechnical collaboration negotiation approach to help an engineering design team structure their negotiation argument with both social and technical factors and guide them through an operational and systematic process where their arguments can be generated, exchanged, the and evaluated. This approach helps stakeholders reconcile design conflicts by analyzing their perspectives and the evolution of these perspectives in social interaction, and then recommending potential conflict management strategies, such as rearranging the design team or refining their proposals and/or objectives. This paper also presents the design, implementation, and application of a computer supported negotiation system that is being developed based on the negotiation approach presented here to support real-life engineering design collaboration.

The rest of this paper is organized as follows: Section 8.2 reviews the literatures relevant to this research work and discusses several underlying theoretical backgrounds for the proposed approach. The overall sociotechnical collaborative negotiation approach is presented in Section 8.3. It describes the integration between a sociotechnical co-construction process and a generic argument structure to build a negotiation approach for engineering design. The section explains how the design arguments are generated, exchanged, and evaluated. It also illustrates how we analyze stakeholders' perspectives and their evolution in order to resolve the design conflicts. Section 8.4 presents the architecture and functionalities of a software prototype, called IWANT, which implements, and demonstrates the application of, the proposed approach. As well, some ongoing case studies and empirical results are described. Lastly, Section 8.5 summarizes this presented research and outlines our planned future work.

8.2 Reviews of Related Studies

As mentioned in Section 8.1, the engineering design is a collaborative negotiation process between various departments which have to socially interact and make technical decisions for engineering design tasks. This process is involved with multiple stakeholders who are geographically distributed, cross-disciplinary, and asynchronously communicating. Our challenge is to identify and organize these stakeholders' objectives and perspectives, and then structure their arguments with this organized information in order to support their group decisions and resolve the decision conflicts through the collaborative negotiation process. To put the discussion in perspective, this section reviews a variety of disciplines in relations to group decision and conflict resolution. Our previous work in collaborative negotiation is also discussed in this section.

8.2.1 Group Decision Studies

Decision scientists interested in group decisions have investigated various negotiation models and decision analysis functionalities that help to achieve group consensus among multiple interests and competing positions of stakeholders. However, these models and functionalities have not provided full support to decision makers who have to identify, organize, and integrate their multidisciplinary objectives and perspectives from distributed locations and asynchronous communications. The schools of study in this field include game-theoretic analysis [Rosenschein and Zlotkin 1994, Kraus 2001, Sandholm 2002a]; heuristic-based approaches [Faratin 2000, Kowalczyk and Bui 2001, Fatima et al. 2002, Kraus 2001, Klein 1995]; and argumentation-based approaches [Kraus et al. 1998; Parsons et al. 1998; Sierra et al. 1998]. The details of each study in relations to our work are explained below.

Rooted in economics, game theory studies interactions between self-interested agents. The objective of game theory is to determine the best (i.e., most rational) decision a player can make, using mathematical modeling. In order to do so, the player must take into account the decisions that other agents can make and must assume that they will act rationally as well. A solution in game theory is generally found when players' strategies are in equilibrium: a player's strategy is the best response to the others' strategies. Tools from game theory can help decision makers understand and predict the outcome of a negotiation and then help them make strategic decisions in group decision-making process [Nagarajan and Sosic 2008]. Game theory can be divided into two main approaches. Noncooperative game theory is strategy oriented, meaning it studies what players will do in a specific context in order to win over their opponent. In contrast, cooperative game theory studies how players can cooperate to reach a win-win situation when the global gains are higher with cooperation than without. A frequently mentioned drawback of game theoretic approaches is the perfect rationality assumption. In order to select the best strategy, the player must know the entire environment as well as the opponent's knowledge. Otherwise, it is not possible for the player to estimate the most rational choice. Unfortunately, in real world situations, players can hide some information from their partners in the decision-making process. So an effective and systematic method to elicit and organize the information from each team member is still in need to make rational group decision using game theoretical approaches.

A way to overcome the game theory limitations described previously is to use heuristic approaches. Heuristic-based negotiation is based on search strategies where the objective, instead of finding the optimal solution, is to find a good solution in a reasonable time. Multiple approaches can be used, depending on the search strategy deployed. Stakeholders do not need to be perfectly rational, and information can be kept private. Basically, the space of possible agreements is represented by contracts having different values for each issue. Using its own utility function, a stakeholder must compute the value of each contract. Proposals and counter-proposals are exchanged over the different contracts and search terminates either when the time limit has been reached or when a mutually acceptable solution has been found. Kraus presented a review of applications of heuristics to negotiations and pointed out where it represents an advantage over other approaches [Kraus 1998]. Klein worked on a simulated annealing-based approach for negotiation of multi-interdependent issues in contracts [Klein et al. 2003]. Rahwan has worked on defining a method for designing heuristics-based negotiation strategies for negotiation agents by analyzing the environment and the agent capabilities [Rahwan et al. 2007]. While heuristic methods do indeed overcome some of the shortcomings of game-theoretic approaches, they also have a number of disadvantages [Jennings et al. 2001]. First, the models often lead to outcomes that are suboptimal, because the information and space that the negotiation team can explore is always limited by the design of the heuristics method, which is usually ad hoc. Second, because of the ad hoc design of the heuristic method, it is very difficult to predict precisely how the team and stakeholders will behave and there is usually no guaranteed solution at the end of the execution of the heuristics. Consequently, these approaches usually need extensive evaluation through simulations and empirical analysis, which is not often available due to the resource limitation in engineering processes.

Argument-based negotiation approaches follow a generic structure of arguments defined in [Toulmin 1958] which helps stakeholders lay out their negotiation information and meta-information into various components, and this information includes major claims, support data, and additional persuasive perspectives such as justification, degree of desire, and rebuttal condition. In the negotiation approaches presented previously, stakeholders cannot justify to their partner why they refuse an offer or what part of the offer was problematic. Proposals do not include the explanations of the positions and considerably limit the potential of negotiation. The idea behind argumentation-based negotiations is precisely to give this additional information (e.g., a justification about why the partner should accept a proposal) to stakeholders, helping the negotiation process by identifying part of the support data and background information that does not get explored otherwise. Different authors have presented applications of argumentation-based negotiation models [Buttner 2006, Atkinson et al. 2005, Capobianco et al. 2005, Jennings et al. 2001]. These approaches can increase the efficiency of the negotiation process by adding information that was not used before. By revealing new information, the partner can be persuaded that a certain proposal is better than thought. Based on the advantage of these approaches in systematically and effectively organizing and conveying stakeholders' perspectives, argument-based negotiation approaches have been our major concern in this work. One of the main limitations of these approaches is that the stakeholder must be able to analyze the arguments and calculate their value in order to better understand the relationship between the arguments, or choose one best argument. This is because, although Toulmin defined the generic and well-adopted argument structure, he proposed his views on argumentation informally in loosely specifying how arguments relate to other arguments and providing little guidance as how to evaluate the best [Zeleznikow 2002]. It is still more intended as a way of checking and arranging arguments for overlooked flaws [Houp, Pearsall, and Tebeaux 1998] instead of directly supporting group decision-making such as specifying the relationship between the structured argument and the governing factors in decision making (e.g., stakeholders' objectives and perspectives).

8.2.2 Conflict Resolution Studies

The effective ways to solve the conflict problems will enhance the team productivity and improve the quality of the product. One of the critical objectives of this proposed approach is to derive a theoretical basis that can be used to solve the different types of conflict during the design process. The current research approaches on design conflict management can be generally divided into three areas according to their theoretical backgrounds. They are the artificial intelligence approach, economic and behavioral approach, and explicit engineering design models. Their details are briefly introduced below.

Many AI researchers take the problem-solving approaches to resolve design conflict. Their approaches build searching algorithms, capture agent dependencies, or develop knowledge-base systems. Some of them view collaborative design as a distributed dynamic interval constraint-satisfaction problem and develop algorithms that use heuristics for distributed design [Campbell 1999, Tiwari and Gupta 1995]. Klein introduced the concept of conflict resolution expertise. His approach used computational models that actually encode conflict resolution expertise more explicitly and use it to maintain the dependencies during cooperative problem solving. In his cooperative design model, design agents can be viewed as being made up of a design component that can update and critique designs, as well as a conflict resolution component that resolves design agent conflict [Klein 1995]. Dunsus tried to use many small, cooperating, and limited-function expert systems to build an integrated system to investigate conflict. It provides ways of discovering and testing the components of negotiation, patterns of communication, functional primitives of design, and the types of knowledge needed [Dunskus 1995]. Wong proposed a cooperative problem-solving approach to handle the conflicts among distributed design agents [Wong 1997]. He classified conflicts into schema conflicts, data conflicts, and knowledge conflicts, and proposed four modes of conflict resolution (Inquiry, Arbitration, Persuasion, and Accommodation).

Other research works focus on the negotiation strategies of conflict resolution based on economic or behavioral theory. Bahler introduced a protocol of evaluating compromise solutions to conflicts in collaborative negotiations [Bahler 1995]. The protocol is based on the notions of economic utility by which design advice systems can recognize conflict and mediate negotiation fairly. The basic idea is to allow expressed preferences of design teams to be qualitative as well as quantitative. Several approaches are proposed to handle conflicts in design by modeling conflict as the multi-objective decision problem [Kannapan and Taylor 1994, Kraus, Wilkenfeld, and Zlotkin 1995, Petrie et al. 1995, Lewis and Mistree 1997, Wellman 1995]. One of them is concerned with global metrics for optimization, decision support, and negotiation. The coordination function is supported by some optimization methodology, such as Pareto optimality and multi-attribute utility [Petrie et al. 1995]. Game theory has been used as a typical method for generating compromise solutions in many research approaches. Vincent examined the role of game theory in the engineering design process in 1983. He examined the multi-criteria optimization task from the perspective of team design [Vincent 1993]. A modified game theory approach to multi-objective optimization has been used in conflict resolution as a combination of optimization steps [Rao and Freiheit 1991].

The engineering design models also have some mechanisms applicable to resolving design conflict. For instance, QFD (Quality Function Deployment) is a structured process that establishes customer value using the "voice of the customer" and transforms that value to design, production, and supportability process characteristics [Hauser and Clausing 1988]. The result of QFD analysis is a systems engineering process that ensures product quality as defined by the customers. This is essentially a methodology to solve/mitigate the conflicts among the diversified customer needs, which mainly exist in the early phases of engineering design. The Independence Axiom in Axiomatic design [Suh 1990] states that the independence of Functional Requirements must be always maintained to reduce the random search process and minimize the iterative trial-and-error process. It claims that a product design that ignores this axiom will face substantial conflicts.

To summarize the above, we now discuss the contributions and limitations of the previous works on conflict resolution. The AI-based approaches and the economic/

behavioral approaches mainly focus on conflict resolution itself rather than its origin and influence in the whole process of engineering design. However, as the design process is being conducted and the design environment evolving, it is difficult to use one category of methods to deal with all of the conflicts [Kilker 1999]. Most of them assume that design stakeholders are purely reasonable and their preferences can be represented by utility functions. However, utility theory has intrinsic limitations on conflict resolution and collaboration support [Binmore 1987]. The critical reason is that in collaborative design, the meanings and concepts are defined during the interaction rather than before the interaction. Many conflicts are actually caused by the different objectives and competing perspectives of stakeholders. Only after these objectives and perspectives are identified and shared among the stakeholders, can utility theory take effect to handle conflict. Conflict resolution is highly coupled with the technical decisions and social interaction. For example, although game theory provides quite complicated methodologies to solve the conflict problems in economics, the use of them in engineering design requires a deep understanding of the nature of design decision making (e.g., collaborative negotiation) in order to adapt the game-playing models. The rightness of the analysis (e.g., build utility functions and determine the strategies of players) depends on the comprehension of the attributes of design participants, the design tasks, and the design situation.

The other deficiency of these approaches is that they mainly can contribute to how to resolve the conflicts after they show up, rather than identify the source of these conflicts and prevent them from happening, which is actually a very effective way for conflict resolution. Using the engineering design models to resolve conflict is a prospective approach to solve the problem. But most of the current design models do not take supporting collaborative design as one of their primary goals. They assume that strictly following their guidelines will significantly reduce the chance of conflict. Overall, all works mentioned above suggest conflict detection mechanisms, define conflict resolution strategies, and provide support to manage the negotiation between different actors involved in the conflict. However, none of them identifies the objectives and analyses the perspectives of involved stakeholders leading to recognizing the source of conflicts, resolving these conflicts with more focused and operational strategy, and preventing them from happening again. This objective identification and perspective analysis is a critical phase for conflict resolution since conflicts originate from different objectives and competing perspectives. How to effectively handle this phase by structuring stakeholders' negotiation arguments with this information is still a critical challenge in supporting group decisions and conflict resolution in engineering design.

8.2.3 Collaborative Negotiation in Engineering

As mentioned earlier, though extensive research has been done in the field of negotiation, various limitations exist. Most of the existing practices have not specified a practical means to identify and organize objectives and perspectives among multiple stakeholders, nor an operational approach to guide the stakeholders through a negotiation process where their perspectives are analyzed for conflict resolution. In order to resolve this challenge in our work, in this section we will review our previous work in a well-designed Socio-Technical Co-construction Process (STCP) which is rooted in an Engineering Collaboration via Negotiation (ECN) paradigm and a Sociotechnical Framework (STF). This work helps us specify operational guidance for the engineering design team to carry out a negotiation process utilizing structured arguments for negotiation tasks. This section will explain these concepts (i.e., ECN, STF, and STCP) in details.

8.2.3.1 Engineering Collaboration via Negotiation Paradigm

Real-world negotiation tasks undertaken by engineering teams are always driven by many conflicting social, economical, and technical (SET) factors. Traditional engineering research has mainly focused on technical factors, with some recent efforts being extended to consider the economic factors. While recognizing the importance of both technical and economical considerations, our past research has been focusing on social factors and, more specifically, on their interactions with technical factors. We view an engineering team activity as a technical activity with a human purpose. Therefore, when a team of engineers (i.e., multiple stakeholders) with differing life cycle concerns come together to develop new software, it can lead to a complex sociotechnical campaign. To resolve this challenge, an Engineering Collaboration via Negotiation (ECN) paradigm is developed in our past work and can best support this type of sociotechnical campaign.

In this paradigm, we have defined the meanings of several key concepts that lay down the foundation for the research framework and process. Now we first give the definition of ECN: a sociotechnical negotiation activity, where a team of stakeholders with different expertise and mixed objectives co-construct consensual agreements of some engineering matter.

More details regarding the concepts used in this definition are explained as follows:

8.2.3.1.1 Sociotechnical

Compared with traditional approaches, ECN treats engineering decision making as a technical activity within dynamic social contexts instead of a purely technical activity.

8.2.3.1.2 Negotiation

With a general definition "to confer with another so as to arrive at the settlement of some matter," given by Webster's dictionary, we limit ourselves in the domain of engineering domain and negotiation is viewed as an on-going activity of social decision making, where two or more interdependent parties with some common or conflicting interests engage in back-and-forth communication aimed at reaching a settlement.

8.2.3.1.3 Stakeholders

Stakeholders are parties with direct or indirect interests in the outcomes of a common undertaking. Regardless of whether stakeholders are directly involved in a decision at a particular moment, they are always given the opportunity to express their perspectives toward that decision in the ECN approach. The stakeholder perspectives evolve dynamically through the co-construction process in ECN.

8.2.3.1.4 Different Expertise

In ECN, engineering expertise must be expanded from purely natural sciences to include not only all social, economical, and technical (S.E.T.) knowledge but also the ability to negotiate effectively with other stakeholders. This expansion requires techniques that go beyond the traditional engineering approaches. The sociotechnical framework developed in our research is an example of these new techniques and will be discussed in the next section.

8.2.3.1.5 Mixed Objectives

ECN focuses on the knowledge of artificial which is based on human agreements. Human agreements are driven by their objectives. Objectives can be in concert or in conflict, which in turn determines stakeholders' various cooperative or adversarial decision behaviors and leads to the final agreement or disagreement.

8.2.3.1.6 Co-Construct/Co-Construction

Co-construction is a key activity in ECN. In ECN, the stakeholders' perspectives are influenced by each other and mutually modified through negotiation, and finally arrive at a shared reality (e.g., new knowledge in the form of consensual agreements) of a particular matter. This makes ECN different from the traditional engineering, in which the perspectives of stakeholders are assumed to be static.

8.2.3.1.7 Consensual Agreements

Unlike traditional engineering approaches that search for precise answers optimized for predefined objectives, the final outcomes of ECN are consensual agreements that suffice to meet the interests of all involved stakeholders. When stakeholders reach consensual agreements, it indicates that, for all parties, the payoffs from the consequences of joint decisions are better than if each party had decided to go-it-alone. In ECN, consensual agreements are the consequences of joint decisions.

They are negotiation process dependent, and change with the stakeholders' objectives and/or social settings.

8.2.3.2 A Sociotechnical Framework

Based on this ECN paradigm, we have developed a Sociotechnical Framework (STF) as a foundation to pursue basic research in collaborative negotiation. The STF has its roots in the Social Construction Theory proposed by Peter Berger and Thomas Luckmann in 1966 [Berger and Luckmann 1967], which states that meaning and institutions (e.g., a collaborative decision during engineering design) are a jointly negotiated and agreed construction between those participating in an endeavor. More specifically, our STF uses perspective models of stakeholders to integrate social interactions with technical decisions, and then uses these models to manage decision conflicts during a co-construction process undertaken by the engineering team. As shown in Figure 8.1, the three core components of our STF research framework are: (1) technical decision processes undertaken by the engineering team, (2) perspective models of stakeholders, and (3) conflict management strategies for collaborative negotiation [Lu and Cai 2001]. The technical decision process refers to a series of tasks and states that must be performed by stakeholders according to some pre-established steps adapted from the specific domain practices or mandated by corporate policies. Perspective models describe stakeholders' viewpoints towards the concepts in a particular design campaign. Conflict management provides guidance to reconcile decision conflicts by managing decision-making processes and helping stakeholders co-construct stakeholders' perspectives.

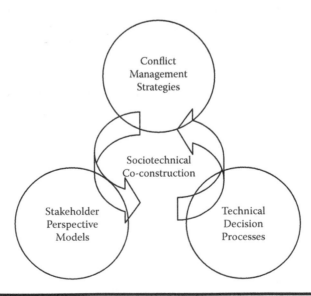

Figure 8.1   The key components of the sociotechnical framework.

8.2.3.3 A Sociotechnical Co-Construction Process

Based on the foundations of ECN diagram and the STF framework, we have taken the next step to develop a generic engineering collaboration process through which can be further detailed into a collaborative negotiation process. This process, which we call the Sociotechnical Co-construction process (STCP), specifies eight steps with sufficient operational details as shown in Figure 8.2:

I. Define a starting "baseline process" for the chosen application domains, as the basis to be co-constructed (i.e., changed) later, upon the agreement by all involved stakeholders.

II. Identify a group of "stakeholders" who have an interest in the outcomes of, and will directly or indirectly participate in, the co-construction process of a particular collaborative campaign.

III. Propose an initial "concept structure" for a particular engineering process to organize the concepts provided by the team.

IV. Establish the initial "perspective model" for all participating stakeholders to express opinions for each concept in the concept structure.

V. Build the "perspective model state diagram" (PMSD) for each concept in the concept structure.

VI. Perform the "perspective analysis" on the current PMSD to understand the closeness or distance of different stakeholders' perspectives at that particular moment.

VII. Conduct the "conflict management" tasks according to the results perspective analysis.

VIII. Obtain a "shared reality" as a result of the co-construction process. This final product of the STC process is a shared reality, which is a broader concept than traditional approaches (e.g., a finished design in terms of a product model).

The sociotechnical co-construction process (STCP) provides us with research context and grounds of building a new negotiation process, as STCP lays out the basic steps to guide the stakeholders through the process of co-constructing group decisions. However, stakeholders who work in STCP are required to fully share their proposals, objectives, and perspectives, yet they have not been guided about how to organize this information to structure the negotiation arguments during the process.

8.3 A Sociotechnical Collaborative Negotiation Approach Using Structured Arguments

Engineering design is a group decision-making process that is often carried by a team of stakeholders who cross geography, disciplinary, and temporal boundaries. One of the practical challenges to support the effective collaborative negotiation

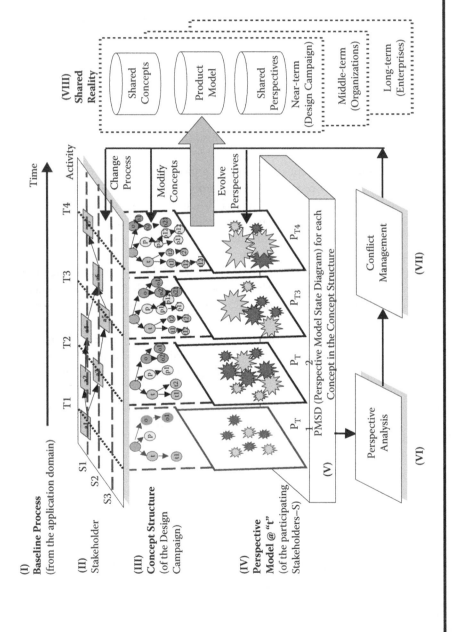

Figure 8.2 The sociotechnical coconstruction process (STCP).

in group decisions is to identify, organize, and integrate the competing objectives and varying perspectives from the distributed, cross-disciplinary, and asynchronous stakeholders. Existing approaches of supporting group decision cannot satisfy these challenges posed by modern engineering design. To address the challenge of supporting collaborative negotiation for group decision making in a distributed and asynchronous workspace like modern engineering design, one of the critical requirements is to structure the negotiation arguments with organized objectives and perspectives from the stakeholders, in order to making sure that all stakeholders have a common ground for achieving mutual understanding and making rational group decisions for engineering design process. With the well-shared information, we can develop specific methods to analyze stakeholders' perspectives and resolve the conflicts caused by the differences in these perspectives.

To address the aforementioned challenges, this work proposes a sociotechnical collaborative negotiation approach to support the group decisions in engineering design. This approach first devises a collaborative negotiation process and then synthesizes it with a generic argument structure. This synthesis entails the negotiation arguments to be structured with both social characteristics (e.g., including stakeholders' objectives and perspectives) and technical factors (e.g., design proposals). With this synthesis, the collaborative negotiation process specifies how the structured arguments can be generated, exchanged, and evaluated in a systematic way. In this process, the stakeholders' perspectives can be analyzed to help stakeholders obtain better understanding of each other's positions and suggest appropriate conflict resolution strategies. The following sections define the key terminologies for this approach (in Section 3.1), give an overview of this sociotechnical collaborative negotiation process (in Section 3.2), propose its synthesis with the generic argument structure (in Section 3.3), and then (in Section 3.4) discuss the process in greater details.

8.3.1 Definitions of Terminologies

This work focuses on managing negotiation tasks in which a team of engineers must collaborate with each other to design an engineering solution. The subject of collaborative negotiation in engineering design is part of an emerging research field, called *collaborative engineering*. In this new research field, collaborative engineering is defined as a sociotechnical group decision-making process, whereby a team of engineers collaborate to resolve conflicts, bargain for individual or collective advantages, agree upon courses of action, and/or craft joint decisions that serve their mutual interests. Unlike traditional engineering tasks, which are often treated as a purely technical decision-making process of "task-work" by an individual, collaborative engineering tasks are, additionally, a social endeavor of teamwork by a team of individuals. In practice, collaborative engineering is best carried out in a "team" environment where, unlike a "work group," all team members have already agreed on a common goal to achieve. Based on this belief, engineering design is essentially a human-based, interdisciplinary teamwork, and must be modeled as sociotechnical collaboration accordingly.

In our research, "social" refers to the behaviors that take the interests of others and the common stakeholder characteristics, which influence collaborative team dynamics during social interactions such as background, objective, and perspectives. The dominant characteristics of design stakeholders (engineer, architect, managers, etc.) tend of be such issues as choice of programming languages, preferred development methodologies, expectation from project work and design team, and career goal in the organization. They are initially brought into the collaborative teamwork by the participating stakeholders, and then continuously co-constructed and evolved during the social interaction process. Based on the above meanings, the term "sociotechnical" signifies the mutual consideration of and the true integration between the social (teamwork) and technical (task-work) aspects of engineering activities.

In order to manage the social interaction in the design team, in our research we also define the "perspective" as the particular attitudes (i.e., viewpoints) via which the stakeholder views his/her own objectives and others' when making decisions (e.g., a strong desire for achieving one's own objective, and supporting or disagreeing with others' objectives). Furthermore, the conflict needs to be defined in this work: its general definition is "an argument about something important or a state of opposition between persons in idea or interests" and specifically in our research, conflict is defined as the argument between stakeholders about the design tasks, At the root of this argument are the differences in stakeholders' perspectives on various points of view, based on their understanding of the design task and their estimation regarding the achievements of the objectives. The conflict is therefore identified in the design task and to resolve it in collaborative design requires the explicit modeling and careful analysis of stakeholder perspectives.

In summary, the above definitions in our research explicitly acknowledge collaborative design tasks as a dynamic interface between individual decisions and group interactions, and as an assimilation of social and technical activities operating in parallel over different time, space, and discipline scales in an engineering team.

8.3.2 Overview of the Collaborative Negotiation Process

The sociotechnical collaborative negotiation process is the main strength of this approach. It describes how the stakeholders structure the negotiation arguments using both social factors (such as stakeholders' objectives and perspectives) and technical decisions (such as design task proposals) and then carries out the negotiation process in order to reach an agreement. Figure 8.3 to follow illustrates this integrated approach, which has three inter-related phases.

First, the *pre-negotiation phase* starts with identifying a set of "stakeholders" who have an interest in the outcome of the co-construction process, in which they will

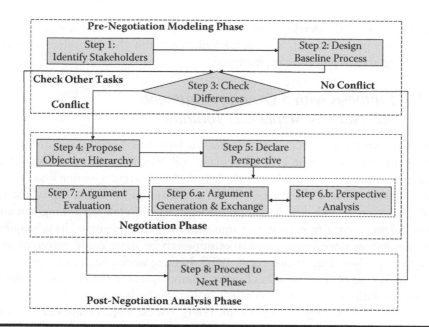

Figure 8.3   A collaborative negotiation process for engineering design.

directly or indirectly participate in the baseline process of engineering design. This approach also needs to employ a baseline process that captures the required technical task-work in a predetermined order. For example, it can be a commonly accepted design "workflow" suggested by the domain experts or standard operating procedures instituted by the company. The team starts the design process, asks each stakeholder to propose an implementation for specific tasks in the design process, and checks the differences (i.e., conflict) between implementation proposals. Then it determines whether to initiate a negotiation by identifying conflicting design proposals.

Second, the *negotiation phase* helps the stakeholders structure their arguments, and guides them into a negotiation process using the structured arguments. In this phase, the stakeholders jointly propose an objective hierarchy that organizes all the objectives and declares their perspectives (e.g., preferences) based on the objectives and design task proposals. Then, based on the design tasks, objectives, and perspectives, the stakeholders are guided to systematically generate and exchange their negotiation arguments. Perspective analysis will be taken to help the stakeholders better understand each other and reconcile their decision conflicts. If no argument is commonly accepted at the end of exchanging the arguments, all the arguments will be evaluated by aggregating stakeholders' preferences and ranked to recommend an optimal choice, or a well-informed team leader will make the choice based on the evaluation results.

Lastly, the *post-negotiation phase* with only one step assures that the stakeholders obtain a commonly accepted engineering design implementation and proceed to the next phase of the development life cycle. The following sections explain these three phases in more detail. Section 8.3.3 discusses how the structured argument in this negotiation process is implemented.

8.3.3 Synthesis with a Generic Argument Structure by Stephen E. Toulmin

The "structured argument" in our approach is built based on the Toulmin structure of argument [Toulmin 1958]. Practicing collaborative design and negotiating dialogue have been found to be positively linked with argumentation and critical thinking skills [Hart 1990, Parsons, Sierra, and Jennings 1998, Jin, Geslin and Lu 2005, Marttunen 1992, Smith 1977]. Furthermore, the work of Buckingham and his colleagues argue that exposing an argument's structure facilitates its subsequent communication since important relationships can be more easily perceived and analyzed by others [Buckingham et al. 1997]. In these works, Stephen E. Toulmin's 1958 work, Uses of Argument, has become commonplace in structuring argumentation. Toulmin acknowledges as much in his the preface to his 1979 text, *An Introduction to Reasoning* [Toulmin et al. 1984]. For example, Houp, Pearsall, and Teheaux's textbook, *Reporting Technical Information*, introduces Toulmin logic as providing "a way of checking your own arguments for those overlooked flaws. It can also help you arrange your argument" [Houp et al. 1998].

Argumentation is a process of making assertions (claims) and providing support and justification for these claims using data, facts, and evidence [Toulmin 1958]. The goal of argumentation in negotiation is to persuade or convince others that one's reasoning is more valid or appropriate. Toulmin's model of argument provides the language symbols and data structure that supports the argumentation process. Toulmin's model, as shown in Figure 8.4, is procedural, and the layout of this model focuses on the movement of accepted data to the claim through a warrant. Toulmin also recognizes three secondary elements that may be present in an argument: backing, qualifier, and rebuttal. Backing is the authority for a warrant and provides credibility for the warrant; it may be introduced when the audience is unwilling to accept the warrant. A qualifier indicates the degree of force or certainty that a claim possesses. Finally, rebuttal represents certain conditions or exceptions under which the claim will fail and hence anticipates objections that might be advanced against the argument to refute the claim [Toulmin 1958]. As such, Toulmin's argument structure becomes a mechanism for structuring argumentation between negotiating stakeholders. It aims to clarify reasoning by encouraging parties to make explicit important assumptions, distinctions, and relationships as they construct and rationalize ideas [Buckingham et al., 1997].

We selected Toulmin's argument structures to investigate negotiation after considering a number of possible approaches and structures applied or developed for negotiation [Janssen and Sage 1996]. Negotiation is a process that involves both qualitative and quantitative concepts. Many of the formal approaches such

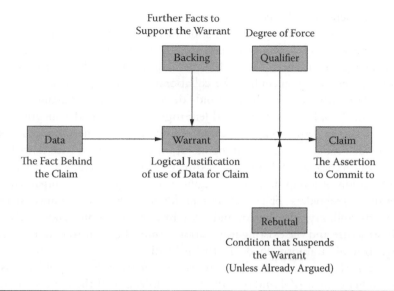

Figure 8.4 Toulmin's argument structure.

as game theory and decision analysis have focused traditionally on the quantitative aspects of negotiation including goals, alternatives, and consequences. The qualitative aspects of negotiation such as argumentation, social interactions, and negotiators' perspectives are typically given low priority and are subsumed in other quantitative concepts, although they are important in their own respect from a practical viewpoint because in many cases negotiation approaches directly impact the negotiation outcome. The negotiation approach proposed in this work will capture these qualitative aspects of negotiation through the use of argumentation methodologies.

Also, Jassen and Sage's study shows there are several advantages to a graphical or structured depiction (i.e., boxes and lines as in Toulmin's argument structure) than natural language description [Janssen and Sage 1996]. They have stated the reasons as follows: first, visualization eases comprehension. The components of the argument are explicitly represented, meaning that it is easier to identify the particular elements of an argument, and these elements of the structure provide stakeholders for the elements, thereby facilitating elicitation of these elements. Second, it is easy for the person filing the boxes to see what is missing as well as the reasoning that has been put forth. In this regard it is easier to compare arguments between multiple experts, and between claims and counterclaims than between statements in generally unstructured discourse [Janssen and Sage 1996].

It is true that using Toulmin's argument structure, which is generally more objective than implicit arguments, it is hard for stakeholders to hide bias because the grounds and backing of an argument are clearly listed and described to support the claims. Therefore, all stakeholders' perspectives are generally relatively easy to be observed by others through examination of the ground and warrants that the stakeholder expresses [Janssen and Sage 1996]. As mentioned earlier in this section, argument structure has been used to build an argument-based negotiation process model in many studies, including the collaborative design previously mentioned and proved to facilitate more objective and fair communication [Chang et al. 1995, Sillince et al. 1999, Parsons, Sierra, and Jennings 1998, Amgoud et al. 2000, Avery et al. 2001, Kraus 2001, Rong et al. 2002]. However, this generic structure is still more intended for checking and arranging arguments for overlooked flaws [Houp, Pearsall, and Tebeaux 1998] instead of directly providing support for collaborative negotiation of group decision in engineering design, such as organizing and integrating stakeholders' objectives and preferences in a well-defined structure for cross-disciplinary, distributed, and asynchronous decision makers. Also, this generic structure and the existing negotiation approaches that were built based on this structure often informally define the utilization of structured arguments and loosely specify how arguments relate to other arguments with little guidance as how best to evaluate them [Zeleznikow 2002]. Therefore, one of the critical challenges to structure arguments to support collaborative negotiation of group decision in engineering design is to structure arguments with organized objectives and perspectives, to develop models that utilize these structured arguments, and to analyze the well-shared perspectives to understand the arguments' relationship and resolve decision conflict for carrying out effective collaborative negotiation.

Our approach has proposed a synthesis between the collaborative negotiation process presented in the last section and this structure to organize the critical information for negotiation based on both social and technical factors. On the technical side, the baseline design tasks model the stakeholders' decisions for the design tasks (i.e., design task proposals) and objective hierarchy helps stakeholders share their understanding of the design tasks in terms of objectives. On the social side, the objective hierarchy helps the stakeholders declare their perspectives on each design task proposals based on how well these proposals achieve the objectives. These perspectives have a great impact on the technical decisions and represent the characteristics of social interaction among the stakeholders. Figure 8.5 describes a synthesis between the data flow in the collaborative negotiation and the argument structure. As shown in the figure, the technical factors in the collaborative negotiation process provide the argument structure with the major elements (e.g., claim, warrant, and data) in the argument data structure. The social factors correspond to the secondary argument elements (e.g., backing, qualifier, and rebuttal).

As shown in Figure 8.5, the claim is proposed by the stakeholder and consists of a sequence of actions/objects to implement the task. The data specifies the current state of team agreement about the design process (e.g., tasks, objectives), and such agreement can be accomplished by previous tasks and arguments. This state of agreement actually describes the initial state of the task and therefore provides

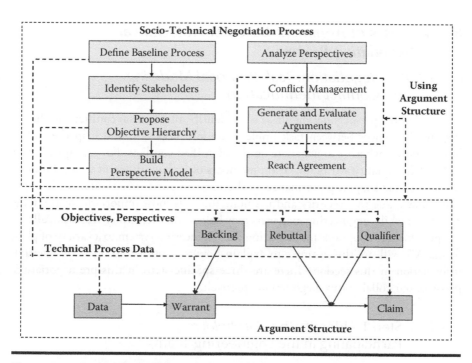

Figure 8.5 Synthesis: Collaborative negotiation process and argument structure.

background facts behind the claim. Stakeholders' objectives are in the place of the warrant, identifying the value that stakeholders want to achieve along with clarification of the relationship between the value and the current state of agreement. These objectives, as warrants, justify that the proposal can achieve the value based on the state of agreement (i.e., data). The attributes of each objective, corresponding to the "backing" component, further explain the objectives by describing their measurement criteria and then validate the relationship among the objectives, the proposal, and the current state of agreement. Based on these objectives and attributes, the measurement result regarding the achievement of the aforementioned objectives by stakeholders' own proposal work as a "qualifier" to indicate the degree of desire of the stakeholders for the proposal. Similar results regarding the achievement of the objectives by others' proposals work as a "rebuttal" and describe possible conditions that could fail the claim or suspend the warrant.

When the stakeholders cannot agree upon task proposal, argument evaluation can be taken based on the level of the objectives to get the best choice. Based on the concrete meanings (proposals, objectives, attributes, measurement results) given to the argument components by its synthesis with the objective hierarchy. The next section will discuss how these structured arguments are utilized in a collaboration negotiation process in the sociotechnical framework.

8.3.4 Phases of Argument-Based Sociotechnical Negotiation Process

8.3.4.1 Pre-Negotiation: Task Proposal Modeling and Conflict Identification

The goal of the pre-negotiation phase is to identify all potential conflicts by checking the differences between task implementation proposals, and help the stakeholders decide whether to negotiate on the identified conflicts. For example, in the task "Define quality attributes," team members often have different views. Product managers may suggest performance as the most important attribute, while engineers may argue that security and maintainability is most important for the long run. Meanwhile, engineering managers may believe that versatility is critical, allowing possible future options for migrating the engineering system to a variety of platforms. We will use this example to explain how to capture and organize relevant information in this section. There are three specific steps in this pre-negotiation phase of our collaborative negotiation approach.

8.3.4.1.1 Step 1—Identify the *Stakeholders* Participating in the Engineering Team

Stakeholders are those engineering team members who have an interest in the process and/or outcome of the decisions (i.e., integration implementations) and may directly or indirectly participate in the negotiation process.

8.3.4.1.2 Step 2—Prescribe a *Baseline Design Process*

A baseline systems integration process is defined as a series of necessary technical task-work that must be undertaken by the team to design an engineering solution. Our approach takes this design process as the baseline to start with. This process and its associated standard design task-works are generally predefined based on the domain practices or chosen for the stakeholders by management. Also in this step, the engineering organization must set up common goals for the team to achieve and define a set of shared values that all team members follow during the design activities. Goals and values set the direction for the design team to identify and define their decision objectives in the negotiation phase.

8.3.4.1.3 Step 3—Ask Stakeholders to Implement the Design Tasks and Check the Difference in Their Implementation Details

Although stakeholders jointly work on the design tasks according to the baseline process prescribed previously, due to their divergent background, interest, experience, and expertise, they will undoubtedly come up with different technical decisions when proposing implementations for these tasks. In our approach, the implementation proposal of a design task is defined as a logical sequence of actions/ objects, combined with necessary resources including time and staff. For example, regarding the example task "define quality attributes," a possible implementation proposal can be specified as:

{Objects: performance, security, and versatility; actions: define performance, security, and usability as quality attributes according to the functional requirements; resources: the design teamwork for one day.}

Therefore, if there are different decisions, objects, or resources in the stakeholders' proposals for a specific design task, the team will declare a decision conflict. A typical conflict could be, for example, that the stakeholders are choosing different objects. Just like the example mentioned at the beginning of this section, the stakeholders' choice of objects (i.e., quality attributes) are different for the task. In case of a conflict, the process will continue on to the negotiation phase where arguments will be generated, exchanged, and evaluated for conflict resolution. Otherwise (i.e., if there is no conflicting decision), the process will move forward directly to the post-negotiation phase (see Section 3.4.3) with mutual agreements on how to implement all design tasks.

8.3.4.2 Negotiation: Utilizing Structured Arguments

In this phase, the participating stakeholders are guided to negotiate with each other based on structured arguments until a mutual agreement is reached. In most of the existing practices, an argument-based negotiation process is generally undertaken according to the following two stages:

- Stakeholders generate argument claims (or counter claims) for concerned issues and provide supporting data.
- Stakeholders exchange and respond to others' claims (or counter claims) and their associated supporting data [Sierra et al. 1998].

However, these practices have not resolved the challenges of analyzing how arguments relate to other arguments for refining conflicting arguments or how best to evaluate the arguments [Zeleznikow 2002]. In addition, most of them provide little guidance in how to generate arguments based on the decision-making process. As mentioned, what is in need is an operational negotiation process built that is based on the arguments to support group decision making. The novelty of our approach is to resolve this challenge by utilizing the structured arguments to design a collaborative negotiation process referencing the sociotechnical co-construction process, where these arguments can be generated, exchanged, and evaluated based on the synthesis between the structured arguments and the objective hierarchy. This phase consists of four steps (4, 5, 6, and 7). Steps 4 and 5 guide the stakeholders to building the objective hierarchy and declare stakeholders' perspectives. Steps 6 and 7 discuss how the perspectives can be analyzed and the arguments evaluated, based on the information collected in Steps 4 and 5.

8.3.4.2.1 Step 4—Propose an *Objective Hierarchy* for Identified Conflicting Design Task

Negotiating conflicting implementation proposals of a design task in the baseline process indicates some differences in the stakeholders' objectives and perspectives (i.e., preferences for arguments against the objectives achievement). These objectives includes the fundamental objectives for which the task is undertaken, the intermediate objectives that help achieve the fundamental objectives, and the objectives' attributes for measuring the proposal degree to which the objectives are achieved. These attributes should be understandable to every stakeholder. If an objective does not have any attributes that are used to interpret the objective (e.g., "network bandwidth of engineering system" is a attribute of the objective "increase the throughput of the system"), the attribute "support versus opposition" will be added. The stakeholders in later steps can declare their perspective as either support or opposition. In line with the goals defined at the beginning of the design process, the team should be able to identify objectives and attributes in this step.

As discussed earlier, our approach uses an objective hierarchy to organize the objectives and capture their differences. This hierarchy is jointly built by the stakeholders based on their understanding and expectations ("values") of the design tasks. And the objectives in this hierarchy will be dynamically changed by the social interactions among the stakeholders. In reference to the information in an objective hierarchy, the stakeholders can declare their preferences regarding how important the objectives (i.e., the weights of the objectives) are, and how much each proposal is supported or opposed. The latter will be obtained in the next step, based on the values assigned by the stakeholders for the objectives' attributes. The objective weights are collected in this step after these concepts are declared in the structure. In details, the relative importance of each objective is defined on a 1-to-10 scale as follows:

10 = Very important
 8 = Somewhat more important
 6 = Important
 4 = Somewhat less important
 2 = Very less important
 1 = Lowest importance

To get more accurate results, the objective weights were collected for each fundamental and means objective. After the perspectives were collected, the weight of each means objective was adjusted as the average value of its weight and the weight of its corresponding fundamental objective. The importance of an attribute was the same as that of its objective.

To explain the concept structure further, we continue to use the task "estimate quality attributes" as an example. Table 8.1 below describes this example objective hierarchy, including information about stakeholders, objectives, and criteria. There

Table 8.1   An Example Objective Hierarchy for Estimate Quality Attributes

Stakeholder	Fundamental objectives	Criteria	Mean objectives
Salesperson	Performance is first priority, especially response time. Security should also be guaranteed.	Sale is most important. All quality attributes should be measured by sale requirements first.	Integrated system needs to beat the previous versions of the systems in performance. Other considerations should yield to this.
Engineer	Performance, easy-to-maintain, security, and usability.	The quality attributes should be determined based on appropriate development resource and proof-of-concept.	Build a prototype to get software quality statistics.
Manager	Portability, performance, security, and usability.	Project responsibility and executive decisions.	Deploy the development environment on different platforms to ensure portability.

are three stakeholders in this example: salesperson, engineer, and manager. The salesperson's fundamental objectives are to guarantee performance and security and mean objective is to at least ensure the integrated system is better in quality than the previous version. Her criteria are that sale is most important and hence every attribute should be evaluated by sale requirements and marketing strength. The engineer, on the other hand, believes that performance, maintainability, security, and usability are most important, which could be achieved by building a prototype of the engineering system to test those attributes, and all decisions must be based on these criteria. Meanwhile, the objectives of the third stakeholder, the manager, include performance, security, usability, and portability, and his criteria may also include project responsibility and other executive decisions.

8.3.4.2.2 Step 5—Each Stakeholder Declares a Perspective Based on an Objective Hierarchy

Once an objective hierarchy is established by the team, each attribute of each objective should be assigned a value before the arguments are evaluated. In case of a natural attribute, the value was generally numeric and calculated by a commonly accepted method based on the individual case, such as average number of the clicks per use case or the total count of supported handset platform. In case of the added attribute "support versus opposition," each stakeholder can express their own perspectives via social interaction based on their expertise and understanding, and this opinion should describe their position of either supporting or opposing the argument according to how much the objective (to which the attribute belongs) can be accomplished if the argument is accepted.

Negotiation, where the stakeholders express and exchange their own opinions about the objectives and attributes, is generally a very complex human phenomenon in teamwork that consists of many inter-related psychological and organizational factors. There is no practical way that a complete analytical modeling of negotiation can be fully developed and incorporated for a group of decision makers. As a result, our approach takes a rather simplified view by focusing on modeling the dynamic impacts of negotiation (i.e., on the evolving "perspectives" of the stakeholders), as they express their opinions toward the design arguments and the objective hierarchy. These dynamically evolving perspectives are declared for the proposed objectives of which the stakeholders have common interests or some expertise. In other words, the perspective dynamically depicts a stakeholder's perceptions of his or others' design arguments based on the objectives. These perceptions could include the stakeholders' desire for their ideas to succeed and their support for or disagreement with how well their own or others' arguments can achieve the objectives, either proposed by themselves or others. Therefore, the perspectives indicate the difference in the stakeholders' perceptions that cause the conflict in the technical proposals of the tasks and put the negotiation into necessity. Moreover, these perspectives will be further analyzed in order to systematically evaluate the arguments in our negotiation approach.

Although stakeholder perspectives are often highly subjective in nature, some quantitative methods are needed in order to define the measurement scales of the perspectives and further analyze these perspectives for argument evaluation. In our research, we define a 1–10 measurement scale to quantify the stakeholders' perspectives of either supporting or opposing the arguments. In other words, when the task proposals were being evaluated, for the support-versus-opposition attribute, stakeholders declared their perspectives about the proposal's value based on their expertise and understanding. The perspective will be one of the following:

10 = Strong support, that is, the proposal will most likely help achieve the objective
 8 = Support, that is, the proposal will likely help achieve the objective
 6 = Neutrality (fair, unknown, or disinterested), that is, the proposal may not either contribute to or harm the achievement of the objective; or controversy, that is, the proposal may have some effect in achieving the objective, but the decision maker is not clear about what kind of effect it may have
 4 = Opposition, that is, the proposal will likely bring negative effects in achieving the objective

2 = Strong opposition, that is, the proposal will most likely bring detrimental effects in achieving the objective

1 = Strongest opposition, that is, the proposal will definitely bring detrimental effects in achieving the objective

For example, in the above "define quality attributes" design task, the proposal from the product manager is to define performance and usability. Her proposal will be measured by each stakeholder against every objective attribute. Table 8.2 describes the measurement results, which are either calculated by numeric value in case of a natural attribute or stakeholders' perspectives in case of a support-versus-opposition attribute.

8.3.4.2.3 Step 6a—Argument Generation and Exchange

In generating the negotiation arguments, claims and data are collected from the baseline process representing technical decisions. Warrant, backing, qualifiers, and rebuttals are obtained from the objective hierarchy and stakeholders' perspective models. Based on Toulmin's definition of structure, the claim is the proposal of the argument. In our approach, the claim is how a stakeholder proposes to implement the design task in terms of the sequence of the actions/objects. The data consists of the initial state of the task—the joint agreement achieved by the design team before they work on this task. The warrant is the set of the objectives that the team wants to achieve from this task based on the initial state. Therefore, the data actually validates the feasibility and applicability of the claim, and the warrant justifies validation between the data and the claim. The backing consists of the attributes of each objective that further explain the objectives by describing their measurement criteria and then validating the relationship among the objectives, the proposal, and the current state of agreement. Qualifier and rebuttal are actually the measurement results regarding how well the proposal achieves its own objectives and the objectives proposed by the team. The measurement results (qualifier) can indicate the degree of desire of the stakeholder for the proposal, while the measurement results (rebuttal) describe the possibility that the proposal (claim) fails.

To build a negotiation argument in this way, stakeholders will have a better understanding of each other because they share not only their claims but also their underlining reasons and desires (e.g., perspectives). Figure 8.6 describes an argument example from an engineer's perspective. As shown in the figure, the claim for the task "define quality attributes" is to define the attributes of performance and security for the engineering system. The data describes the initial state (of this task), which includes design requirements, application constraints, and architecture style. To justify the use of the data, the warrant has fundamental and intermediate objectives that state why the claim is proposed. The backing of this argument is the attributes that further explain the warrant by providing its measurement scales. The measurement result given by the engineer for his/her own objectives is included in a qualifier, while the measurement result for the team's objectives is the rebuttal that describes

Table 8.2   Stakeholders' Perspectives (Attribute Values) for Product Manager's Proposal

Objectives/attributes	Product manager	Engineer	Engineering manager	Average value
Performance–beat the performance of the previous versions of the systems.	Strong support (10)	Support (8)	Neutrality (6)	0.67
Usability–build a friendly user interface in the integrated system	Support (8)	Strong support (10)	Neutrality (6)	0.67
Maintainability–build a prototype system for estimating the efforts taken to integrate the systems-support versus opposition	Neutrality (6)	Support (8)	Controversy (6)	0
Security–build a prototype system for checking the best level of the data encryption which can be achieved—the maximum number of bits in the encryption algorithm which can be applied-support versus opposition	256	256	256	256
Portability–estimate the efforts of migrating the integrated system to a new engineering platform-support versus opposition	Support (8)	Neutrality (6)	Support (8)	0.67
Development cost– build a project roadmap having the workload estimation-support versus opposition	Controversy (6)	Neutrality (6)	Support (1)	0

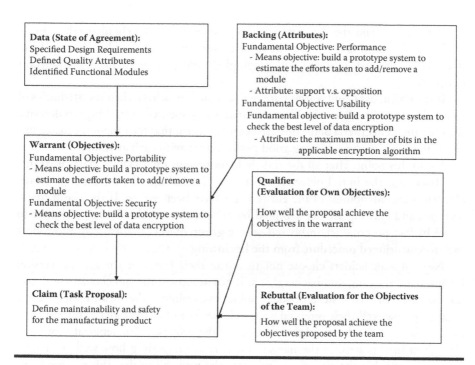

Figure 8.6   An example argument (by the engineer).

his perspective regarding the performance—how well his argument may achieve the objectives proposed by the entire team.

Different argument components can be exchanged in an order, instead of all at once; this exchange will continue only if the stakeholders have not reached a consensual agreement. Such an order of exchanging argument components is actually defined by the logic flow between the argument components. The claim should always be proposed first to clearly state the stakeholders' position. The data can be exchanged with the claim as it shows the facts behind the claim. In fact, we suggest that the claim and data should be exchanged together since presumably the claims are actually conflicting (otherwise negotiations aren't necessary) and thus it is necessary to present data in this step. After the data it should be the warrant that justifies the use of data for proving the claim. Backing comes next as further facts to support the warrant. The last two components that should be exchanged are qualifiers indicating the degree of desire for the proposal and the rebuttal indicating the condition that may suspend the warrant.

In details, the order of exchanging the arguments is defined as follows:

First, the stakeholder begins to work on the design task and develops her claim based on the data, that is, her task implementation proposal based on the state of agreement that can validate the proposal is a further effort to achieve the goals.

If the claim and the data are not accepted by other stakeholders who jointly work with her on this task, then the stakeholder must begin to identify the objectives which the task proposal will accomplish and present them as the warrant to others.

If the claim, data, and warrant are not accepted by others, then the attributes of those objectives (in warrant) will be declared and presented as backings to describe the measurement criteria of the objectives and confirm that the proposal can accomplish the objectives by achieving good performance with each attribute.

Up to this point, after all the stakeholders present their claims, data, warrants and backings, the initial objectives hierarchy (including all fundamental/means objectives and attributes) of the entire team have been set up. If the claim, data, warrant, and backing are not accepted by others, the stakeholder has a chance to refine his/her proposal (claim) based on the group objectives hierarchy and follow the aforementioned procedure from the beginning.

Next, if stakeholders choose not to refine their claim or the refined version (claim, data, warrant, and backing) is still not accepted, the stakeholders will give the qualifier, that is, instead of solely subjective opinion, the measurement result regarding how well their proposal accomplishes the objectives given in their warrant, indicating the degree of their desire for the proposal. The rebuttal should be also given in this step, as the measurement result regarding how well their proposal accomplishes the objectives, indicates the probability that this proposal can be rejected if this result is rather unsatisfactory. In this step, when all the involved stakeholders give qualifiers and rebuttals for their proposals, they should be offered one more chance to refine the proposal based on the measurement results and then follow the steps.

If the stakeholder chooses not to refine his or her claim or the refined version is still not accepted, all the arguments will be evaluated and ranked based on deterministic analysis. The argument with best evaluation result will be recommended to the group leader.

8.3.4.2.4 Step 6b—Perspective Analysis

With the well shared and reviewed objectives and perspectives in the arguments exchange, it is possible to compare and analyze stakeholders' perspective models and to determine the similarity of two stakeholders' perspectives for one argument against a shared objective and the degree of agreement among these stakeholders for choosing the arguments. We can also aggregate multiple stakeholders' perspective models and compare their general attitudes towards each other's arguments at different levels of abstraction. Based on these analysis results, certain conflict resolution strategies can be suggested to the corresponding design team members.

First, we define the similarity of two perspectives (e.g., i and j) as the "distance" $d_{i,j}$. If $d_{i,j}$ equals 0, it means two perspectives are compatible. If $d_{i,j}$ equals 1, then the two perspectives are opposite each other. There are two approaches to determine the "distance" between perspectives: the intuitive approach and the analysis approach. The intuitive approach solely relies on the subjective insights of the stakeholder. The analysis approach uses mathematical algorithms to compare two perspectives. Here, we will discuss the latter, which is to compare the perspectives through "positional analysis," based on a formal method used in social network analysis [Wasserman and Faust 1994]. In this case, the perspective models of a group of stakeholders toward a single concept are viewed as a network of opinions associated with each other (an example is shown in Figure 8.7).

In this network, a stakeholder who possesses a perspective model has relationships with other prospective models. We define the relations as their perceptional attitudes toward each other. The rules are defined as:

If stakeholder P_i agrees to stakeholder P_j's perspective model of concept C_f (i.e., $\rho_i^{C_f}$), the perception relation is $x_{ij} = 1$.

If stakeholder P_i disagrees to $\rho_i^{C_f}$, the perception relation is $x_{ij} = -1$.

If stakeholder P_i has no comments to $\rho_i^{C_f}$, the relation is $x_{ij} = 0$.

For a given objective, a group of perspective models are placed as a graph

(i.e., perspective model network). The solid line indicates an "agreement" and the dotted line indicates a "disagreement."

The way we compare the perspective models is based on analysis of the structure of the perspective network. Two perspective models are compatible (or similar) if they are in the same "position" in the network. In social network analysis, position refers to a collection of individuals who are similarly embedded in networks of relations. To precisely determine how the perspectives are involved (i.e., the positional analysis), we need a formal definition of equivalence and a measure of the degree to which a subset of actors approach that definition in a given set of network data.

If two perspective models are structural equivalent (i.e., their relationships with other perspective models are the same), we assume they are purely compatible, and there are no detectable differences. That means they have the same perception

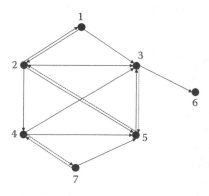

Figure 8.7   A perspective model network.

to others and others have the same perception to them. In this case, these two perspective models are structural equivalent. Structural equivalence is defined as:

Definition 1: Perspective models $\rho_i^{C_f}$ and $\rho_j^{C_f}$ toward a objective C_f are structurally equivalent if the relation $x_{ki} = x_{kj}$ and $x_{ik} = x_{jk}$ for $k = 1, 2, ..., g$.

Since structural equivalence is a mathematical property, which is seldom actually realized in collected perspective data, we use Euclidean distance as a measurement of structural equivalence. Different from the $d_{i,j}$ defined in the intuitive approach, the Euclidean distance quantifies the similarity of the perspective models based on the analysis of stakeholders' responses to each other.

Definition 2: For perspectives $\rho_i^{C_f}$ and $\rho_j^{C_f}$, $d_{i,j}$ is the distance between rows i and j, and columns i and j of the perspective interaction matrix:

$$d_{i,j} = \sqrt{\sum_{k=1}^{g}\left[(x_{ik} - x_{jk})^2 + (x_{ki} - x_{kj})^2\right]}$$

The normalized distance is $d'_{i,j} = d_{i,j}/2\sqrt{2g}$.

If $\rho_i^{C_f}$ and $\rho_j^{C_f}$ are structurally equivalent, then the Euclidean distance between them will be equal to 0.

If we want to compare stakeholders' perspective models for one argument against more than one objective, we can generalize the above equation to measure structural equivalence across the collection of several perspective models (i.e., a perspective model set).

Definition 3: For perspective sets $\{\rho_i^{C_1}, \rho_i^{C_2}, ..., \rho_i^{C_R}\}$ and $\{\rho_j^{C_1}, \rho_j^{C_2}, ..., \rho_j^{C_R}\}$ for objectives $C_1, ..., C_R$, x_{ijr} is the perception relation from stakeholder i to stakeholder j on objective C_r. The value of $d_{i,j}$ is the distance between the perceptions from and to stakeholder i and j across the collection of R relations:

$$d_{i,j} = \sqrt{\sum_{r=1}^{R}\sum_{k=1}^{g}\left[(x_{ikr} - x_{jkr})^2 + (x_{kir} - x_{kjr})^2\right]}$$

The normalized distance is $d'_{i,j} = d_{i,j}/2\sqrt{2Rg}$.

There exist different measures of structural equivalence. Euclidean distance and correlation are two typical methods in measuring positional structural equivalence. Correlation is preferred in measuring the pattern of perceptions between two perspectives (i.e., two stakeholders' opinions). Euclidean distance is preferred in measuring the identity of the perspective relations. In our perspective model comparison, we use Euclidean distance since the purpose is to determine the similarity of the perspectives' responses toward each other rather than the resemblance of the arrangements of the linkages in the graph.

The more similarity or exact structural equivalence found in the stakeholders' perspectives, the higher level of agreement they may have when choosing the argument as the final solution of this negotiation process. This analysis result will provide the design team or the team leader with recommendations to refine the arguments for more effective conflict resolution and collaborative negotiation. The following describes some of the typical argument refinement strategies.

8.3.4.3 Refine Design Proposals/Process

In cases where there is high similarity in stakeholders' perspectives but a different task proposal, stakeholders can refine the task proposals and/or the design process to increase the similarity of stakeholders' perspectives and the level of agreement in their attitude for arguments to work towards a consensual agreement.

1. Identify further means objectives to achieve the fundamental objectives and add more actions/objects accordingly.
2. Add or remove stakeholders from a given task. It is even possible to add/remove stakeholders associated with a task to avoid the conflict situation.
3. By evaluating the feasibility of planned design tasks, we can prevent a scenario of distant arguments by noticing their potential existence earlier to the stakeholder.
4. Identify the perspectives with low similarities and reveal the differences earlier.

8.3.4.4 Refine Objectives and Perspectives

In the case of little similarity of stakeholders' perspectives and low level of agreement in their arguments, it is possible to directly refine stakeholders' objectives and perspectives to increase the similarity of stakeholders' perspectives and promote the level of their agreement to work towards a consensual agreement.

1. Focus on the stakeholders who have "separated" arguments (from other clusters) and ask them to consider refining or adding objectives.
2. Ask the stakeholder with different distant models to talk to each other on certain issues. Build communication channels to increase their interaction chances.
3. Clarify the meaning/definition of fundamental objectives so that people have shared understanding.
4. Help stakeholder generate more objectives (e.g., separate objectives, generate more means objectives) to isolate their perspectives.

8.3.4.5 Rearrange Design Team

The perspective analysis presented above provides feasibility to analyze the similarity of stakeholders' perspectives, understand the degree of their agreement for argument, and better control the design teamwork.

a. The clustering tree shows the grouping features of the arguments. If two stakeholders have very distant perspectives, the team can apply certain methods of promoting their interaction, such as suitable cross-trainings based on their expertise and backgrounds.
b. Ask the stakeholder with similar perspectives to communicate more and explore the possibility of combining their arguments.
c. Suggest that the stakeholders review the relevant product information during certain tasks.
d. Provide the stakeholders with the information of the negotiation and solutions for similar design tasks in the past.

8.3.4.5.1 Step 7—Argument Evaluation

As the stakeholders' arguments are generated and exchanged during negotiation, their objectives and perspective models may evolve due to deepened understanding of each other. If all the stakeholders can jointly agree on a particular argument claim, they can take that claim as the final resolution. Otherwise, all the arguments must be carefully evaluated for resolutions. The evaluation method further works on the stakeholder perspectives of the objectives within the arguments and compares the argument claims based on the result. In this work, an intuitive additive weighting function (a.k.a. weighted average) is used to build the evaluation method, which ranks the arguments from most desired to least desired assuming stakeholders can characterize the consequences of each argument with certainty. Furthermore, "weighted average" is also applied when evaluating the arguments based on their value for the objective attributes with varying importance. Weighted average, by its definition, means an average that takes into account the proportional relevance and strength of each component, rather than treating each component equally.

The argument evaluation in our work includes four steps: define measurement scale, assign objective weights, score the arguments, and aggregate the preferences. In these four steps, the measurement scale has been defined, the objective weights have been defined in Step 4, and the arguments are scored in attribute values (either natural attributes' values or stakeholders' perspectives) in Step 5, both as stakeholders' perspectives. In this step, the perspectives and weights are aggregated to derive final argument evaluation results, which are used to rank the arguments and select the one that is most preferred by the team. The calculation of a final score for an argument is defined as follows:

Definition 4: For a given argument, A_j,

$$f_j = \sum_{i=1}^{m} c_i g_{ij}, j = 1...n$$

where f_j is the final score for alternative A_j,

n is the number of arguments,

m is the number of criteria,

c_i is the normalized weight of the attribute c_i, and

g_{ij} is the performance grade (score) for argument A_j with respect to attribute c_i.

Before the arguments were measured, all the attributes values should also be first normalized into a range of [0,1] in order to decrease the effects of differences in the numeric range of attribute values and thus allow easier and better cross-attribute comparisons.

For normalizing the values of natural attributes, since the value of the attributes is usually either zero or positive, but we do not know the maximum value of an attribute, the normalized value is:

$$\delta = \frac{d_i}{\sum_{i=1}^{n} d_i}$$

where d_i is the attribute value, and n is the number of the proposals.

For normalizing the values of "support versus opposition," since we already knew the maximum value ("10" as "strongest support") and minimum value ("1" as "strongest opposition") of this attribute, then the value can be normalized as:

$$\delta = \frac{d - d^{min}}{d^{max} - d^{min}}$$

where d_i is the attribute value, $d_{max} = 10$, and $d_{min} = 1$

A final evaluation score is calculated based on the attribute values and their normalization results. For example, the evaluation of the product manager's proposal is:

$$\text{Score} = \frac{(\text{rendering\_quality} + \text{friendly\_UI} + \text{modularity} + \text{encryption} + \text{migration} + \text{development\_cost})}{6}$$

$$= \frac{(0.89 * 8.9 + 0.89 * 8.3 + 0.66 * 7.3 + 0.75 * 6.3 + 0.89 * 7.9 + 0.66 * 6.9)}{6} = 5.95$$

Based on the evaluation results, a most preferred argument (i.e., the one with highest evaluation score) will be recommended as the final agreement of the negotiation for the design task. They will move back to Step 3 in Section 8.3.4.1.3 to check for further decision conflicts with other tasks. These iterations continue until no more conflict is found (i.e., no more negotiation is necessary), and the team moves to the post-negotiation phase as described in the coming text.

8.3.4.6 Post-Negotiation: Consensual Agreement and Move to Next Phase

In the post-negotiation phase, the stakeholders have achieved consensual agreement for the design process: they have completed all negotiation activities and are committed to accept one jointly-agreed design that consists of agreements for each design task. The step in this last phase is described in the coming text.

8.3.4.6.1 Step 8—Obtain a Commonly Accepted Design

At the end of the collaborative negotiation process for each task, the design team should either agree on a commonly appraised argument, or take the evaluation results and accept the argument with the top evaluation score as the agreement. After this process runs for all the design tasks, the team should be ready to continue to the next phase of the engineering design process with the implementation proposals in the agreed arguments for all the tasks. In addition, the result of the collaborative negotiation processes also includes the objectives and perspectives which have been collected and constructed in the negotiation phase and can be very useful for future collaboration within the same group of stakeholders on similar design tasks.

8.4 Prototype Implementation and System Applications

Using the sociotechnical collaborative negotiation approach presented in the previous section, in this work we are developing an Intelligent Web-Based Argument Negotiation Toolkit (IWANT). IWANT is a computer-supported collaborative negotiation management system based on our approach for group decision in engineering design processes. The unique contribution of this system is in its management of a negotiation process based on structured argument that is built upon the synthesis of a value-focused objective hierarchy and the generic argument structure. It provides a toolkit to help the stakeholders to systematically carry out a collaborative negotiation process for group decision in engineering design and also help us justify our research approach in improving the effectiveness of collaborative negotiation. This section briefly explains the functionality, architecture, and implementation of this research prototype and a case study of collaborative negotiation in software engineering design using IWANT.

8.4.1 System Functionality and Architecture Design of IWANT

The major functionality of IWANT is to help stakeholders to systematically carry out this negotiation process by providing a step-by-step procedure based on our approach. When stakeholders realize that there are different implementations in their decision tasks, they can activate the negotiation process by logging into the IWANT system and launching a new process instance. The new instance first collects argument information from the stakeholders by identifying their objectives and perspectives and building the objective hierarchy. After that, the IWANT system shares the argument claims within all members in the design team. It can also track the evolving objectives and stakeholders' perspectives, and make relevant changes in the negotiation arguments. If the stakeholders cannot choose a claim by themselves, IWANT can provide them with a few evaluation approach options (e.g., weighted average) and then evaluate all the claims using the approach chosen by the stakeholders. After that, the team takes the claim with the best score and continues their design work.

In more details, the system is designed based on three layers, in accordance with widely accepted Model-View-Controller standard [Alur et al. 2001] in system design domain:

■ The view layer is the user interface component running on the client side, developed using various Web technology (e.g., HTML/Java Script and Java Applet). It can display the information requested by the users for different purposes; for example, the user initializes the baseline technical process, launches the negotiation process when facing a conflicting issue, and reviews the negotiation result after coming to an agreement.

■ The controller layer implements the business logic in order to manage the data modules (stakeholder, process, and negotiation). The process management module manipulates the design process and models the tasks that the stakeholders work on. The negotiation management module helps stakeholders plan, enact, and complete a negotiation process centered on the argument-based approach. It also can help the design team obtain the agreement of the negotiation process using argument evaluation functions. The stakeholder management module administrates the user account, background, preference, skills, and other information.

■ The model layer is responsible for accessing and manipulating the data for different objects, including processes, users, and negotiations.

Based on the functionalities specification and architecture, a Web-based negotiation process management system is built and utilized for the case study in this research project. In this prototype system, users can register their own profiles, build objective hierarchy, declare individual perspectives, generate an argument structure based on objectives and perspectives, exchange arguments with each other using Web technology, view related negotiation information collected by the system, and apply argument evaluation techniques for negotiations.

8.4.2 IWANT Prototype Implementation

A prototype of IWANT is being implemented in Java language, and is being deployed to support a few software development projects. The prototype is implemented as a Web service on the Apache Web server so that the stakeholders (users) can access this system via the Internet [Fielding et al. 2006]. To better illustrate the use of this prototype, three screen snapshots are taken in the prototype and provided in the figures below. Figure 8.8 is an example of showing the claims related with one task, which the stakeholders have different opinions of. The stakeholders can add a new claim (e.g., the manager can add his claim following those made by the engineer and salesperson), view the objective hierarchy (related with the conflicting task), or enter the conflict resolution phase. In the claims table, more user-friendly terms have been implemented, for instance, reason (as data in argument structure) and proof (as warrant), to improve the user experience.

Figure 8.9 presents the conflict management interface. The stakeholders review all the relevant claims and then either agree on one claim or use the system to rank all the claims by a weighted average method. Figure 8.10 shows the ranking result in an ordered list.

8.4.3 IWANT Applications: Case Studies

This case study is to design an engineering software system for a specific user community. Before the experiment, the collaborative negotiation approach was introduced to the design team with examples and detailed guidelines to make sure the team has sufficient understanding and abilities to use our approach in the process. For demonstration purpose, only the case study of applying our approach is presented (previously case studies without applying this approach were also undertaken). The research data and analysis of a common design task "Build Communication Protocol" is also presented.

8.4.3.1 The Negotiation Process

For each design task in this case study, a 6-step procedure was suggested, in which a combination of our collaborative negotiation process and the common practice was previously taken by the design team.

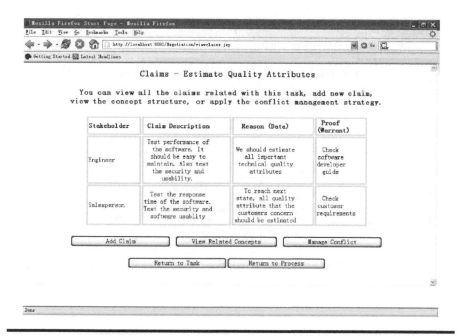

Figure 8.8   A snapshot of argument claims.

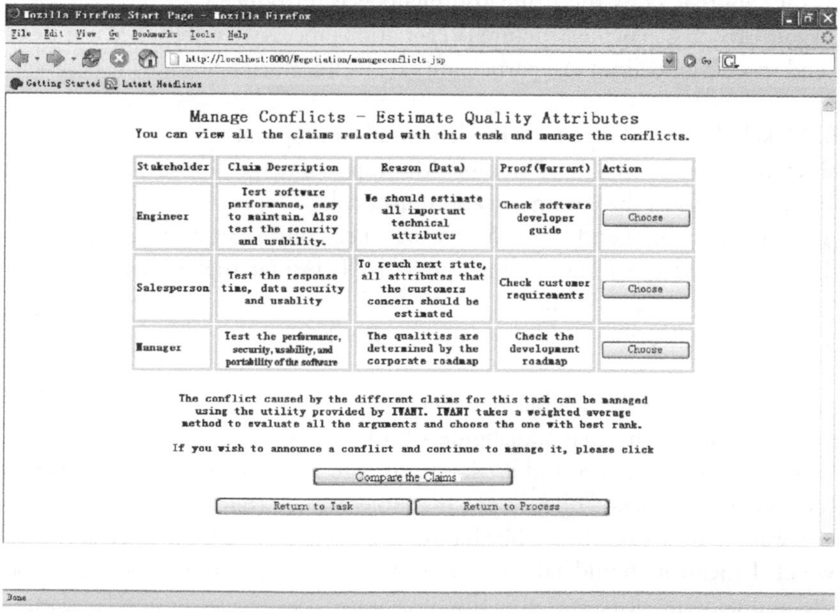

Figure 8.9   A snapshot of conflict management.

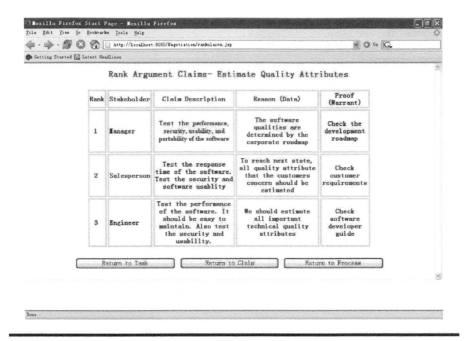

Figure 8.10 A snapshot of ranking argument claims.

a. Our approach of structuring arguments was introduced.
The details of each step in the structured negotiation process were presented using examples and specific guidelines. All participants are well-trained before the experiment.

b. Stakeholders developed the implementation proposals.
Product manager: use XML (eXtensible Markup Language) format specified by the company partners as the communication protocol.

Engineering manager: Use a CSV format, i.e., comma separated values.

Engineers: use open and well-adopted XML format that is used for general device and software specification.

Engineering director: build a proprietary XML format.

c. Stakeholders built the objective hierarchy.
The objective hierarchy that stakeholders built in this case study was a flowchart including all the objectives and attributes as well as the relationship between the objectives and attributes. For example, if a subject stated that "We should maximize the software usability on the mobile handsets by keeping UI (user interface) simple, by which I mean it should take the user as little navigation as possible to locate the desired content," this was actually interpreted as suggesting one fundamental objective, "maximize usability on handsets," and two means objectives, "keep UI simple on handset browsers" and "require little navigation to locate content." One

attribute, "average number of clicks per use case," was also added by us for the objective "require little navigation to locate content" to measure this.

If an objective does not have any means objectives or any attributes that are naturally used to interpret the objective (also called natural attributes below), an attribute "support vs. opposition" was added by the researcher.

In this work, additive weighting function (a.k.a. weighted average) was used to measure the arguments, i.e., the proposals were measured based on the attribute values and the "importance" of the attributes. Therefore, the stakeholders had to give the relative importance of each objective in a 1-to-10 scale as follows:

10 = Very important
 8 = Somewhat more important
 6 = Important
 4 = Somewhat less important
 2 = Very less important

To get more accurate results, these "importance" value were collected for each fundamental and means objectives. After then the importance of each means objective was calculated as the average value of its importance and the importance of its corresponding fundamental objective. The importance of an attribute was the same as that of its objective.

Table 3 shows the relative importance of several objectives and attributes in the task "Build Communication Protocol."

d. Stakeholders declared their perspectives.
When the task proposals were being evaluated, each attribute of each objective was assigned a value. Following our approach, the stakeholders' preferences for each argument regarding how well it achieves each objective are shown in Figure 8.11 and these perspectives are represented by values for attributes of the objective.

e. Stakeholders generated and exchanged arguments.
Up to this step, stakeholders had prepared task proposals, objectives, and perspectives. They used this information to generate the arguments. Based on the Toulmin's definition of structure, the claim was the design task proposal. The data consist of the initial state of the task—the joint agreement achieved by the design team before they work on this task. The warrant was the set of the objectives that the team wanted to achieve from this task based on the initial state. Backing was the attributes of each objective that further explained the objectives by describing their measurement criteria and then validated the relationship amongst the objectives, the proposal, and the current state of agreement. Qualifier and rebuttal were actually the measurement results regarding how well the proposal achieved her own objectives and the objectives proposed by the team, so that the measurement result for own objectives (qualifier) could indicate the degree of desire of

Table 8.3 Objectives and Attributes

Objectives	Product manager	Manager	Engineering director	Engineer	Importance
Maximize usability	8	8	8	8	8
Maximize usability Keep UI simple on handheld browser	8	8	8	8	9
Maximize usability Keep UI simple on handheld browser Use less navigation to locate content	10	8	8	8	8.5
Maximize usability Reduce data entry Easy-to-build data category	8	6	6	6	6.5
Maximize usability Reduce data entry More choice than input	8	8	6	6	7

the stakeholder for the proposal while the measurement results for team objectives (rebuttal) described the chances that could fail the proposal (claim).

In the process of generating the arguments, the stakeholders were also guided to exchange each component of their arguments. The order of exchanging these components was defined based on the logic flow between the components: the component was exchanged only if the components that stayed ahead of it were not accepted.

Objective Attribute	(1)	(2)	(3)	(4)
A	3 clicks	3 clicks	3 clicks	3 clicks
B	PM (S) E (N) EM (O) ED (O)	PM (S) E (S) EM (O) ED (N)	PM (N) E (N) EM (S) ED (O)	PM (N) E (S) EM (C) ED (S)
C	22:2	22:2	22:2	22:2

Figure 8.11 Stakeholders' perspectives: attribute values per proposal for build communication protocol.

For example, the claim and the data in one argument were exchanged first before all other components were exchanged or even generated. If they were not accepted, the warrant was provided. If still not accepted, the backing was exchanged. If the combination of claim, data, warrant and backing were not accepted, the qualifier and rebuttal were the final batch to be exchanged before all the arguments were evaluated to find out the one which were most preferred.

f. Arguments were evaluated and the one with highest ranking was recommended Based on the measurements results and calculated preference order, the argument from the engineering director was most preferred and recommended as the resolution of the negotiation. In this case study, it took the design team around 2 and half days (around 21 hours) to complete the entire design process. The average number in the rounds of generating and exchanging the arguments was 6 before the stakeholders reached an agreement for each design task. Compared with the 37 hours for the entire design process and 9 rounds in average for the arguments generation and exchange in a previous case study where this approach was not applied, it showed both the total time taken for the design phase and the average number in the rounds of generating and exchanging the arguments (before an agreement is reached) had been reduced. Also our analysis showed the commonality of stakeholders' objectives (i.e. the compatibility of their arguments) has been improved after each round of arguments generation and exchange. Overall, the decrease in the negotiation time and the improvement in the commonality of stakeholders' objectives have justified our research approach.

8.5 Conclusion and Future Work

This paper describes a research framework to structure arguments with organized objectives and preferences of multiple stakeholders to support their collaborative negotiation of group decision in engineering design. Based on this framework, this work has developed a research approach that utilizes these structured arguments to carry out effective collaborative negotiation and analyze stakeholders' perspectives for decision conflict resolution. With this approach, stakeholders can be guided through a systematic negotiation process where structure arguments are generated from stakeholders' objectives and preferences. There is an exchange that helps stakeholders share their arguments based on the logic flow of argument components, and these are evaluated to choose a most preferred argument based on how well the objectives have been achieved.

We start with a review of a variety of disciplines that have contributed to group decision, conflict resolution, and a discussion about the contributions and limitations of the approaches in each discipline. In addition, we have reviewed our previous work in collaborative negotiation: an engineering collaboration via the negotiation paradigm, a sociotechnical framework, and a sociotechnical co-construction process. These works have built research foundations and provided operational guidance to devise a collaborative negotiation process for the engineering design team. Based on the summary of all the above studies, we have developed and hereby presented a sociotechnical collaboration negotiation approach based on structured arguments. The main strength of this approach is a collaborative negotiation process with clearly specified phases and steps for stakeholders to carry out negotiation activities. The framework of grounding the structure arguments is built upon a synthesis between the collaborative negotiation process and a generic argument structure. This synthesis explains how stakeholders can generate the structured arguments according to their objectives and preferences. With this synthesis framework it helps us to overcome the challenges in existing practices of generic argument structure by incorporating the important decision-making factors from both social and technical aspects and developing feasible ways to evaluate the arguments for the most preferred by the team. Based on this synthesis, we further discuss the details of the collaborative negotiation process where the structured arguments can be generated, exchanged, and evaluated. In addition, this paper described a research software prototype IWANT that is being developed to validate the proposed work and evaluated in several real-life engineering projects. It has been used to collect experimental data and user feedback both of which are used to demonstrate the application of our approach and validate its effectiveness in supporting collaborative negotiation.

In conclusion, this research is expected to provide a more comprehensive yet practical method for engineering design teams to effectively carry out collaborative negotiation and develop a shared decision for the design tasks. We also wish to transfer the lessons learned to other specific fields of engineering designs, such as new product developments, to broaden the research impacts. Our future research work will develop more objective hierarchy templates based on individual domain and build more accurate and comprehensive models to quantify stakeholders' perspectives. Furthermore, we plan to thoroughly validate this research framework and exercise the software prototype by conducting more case studies with the engineering organizations. When richer application results are gathered, the framework and system will be continuously improved, eventually leading to the establishment of a scientific foundation for collaborative engineering.

References

Alur, D., Crupi, J., and Malks, D. (2001), *Core J2EE Patterns: Best Practices and Design Strategies*, Prentice-Hall. USA.

Amgoud, L., Maudet, N., and Parsons, S. (2000), Modeling dialogues using argumentation, *Proceedings of the Fourth International Conference on MultiAgent Systems*, July 10–12, 2000, pp. 31–38. Boston, MA.

Atkinson, K., Bench-Capon, T., and Mcburney, P. (2005), A dialogue game protocol for multi-agent argument over proposal for action, *Autonomous Agents and Multi-Agent Systems*, Vol. 11, No. 2, pp. 153–171.

Avery, J., Yearwood, J., and Stranieri, A. (2001), An argumentation based multi-agent system for eTourism dialogue, *Proceedings of International Workshop on Hybrid Intelligent Systems (HIS'01)*, December 2001, Adelaide, Australia, pp.194–210.

Bahler, D. (1995), Mixed quantitative/qualitative method for evaluating compromise solutions to conflict in collaborative design, *AIEDAM*, Vol. 9. pp. 325–326. Cambridge University Press.

Berger, P. L. and Luckmann, T. (1967), *The Social Construction of Reality*, Anchor Books, 1967. ISBN 0385-05898-5

Binmore, K. G. (1987), Why Game Theory "doesn't work," in *Analyzing Conflict and Its Resolutions: Some Mathematical Contributions* (Bennett, P.G., Ed.), 23–42.Oxford University Press, Oxford. UK.

Buckingham, S., MacLean, A., Bellotti, V., and Hammond, N. (1997), Graphical argumentation and design cognition, *Human-Computer Interaction*, 12(3), pp. 267–300.

Bui, T. (1987), *Co-op: A Group Decision Support System for Cooperative Multiple Criteria Group Decision-Making*, Springer-Verlag. Berlin, Germany.

Bui, T. (1993), Designing multiple criteria negotiation support systems: Framework, issues and implementation, in *MCDM: Expand and Enrich the Domains of Thinking and Application*, Eds. Tzeng et al., Springer Verlag. Berlin, Germany.

Bui, T. (1994), Evaluating negotiation support systems: A conceptualization, in *Proceedings of the 27th Annual Hawaii International Conference on Systems Sciences*, Vol. 4, 316–324. Hawaii, USA.

Buttner, R. (2006), The state of the art in automated negotiation models of the Behavior and Information perspective, *International Transactions on Systems Science and Applications*, Vol. 1, No. 4, pp. 351–356.

Campbell, M. I. et al. (1999), A-design: An agent-based approach to conceptual design in a dynamic environment, *Research in Engineering Design*, Vol. 11, 172–192.

Capobianco, M., Chesnevar, C. I. and Simari, G. R. (2005), Argumentation and the Dynamics of Warranted Beliefs in Changing Environments, *Autonomous Agents and Multi-Agent Systems*, Vol. 11, No. 2, pp. 127–151.

Chang, A. M. and Han, T. D. (1995), Design of an argumentation-based negotiation support system, Vol. IV. *Proceedings of the Twenty-Eighth Hawaii International Conference on System Sciences*, Vol. 4, January 3–6 1995, pp. 242–251.

Davis, R. and Smith R. G., (1983), Negotiation as a metaphor for distributed problem solving, *Artificial Intelligence*, Vol. 20, 63–109.

Dunskus, B. V. (1995), Using Single Function Agents to investigate conflict, *AIEDAM*, Vol. 9, No. 4, 299–313.

Durfee, E. H. and Lesser, V. R. (1989), Negotiating task decomposition and allocation using Partial Global Planning, in *Distributed Artificial Intelligence*, Vol. 2, Eds. M. Huhns and L. Gasser, San Mateo, CA: Morgan Kaufmann.

Faratin, P. (2000), Automated Service Negotiation between Autonomous Computational Agents, Ph.D. thesis, Department of Electronic Engineering, Queen Mary and Westfield College, University of London.

Fatima, S., Wooldridge, M., and Jennings, N. R. (2002), Multi-issue negotiation under time constraints, in Castelfranchi, C. and Johnson, L. (Eds.), *Proceedings of the 1st International Joint Conference on Autonomous Agents and Multiagent Systems (AAMAS-2002)*, New York, ACM Press, pp. 143–150.

Fielding, R. T. and Kaiser, G. (2006), The Apache HTTP server project, *Internet Computing, IEEE*, Vol. 1, Issue 4, July–Aug. 1997, pp. 88–90.

Hart, K. A. (1990), Teaching thinking in college. Accent on improving college teaching and learning. (ERIC Document Reproduction service No. ED 332 613.)

Hauser, J. R. and Clausing, D. (1988), The house of quality, *Harvard Business Review*, May–June, 63–73.

Houp, K.W., Pearsall, T.E., and Tebeaux, E. (1998), *Reporting Technical Information*, 9th Edition, Oxford UP: New York. 1998.

Huhns, M. and Gasser, L. (1989), (Eds.), *Distributed Artificial Intelligence*, Vol. 2, San Mateo, CA: Morgan Kaufmann.

Janssen, T. and Sage, A.P. (1996), Group decision support using Toulmin argument structures, *IEEE International Conference on Systems, Man, and Cybernetics*, Vol. 4, pp. 2704–2709, October 1996.

Jelassi, M. T. and Foroughi, A. (1989), Negotiation support systems: An overview of design issues and existing software, *Decision Support Systems*, Vol. 5, 32–49.

Jennings, N.R., Faratin, P., Lomuscio, A.R., Parsons, S., Wooldridge, M., and Sierra, C. (2001), Automated negotiations: Prospects, methods and challenges, *Group Decision and Negotiation*, Vol. 10. pp. 199–215.

Jin, Y., Geslin, M., and Lu, S. C.-Y. (2005), Impact of Argumentative Negotiation on Collaborative Engineering, IMPACT Laboratory, Department of Aerospace and Mechanical Engineering, University of Southern California, Los Angeles, 2005.

Kannapan, S. and Taylor, D. (1994), The interplay of context, process, and conflict in concurrent engineering, *Journal of Concurrent Engineering Research and Applications*, Vol. 2, 183–196.

Keeney, R. L. and Raiffa, H. (1976), *Decision with Multiple Objectives*, New York: John Wiley & Sons.

Kersten, G. E. (1985), NEGO—Group decision support system, *Information and Management*, Vol. 8, No. 5, 237–246.

Kersten, G. E., Michalowski, W., Szpakowicz S., and Koperczak, Z. (1991), Restructurable representations of negotiation, *Management Science*, Vol. 37, No. 10, 1269–1290.

Kilker, J. (1999), Conflict on collaborative design teams: Understanding the role of social identities, *IEEE Technology and Society Magazine*, Fall, 12–21.

Klein, M., Faratin, P., Sayama, H., and Bar-Yam, Y. (2003), Negotiating complex contracts, *Group Decision and Negotiation*, Vol. 12, pp. 111–125.

Klein, M. (1995), Conflict management as a part of an integrated exception handing approach, *AIEDAM*, Vol. 9, 259–267.

Kowalczyk, R. and Bui, V. (2001), On constraint-based reasoning in e-negotiation agents, In Dighum, F. and Cortes, U. (Eds.), *Agent-Mediated Electronic Commerce III (Lecture Notes in Computer Science*, Vol. 2003), Berlin: Springer-Verlag, pp. 31–46.

Kraus, S., Wilkenfeld, J., and Zlotkin, G. (1995), Multiagent negotiation under time constraints, *Artificial Intelligence*, Vol. 75, 297–345.

Kraus, S. (2001), Automated negotiation and decision making in multiagent environments, *Lecture Notes in Artificial Intelligence*, 2086, p. 150.

Kraus, S. (2001), *Strategic Negotiation in Multi-Agent Environments*, Cambridge, MA, MIT Press.

Kraus, S., Sycara, K., and Evenchik, A. (1998), Reaching agreements through argumentation: A logical model and implementation, *Artificial Intelligence*, 104 (1–2), 1–69.

Lewis, K., and Mistree, F. (1997), Modeling interactions in multidisciplinary decision: A game theoretic approach, *AIAA Journal*, August, Vol. 35.

Lim, L-H. and Benbasat, I. (1991), From Negotiation to Negotiation Support Systems: A Theoretical Perspective, Working Paper, Faculty of Commerce and Business Administration, University of British Columbia, Vancouver, B. C., Canada.

Lu, S. C-Y. and Cai, J. (2001), A Collaborative Design Process Model in the Sociotechnical Engineering Design Framework, Artificial Intelligence for Engineering Design, Analysis and Manufacturing, Vol. 15, 3–20, 2001.

Marttunen, M. (1992), Commenting on written arguments as a part of argumentation skills – comparison between students engaged in traditional vs. on-line study, *Scandinavian Journal of Educational Research*, 36(4), 289–302.

Nagarajan, M. and Sosic, G. (2008), Game-theoretic analysis of cooperation among supply chain agents: Review and extensions, *European Journal of Operational Research*, 187(3), 719–745.

Nash, J. (1950), The bargaining problem, *Econometrica*, Vol. 18, 155–162.

Parsons, S., Sierra, C., and Jennings, N. (1998), Agents that reason and negotiate by arguing, *Journal of Logic and Computation*, 8 (3), 261–292.

Petrie, C. J. et al. (1995), Using Pareto optimality to coordinate distributed agents, *AIEDAM*, Vol. 9, 269–281.

Rahwan, I., Sonenberg, L., Jennings, N.R., and McBurney, P. (2007), STRATUM: A methodology for designing heuristic agent negotiation strategies, *Applied Artificial Intelligence*, Vol. 21, pp. 489–527.

Raiffa, H. (1982), *The Art and Science of Negotiation*, Cambridge, MA: Harvard University Press.

Rao, S. S. and Freiheit, T. I. (1991), A modified game theory approach to multi-objective optimization, *Transactions of ASME*, September. Vol. 113.

Rong, J., Geng, S. J., Valasek, J., Ioerger, T. R. (2002), Air traffic conflict negotiation and resolution using an onboard multi-agent system, *Proceedings of the 21st Digital Avionics Systems Conference*, 2002. Volume 2, 2002, pp. 7B2-1–7B2-12.

Rosenschein, J. and Zlotkin, G. (1994), *Rules of Encounter: Designing Conventions for Automated Negotiation among Computers*, Cambridge, MA, MIT Press

Sandholm, T. (2002a), Algorithm for optimal winner determination in combinatorial auctions, *Artificial Intelligence*, 135 (1–2), 1–54.

Sandholm, T. (2002b), eMediator: a next generation electronic commerce server, Computational Intelligence, *Special Issue on Agent Technology for Electronic Commerce*, 18 (4), 656–676.

Shakun, M. F. (1988), *Evolutionary Systems Design: Policy Making under Complex@ and Group Decision Support Systems*. Holden-Day, Oakland, CA, 1988.

Shakun, M. F. (1992), "Defining a right problem in group decision and negotiation: feeling and evolutionary generating procedures," *Group Decision and Negotiation*, Vol. No 1, April 1992. pages 27–40.

Sierra, C., Jennings, N. R., Noriega, P., and Parsons, S. (1998), A framework for argumentation-based negotiation, in Singh, M., Rao, A., and Wooldridge, M. (Eds.), *Intelligent Agent IV: 4th International Workshop on Agent Theories, Architectures and Languages (ATAL-1997)* (*Lecture Notes in Artificial Intelligence*, Vol. 1365), Berlin, Springer-Verlag, pp. 177–192.

Sillince, J. A. A. and Saeedi, M. H. (1999), Computer-mediated communication: Problems and potentials of argumentation support systems, *Decision Support Systems*, 26, 287–306.

Smith, D. G. (1977), College classroom interactions and critical thinking, *Journal of Educational Psychology*, 69(2), 180–190.

Suh, N. P., (1990), *The Principle of Design*, Oxford University Press, Oxford

Sycara, K.(1989), Multiagent compromise via negotiation, in *Distributed Artificial Intelligence*, Vol. 2, Eds. M. Huhns and L. Gasser, San Mateo, CA: Morgan Kaufmann.

Sycara, K. (1990), Negotiation planning: An AI approach, *European Journal of Operational Research*, 46 (1990), 216–234.

Sycara, K. (1991), Problem restructuring in negotiation, *Management Science*, Vol. 37, No. 10, 1248–1268.

Tiwari, S. and Gupta, A. (1995), Constraint management on distributed design configurations, *Engineering with Computers*, 199–210.

Toulmin, S., Rieke, R., and Janik, A. (1984), *An Introduction to Reasoning*, Macmillan Publishing, New York, 1984.

Toulmin, S. (1958), *The Uses of Argument*, Cambridge University Press, London.

Vincent, T. L. (1983), Game theory as a design tool, *Journal of Mechanisms, Transmissions, and Automation in Design*, Vol.105, pages 165–170.

Wasserman, S., Faust, K. (1994), *Social Network Analysis: Methods and Applications*, New York: Cambridge University Press.

Wellman, M. P., (1995), A computational market model for distributed configuration design, *AIEDAM*, Vol. 9, 125–133.

Wong, S. T. C. (1997), Coping with conflict in cooperative knowledge-based systems, *IEEE Transactions on Systems, Man, and Cybernetics—Part A: Systems and Humans*, Vol. 27, No. 1, 57–71.

Zeleznikow, J. (2002), Risk, negotiation and argumentation—a decision support system based approach, *Law, Probability and Risk*, Vol. 1, pp. 37–48, July 2002.

Chapter 9

Risk Analysis in Sociotechnical System

Jonathan Scott Corley and Fei Hu

Contents

9.1 Introduction

Risk analysis of sociotechnical systems is an important means of defining and analyzing possible threats to individuals, businesses, or the environments or systems in which they function or participate. Risk analysis is performed in a multitude of occupations ranging from engineering, computer science, social scientists, etc. Civil engineers, for instance, will examine the performance of various structures, possibly a building or bridge, by examining their ability to handle different conditions of threat. Increasingly heavy loads could be applied to a small-scale bridge in order to identify points of failure in regards to the structural integrity of the bridge. Once identified, these points of failure allow the engineers to determine what degrees of improvement need to be implemented in order to construct a safe and dependable bridge. In general, the characteristics of a given system can only be

229

improved by identifying the points of failure through application of various conditions of threat.

Risk analysis is a widely studied topic. In order to assess risk, it must first be defined. Risk is generally defined as the combination of the occurrence probability of damage and its gravity. Likewise, risk assessment is defined as the series of logical steps used to systematically examine the risks associated with an operational system [15]. But the difficulty in determining or defining which steps should be taken to analyze the system increases as the complexity of the system increases. This is the case for applying risk analysis to sociotechnical systems, where this system is defined as one in which influential interactions occur between humans and some organizational infrastructure. Sociotechnical systems are inherently multi-dimensional and highly complex. A means of defining the method for performing risk analysis to a given sociotechnical system is not necessarily applicable to other systems. Each application is typically unique and highly dependent on the domain of interest.

Different studies addressing the difficulty of applying risk analysis to a sociotechnical system are summarized in this chapter. Each describes the complexities that arise in accurately representing the system of interest, as well as, consideration of identifying all contributing factors.

9.2 Bayesian Belief Network Approach for Risk Analysis [5]

It is widely accepted that the human element plays a major role in most accidents involving modern ships. The Transportation Safety Board of Canada (TSB) [2] concluded that 74% of accidents at sea are attributed to human error whereas only 1% is attributed to technical failures. The chart in Figure 9.1 displays the results of these statistics. Of the cases involving human error, 45% of accidents are attributed to the pilot or master's misjudgment, 10% to a lack of communication, 10% to inattention by the officer on watch, 13% to inattention of the pilot, and 9% to misunderstanding [2]. The chart concerning the breakdown of human error cases is displayed in Figure 9.2.

In addition to the statistics provided by the Transportation Safety Board, data from Lloyds Informative Maritime Service [3] help to support the link between accidents and human error. The statistics claim that half of all maritime accidents are attributed to excessive speeds and an uncorrected course with respect to the traffic in the sea zone.

Ensuring safety for maritime transport would require a more in-depth understanding of the human role and its contribution to accidents. Even so, it seems there are additional factors that need to be considered in the analysis of risk. The Zeebrugge incident [4], where a passenger ship capsized, was reportedly a result of "systematic change in the organizational behavior of operators under the influence

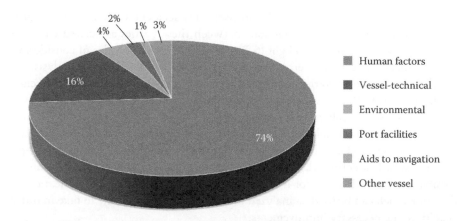

Figure 9.1   Incidence of the typologies of accident causes. (From Transportation Safety Board of Canada, (TSB), 1998, http://www.bst.gc.ca.)

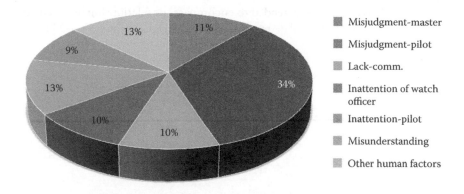

Figure 9.2   Typology of human factors associated with causing an accident. (From Transportation Safety Board of Canada, (TSB), 1998, http://www.bst.gc.ca.)

of economic pressure in a strongly competitive environment" [5]. The incident was not a result of human error, possibly associated with technical failures, based on the official report. Thus, the scope of the safety analysis of the Maritime Transport System must be broadened to include all relevant, outside factors and actors whose decisions contribute to the safety of the system.

The most critical issue in developing an effective risk or accident analysis is identifying the various parties involved and determining to what degree they affect the sequence of events leading up to the occurrence of an accident. In the case of the Maritime Transport System, the various parties may include but are not limited to ship operators, shipyards, government bodies, or company investors. These actors may directly or indirectly serve a role in the sequence of events contributing to the final act of a ship operator's error. Rasmussen's [4] accident analysis of oil tankers and ferryboats brought the interactions between these parties associated with the Maritime Transport System to light [6,7,8], which supports the idea of considering other factors beyond human error into the systematic approach of risk analysis.

The International Maritime Organization (IMO) used Regulatory Influence Diagrams (RID) [9] as a systematic approach to access risks for shipping activity. The RID is used to achieve a better understanding of all influencing factors and how they related to possible accidents. Figure 9.3 illustrates the structure of a RID. The RID serves as a basis for establishing the contribution of relevant factors for all system levels. It identifies the hierarchy of factors at every level that contribute to possible accidents. Each factor is an idea for improvement. Upon identification of all factors, each can be further analyzed to determine the best route to take in order to achieve the necessary improvements.

A Bayesian Belief Network (BBN) is a probabilistic model used to represent a set of random variables and their conditional independences via a directed acyclic graph (DAG) [11]. The Bayesian Belief Network directly correlates to an influence diagram in which the effects of the represented factors are in terms of conditional probabilities. This idea can be extended to encompass the relationship between considered factors and how they relate to possible accidents occurring in the Maritime Transport System.

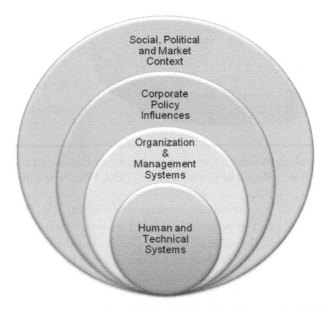

Figure 9.3 Nested system of influences in a Regulatory Influence Diagram. (From International Maritime Organization (IMO), Guidelines for the application of Formal Safety Assessment (FSA) for use in the IMO rule-making process, Publisher: IMO. London, England, April 2002.

A functional model (FM) has been developed for the Maritime Transport System in the Safety at Speed [12] project which was funded by the European Commission. The FModel is another means of determining what factors contribute to undesired events and possibly help to find out what aspects of it can be fixed to improve the situation.

The objective of the Safety at Speed project was to develop a formal methodology for designing high speed crafts safely. Fault Trees were applied to the project in order to determine the best risk control option in designing the High Speed Craft. The Fault Trees included hazardous scenarios that considered hazardous factors such as collision, grounding, fire, flooding, etc.

The foundation of an FM of the Maritime Transport System was to identify the activities that each group performed according to their roles. The activities were then represented as a function, so the FM would signify the influence of each party on one another as well as how the different activities correspond and relate. This network of interdependence provides implication of how changes made within the Maritime Transport System (MTS) can produce growth and affect safety.

In [5] a means is introduced of producing a comprehensive model for the study of Risk Analysis based on Fault Tree Analysis and Bayesian Belief Network, which incorporate human organizational factors. It differs from previous works, as it includes the development of the model and an explanation of the comprehensive approach, as well as those factors or variables that contribute to the overall safety performance of the Maritime Transport System. Figure 9.4 illustrates how the Fault Tree and Bayesian Belief Network are linked. The equation presented will be discussed later.

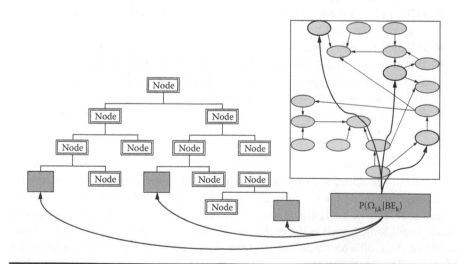

Figure 9.4   The Bayesian Belief Network and Fault Tree linkage. (From Bayesian Belief Network approach ([paper].)

BBN serves as a tool for exploiting information from the complex relationships between large numbers of variables emerging from the real-world scenarios or systems. It provides a graphic aid for mapping relationships between complex relationships between variables, which helps aid in decision making and performing numerical procedures. More specifically, the BBN used in this research serves as a graphical tool for quantifying the FM of the Maritime Transport System in order to determine an estimation of the probabilistic occurrence of an accident in relation to specific contribution of human organizational factors. This application will allow the influencing factors to be extrapolated amongst the contributing parties within the Maritime Transport System. The BBN will then aid in modifying probabilistic occurrences of different factors in the Fault Tree based on what knowledge is present for the specific configuration of relevant human organizational factors.

Bayes theorem was used to estimate the influence of organizational factors on the probability of occurrence for single basic events. The equation for calculating the probability of occurrence of both technical and human basic is given as follows:

$$P(BEk \mid \Omega j, k) \frac{P(\Omega_{j,k} \mid BEk) \cdot P(BEk)}{P(\Omega_{j,k})}$$

where

- $\Omega_{j,k}$ the j-th phase of the "organizational scenario variable" which indicates the influence of HOF on BE_k.
- $P(BE_k \mid \Omega_{j,k})$ is the posterior probability, or the probability of BE after considering the effect of $\Omega_{j,k}$.
- $P(BE_k)$ is the prior probability of BE occurring based on past statistical analysis.
- $P(\Omega_{j,k})$ is the probability that state j of the k "organizational scenario variable" that has been approximated from the Bayesian Belief Network given the probability distribution of variable for the root nodes.
- $P(\Omega_{j,k} \mid BE_k)$ is the degree of belief in the occurrence of $\Omega_{j,k}$ given the occurrence of BE_k.

In light of these applications, this research focuses on the Fault Tree Analysis developed within the Speed at Sea project as the case study of interest. This particular project identified 38 human errors, 26 technical failures, and 64 organizational scenario variables. The analysis was used to identify and evaluate risk control options for ship collisions, as well as the probabilistic correlation between the multiple basic events of the Collision Fault Tree and the Bayesian Belief Network model of the Maritime Transport System.

In short, the analysis of the Speed at Sea project illustrates the use of applying the Bayesian Belief Network model to identify the relevant causal factors related to ship collisions occurring on the Maritime Transport System. This application identified those contributing factors as well as the conditions and/or scenarios that increase the possibility of ship accidents between two high-speed crafts on the open sea. Additionally, the case study provided support for illustrating the characteristics associated with the Bayesian Belief Network, which are as follows:

- Modeling of human and organizational factors in a Bayesian Belief Network can be used as a tool for tuning parameters within other probabilistic models and performing risk analysis.
- Simplify the identification of failures or causal factors at the organizational level.
- Probabilities of a Bayesian Belief Network model are easily updateable, which is beneficial upon introduction of future evidence related to existing factors over time.
- The Bayesian Belief Network model has the potential for further application in that it can be used as a tool for safety management processes and decision making at different levels.

9.3 Interagency Antiterrorism Information-Sharing Systems [14]

A growing concern for interagency communication between counter-terrorism and emergency management agencies in regard to information sharing and coordination has come out of the terrorist attacks of 9/11 in 2001, as well as the government's response to Hurricane Katrina in 2005. These occurrences are sufficient evidence to support that emergency management agencies need to improve their means of information sharing and coordination.

A study was conducted to analyze counterterrorism organizations' acceptance of inter-organizational information-sharing systems in terms of sociotechnical factors at a station level [14]. These factors include information sharing between partners, sensitivity of shared information, organizational norm of interagency information sharing, and IT infrastructure [14]. A station is considered to be a physical structure or establishment of a counterterrorism organization located within a small geographical area [14]. By defining the study on the station level, data collection from individuals can be aggregated and for multiple responses from a single station, it is required that confidentiality be maintained of the surveyed counterterrorism organization.

Information sharing commonly occurs among business partners for the purpose of achieving some degree of financial or economic benefit. These information-sharing relationships have limited confidentiality in regards to public safety and national security. For this reason, the information sharing between businesses and government organizations do not directly correlate although they are somewhat comparable. Cooperation between various counterterrorism organizations is sometimes limited because these organizations are assigned to different roles, including intelligence gathering overseas, terrorism investigation in the U.S. homeland, and public control and assistance, in which they compete with each other for political power, budget, or pride [14].

A national e-government may implement the means of sharing information between counterterrorism organizations but the competition between agencies will still exist, depending on how the system is implemented and utilized [14]. This study defines information sharing systems acceptance as "the level of provision of proprietary information to relevant external parties through information systems [14]." Other researchers have proposed the idea of implementing a system for information sharing based on the social exchange theory. The social exchange theory argues that when exchange partners conform and adhere to reciprocal rules of exchange a quality relationship will develop. In the context of sharing information between counterterrorism organizations, the social exchange theory would suggest that when one counter-terrorism organization discloses its information to other counterterrorism organizations, the behavior should be compensated by other counterterrorism organizations with information or actions of equal value. However, due to the classified nature of information within a given counterorganization, the act of making such private information available is associated with the inherent risk that the ability to maintain national security in compromised. The risk understandably increases as the sensitivity of information increases. Likewise, as the sensitivity of the information disclosed to other counterterrorism organizations increases, the supplemental information exchanged in return must be of equal sensitivity. This exchange system emphasizes the ability of counterterrorism organizations to provide adequate proof of a high level of information assurance to other organizations before providing sensitive information.

In addition to the risk of sharing sensitive information, the IT infrastructure and system utilization can also influence the acceptance and use of information sharing systems. Integrating an information sharing system into an already widely used internal-information sharing system could result in the system's being more readily accepted and utilized.

Another factor that contributes to the degree of acceptance of information sharing systems is how a given counterterrorism organization utilizes the system. Typically, in the domain of counterterrorism, information sharing is controlled by, or at least influenced, by a supervisory authority or regulations for many organizations [14]. This control implies the expectation of information-sharing systems to experience authoritative pressures through defined standards put in place by these authoritative bodies. The model of counterterrorism information-sharing systems acceptance is displayed in Figure 9.5.

An online survey questionnaire was administered to emergency responders to empirically test the suggested model of counterterrorism information-sharing systems acceptance. The presented results are that of a pilot study conducted using the first wave of survey results. The survey results uncovered an inconsistency between the use of information-sharing systems and organizational needs [14]. Results gave

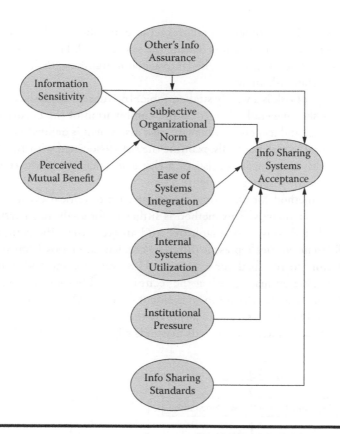

Figure 9.5 The information-sharing systems acceptance model. (From Lee, J. and Rao, H., 2007, Understanding sociotechnical environments for acceptance of inter-agency counterterrorism information sharing systems, *Hawaii International Conference on System Sciences*, 2007. IEEE Computer Society, Washington, DC.)

evidence to information-sharing systems acceptance being mainly influenced by concerns for information security and institutional standards or conditions rather than the value of the information being shared with other organizations. From the results, the continuing study can be improved and revised in expectation to obtain further evidence to support the information-sharing system acceptance model.

9.4 Risk Analysis of Complex Sociotechnical Systems [15]

The occurrence of a critical event, or major accident, is not acceptable within an operational installation when it presents any degree of risk for the environment. The Major Accident Reporting System database associated with the European

Union presents evidence of human failures representing 64% of declared accidents. Risk analysis must consider factors outside the system level. Human operation and organizational influence must be taken into account to sufficiently implement some practice of accurate risk analysis.

The concept of risk is a widely studied topic. In order to assess risk, it must first be defined. Risk is generally defined as the combination of the occurrence probability of damage and its gravity. Likewise, risk assessment is defined as the series of logical steps used to systematically examine the risks associated with an operational system [15]. This assessment consists of a risk assessment and reduction process, which is graphically displayed in Figure 9.6.

A popular method for analyzing the occurrence of critical events is to apply the "bow-tie" risk analysis. This method is sufficient for analyzing a system at the technical level, and consists of a fault tree and an event tree. The paths that exist between different entities represent different accident scenarios from initial contributing factors to the final consequences. However, this method is limited. It adequately handles evaluating risk at the technical level but fails to consider contributing factors that are relevant to an accident scenario. Modification of the bow-tie method would be necessary to incorporate the contributing factors into the risk analysis. Likewise, present risk analysis methods require modification because they

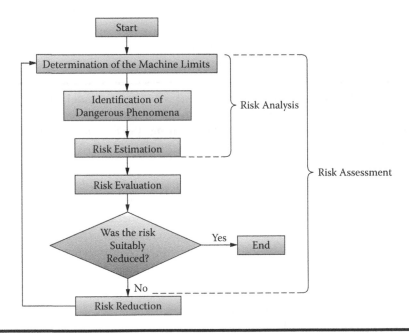

Figure 9.6   Risk assessment and risk reduction processes. (From Léger, A., Duval, C., Weber, P., Levrat, E., and Farret, R., Risk Analysis of Complex Socio Technical Systems by Using Bayesian Network Modeling, available from: http://www.cpermisn-sectaf.cran.uhp-nancy.fr/Files/ACD/p42.pdf.)

are limited to Boolean variables and uncorrelated relations, and they do not include repairing notions and temporal dependencies [15].

As previously stated, risk analysis applied to the technical layer alone does not produce an accurate depiction of every contributing factor for a given critical event. A higher degree of analysis must be used to consider all relevant factors: a global risk analysis. At the global level, the constraining external processes for an operational system are divided into four categories or layers:

1. Decisions and actions layer
2. Internal organizational layer
3. External organizational layer
4. Natural environment layer

The decisions and actions layer represents processes linked with the decision making at the individual level, the internal organizational layer represents processes linked with the management of the enterprise, the external organizational later represents processes linked with the climate in which this enterprise evolves, and the natural environment layer represents processes linked with the evolution of the physical and natural climate [15].

Understandably, there exists the need to accurately identify the relations between these defined layers with an operational system of interest. Additionally, it is highly important to identify the relations existing between the technical layer and the human/organizational layer. The technical layer is typically qualified as a closed-loop system consisting of limitations or constraints, multiple causality relations, and identifiable interactions [15]. On the other hand, the human/organizational layer is typically qualified as a dynamic, open-loop system where limits are difficult to determine and the systems experience high rates of change. A high-level flow chart illustrating the steps taken in global risk analysis with respect for decision-making support is displayed in Figure 9.7.

On top of performing global risk analysis, it may be desirable to incorporate barriers into the system. A risk reduction barrier is defined as an entity installed in the system to prevent the occurrence of a risky scenario [15]. Risk reduction barriers are categorized as preventive or protective; a preventive barrier is typically located upstream for the purpose of preventing or limiting the critical event and a protective barrier is typically located downstream for the purpose of reducing the consequences of the critical event. Risk reduction barriers can be further categorized based on the contributing resources into the three following categories:

■ Organizational barrier: composed of management activity
■ Human barrier: composed of human activity
■ Technical barrier: composed of a safety device
■ Combined barrier: combination of barriers

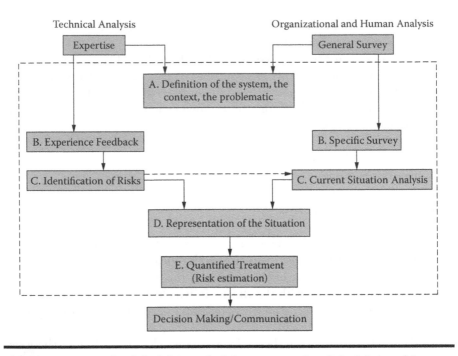

Figure 9.7 **Steps of a global risk analysis in a perspective of decision-making support. (From Léger, A., Duval, C., Weber, P., Levrat, E., and Farret, R., Risk Analysis of Complex Socio Technical Systems by Using Bayesian Network Modeling, available from: http://www.cper-misn-sectaf.cran.uhp-nancy.fr/Files/ACD/p42.pdf.), November 2006. IAR Annual Meeting.**

These barriers need to be integrated into the risk analysis model in order to determine the impact the barriers have on the system as a whole. Performing a risk analysis model with the idea of integrating these barriers requires that presently operating barriers be identified. Next, the model gives light to locations where additional barriers may be incorporated into the system. In doing so, the model must be updated to represent the barriers resulting in an explicit representation of a barrier impact on the entire system.

Of the existing tools to construct the risk analysis model, Bayesian network models are most applicable to this modeling problem because they allow for the use of qualitative and/or quantitative models [15]. Bayesian network models lend themselves easily to generalizing the translation from fault trees and event trees. With respect to the technical layer, a Bayesian network model is beneficial because it allows for the representation of reconfigurations of the system, treatment of partially correlated failures, and modeling and propagation of uncertainties in the model from initiators to the output indicators [15]. With respect to the human/ organizational layer, a Bayesian network model is beneficial because it allows correlations between variables, integration and updating of various kinds of knowledge, different abstraction layers to be structurally modeled, and the use of multi-model variables [15].

Implementing the Bayesian network model requires intimate knowledge of the technical layer as well as the human/organizational level. Integrating the risk reduction barriers requires some degree of modification to the existing modeling tool. Upon integrating the risk reduction barriers, each barrier is incorporated as a parent entity of the event it protects or prevents. Ideally, when constructing the Bayesian network model, all entities are organized so that the high-level influences are parents of the low-level influences, which is a realistic and practical representation. Or in other words, the model will illustrate the influence streaming from management to the actors and then to the technical layer [15]. It is also important to note that when the risk reduction barriers are incorporated into the Bayesian network model the implementation of one barrier does not directly influence the functionality of another barrier, or they are independent of one another.

The industrial storage tank displayed in Figure 9.8 was the system of interest for the case-study for application of the proposed modeling techniques. The storage tank houses liquid pentane for a short period of time, which is extremely flammable in open air. The storage of the liquid pentane is performed in the presence of

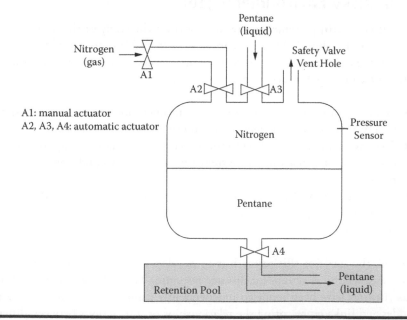

Figure 9.8   Industrial storage tank. (From Léger, A., Duval, C., Weber, P., Levrat, E., and Farret, R., Risk Analysis of Complex Socio Technical Systems by Using Bayesian Network Modeling, available from: http://www.cper-misn-sectaf.cran. uhp-nancy.fr/Files/ACD/p42.pdf.), November 2006. IAR Annual Meeting.

gaseous nitrogen, which prevents any reaction or ignition from the air. Actuators are used to systematically control the amount of input and output of the pentane liquid and the nitrogen gas, as well as control the output of pressure from the tank. A vent hole, safety valve, and retention pool are present for sustaining a safe amount of liquid in the tank and also for balancing the amount of pressure buildup inside the tank.

A global risk analysis was performed on the storage tank scenario previously described. The first step of achieving the global risk analysis was to perform a technical analysis that would identify the contributing factors that make up the technical layer of the model. Next, the human and organizational factors were identified with respect to decision-making support. Lastly, all risk reduction barriers were identified as well as the resources they influence. All these variables were then incorporated to construct the Bayesian network model. This constructed model served as the basis for determining the probabilistic occurrence of the critical event in the month of August.

9.5 Dynamic Networks: Modeling Change in Risky Environments [16]

The research in [16] presents an interim report on the study of the transportation system in the Pittsburgh Metropolitan Region in reaction to a range of extreme events on the existing infrastructure. Certain aspects of this research are ongoing but the three principal objectives are as follows:

- To identify the metrics associated with the operation of a regional transportation system for both the technical and organizational networks
- To construct a model for determining patterns of adaptive response through simulation of threats to the system under different conditions of risk and resilience
- To provide a model as a means of supporting decision making at the management level to improve efficiency and effectiveness handling risk to transportation systems

As stated, the focus of this research is to develop a model that accurately represents a sociotechnical system for disaster response. Typically, social and technical infrastructures have been modeled independently using an interconnected system of nodes and links representing the relationships or interactions between different entities. Relative to the goals of this research, the relationships and interactions between the social and technical infrastructures are substantially important for assessing the fragility or performance of a transportation system within a metropolitan region under threat.

The research concerning the previous stated objectives was conducted in several phases. First, a generic set of metrics are developed to characterize the sociotechnical infrastructure of the emergency response operations concerning threats to the transportation within the Pittsburgh Metropolitan Region. The particular transportation system consists of a highly complex technical network of different means of transportation and a highly complex social network of emergency response organizations. The generic set of measurements will be determined from a subsection of the transportation system [16].

Next, the characterization of the transportation infrastructure will used to construct the simulation framework to represent the Pittsburgh Metro Region in order to simulate the response of the regional transportation system under the influence of different types of threats, available information, resource availability, and time stress [16].

Next, the results of the simulation of the transportation infrastructure will be used to develop probabilistic models for the Pittsburgh Metro Region. These models will accurately describe the spread of congestion due to the occurrence of different critical events. The model will also help to identify the threshold of the transportation system under various conditions in response to the different types of threat. The results will help contribute to determining what proactive barriers can be instituted to prevent the occurrence of the damaging event as well as how to handled them through efficient use of resources from the emergency response organizations. These risk reduction barriers may include improving the shared information and coordination between the organizational systems, which in turn will improve proper organization to best handle the occurrence of the critical event.

In developing the necessary metrics, modeling of the infrastructure's fragility is based on an the percolation theory [16]. Percolation analysis is the study of the distribution of failure cluster size and phase transition which provides a means of determining when a system transitions from a stable phase into an unstable phase [16]. Specifically, a system reaches a point of instability when the failure cluster grows to the extent that the network is no longer connected [16]. Applying this idea will assist in concluding whether or not an infrastructure of an area will maintain its operational capacity in response to various disasters.

The first task of characterizing the sociotechnical infrastructure systems is to model the vulnerability of the technical infrastructure for transportation. The initial study focused on an area of highway network near Allegheny County, Pennsylvania. The particular highway network of interest was limited to consider only those sections that incurred daily traffic of over 10,000 vehicles [16]. These highway sections include highways that are maintained by the state in the city of Pittsburgh [16]. The longest distance to which one can travel defines the stressed diameter and the average distance that can be traveled defines the stressed characteristics. To indicate risk, a dynamic variable will represent the flow of traffic through the system. The Pennsylvania Department of Transportation is assisting with the collection of data regarding traffic flow in the area of interest. This data will assist in determining which sections or vertices are most significant to the highway network or which vertex will introduce the most damage into the transportation system upon removal.

The second task of characterizing the sociotechnical infrastructure systems is to model the vulnerability of the organizational infrastructure for disaster management. Comparable analysis, as previously described, is being applied to characterize the emergency response network responsible for monitoring and handling disruptions within the transportation system. Once again, the study is limited to the sub-sectioned, area of interest. Those organizations contributing the maintenance of this highway section are being modeled as a single organizational network where each of the authoritative organizations responsible for responding to their given jurisdiction will be represented as a vertex. Edges between the different organizational vertices represent the laws, policies, and procedures shared between the different organizations pertaining to communication and action responsibilities [16]. As a measure of the capacity for action, calculation of the cost of time and resources required to respond and handle the occurrence of a critical event in the highway network will be necessary. The resilience indicator will be a dynamic variable representing the total number of messages communicated between the different organizations in the network in when responding to a critical event in the transportation system. Likewise, the resulting measures will illustrate the most significant vertices in the organizational network which will also identify which one will introduce the most damage into the network's ability to respond and act to critical events upon removal that vertex.

The last task in characterizing the sociotechnical infrastructure systems is to model the interaction between the social and technical infrastructure systems. It is desirable to determine how the interactions between the two infrastructures impact the operation of the regional transportation system [16]. The two infrastructures must be analyzed in parallel to determine how a given critical event affects the ability of the emergency response organizations to coordinate and efficiently act. The analysis will be extended to determine the patterns of failure or the extent of failure within the transportation system, or technical infrastructure, that reduces the organizational response systems ability to respond. The results of these analyses on the interaction between the two technical and organizational systems will contribute to the process of identifying the different points of failure, which, in turn, points out what aspects of the systems need to be improved to prevent future occurrences of a critical event or a better means of addressing the occurrence of the critical event.

The next phase is to construct the simulation framework to represent the Pittsburgh Metro Region. This framework will be modeled after the identified relationships, measures, and network models produced from the analysis of characterizing the sociotechnical infrastructure systems.

The first step toward building the simulation framework is simulating the transportation network. For each vertex of the constructed transportation network model, a small number of surrounding intersections will be considered in conducting an analysis of traffic. Within each analysis, sufficient data for different scenarios will be generated to produce an accurate characterization of each region of the transportation system. Multiple transportation agencies are assisting in the process of gathering data by monitoring traffic flow within the transportation system [16]. This data will be used to model the rules of interaction between the transportation system and the emergency response organizations under the influence of some critical event.

The second step toward building the simulation framework is simulating the emergency response network. Data relating to this simulation has been extracted from emergency plans, protocols and policies for emergency response, and operation logs of past incidents occurring on the transportation system. Additionally, the flow of information between the various emergency response organizations will contribute to the data. This informational data includes the number of messages sent, the direction of message flow, and urgency of need. The data extracted from the emergency response organizations in the Pittsburgh Metropolitan Region will be used to establish parameters of information flow in characterizing the simulation behavior in response to different critical events. Also, to investigate decision making in the management of these emergency response organizations, a meta-agent, or means of simulated coordination and control, is introduced, as well as the use of the Bayesian network model, which allows for the modeling of incomplete information and uncertainty related to human decision making [16].

The last step toward building the simulation framework is simultaneously simulating the social and transportation network. The simultaneous simulation will allow both the physical infrastructure and the organizational infrastructure to be analyzed in relation to one another. The results of these analyses on the interaction between the two technical and organizational systems will, once again, contribute to the process of identifying the different points of failure, which, in turn, points out what aspects of the systems need to be improved to prevent future occurrences of a critical event or a better means of addressing the occurrence of the critical event.

The final phase is to establish a module for decision support. To complete the characterization and modeling of the Pittsburgh Metropolitan Region's transportation system, a decision module will be produced to assist decision making authorities in efficiently handling critical events in the transportation system.

9.6 Conclusions

Risk analysis is an important means of defining and analyzing possible threats to individuals, businesses, or the environments or systems in which they function or participate in. Risk analysis is performed by a multitude of occupations ranging from engineering, computer science, social scientists, etc. The presented studies illustrate that the process of implementing risk analysis to sociotechnical systems is evolving. Regarding the study performed on the Maritime Transport System, initial application of the presented analysis limited the contributing factors to accidents occurring at sea to the mechanical functionality of the ship itself, environmental conditions such as wind, time of day, etc., and human error. Human error was considered to be the major factor contributing to accidents occurring at sea but it was introduced that external factors outside the present system need to be considered under the risk analysis. To accurately represent the system of interest all relevant parties at every level must be identified. This includes government bodies, shipyard owners, company investors, and any other organizational body that is involved or associated with the decision-making process related to the well-being of the company.

Each of the above discussed works describes the complexities associated with accurately representing the different systems. A sociotechnical system consists of interactions between a social and technical infrastructure. The degree of complexity associated with each infrastructure varies but, regardless of the complexity, each one must be accurately represented to produce accurate results upon performing risk analysis. The two infrastructures must first be studied independently of one another, identifying the variables of interest and identifying how these variables can be extracted from real-time operation of a given infrastructure. A model for each infrastructure will then be constructed to represent the relevant entities and relationships identified previously. The modeled systems can then be subdued to different conditions of threat to characterize how it affects the functionality of the model. It will also assist in identifying which entities are most significant on the infrastructure of interest.

Upon completion of analyzing the social and technical infrastructures independently, analysis must be performed on the two with respect to the other. The two infrastructures must be further studied to determine what relationships are occurring between them. The independently constructed models are combined or linked together with the identified relationships between them, representing the sociotechnical system as a single model. Once again, the model is subdued to different conditions of threat to determine how each infrastructure responds in relation to the other. This analysis will provide a measure of performance for the whole system consisting of all relationships occurring within and between both infrastructures. In conclusion of this risk analysis, a system of support for decision making can be constructed to determine what aspects of the two infrastructures need to be improved to prevent future threats from occurring or improving the system's ability to handle or respond the occurrence.

References

1. European Transport Safety Council (ETSC), 2001, EU Transport Accident, Incident and Casualty Databases: Current Status and Future Needs, http://www.etsc.be.
2. Transportation Safety Board of Canada (TSB), 1998, Safety Study of the Operational Relationship between Ship Master/Watchkeeping Officers and Marine Pilots, http://www.bst.gc.ca.

3. Mathes, S., Nielsen, K., Engen, J., and Haaland, E., 1997, ATO-MOSR II—Final Report. Brussels: European Commission.
4. Rasmussen, J. 1997 Risk management in a dynamic society: A modeling problem. *Safety Science*, 27, 183–213.
5. Ruggeri, F., Pedrali, M., Trucco, P., and Cagno, E., 2004, On the use of Bayesian Belief Networks in Modelling Human and Organisational Causes of Maritime Accidents, *ENBIS*, Copenhagen, Denmark.
6. Shell, 1992, A Study of Standards in the Oil Tanker Industry, Shell International Marine Ltd., May.
7. Estonia, 1995, Accident investigation report; part report covering technical issues on the capsizing on 28 September 1994 in the Baltic Sea of the Ro-Ro passenger vessel *MV Estonia*, The Joint Accident Investigation Commission, Stockholm: Board of Accident Investigation.
8. Stenstrom, B., 1995, What can we learn from the *Estonia* accident? Some observation on technical and human shortcomings, in *The Cologne Re Marine Safety: Seminar,* April 27–28, Rotterdam.
9. International Maritime Organization (IMO), 2002, Guidelines for the Application of Formal Safety Assessment (FSA) for Use in the IMO Rule-Making Process, http://www.imo.org. Publisher: IMO, London, England. April 2002.
10. Maritime and Coastguard Agency (MCA).
11. http://en.wikipedia.org/wiki/Bayesian_network.
12. P. Trucco, E. Cagno & O. Grande, F. Ruggeri, "A Bayesian Belief Network Approach for Integrating Human and Organisational Factors in Rish analysis: A case study for the Martime Industry," Fourth Worshop on Bayesian Interence In stockastic processes, Villa Monastero, Varenna (LC), Italy, June 2005.
13. Jensen, F.V., 2001, *Bayesian Networks and Decision Graphs*, Springer-Verlag, New York.
14. Lee, J. and Rao, H., 2007, Understanding sociotechnical environments for acceptance of inter-agency counterterrorism information sharing systems, *Hawaii International Conference on System Sciences*, Oklahoma State University, University of Buffalo.
15. Léger, A., Duval, C., Weber, P., Levrat, E., and Farret, R., Risk Analysis of Complex Socio Technical Systems by Using Bayesian Network Modeling, available from: http://www.cper-misn-sectaf.cran.uhp-nancy.fr/Files/ACD/p42.pdf.
16. Comfort, L., Hauskrecht, M., and Lin, J., 2005, Dynamic networks: Modeling change in environments exposed to risk, University of Pittsburgh. *Proceedings of the 5th International ISCRAM Conference*, Washington, DC, USA, May 2008.

Chapter 10

Privacy Support in Cloud-Computing-Based Sociotechnical Networks

Yao Wu, Fei Hu, and Qi Hao

Contents

10.1 Introduction

Sociotechnical networks (STN) have been becoming prevalent in many applications (see previous chapters on different applications). However, information sharing in the STNs also results in the vulnerabilities and difficulties in privacy preservation. A malicious person can easily take advantage of the public profiles and friendships to exploit the private information of the target such as locations, transaction records, and identities. Thus, it is necessary to provide appropriate privacy policies or algorithms to limit the information leakage as well as to ensure the stability in keeping the dataflow among users and maintaining the accessibility.

Today, cloud computing [20] has become an important physical infrastructure to support STN. Cloud computing is the evolution of grid computing. It maps real user applications to different virtual resources. Figure 10.1 shows an example scenario of cloud computing. When a user issues resources dispatch commands to the cloud computing core, a series of virtual resource connections will be mapped to

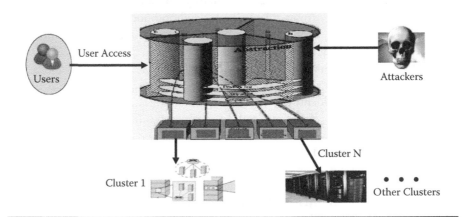

Figure 10.1 Cloud computing architecture (example).

real physical clusters. Those clusters in different places form an STN. The attackers can try to interpret users' data and infringe STN privacy.

In this chapter, we will provide a review on the privacy preserving schemes in the cloud-computing-based STNs. As an important requirement for privacy, anonymity is considered in many application domains. For instance, *K-anonymity* (to be discussed later) hides the identity of an entity by forming a group of similar entities. Thus, the probability of identifying the entity is less than $1/k$. Group formation depends on broadcast and multicast to hide the identity of the receiver side.

STNs should be anonymized effectively in order to compromise the privacy attacks. However, there are more challenges in privacy preservation in STNs such as the difficulty in modeling the background knowledge of social attacks, to measure the data loss, and to anonymize the social identities and relationships.

In terms of STN privacy preservation, we are concerned about end-to-end confidentiality, access control, data integrity, authentication, and availability [8]. Some attacks such as man-in-the-middle, impersonation attack, sybil attack [9], denial of service, and black hole attack can breach privacy preservation.

In the following sections we will introduce a few efficient methods to preserve privacy in STNs.

10.2 Privacy Preserving (Anonymization) Based on Graph Model

In [1], the authors have introduced *neighborhood attacks*, a prevalent type of privacy attacks in STNs. Even if we mask all the identities of vertices (a vertex in network graph represents a node in STNs), a malicious person can still infer part of the private information of the target vertex with some available information published in the networks. For example, in Figure 10.2, several users are identified. The figure shows that an anonymized STN graph Ada can be identified with the knowledge of Ada's unique 1-neighborhood graph (Figure 10.2c). A malicious person can find Bob through such a graph.

In [1], it makes use of the k-anonymity model [2] by adding a noise edge between Harry and Irene as shown in Figure 10.2d; k-anonymity is defined as that any vertices in the anonymized network can be identified with a probability lower than $1/k$. In Figure 10.2d, k equals 2.

In [1], it applies graph theory to model a network as $G = (V, E, L, \varphi)$, where V is a set of vertices, E is a set of edges, L is a set of labels, and $\varphi: V \to L$ is a labeling function. For a graph G, $V(G)$, $E(G)$, L_G, and φ_G are the set of vertices, the set of edges, the set of labels, and the labeling function in G, respectively.

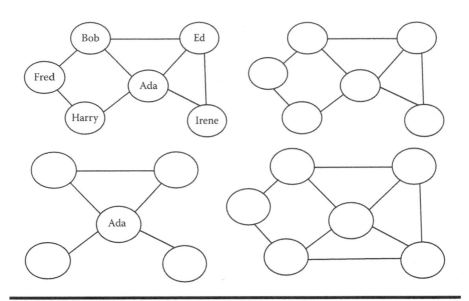

Figure 10.2   Neighborhood attacks in an STN. (From Bin Zhou and Jian Pei. Data Engineering, 2008. *IEEE 24th International Conference on ICDE 2008.* April 7–12, 2008, pp. 506–515.)

The labels in L are hierarchical. For two labels $l_1, l_2 \in L$, if l_1 is more general than l_2, then $l_1 \prec l_2$; as a example: *scientist* $\prec$ *physicist*. If $l_1 = l_2$ then $l_1 \leq l_2$. $G(S) = (S, E_s, L_g, \varphi_g)$ is defined as the subgraph of G if $S \subseteq V(G)$ and $E_s = \{(u,v) \mid (u,v) \in E(G) \wedge u, v \in S\}$.

Given $u \in V(G)$, we define the neighborhood of u as $Neighbor_G = G(N_u)$ where $N_u = \{v \mid (u,v) \in E(G)\}$. For two graphs $G = (V, E, L, \varphi)$ and $H = (V_H, E_H, L, \varphi)$, an instance of H in G is a tuple (H', f) where $H' = (V_{H'}, E_{H'}, L, \varphi)$ is a subgraph in G and $f : V_H \to V_{H'}$ is a bisection function such that (a) given $\forall u \in V_H$, $\varphi(f(u)) \leq \varphi(u)$, and (b) $(u,v) \in E_H$ if and only if $(f(u), f(v)) \in E_{H'}$.

In [1], four issues are addressed in order to preserve privacy in publishing network data:

1. Privacy in social networks and anonymization: Given a network $G = (V, E, L, \varphi)$ and the anonymization $G' = (V', E', L', \varphi')$ for publishing, Reference 1 provides a bijection function $A : V \to V'$ under the assumption that no fake vertices are induced. Besides, [1] assumes that for $(u,v) \in E$, $(A(u), A(v)) \in E'$. As an adversary can identity a vertex by the similarity and difference of relationships among the vertices in G and G', Reference 1 induces k-anonymity into the process $G \to G'$.

2. Adversary background knowledge: An adversary needs certain background knowledge of networks to reidentify the vertex. Different kind of background

knowledge can lead to different types of privacy attacks. Reference [1] just focuses on the background knowledge about the immediate neighbors of the target vertex.

Given a vertex $u \in V(G)$, u is k-anonymous in anonymization G' if there are at least $(k-1)$ other vertices, denoted as $v_1, ... v_{k-1} \in V(G)$, such that the neighborhoods $Neighbor_{G'}(A(u)), Neighbor_{G'}(A(v_1)), ..., Neighbor_{G'}(A(v_{k-1}))$ are isomorphic. Thus, G' is k-anonymous if any vertex in G is k-anonymous in G'.

3. Usage of anonymized social networks: Different applications should adopt various anonymization schemes. In Reference [1], the anonymization scheme applied is based on aggregate network queries that are popularly used in many network applications whenever aggregated data needs to be queried.

4. Problem complexity: The complexity of k-anonymity problem defined in Reference [1] is NP-hard.

Reference [1] also proposes an effective anonymization method, which consists of two steps:

10.2.1 Neighborhood Extraction and Coding

According to the requirements of k-anonymity, the vertices should be divided into groups and their neighborhoods need to be anonymized. As a graph iso-morphism problem, Reference 1 introduces neighborhood component coding technique to tackle the isomorphism NP-hard problem [3]. As a result, isomor-phism can be determined by the corresponding codes. A neighborhood com-ponent C is defined as a maximal connected subgraph in $Neighbor_G(u)$. As shown in Figure 10.3, there are three neighborhood components, C_1, C_2, C_3, in $Neighbor_G(u)$.

Thus, in order to encode the whole neighborhood, the components should be coded first. Reference 1 suggests the use of *DFS-tree* (*depth-first search tree*) [4] to encode the vertices in the preorder of T. As shown in Figure 10.4a,b,c, (b) and (c) are two different DFS-trees of graph G in (a). *The forward edges* included in the DFS-trees and *the backward edges* excluded from the DFS-trees are illustrated as the thick edges and the thin edges, respectively, in Figure 10.4b,c. Then the vertices are encoded form v_0 to v_3 based on the preorder of the corresponding DFS-trees. Thus, the DFS-tree for a graph G is not unique. To tackle this problem, Reference 1 uses a *minimum DFS* code notation proposed in Reference 5.

To identify the *minimum DFS code*, it is necessary to give the definition of a lin-ear order $\prec$ on edges. For edges $e = (v_i, v_j)$ and $e' = (v_{i'}, v_{j'})$ (in any edge (v_i, v_j), $i < j$), $e \prec e'$ if (a) when both e and e' are forward edges, $j < j'$ or $(i > i' \wedge j = j')$; (b) when both e and e' are backward edges, $i < i'$ or $(i = i' \wedge j < j')$; (c) when e is a forward edge and e' is a backward edge, $j \leq i'$; or (d) when e is a backward edge and e' is a forward edge, $i < j'$.

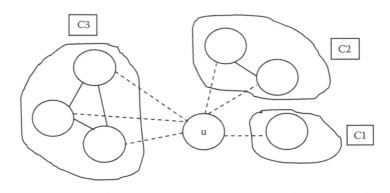

Figure 10.3 Neighborhood and its components (the dashed edges are just for illustration purpose and are not in the neighborhood subgraph). (From Bin Zhou and Jian Pei. Data Engineering, 2008. *IEEE 24th International Conference on ICDE 2008.* April 7–12, 2008, pp. 506–515.)

The *DFS code* of G with respect to T, $code(G, T)$, is a list of all edges in $E(G)$ according to the order $\prec$. For instance, the DFS code in Figure 4b is

$$code(G,T_1) = \langle (v_0,v_1,x,x)-(v_1,v_2,x,z)-(v_2,v_0,z,x)-(v_1,v_3,x,y)\rangle,$$

where an edge is denoted as $(v_i,v_j,\varphi(v_i),\varphi(v_j))$.

In Figure 4c,

$$code(G,T_2) = \langle (v_0,v_1,y,x)-(v_1,v_2,x,x)-(v_2,v_3,x,z)-(v_3,v_1,z,x)\rangle.$$

A predefined linear order in the label set L can produce the order of edges which determines the lexically *minimum DFS code*, denoted as $DFS(G)$. For example, $DFS(G) = \min(code(G,T_1),code(G,T_2)) = code(G,T_1)$ in Figure 10.4. The property of minimum DFS code (two graphs G and G' are isomorphic if and only if $DFS(G) = DFS(G')$ [5]) is useful for coding the components of the neighborhood of a vertex. The minimum DFS code of all components can be combined to one code according to the neighborhood component order.

Given two neighborhood components C_i and C_j in $Neighbor_G(u)$, $C_i \prec C_j$ if (a) $|V(C_i)| < V(C_j)|$; or (b) $|V(C_i)| = V(C_j)|$ and $|E(C_i)| < E(C_j)|$; or (c) $|V(C_i)| = V(C_j)|$ $|E(C_i)| = E(C_j)|$, and $|DFS(C_i) < DFS(C_j)|$. Thus, the neighborhood component code of $Neighbor_G(u)$ is a vector $NCC(u) = (DFS(C_1),...,DFS(C_m))$ where $C_1,...,C_m$ are the neighborhood components of $Neighbor_G(u)$, i.e., $Neighbor_G(u) = \bigcup_{i=1}^m C_i$, $C_i \preceq C_j$ for $1 \le i < j \le m$. For example, $NCC(u) = (DFS(C_1),DFS(C_2),DFS(C_3))$ in Figure 10.4. According to the property of minimum DFS codes, two neighborhoods $Neighbor_G(u)$ and $Neighbor_G(v)$ are isomorphic if and only if

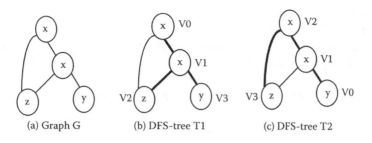

(a) Graph G   (b) DFS-tree T1   (c) DFS-tree T2

Figure 10.4 DFS codes, starting from different vertices. (From Bin Zhou and Jian Pei. Data Engineering, 2008. *IEEE 24th International Conference on ICDE 2008.* April 7–12, 2008, pp. 506–515.)

$NCC(u) = NCC(v)$. Thus, it is easy to compare the isomorphism and to calculate the similarity between two neighborhoods where information loss is reduced during anonymizing similar components.

10.2.2 STNs Anonymization

Based on the predominant properties of STNs such as power law distribution of node degree and small world theory, we can anonymize a network as well as preserve the neighborhoods and properties of original networks. k vertices with same degrees should be divided in a group according to the requirements of k-anonymity. Besides, such a process should follow the descending order based on the power law distribution.

10.2.2.1 Anonymization Quality Measure

Reference 1 proposes two methods to anonymize the neighborhoods of vertices: generalizing vertex labels and adding edges, both of which result in some information loss.

The information loss caused by generalizing vertex labels can be measured by normalized certainty penalty [6]. Suppose label l_1 of the vertex u is a leaf in the label hierarchy and $l_2 \prec l_1$. The number of leaves of l_2 is denoted as $size(l_2)$. $size(*)$ (* represents the most general category in the label hierarchy) is the total number of leafs in the label hierarchy. The normalized certainty penalty of l_2 is

$$NCP(l_2) = \frac{size(l_2)}{size(*)}$$

The information loss caused by adding edges can be measured by the total number of edges added and the number of vertices induced from other neighborhood for anonymization. Consider $Neighbor_G(u_1)$ and $Neighbor_G(u_2)$ are generalized to $Neighbor_{G'}(A(u_1))$ and $Neighbor_{G'}(A(u_2))$. Given

$$H = Neighbor_G(A(u_1)) \cup Neighbor_G(A(u_2))$$

and

$$H' = Neighbor_{G'}(A(u_1)) \cup Neighbor_{G'}(A(u_2)),$$

The anonymization cost is

$$Cost(u,v) = \alpha \cdot \sum_{v' \in H'} NCP(v') + \beta \cdot |\{(v_1,v_2) \mid (v_1,v_2) \notin E(H),$$

$$(A(v_1), A(v_2)) \in E(H')\}| + \gamma \cdot (|V(H')| - |V(H)|)$$

where α, β, and γ are the weights of three parts of cost predefined by users. The first part is the normalized certainty penalty; the second part calculates the cost of adding edges; the third part takes the number of vertices associated with the anonymized neighborhood. We can balance these three parts by tuning the three parameters. Thus, the similarity between two neighborhoods is measured by the anonymization cost.

10.2.2.2 Anonymizing Two Neighborhoods

First, we select all neighborhood components that totally match each other according to the same minimum DFS code. For example, as shown in Figure 10.5, the neighborhood component $C_2(u) \in Neighbor_G(u)$ matches $C_3(v) \in Neighbor_G(v)$ exactly.

Then Reference 1 uses a greedy method to group these not completely matched components based on the anonymization cost. Initially, we find two vertices with the same degree and the same label in the two components. Select the pair with the highest vertex degree when there are more than one pair of such vertices.

If there is not such a pair of matching vertices, we relax the requirements of vertex degree or label, compute the difference of degrees and the normalized certainty penalty of generalizing the labels in the label hierarchy, and select the pair with the minimum anonymization cost. Then, take a breadth-first search to match vertices one by one. Thus, the similarity between the two components can be calculated by the anonymization cost according to the matching process.

Regarding the components $C_1(u)$ and $C_1(v)$ in Figure 10.5, we select the pair of vertices $(u_1 \ v_1)$ and take a breadth-first search ($u_2 \ v_2$ and $u_3 \ v_3$). However, there is

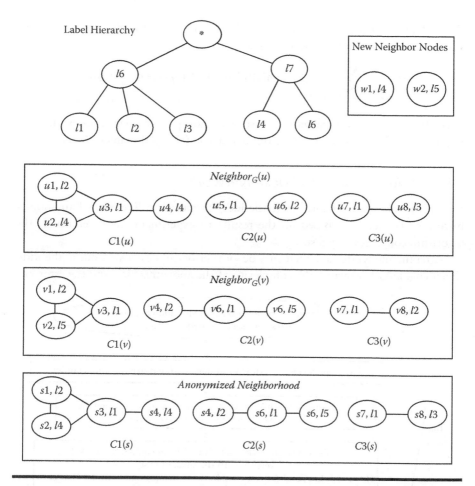

Figure 10.5 Anonymizing two neighborhoods. (From Bin Zhou and Jian Pei. Data Engineering, 2008. *IEEE 24th International Conference on ICDE 2008.* April 7–12, 2008, pp. 506–515.)

no vertex in $C_1(v)$ matching with u_4 in $C_1(u)$. In such a case, we should find a vertex $w_1 \in V(G)$ which is not included in $C_1(u)$ or $C_1(v)$, and add w_1 to $C_1(v)$. As a result, $C_1(u)$ and $C_1(v)$ can be anonymized to the same structure. The process of selection of w_1 is introduced as below.

First, select such a vertex in $V(G)$ that is unanonymized and with the smallest degree. If there is more than one vertex that satisfy the requirements, we can choose the one with the closest label according to the normalized certainty penalty. If there is no unanonymized vertex, we then select an anonymized vertex w satisfying the requirements of the degree and the label, and categorize w and other $(k-1)$ vertices in its same group as unanonymized.

In Figure 10.5, given an unanonymized vertex (w_1, l_4) added to $C_1(u)$, the anonymization cost of $C_1(u)$ and $C_1(v)$ is

$$\alpha \cdot \sum_{v' \in V(C_1(u)) \cup V(C_1(v))} NCP(\varphi(A(v'))) + \beta \cdot 1 + \gamma \cdot 1 = \alpha \cdot \frac{4}{5} + \beta + \gamma.$$

According to the anonymization cost, we can pair similar components. In Figure 10.5, $C_1(u)$ matches $C_1(v)$, $C_2(u)$ matches $C_3(v)$, $C_3(u)$ matches $C_2(v)$.

10.2.2.3 Anonymizing a Social Network

Figure 10.6 shows the algorithm (basic idea) proposed in Reference 1 to anonymize a social network. Based on the results of experiments in Reference 1, the algorithm converges very fast.

After the anonymization, there may be some errors in the network due to the additional edges. As k increases, the complexity of the anonymization and the error rate

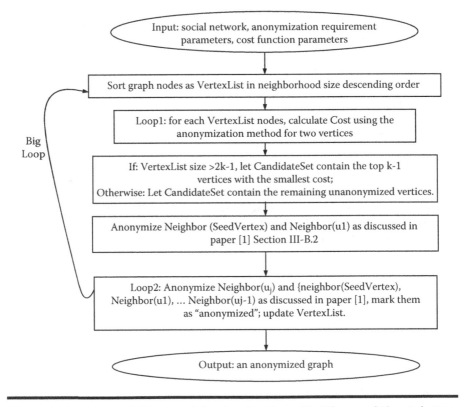

Figure 10.6 Anonymizing a social network. (From Bin Zhou and Jian Pei. Data Engineering, 2008. *IEEE 24th International Conference on ICDE 2008*. April 7–12, 2008, pp. 506–515.)

in the network will increase. Actually, an adversary maybe knows only a part of the neighborhood of a target vertex. This results in better performance of the algorithm.

Although the algorithm has some advantage as we mentioned above, we should extend the method to handle the case where not only vertices but also edges have labels. Besides, we could induce some faked vertices in the process of anonymization as well as considering the network structure preservation. We also can extend 1-neighborhood in Reference 1 to d-neighborhood to enhance the privacy preservation. k-anonymize has some privacy problems because of the lack of diversity in sensitive attributes. Thus, l-diversity [7] is more desirable.

10.3 Privacy Preserving Based on Trust Relationships

Reference 8 proposes a distributed privacy preservation method based on the trust relationships. This anonymization method makes use of the multi-hop routing among cooperative nodes. The node, which represents a user in network, is uniquely identified by a pseudonym and a node identifier.

As shown in Figure 10.7, there are three components in the system proposed in Reference 8.

10.3.1 Matryoshkas

The matryoshkas is defined as a hierarchical structure of relationship between the node (the owner of the matryoshkas) that is located on the core and other trusted nodes on the concentric rings. The innermost ring consists of a set of nodes which are trusted by the owner of the matryoshkas. The second ring consists of a set of nodes which are trusted by the nodes in the first ring. Other rings are established

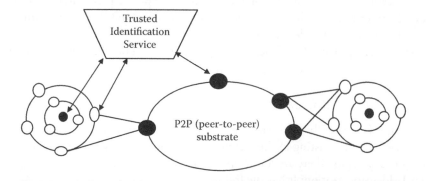

Figure 10.7 System main entities: peer to peer substrate, matryoshkas, and trusted identification service [8]. (From Cutillo, L.A., Molva, R., and Strufe, T. Wireless On-Demand Network Systems and Services, 2009. *Sixth International Conference on WONS 2009.* February 2–4, 2009, pp. 145–152.)

according to the same rules. Besides, it is not necessary for the nodes on the same ring to trust each other, except for the first ring. Under certain encryption operations, the information of the core node is made copies on all the nodes in the first ring. Thus, the messages go through the concentric rings from an outermost node to an innermost node. Every node must establish its matryoshka once it enters the system and keep updating it. The privacy is preserved based on the hop-by-hop trust relationships.

10.3.2 Peer-To-Peer Substrate

According to users' identifiers, the peer-to-peer substrate provides the global access to its data. Each node in the peer-to-peer substrate is arranged in a distribute hash table (DHT) associating with the distributed systems. The pseudonym of each node is used to identify its location in the DHT according to the DHT protocol. Thus, the location data include the pointers to nodes on the outermost ring of the requested user's matryoshka. The node in peer-to-peer substrate works as an entry to access the information of the target node.

10.3.3 Trusted Identification Service

Each node gets a unique pseudonym, a unique node identifier, and two certificates for the authentication for each type of identifiers from the trusted identification service. The pseudonym is used as an identifier in the peer-to-peer system, and the node identifier is used to identify a member of the STN. Such mechanism leads to the protection of Sybil attacks, impersonation attacks, and attacks on the DHT overlay.

Reference 8 uses a straightforward public key cryptography in order to realize the privacy preservation. Each node has a set of properties N such as the pseudonym and the node identifier. It generates two key pairs: I and P. The identification service certifies the authenticity of I and P to encrypt the pseudonym P and the node identifier respectively. The relationship among I, P and P cannot be inferred, except for the trusted nodes of a user.

The system proposed in Reference 8 provides the following six operations in order to realize the service required in the network:

10.3.3.1 Account Creation

An account is created by an invitation initiated from a user u to a different user v (u is a user already existing in the system; v is denoted as a user who wants to take part in the system.). There are four steps for account creation:
(Step 1) Identity creation: It has the following smaller steps:

a. v creates the two key pairs I and P;
b. v sends a request to u for obtaining pseudonym, node identifier, and certificates;

c. u relays this request to the trusted identification service based on the DHT;

d. the trusted identification service derives node's pseudonym $P_v = h_1(N)$ and its node identifier $v = h_1(N)$ from node's properties $N = (h_1, h_2$ are two cryptographic hash functions). It also grants two certificates $\{I^+, v\}_{S_{TTP}}$ and $\{P^+, P_v\}_{S_{TTP}}$, where S_{TTP} is the signature of the identification service;

e. once u receives the response from the identification, it will relay the response to v.

(Step 2) Joining the P2P substrate:
According to the received certifications, v joins the P2P substrate using u as a bootstrapping host and P_v as its pseudonym.

(Step 3) Creation of the profile:
v can independently generate its profile consisting of several attributes for each entry, and generates public key pairs, which it signs with I^+, for each attribute in order to share it with preferred users. Then each attribute is encrypted with its respective private key. The friend list is an important attribute in Reference 8, v retrieves the name attribute from its contacts like u in their encrypted form and lists these as the friend list, finally encrypted with its own respective key. Thus, a user is able to access the profile only if it is admitted by the nodes in the chain from the outmost to the innermost ring in the matryoshka.

(Step 4) Matryoshka creation:
Figure 10.8 illustrates the process of matryoshka creation for v. Initially, v only knows u. Step 4 further includes the following smaller steps:

a. v stores its encrypted profile in u;

b. It sends a request to register to DHT and a time-to-live counter, ttl, to u; $E_{P_u}\{M_{vu}, ttl\}$ with $M_{vu} = \{k, v, P_u, \{I_v^+, v\}_{S_{TTP}}\}_{S_{I_v}}$ where k is the lookup key for the DHT;

c. Once u receives the message from v, it selects a node from its contact list arbitrarily, for example, w, and encapsulates M_{vu}, then sends it together with the decreased ttl counter ttl' to w:

$$E_{P_w}\{M_{uw}, ttl'\}$$

with $M_{uw} = \{k, P_u, P_w, \{P_u^+, P_u\}_{S_{TTP}}, M_{vu}\}_{S_{P_u}}$;

d. repeat (c) recursively until the ttl expires (ttl is set according to the requirement of the number of the rings in a matryoshka).

e. Once the message reaches the outermost ring, the node will register the key and authenticate it according to the chain of encapsulated signatures.

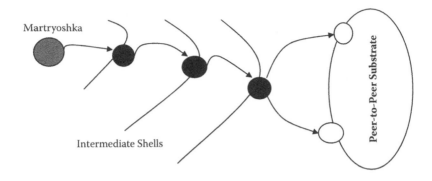

Figure 10.8 Account and matryoshka creation with key registration for node. (From Cutillo, L.A., Molva, R., and Strufe, T. *Wireless* On-Demand Network Systems and Services, 2009. *Sixth International Conference on WONS 2009.* February 2–4, 2009, pp. 145–152.)

10.3.3.2 Profile Publication

Any data can be classified as public, protected, private data. Public data is signed by the originator, published by the owner, and replicated at the trusted contacts of a user on the innermost matryoshka ring. Protected data is managed almost in the same way as the public data, except it needs to be encrypted by the owner. Private data is stored by the owner itself and not published. Each node in the system may dispose three different kinds of data: profile information, trusted contact relations, and message.

10.3.3.3 Data Retrieval

The lookup of data follows the opposite path compared to the registration. The requesting node can access the data based on the respective keys the owner provides.

10.3.3.4 Contact Request and Acceptance

Contact request is sent in the same way as the data request. If the target accepts the contact relation, it replies by a direct trusted link to *v* and both expand their inner ring of their matryoshka and executing profile replication and profile registration.

10.3.3.5 Message Management

Messages are sent in the same way as data retrieval requests. However, they are only served by the owner of the matryoshka. Besides, the sender signs its message with its own private node id key and encrypts it for the receiver.

10.3.3.6 Matryoshka Maintenance

In case that a node in a matryoshka leaves the network, it sends a path invalidation message to the nodes on the next inner and outer rings of the matryoshka. In the system, all nodes check their links in the matryoshkas they participate in to detect the failure of nodes.

Due to the utilization of the cryptographic mechanism (the public key and the private key), trust relationship, and trusted identification service, the system in Reference 8 is able to anonymize the network so effectively that it preserves the privacy. Besides, it can resist the kind of attacks we mentioned above, as well as keep the availability of the network by the replication of data on the innermost ring. However, the storage of a node must be taken account of as the profile duplication exhausts the cache of the system. Besides, the response time should be considered because of the distributed structure and the hop-by-hop communication. We can make use of a Kademlia-based approach [10] instead of a ring-based DHT for shorter response times. We can optimize the authentication by a distributed TTP based on threshold cryptography, or even without a TTP [11]. The group key management is a major issue in the system of [8]. We can employ a degradable crypto scheme to simplify this management.

10.4 *Clarke Tax* Mechanism

In Reference 14, a simple mechanism, the Clarke Tax mechanism [12] [13], is proposed for collaborative management of privacy policies on the shared data based on game theory. The Clarke Tax mechanism can be used as an incentive for trust and coownership.

In Reference 14, data access is based on the distance which is defined as the path with minimal length between two nodes. A privacy policy can be summarized by the predicate $\Pr P(i,n)_{RtSet}$, which means all the users who are connected to i with a minimum path of length n, by relationships in $RtSet$. If $n = 0$, it means that the data is private. If $n = \infty$, it means that the data is public to all users in the system.

In STNs, there are a lot of data shared among different users. Thus, the concept of *co-ownership* in the network is important. In Reference 14 the user collaborative policy requirements are mapped to an auction based on the Clarke Tax mechanism, which selects the privacy policy that will maximize the social utility by encouraging truthfulness among the co-owners [15], who have the right to not only edit data but also manage the access to data. In order to identify co-owners, Reference 14 provides a general classification of users (viewers, originators, and owners) based on their relationships with the data. As in most STNs, Reference 14 makes use of tags corresponding to unique user id to identify the potential owners of the data. The co-ownerships can be automatically established by the originator according to distance-based policy condition.

Due to the co-ownership, the privacy preferences of different owners about the shared data may conflict. As a result, some owners' actions may breach others' privacy. Thus, it is necessary to employ collaborative privacy management that must satisfy the requirements: content integrity, semiautomated, adaptive, and group-preference.

In order to aggregate the privacy setting decisions of the co-owners, it is necessary to balance the time complexity and fairness of the algorithm. Thus, Reference 14 proposes an incentive-based mechanism for users to share data and leverage the decisions about their privacy. It makes use of a credit-based system in which the user earns credits proportional to the amount of data the use discloses, as a co-owner, and to the number of times it grants co-ownership to potential owners. For example, the originator i gains c for sharing data s with n co-owners: elevate $c = m_i + (\beta \times m_i) \times n$, where m_i and $\beta \times m_i$ ($\beta \in [0,1]$) are the credits for the data the originator discloses and for each user accepted as a co-owner respectively. And each user accepted as a co-owner of the data gains $\alpha \times m_i$ ($\alpha \in [0,1]$). It can be inferred that the credit of a user is based on the importance of the user's preferences in making the group decision. $v_i(g)$ represents the value of the user i choosing the privacy g. Thus, the collective decision value is defined as $F(v_1(g),...,v_n(g)) = X$, where $F(.)$ is a collective function which is designed for the optimality characteristics according to Game Theory in Reference 14, maximizing the collective value. This approach has three advantages. It is (1) simple, (2) nonmanipulable, and (3) fair.

Reference 14 adopts the additive social utility, which means that $F(v_1(g),...,v_n(g)) = \sum_{i=1}^{n} v_i(g)$. Thus, we select the privacy setting which maximizes the collective social value: $g^* = \arg\max \sum_{i=1}^{n} v_i(g)$. After selecting g, each user is required to pay tax π_i. The utility of the choice $c = (g, \pi_1,...,\pi_n)$ is represented by $u_i(c) = v_i(g) - \pi_i$. Reference 14 utilizes the Clarke Tax mechanism that maximizes the social utility function by encouraging truthfulness among the individuals, regardless of other individuals' choices. Thus, the tax of a user is computed as below:

$$\pi_i(g^*) = \sum_{j \neq i} v_j(\arg\max_{g \in G} \sum_{k \neq i} v_k(g)) - \sum_{j \neq i} v_j(g^*).$$

The most important feature of the Clarke Tax mechanism is that it ensures the incentive of users to keep honest in their transactions. The evidence can be found in Reference 15.

In order to automatically select the privacy preferences for each item of data, Reference 14 makes use of inference-based techniques that use tags and similarity analysis to infer the best privacy policy based on previous preferences of users about shared data. An item of data having k tags can be defined as a vector of tags: $\vec{t} = \{t_1,...,t_k\}$. A set of shared items is denoted as $T = \{\vec{t_1}, \vec{t_2},...,\vec{t_n}\}$. Based on folksonomy [16], items represented by corresponding tags can be compared using several metrics [17,18] such as occurrence of tag pairs:

$$w(t_1;t_2) := card\{(u;r) \in U \times R \mid t_1;t_2 \in T_{ur}\}.$$

(A folksonomy is a tuple $F := (U;T;R;Y)$ where U, T, and R are finite sets of users, tags, and resources respectively. Y is a ternary relation among them, i.e., $Y \subseteq U \times T \times R$. A post is a triple $(u;T_{ur};r)$ with $u \in U$, $r \in R$, and $T_{ur} := \{t \in T \mid (u;t;r) \in Y\}$.

The similarity between $\vec{t}$ and $\vec{t}'$ is represented as follows:

$$sim(\vec{t},\vec{t}') = sim(\vec{t}',\vec{t}) = \sum_{i=1}^{k} \sum_{j=1}^{n} w(t_i,t_j') \geq 0$$

$$champ = \max\left\{ sim(\vec{t},\vec{t}'), sim(\vec{t},\vec{t}_1),...,sim(\vec{t},\vec{t}_n) \right\}.$$

Thus, the privacy policy associated with *champ* is prompted to all the users in the same set.

Disadvantages: The approach proposed in Reference 14 should be extended for a hierarchical relationship structure. Besides, it is necessary to take the type of access privilege into account. In order to determine the optimal privacy policy and calculate the tax, Reference 14 requires every user to publish their social value $v_i(g)$ simultaneously. However, this requirement, which needs an effective synchronization mechanism, may not be achieved in distributed networks. The Clark Tax approach is not perfect because of the assumption that users should be able to calculate the value of different privacy policies. This assumption cannot be achieved easily. Fortunately, the approach is implemented with short execution time.

10.5. Privacy Preserving in Collaborative STNs

Reference 19 proposes a method to preserve the privacy while extending the individual STN to multiple collaborative STNs. This kind of collaborative network must address three problems as follows:

10.5.1 Privacy Problem 1

Combine the multiple and sometimes conflicting data from different providers in different STNs into a single network.

This step not only is a mere extension of the existing algorithm for creating the network but also should concern about collaborations among STNs:

Criteria 1: Given the collaborative STN S, which contains n social networks, n_1 cannot determine the contents of n_2 when $n_1 \neq n_2$.

Besides, Reference 19 proposes a client-server physical architecture which can minimize the data leakage. A server in the architecture can separate the data and communications that are encrypted between the server and client. In Reference 19, there must be a third party managing the server to preserve the privacy.

Reference 19 provides the collaborative social network addition protocol as follows:

10.5.1.1 Protocol Definitions

10.5.1.1.1 Objects

- S: The collaborative social network, which is a set of social networks
  - $S(o,e)$:
- O: A node within the social network n; note that o is already hashed with function $h(\ )$ as it is created from hashed data
  - O_j: The set of social networks that have provided these attributes; this numbering is held at the individual attributes level
- e: A set of edges related to node o
  - e_i: The set of social networks that have provided this edge
  - S_r: The resulting social network from a user query
- N: A social network being added to S
  - $N(d,g)$:
- d: A node within the social network N
- g: A set of edges related to node o
- R: A revocation social network being removed from S; note that $R = N$ for social network identification purposes
  - $R(d,g)$:
- d: A node within the social network R
- g: A set of edges related to node o
- U: A user of S
- U_q: A query containing attributes to look for within S

10.5.1.1.2 Functions

- $a(o)$: An attribute or set of attributes of a node which can be used to uniquely identify the node
- $h(\ )$: A secure hash function. For example, SHA 512

10.5.1.1.3 Protocol Algorithm

For N $(d = [1...n],g)$

N $(h(d),g)$ is sent to S

If any $a(S(o)) == a(N(h(d)))$ then

For each attribute within $h(d)$ that matches in o

$o_j + = h(N)$

Else

Add new attribute from $h(d)$ to o with a $o_j = h(N)$

End

For any edge within e that matches an edge within g

$e_i + = h(N)$

Else

Add non-matching edges within set g to set e with $e_i = h(N)$

End

Else

Add new node and edge set $N(h(d), g)$ to S

End

Next

In Reference 19, the result of the experiment shows that the creation algorithm converges quickly as well as achieves the validation of the data.

10.5.2 Privacy Problem 2: Network Updating Issues

Reference 19 uses a pull architecture where the centralized server periodically pulls updates from the involved STNs. In order to save the bandwidth and the process time, this architecture equips each subnet with an addition list and a revocation list.

10.5.2.1 Collaborative Social Network Revocation Protocol

For $N(d = [1...n], g$

$R(d = [1...n], g)$ *is sent to* S

If any $a(S(o)) == a(R(h(d)))$ then

For each attribute within $h(d)$ that matches in o

$o_j - = h(R)$

If o_j empty then remove o

End

For any edge within *e* that matches an edge within *g*

$$e_i - = h(R)$$

If e_i empty then remove *e*
End
End
Next

3. Privacy Problem 3: Harmonizing Node Behavior

It is necessary to guarantee the privacy of the query, network, and result in the interactions among nodes:

Criteria 2: Given a users query Q, the collaborative STN set S, cannot determine the original attribute values within Q.
Criteria 3: Given a users query Q, STN S_n with S, cannot determine the value of any non-matching attribute values within Q.
Criteria 4: Given a query result set R, a user cannot determine which STN S_n within S matched Q to generate R.

10.5.2.2 Collaborative Social Network Searching Protocol

U generates query U_q which contains attributes of interest

$h(U_q)$ is sent to S
For $S(o)$ with attributes matching $h(U_q)$
    $S_r + = S(o,e)$ not including o_j or e_i
Next
For each *e* within S_r
    If both nodes of *e* are not within S_r then
        Remove *e* from S_r
    End
Next
S_r is sent to U

U uses hash values from U_q to reveal matching attributes in S_r
The searching time depends on the number of required criteria and the scale of the collaborative network.
Disadvantages: The experiments in Reference 19 illustrate that all these four criteria can be achieved in the proposed architecture under communication encryptions like SSL. However, this client-server architecture compromises a central point of failure as well as an obvious target for malicious activity. Besides, the centralized

algorithm is based upon a powerful server which may not be achieved in the environment of sociotechnical networks. Thus, some distributed methods such as the extension of the algorithm mentioned above should be involved. To tackle this problem, the users may directly generate the collaborative STNs to distribute the process of the update and query issues. Because some identification issues must be taken into account, this distributed system is very challenging.

10.6 Conclusions

In this chapter, we have presented some privacy models which are based on STNs and can also be extended to the applications of sociotechnical networks. Furthermore, we have analyzed the advantage and disadvantages of these privacy models. There are still some unsolved problems in the privacy preservation. For example, it is difficult to deploy the anonymity protocols in highly dynamic environments, especially when the nodes leave or add to the network frequently. Besides, it is more effective to associate privacy preservation with trust models. In this way, the trustees (determined by the trust computation) of a node can work coordinately to defend external and internal attacks. In future research, the privacy model should be improved to adapt to the characteristics of STNs, especially considering the privacy between the layers in multilevel STNs.

References

1. Bin Zhou and Jian Pei. Preserving privacy in social networks against neighborhood attacks. Data Engineering, 2008. *IEEE 24th International Conference on ICDE 2008.* April 7–12, 2008, pp. 506–515.
2. Sweeney, L. K-anonymity: a model for protecting privacy, *International Journal on Uncertainty, Fuzziness and Knowledge-Based System*, vol. 10, no. 5, pp. 557–570, 2002.
3. Garey, M. R. and Johnson, D. S. *Computers and Intractability: A Guide to the Theory of NP-Completeness.* New York: W. H. Freeman & Co., 1979.
4. Cormen, T. H. et al. *Introduction to Algorithms*, Second edition. MIT Press and McGraw Hill, 2002.
5. Yan, X. and Han, J. gspan: Graph-based substructure pattern mining, in *Proc. ICDM'02*, pp. 721, 2002, Maebashi city, Japan.
6. Xu, J. et al., Utility-based anonymization using local recoding, in *Proc. KDD '06*, pp. 785–790, 2006, Philadelphia, PA, USA.
7. Machanavajjhala, A. et al. L-diversity: Privacy beyond k-anonymity, in *ACM Transactions on knowledge Discovery from Data*, Vol I, Issue I, March 2007.
8. Cutillo, L. A., Molva, R., and Strufe, T. Privacy preserving social networking through decentralization. *Sixth International Conference on Wireless On-Demand Network Systems and Services (WONS) 2009.* February 2–4, 2009, pp. 145–152.
9. Douceur, J. R. The Sybil attack, in *International Workshop on Peer-to-Peer Systems*, 2002, pp. 251–260.

10. Maymounkov, P. and Mazieres, D. Kademlia: A peer-to-peer information system based on the XOR metric, in *LNCS: International Workshop on P2P-Systems*, vol. 2429, 2002, pp. 53–65.

11. Popescu, B. C., Crispo, B., and Tanenbaum, A. S. Safe and private data sharing with turtle: Friends team-up and beat the system, in *LNCS: Security Protocols, 2006*, pp. 213–220.

12. Clarke, E. H. Multipart pricing of public goods, in *Public Choice* 11, pp. 17–33, 1971.

13. Clarke, E. H. Multipart pricing of public goods: An example, in *Public Price for Public Products*, Urban Inst., 1972.

14. Anna Cinzia Squicciarini, Mohamed Shehab, and Federica Paci. Collective privacy management in social networks. International World Wide Web Conference. *Proceedings of the 18th International Conference on World Wide Web.* pp. 521–530.

15. Ephrati, E. and Rosenschein, J. S. Voting and Multi-Agent Consensus. 1991. Technical report, Computer Science Department, Hebrew University, Jerusalem, Israel.

16. Mathes, A. Folksonomies: Cooperative classification and communication through shared metadata. See http://www.adammathes.com/academic/computer-mediated-communication/folksonomies.html, 2004.

17. Jiang, J. and Conrath, D. Semantic similarity based on corpus statistics and lexical taxonomy, in *Proceedings of ROCLING X*, September 1997.

18. Pirrò, G. and Seco, N. Design, implementation and evaluation of a new semantic similarity metric combining features and intrinsic information content, in *Proceedings of on the Move to Meaningful Internet Systems*, 2008.

19. Blosser, G. and Zhan, J. Privacy preserving collaborative social network, *International Conference on Information Security and Assurance (ISA) 2008*. April 24–26, 2008, pp. 543–548.

20. Armbrust, M. et al. Above the Clouds: A Berkeley View of Cloud Computing, UC Berkeley EECS, February 10, 2009. See http://www.eecs.berkeley.edu/Pubs/TechRpts/2009/EECS-2009-28.pdf.

Chapter 11

Trust Models in Cloud-Computing-Based Sociotechnical Networks

Yao Wu, Fei Hu, and Qi Hao

Contents

11.1 Introduction

11.1.1 Quick Overview on Social Networks

In the early 20th century, social networks emerged as an important research field in sociology. Due to some interesting properties of social networks, they have been used extensively in sociology, as well as in information science, economics, and industrial engineering.

A social network is defined as a networking system that consists of a set of nodes (such as people, organizations, or other social entities) that have a set of relations of ties among them (e.g., friendship, conflict, information exchange, etc.) [1]. In order to measure the social structure, social relationships, and social behaviors, social networks analysis therefore is an essential and important technique.

In social networks analysis, there are two main measurements—extraction and visualization. The extracted relational data can be used to construct a social network. Through visualization, the characteristics of the social networks such as the structure of networks, the distribution of nodes, the links (relationships) between nodes, and the clusters and groups in the social networks can be more easily understood [2].

Typically, social networks have some fundamental properties such as degree, size, density, distance, and geodesic distance (see Table 11.1). Besides, there are some more complicated properties utilized in social network analysis as follows [3]:

- **Maximum flow**, which is defined as the number of different nodes the source can choose to initiate the path to the target. It focuses on the vulnerability or redundancy of connections between pairs of nodes;
- *The Hubbell and Katz cohesion,* which considers the whole range of connections between the two nodes;
- *Centrality and power,* which define the importance of the node in a network. These include several aspects such as degree, closeness, and betweenness (Table 11.1).
- In a clique that belongs to the subset of a network, its nodes have closer and more intense relationships than other nodes in the network. There are four types of cliques [1]: N-cliques; N-Clans; K-plexes; K-cores (Table 11.2).

By considering the social network properties, the social network model has evolved through several phases. Initially the random network theory was explored. And then

Table 11.1   Three Aspects of Power

Node power parameters	Definitions	Effects
Degree	Number of connections around a node	Having more opportunities and alternatives
Closeness	Length of paths to other nodes	Direct communication with other nodes
Betweenness	Lying between pairs of nodes	Breaking contacts among nodes to isolate them or prevent connections

Source: Jamali, M. and Abolhassani, Web Intelligence (2006). *IEEE/WIC/ACM International Conference on WI* 2006. December 18–22, 2006, pp. 66–72.

Table 11.2   Four Types of Cliques

Types	Definition
N-cliques	Nodes are tied to each of the group members at a distance within N links
N-Clans	All the ties among the nodes in N-cliques occur through other members of the group
K-plexes	A node is a member of a clique of size *n* if it has direct ties to *n-k* members of that clique
K-cores	Nodes are connected to *k* members of the group

Source: Zhai Dongsheng and Pan Hong. A social network-based trust model for E-commerce. *Wireless Communications, Networking and Mobile Computing,* 2008. *4th International Conference on WiCOM '08.* October 12–14, 2008, pp. 1–5.

the establishment of the notion of *six degree of separation,* also known as the small world property of social networks, contributed to its significant evolvement. The scale-free link distribution was also taken into account in the modeling process.

Generally there are two techniques: mathematical and graphical techniques, which are used to describe the network compactly and systematically in social network modeling. Network analysis uses graphic display that consists of nodes to represent actors and edges to represent ties or relation. Besides, adjacent matrix is used in social network analysis: if a relationship exits a one is written in a cell; if there is no relationship a zero is entered.

	A	B	C	D
A	0	1	1	1
B	1	0	0	0
C	0	0	0	1
D	0	0	0	0

Figure 11.1   Graph and matrix.

Figure 11.1 illustrates these two techniques in detail. Statistical analysis is an advanced approach to establish a social network model. It aims at modeling probabilities of relational ties between nodes.

11.1.2 Transition to Sociotechnical Networks (STNs)

Based on the characteristics of social networks, sociotechnical networks (STNs) incorporate some new technical elements. An STN includes the technologies that sustain human interaction, and the technologies that people construct and use in collaborations. In STNs, the social and the technical are essentially inseparable and coconstitutive [4,5]. Online social network Web sites such as MySpace, Facebook, and Wikipedia pertain to STNs. Other examples are the electrical power grid and the transportation network. The main purpose of an STN is to facilitate the communication among users and to exchange and share information.

Cloud-computing-based STN: Recently a concept called "cloud computing" has been proposed to reflect the fact that lots of network users collaborate through a virtual organization that includes a series of computing resources, which are essentially mapped to realistic physical facilities such as different clusters located everywhere in the Internet. Such a cloud-computing-based architecture is an excellent medium to form an STN since humans and physical infrastructure can interact with each other through virtual network resource access under some type of access rules.

In this chapter, we will target security issues, especially trust models in such a cloud-computing-based STN.

11.1.3 Security in Sociotechnical Networks

The benefits from STNs do not come without a price. When considering the security, privacy, and trust of the STN services, several serious matters emerge. Malicious participants can easily exploit social relationships and attack these communities by disseminating misinformation, impersonating digital identities, and with social-network-enhanced phishing. Generally, STN services contain a lot of information that may be protected so that they are inaccessible. Unfortunately, there are still some "back doors" opened for malicious participants to access, based on complicated social relationships. What's worse, group attacks have come into vogue. For example in a gang attack, a group of attackers within a community collude to reduce the reputation of the target. Thus, the protection of the privacy data and detecting/mitigating the reputation attacks are challenging problems that need more sophisticated strategies and more robust models.

The aim of security is to make the system both correct and dependable by handling threats effectively. It has been argued in Reference 6 that dependability plays a more important role in security research than usually considered. To become a secure system, the social and technical components in an STN should cooperate not only for the achievement of production tasks but also for the achievement of dependability, which is defined by the degree to which the sociotechnical system behaves in the way it is expected to be [7].

Although technical components perform well on well-defined, predictable, and repetitive security tasks such as access control, they become complex and expensive when the requirements of the task are vague and need a lot of flexibilities like abnormal detection. Fortunately, some schemes have been proposed to effectively address these disadvantages of technical components (such as in Reference 8). Thus, despite the uncertainty induced by the social component, both technical and social measures are equally important in the role of mitigating the risks and improving the reliability of a system. Good security in the STN environment must take into consideration the human element, and designs must incorporate an easy interface to ensure security and reduce costs for applying security.

Table 11.3 shows the different types of social attacks.

Table 11.3   Classification of Sociocommunal Attacks

Inflation attack		Deflation attack		
One-on-self	Aggrandizement		Inferiority complex	
One-on-one	Shilling kickback	Vilification vendetta		
One-on-many	Dr. Jekyll & Mr. Hide			
Many-on-one	Praise planting	Godfather	Gang attack	
Many-on-many (intra)	Elite clique	Supra society	Cultural cringe	Civil war
Many-on-many (exo)	Cartel	Mutual boosting	Reputation racism	Reputation war

Source: Javed I. Khan and Sajid S. Shaikh. A phenotype reputation estimation function and its study of resilience to social attacks. *Journal of Network and Computer Applications* Volume 32, Issue 4, Pages 913–924, 2009. Elsevier Ltd.

11.2 Trust in Sociotechnical Network

Social norms that are based on the moral or spiritual values of people influence all the interactions in the STNs. They evolve to adapt to the development of the network [8]. Trust is essential in social norms. In social sciences the widely accepted definition of trust is "an attitude of positive expectation that one's vulnerabilities will not be exploited" [9,10]. However, in security, trust has been recently defined as a "system or component whose failure can break the security policy" [11]. The main difference between the two definitions is that the one from the social perspective pays attention to the interaction between people and the one from security perspective emphasizes the feature of a secure system. Figure 11.2 is from the research presented in [8,12]; it illustrates the model of trust that consists of some factors determining the relationship between a trustor and trustee. The main factors include Intrinsic Properties (Motivation, Ability, Internalized Norms, and Benevolence) and Contextual Properties (Temporal, Social, and Institutional Embeddedness).

The establishment of a trust relationship depends upon both intrinsic properties and contextual properties. Intrinsic properties, such as the propensity to take risks, the benefits of engaging in a trust relationship, and the personal cost of breaking trust, are defined as the factors that are internal to the trustor and trustee; law enforcement, expectations of future interactions, or reputation properties are defined as the factors that exist outside both actors [8].

Trust plays a very important role in improving dependability of the social component in STNs. Trust and the factors it includes seem to be consistent with security policies, but sometimes they are contradictory and even worse; for instance,

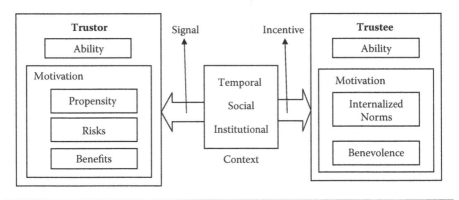

Figure 11.2 Model of trust. (From Ivan Flechais et al. Divide and conquer: The role of trust and assurance in the design of secure socio-technical systems. September 2005, *NSPW '05: Proceedings of the 2005 Workshop on New Security Paradigms*; Riegelsberger, J. et al. The mechanics of trust: A framework for research and design. *International Journal of Human Computer Studies* 2004. 62(3), pp. 381–422.)

they tend to suppress each other. In the former situation, for instance, due to the internalized norms of trust, the trustee is induced to adhere to the security rules that are beneficial to the trustor. However, because of the restriction of the ability of trustors and trustees and the weakness of their motivations, trust actions can lead to violating the security policies, especially under the influence of benefit and benevolence, which may be exploited by the network attackers for malicious purpose, such as phishing and getting private information. Besides, external elements in trust should also be taken into account in security. A good environment where most people comply with the security rules encourages both the member and newcomer to behave normally. Actually security policies enforce the actions that keep the trust relationship.

So how can trust and security policies work compatibly? This is a challenging issue in system security. As mentioned before, technical components and social components should be made use of in a balanced manner. This means that stringent enforcement should be balanced by flexible encouragement such as creating the environment where everyone is concerned about the importance of security policies and executing punishment. Thus, these factors of trust can be used to improve dependability.

11.3 Trust Model in a Sociotechnical Network

The key point in trust modeling is how to compute trust as a security mechanism in STNs. Trust computing security architecture should consist of four components: entity recognition, trustworthiness evaluation, trust propagation, and risk assessment [14]. All components are based on the characteristics of STN such as the small world property and the scale-free link distribution. This means that a target in STN can be found on a short path created by local information. The framework of trust computing is shown in Figure 11.3 [14].

Entity recognition, which is decided by the memory of previous interactions, is the first step to facilitate determination of the trust level of the node communicated with. Without correct entity recognition, trustworthiness evaluation and risk assessment become meaningless. Thus, recognition is fundamental and necessary for following trust computing.

Trustworthiness evaluation also plays a very important role in the whole framework. Generally, it should be considered in two aspects. The first is direct trust that is obtained from the direct connection between the source and the target; the node that wants to compute its trust value to another one is defined as a source. On the other hand, the node that source wants to interact with is defined as a target. The second aspect is indirect trust that is based on the information provided by other nodes having had experiences in transactions with the target in the past. There are also several fundamental factors that affect direct and indirect trust. The existence of risk in every transaction in STNs leads to uncertain results that might

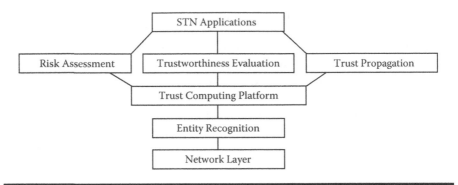

Figure 11.3 Trust computing security architecture. (From Fengming Liu and Yongsheng Ding. Social network-based trust computing in P2P environments intelligent control and automation, 2008. *7th World Congress on WCICA 2008.* June 25–27, 2008, pp. 2130–2135.)

harm the benefits of the nodes (e.g., the more investment put in a transaction, the more risk will be generated).

Thus, a risk assessment mechanism is needed to calculate the risk involved in cooperation to avoid some kind of loss. The risk information can be disseminated by mutual acquaintances [14]. Trust can be propagated through the relationship among nodes, which could be a trust decreasing procedure. Finally, the web of trust will be established in an STN.

11.4 Trust Computation

In this section we will focus on how to calculate trustworthiness. As an important indicator of the degree of trust, reputation is used widely in the trust modeling. Reputation is a form of collective opinion about a subject by the community that is part of a larger sociocognitive mechanism [13]. It can be used to direct the transaction and communication cooperatively in social technical systems.

The factors that affect reputation must be considered when modeling trust. There might be several essential issues [19]:

1. The opinion in terms of amount of satisfaction a peer receives from another peer (O)
2. The total number of transactions/interactions a peer has performed (N)
3. The reputation of the opinion provider, reflecting his/her credibility (R)
4. Temporal adaptability of opinion factor (T)
5. The community context factor (W)

The importance of factor (O) is obvious. Reputation is determined mostly by the feedback from other nodes. The opinion providers who have a good reputation tend to express truthfully, so (R) should be also taken into account. The factor (N) extends the factor (O) to a distribution level that makes factor (O) more reliable. Age of the opinion (T) indicates the freshness of the opinion. The influence of the opinion on reputation will become weakened when the opinion exits for a long time in the sociotechnical network. Reputation attaches importance to community context factor (W).

The node in an environment where most of the nodes communicate so honestly (such that the community has a high overall reputation) is prone to be reliable. Besides, another issue should be considered in reputation modeling; for example, node *i* trusts node *j* for his advising about cars but does not trust *j* with his recommendation about computers. Thus, reputation should be expressed by a trust space like *Trust₁*, *Trust₂*, *Trust₃*, ... *Trustₙ*. Every *Trust* represents one aspect of the reputation in a particular context, so we just discuss one aspect of reputation. Other aspects can be calculated in the same way.

11.4.1 Generic Reputation Function [19]

The Generic Reputation Function described in Reference 19 is shown below:

$$Trust(t) = \sum_{k=1}^{N} W_k \left[\frac{\sum_{j=1}^{N} R_j^{\alpha^R X^R} O_j^{\alpha^O X^O} e_j^{(-\lambda Tj)\alpha^T X^T}}{N^{\alpha^N X^N} + \sum_{j=1}^{m} W^{\alpha^W X^W}} \right] + \Phi e^{-\lambda/T_n} \qquad (11.1)$$

In this function there are two types of impact parameters: the impact variable (X) and the impact weight (α). They are used to control the direction of influence and the amount of influence factors (O, R, T, N, W) on the reputation of the node [19]. Each factor has its own impact factors. The freshness of the opinion should decay gradually not suddenly, so an exponential function is involved. The variable λ is the opinion decaying rate. The variable ϕ is used to assign the initial reputation value, and it serves the dual purpose of stabilization.

This generic reputation function is the foundation of many other reputation computation models. These models may change somewhere in the format but they all consider a part of the factors mentioned in the generic reputation function. According to the requirements of the environment, the factors in the function can be changed to emphasize the influence of several factors. In the experimental evaluation of the function in Reference 19, during the period when the attackers express their dishonest opinions to the target, if attacker frequency is higher than the evaluator frequency, the reputation of the target will be affected seriously, especially in the case where attacker frequency overwhelms evaluator frequency totally. On the other hand, if the attacker frequency is lower, the reputation of the target will be hardly influenced. Thus, the sudden change in reputation slope should be paid attention to as a possible attack. Generally, the reputation function cannot detect and resist attack fully, although it can contribute to system security. Other components are needed such as authentication and identity management.

11.4.2 SocialTrust [15]

In Reference 15 another trust model called *SocialTrust* is proposed. It also has a reputation for tamper resistance. SocialTrust provides community nodes with dynamic trust values by (1) distinguishing relationship quality from trust, (2) incorporating a personalized feedback mechanism for adapting as the community evolves, and (3) tracking user behaviors [15]. These features are embodied in three components in the SocialTrust model [15] as shown in (2).

$$Trust(i,t) = \alpha \cdot Tr_q(i,t) + \beta \cdot \frac{1}{t} \int_0^t Trust(i,x)dx + \gamma \cdot Tr_q'(i,t) \qquad (11.2)$$

In Equation 11.2, i is denoted as a node i, and t represents time.

1. Quality Component of Trust $[Tr_q(i, t)]$ represents the current trustworthiness of the node. As a basic trust metric, quality component of trust is the most important in the SocialTrust model.

$$Tr_q(i) = \lambda \sum_{j \in rel(i)} L(j) \cdot Tr_q(j) / |rel(j)| + (1-\lambda)F(i) \qquad (11.3)$$

In Equation 11.3, $rel(i)z$ represents node i's set of relationships and $|rel(i)|$ is the total number of node i's relationships.

Three main factors should be taken into account in trust establishment [15].
   a. Trust Establishment Scope: It defines which nodes in STN a node can judge.
   b. Trust Group Feedback: $F(i)$ is denoted as the feedback rating, which can be obtained by a voting scheme.
   c. Relationship Link Quality: Link Quality $L(i)$ of a node depends upon the node's direct relationship links and possibly its neighbors' relationship links until several hops away. We can use the feedback rating along the relationship chain to calculate $L(i)$ iteratively.
   λ is used to adjust the weight of feedback rating and link quality on trust establishment.

2. History Component of Trust $[1\backslash 4 \int_0^t Trust(i,x)dx]$ represents the evolution of the trustworthiness of a node. It makes the nodes tend to behave well over a long time. Besides, the history component of trust leads to more accurate computation of the current trust value. *Trust* (i, x) is denoted as the trust rating of a node i at time t.

3. Adaptation to Change Component of Trust $[Tr_q'(i, t)]$ is used to track changes of the behaviors of a node and detect the nodes that suddenly turn malicious.

The SocialTrust model can be optimized to balance the influence among the three components by tuning the parameters α, β, and γ.

11.4.3 Indirect/Direct Trust Models

The models mentioned above are used to calculate the global reputation of the target based on the assumption that all information is available (there must be a centralized trust management center that assembles and processes the trust information) and every node has the same trust value towards the target. Possibly this assumption is unrealistic in the distributed and complicated environment of the STNs, for example, x may trust z while y does not.

Thus, we need to establish a distributed trust management system between source and target in STNs. The overall trust consists of direct trust and indirect trust [16] that are reflected by the recommendation obtained from the other nodes' transactions with the recommended node. A source can query other nodes to get the recommendation of the target according to the characteristics of STNs.

For example, in Reference 16 direct trust is denoted as

$$dr_{ij} = \frac{Suc_{ij}}{N_{ij}} \tag{11.4}$$

where Suc_{ij} denotes the number of successful transactions between node i and node j. N_{ij} denotes the total number of transactions. T_{ij} denotes the value of recommendation from i to j.

$$T_{ij} = \frac{Suc_{ij} - (N_{ij} - Suc_{ij})}{\sum_{k} Suc_{ik}} \tag{11.5}$$

Indirect trust is denoted as

$$ir_{ij} = \frac{\sum_{i=1}^{k} R_{ij} \cdot (T_{ij} + \lambda)}{k} \tag{11.6}$$

where R_{ij} denotes reputation from i to j. It decreases exponentially due to the punishment for the false recommendation and increases linearly as the recommendation is accurate. The variable λ denotes the adjustment coefficient to ensure that the network is stable. Thus, the overall trust is

$$Trust_{ij} = \alpha \cdot dr_{ij} + (1 - \alpha) \cdot ir_{ij} \tag{11.7}$$

This model in Reference 16 is simple and just considers a few factors that affect trustworthiness.

A more sophisticated model which takes more factors into account in trust computation is proposed in Reference 1.

1. Direct trust:

$$dr_{ij} = dr_{t-1} \times t + M(i,j) \times L(i,j) \times w(L(i,j)) \times F(j) \\ + K(j) \times f(x) \times P(x) \times F(y) \tag{11.8}$$

dr_{t-1} is the accumulative direct trust values of node j until $t{-}1$ times.

$$t = 1 - (L(i,j) \cdot M(i,j)) \tag{11.9}$$

The above is defined as the trust decay in terms of time. $M(i,j)$ is the satisfaction degree from node i to node j. $L(i,j)$ is the shortest length between node i and node j.

$$w(L(i,j)) = \exp(-L(i,j)) \tag{11.10}$$

The above is the weight of the link.

$$P(x) = 1/(1 + \exp(-n)) \tag{11.11}$$

The above is the recommendation punishment and n is the number of false recommendations. $F(j)$ is the risk that node j takes in the transaction. $F(y)$ is the transaction risk of node y which is recommended by node j. If node j is the member of the clique, $K(j)$ equals 1. Otherwise $K(j)$ is 0. If the recommendation is false, $f(x)$ equals -0.5. Otherwise $f(x)$ is 0.

2. Indirect trust:

$$ir_{xj} = ir_{t-1} \times t + \frac{1}{N} \left\{ \sum_{1}^{N} \left[\frac{Cxi}{Cxi + Rxi} \times L(x,j) \times w(L(x,j)) \times M(x,j) \right] \right\} \tag{11.12}$$

N is the number of recommendation nodes. $Cxi/(Cxi + Rxi)$ is the trust degree of recommendation nodes.

The expression of the overall trust is the same as Equation 11.7. According to simulation results of [1,16], these two models can recognize malicious behaviors such as boast and cheating in STNs. Based on the small world theory they can efficiently handle relationships such as establishing new connections and terminating old connections. The trust feedback mechanism, which consists of service effectiveness and recommendation accuracy, also plays an important role in these two models. Besides, when the coefficient α decreases, malicious nodes can be detected and punished quickly and the amount of successful transactions increases stably.

11.4.4 Information Theoretic Trust

The information theoretic trust scheme [30,31] can be used to compute the trust values. Every interaction node i updates the direct trust value of node j in the case that node i is connected with node j directly as below:

$$Trust_{i,j} = \begin{cases} 1 - h_b(p) & 0.5 \le p \le 1 \\ h_b(p) - 1 & 0 \le p \le 0.5 \end{cases}$$

$$p = pr(v(n+1) = 1 \mid n(N) = s) = \frac{s+1}{N=2}$$

$$h_p(p) = -\sum_x p(x) \log p(x)$$

$$V(m) = \begin{cases} 1 & node\ i,j\ interact\ successfully\ in\ the\ m^{th}\ transaction \\ 0 & otherwise \end{cases}$$

$$n(N) = \sum_{m=1}^{N} V(m)$$

Node i computes the indirect trust value of the node j if node j is not included in the neighborhood of node i as follows:

$$Trust_{i,j} = \sum_{k \in N} w_k Trust_{i,k} Trust_{k,j}$$

$$w_k = \frac{Trust_{i,k}}{\displaystyle\sum_{k \in N} Trust_{i,k}}$$

where N is the set of the neighbors of node i with $Trust_{i,k} > 0$. A threshold trust value $Trust_{i,j}(H') = \hat{H}$ is set statically.

11.4.5 Confident

In the CONFIDANT scheme [31,32] direct trust values are updated according to a Beta distribution $Beta(\alpha,\beta)$, where α and β represent the total number of unsuccessful and successful interactions, respectively.

$$DirectTrust_{i,j} = 1 - CDT_{i,j}$$

$$CDT_{i,j} =\in (Beta(F_{i,j})) = \frac{\alpha}{\alpha + \beta}$$

where $F_{i,j} = (\alpha, \beta)$ is initialized to $(1, 1)$. α and β are updated as below:

$$\alpha = \alpha + s, \beta = \beta + (1 - s)$$

where s indicates the unsuccessful interaction.

In CONFIDANT the *indirect trust* values are calculated in the same way as the direct trust values.

$$IndirectTrust_{i,j} = 1 - CIT_{i,}$$

$$CiT_{i,j} = E(Beta(R_{i,j})) = \frac{\alpha'}{\alpha' + \beta'}$$

where $R_{i,j} = (\alpha' > 0, \beta' > 0)$is initialized to $(0, 0)$ and then updated as follows:

$$R_{i,j} = R_{i,j} + w_k F_{k,j} = (\alpha', \beta')$$

Note that w_k and the threshold trust value H' are set statically.

In Reference 31 a new trust scheme is proposed which involves the observation of the mutual neighbors of both nodes into the trust value computation based on Heider's theory and introduces a dynamic threshold. $Trust_{i,j} = (s, u)$ is initialized to $(1,1)$ and then updated as below:

$$Trust_{i,j} = (s,u) + \sum_{k \in N} f(Trust_{i,k})Trust'_{k,j}$$

$$u = u + e, \ s = s + (1 - e)$$

$$Trust_{k,j} = (x, y) \Rightarrow Trust'_{k,j} = (x - 1, y - 1)$$

$$Trust_{i,j} = (x, y) \Rightarrow f(Trust_{i,j}) = \frac{x}{x + y}$$

N is the set of direct mutual neighbors of nodes i and j. e indicates the number of unsuccessful interaction.

$$DirectTrustValue_{i,j} = f(Trust_{i,j})$$

The computation of the *indirect trust* is the same as the *direct trust* value and just needs to replace N by M, which is denoted as the set of all the neighbors of i which are connected to node j directly.

From the simulation and scenario analysis in Reference 31 we can see that this new model revokes malicious nodes more quickly and performs with better tolerance for the node's occasional failure than the other two schemes we mentioned above.

11.4.6 Gravity-Based Trust Model

In Reference 18 there is an interesting trust model called the gravity-based trust model according to the mechanics theory in physics. It considers the trust attenuation with time and trust context. Its goal is to use the local values to calculate the global trust. This model includes two steps: computing trusted social neighborhoods and computing trust flows.

Step 1. Computing a trusted social neighborhood
According to the small world theory, a node usually interacts with only a small fraction of nodes in an STN. Thus, the trust distance, which is defined as the distance in the trust spaces can be calculated only based on partial and local information in whole STNs. The idea of computing the trust distance comes from distributed virtual coordinate systems from the network area [20,21].

According to the theory of the virtual coordinates, the nodes in STNs are mapped onto a Cartesian space based on the delay measurements in the network.

In Reference 18 a virtual coordinate y_i is associated with the trust space of the node i. The initial value of the virtual coordinate is assigned randomly. d_{ij} is denoted as the trustworthiness between node i and node j. Reference 18 defines the total error as a sum of a squared-error function as below:

$$E = \sum_i \sum_j (d_{ij} - \|y_i - y_j\|)^2 \tag{11.13}$$

Reference 20 demonstrates that simulating a network of mechanical springs produces coordinates that lead to the minimum error function shown previously in

Equation 11.13. It seems that the node i is connected with node j by a spring with natural length d_{ij}. The potential energy resulting from the elongation of the spring represents the error. Base on Hooke's law ($F = -kx$) the distributed algorithm can be used to adjust the spring to minimize the total elongation of the whole system of springs. Thus, Hooke's law in the virtual coordinate system in the gravity-based trust model is shown as below:

$$F_{ij} = -k((y_i - y_j) - d_{ij}) \tag{11.14}$$

When the computation process of the virtual computation converges, each node i will be mapped to a coordinate value y_i. And the trust social neighborhood relies on the coordinate values. During the computation process new trust neighbors will be found. The algorithm is illustrated in Figure 11.4. f_{ij} is the force between node i and node j. The k is spring constant; k_t and k_c represent the different characteristics of the spring under tension and compression.

Step 2. Computing trust flow
The trust model proposed in [18] also takes the node age parameters into account. Thus the gravity-based trust model is shown below:

```
For each node Xi, do:
        yᵢ ← virtual coordinate of node Xi
        For each node Xi, do:
                yⱼ ← virtual coordinate of node Xj
                dᵢⱼ ← observed trust value between Xi and Xj
                fᵢⱼ = ((yᵢ – yⱼ) – dᵢⱼ)
                if ||yᵢ – yⱼ||> ||dᵢⱼ||then
                        k = kₜ
                else
                        k = k_c
                end if
                yᵢ = yᵢ + ukfᵢⱼ  /* u is the time step */
        End For
End For
        Errvar = error variation over last m iterations
If errvar < Threshold, go to beginning
```

Figure 11.4 Pseudo code for centralized trust computation using coordinates. (From Maheswaran, M., Hon Cheong Tang, and Ghunaim, A. Towards a gravity-based trust model for social networking systems. *Distributed computing systems workshops,* 2007. *27th International Conference on ICDCSW '07.* **June 22–29, 2007, pp. 24–24.)**

$$Trust_{ij} = \lambda \frac{T_i^s T_{ij}(d_n - r_{ij})}{r_{ij}^3} \tag{11.15}$$

where T_{ij} is the age of node j as estimated by node i, and T_i^s is the age of the system as estimated by node i. r_{ij} is the distance calculated from the virtual coordinate $r_{ij} = y_i - y_j$.

The simulation results of the gravity-based trust model [18] show that trust estimation error varies with number of nodes, and the spring has no additional stiffness. This means a spring constant equal to 1 is the best scenario.

(a) (b)
However, due to the shortcomings of the small world theory, only the shortest tie between source and target is considered, and some useful information is ignored by eliminating some ties in trust computation. Thus, we will introduce a new model based on electric circuit theory to solve the problem.

In Reference 17, an interesting trust model is proposed called RN-trust where an STN is mapped to a resistive network. A resistive network consists of resistors that are connected in series and parallel. It can reflect some properties of STNs such as transitivity and asymmetry. Every node in the STNs is replaced by a node in the resistive network. A resistor is placed between the nodes that have a trust relationship (see Figure 11.5). An ideal diode is used to realize the asymmetry property of sociotechnical network. Thus, the resistors' values must have a reverse relation with the trust values [17].

$$resistance = -\log trust \tag{11.16}$$

By the methods of circuit analysis the equivalent resistance of the electric circuit can be used as a measure to calculate the trust value from the source to the sink after establishing the resistive network [17]. All links are taken into account in this model so no information is ignored. Besides, the time complexity of RN-trust is comparable to other models. However, now the RN-trust model cannot totally simulate the sociotechnical work so it should be improved by adding more aspects of trust through including more electronic elements to the resistive network.

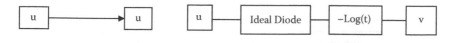

Figure 11.5 **(a) An edge in a trust network with the trust value t from u to v; (b) Corresponding edge in the resistive network. (From Taherian, M. et al. Trust inference in web-based social networks using resistive networks.** *Internet and Web Applications and Services, 2008. Third International Conference on ICIW '08.* **June 8–13, 2008, pp. 233–238.)**

11.4.7 Direct Reciprocation-Based Trust Model [23]

The importance and motivation of trust models is that they can promote the cooperation and reciprocity in the communities where selfish or defective behaviors are limited by some punishment and incentive mechanisms. However, the reciprocity-based technique requires the system to remember the previous interactions among all nodes, which may be impossible [22]. Thus, in Reference 23 it proposes a trust model that considers the direct reciprocation. Direct reciprocity is defined as the direct transactions between two nodes, and indirect reciprocity is defined as the interaction with the involvement of other nodes [22,23,24], as well as the individuals adjusting their behaviors by the direct experience, which leads to limited misreporting of information. So there are no external control mechanisms or any form of reputation in the trust model in Reference 23.

This trust model proposed in Reference 23 is applied to the Prisoner's Dilemma, which is a classical social dilemma where two players have to collaborate with each other, or suppress its opponent for its own maximum profits. The payoff matrix is shown in Table 11.4 [23]. In this model the Prisoner's Dilemma plays iteratively and at least one previous game is recorded.

In this model, also, relationships are formed based on the principle that every node seeks to interact with another that is at least as cooperative as itself [23]. The indicator of the cooperation is the payoff from the previous transaction. Each node can determine whether to invite other players or accept the invitation from other players according to the cooperation threshold [23]:

$$tp_{i,j}/m = \begin{cases} \geq v_i^{inuite} & node\ i\ will\ invite\ node\ j\ to\ play\ the\ game \\ < v_i^{inuite} & node\ i\ will\ not\ invite\ node\ j\ to\ play\ the\ game \end{cases} \quad (11.17)$$

Table 11.4 Payoffs for Different Combination of Player Strategy

	Player B	
Player A	Cooperate	Defect
Cooperate	1,1	−1,2
Defect	2,−1	0,0

Source: Colombo, G. et al. Cooperation in social networks of trust. *Self-Adaptive and Self-Organizing Systems Workshops,* 2008. *Second IEEE International Conference on SASOW 2008.* October 20–24, 2008, pp. 78–83.

$$tp_{i,j}/m = \begin{cases} \geq v_i^{inuite} & node\ i\ will\ accept\ node\ j's\ invitation \\ < v_i^{inuite} & node\ i\ will\ refuse\ node\ j's\ invitation\ or \\ & remove\ the\ relationship\ with\ node\ j \end{cases} \quad (11.18)$$

tP_{ij} is node i's total payoff in the last m transactions with node j. v_i^{invite} is the invitation threshold of node i and

$$v_i^{invite} = v_i^{coop} \quad (11.19)$$

where v_i^{coop} is the cooperation level of node i and can be a constant or variable value, depending on the requirements of the system. v_i^{accept} is the acceptance threshold of node i and

$$v_i^{accept} = v_i^{invite} \cdot \alpha_i \quad (11.20)$$

where α_i represents the risk node i will take with respect to accepting an invitation that is less cooperative than itself [23].

Reference 23 assumes that when a relationship is established from node i to node j, node j will also connect to all the neighbors of node i. However, when node j cuts off the link with node i due to reduction of the payoffs, it will not delete the relationships with the neighbors of node i. The simulation of the algorithm shows that the total payoffs increase as the cooperation level is higher. Based on the cooperation we can also introduce game theory and evolutionary dynamics in the process of trust modeling [29].

11.4.8 Subjective Logic-Based Trust Model

Another trust model which also addresses the problem in many other models that require the explicit and frequent feedbacks or ratings from the nodes to compute the trustworthiness or reputation is presented in Reference 25. According to the subjective aspects of trust, in Reference 25 it establishes the trust model by subjective logic, which includes various logical operators for the opinion combination such as AND, OR, and NOT. In Reference 25, some nontraditional operators as recommendation and consensus are emphasized.

Usually one opinion (O) consists of three parts [25]: belief (b), disbelief (d), and uncertainty (u).

$$O = \{b, d, u\} \quad (11.21)$$

$$b + d + u = 1, \{b, d, u\} \in [0,1] \quad (11.22)$$

In Reference 25 the opinion expressed by node j about given predicate p and the opinion of node i about j are denoted as O_p^j and O_j^i, respectively. Thus, the opinion of node i about p is calculated by the recommendation operator denoted by ⊗ [25]:

$$O_p^{ij} = O_j^i \otimes O_p^j = \left\langle b_j^i b_p^j, b_j^i d_p^j, d_j^i + u_j^i + b_j^i u_p^j \right\rangle \qquad (11.23)$$

From the equation we can see that the result of recommendation is based on the order of the opinions. The joint opinion of node i and node j about the given predicate is calculated by the consensus operator denoted by ⊕ [25]:

$$O_p^{ij} = O_p^i \oplus O_p^j = \left\langle (b_p^i u_p^j + b_p^j u_p^i)/k, (d_p^i u_p^j + d_p^j u_p^i)/k, u_p^i u_p^j/k \right\rangle \qquad (11.24)$$

$$k = u_p^i + u_p^j - u_p^i u_p^j \qquad (11.25)$$

Based on the small world and scale free theory the trust model in [25] only considers two parameters in STNs: clustering coefficient and centrality. Centrality determines the relative importance of a node in the STN. Many centrality measures can be used to compute this parameter. The clustering coefficient of a node in STN is used to represent the closeness of the node and neighbors as a clique. It can be computed as follows:

$$C_i = \frac{\left|\{e_{ik}\}\right|}{k_i(k_i - 1)}, \ v_i, v_k \in N_i, e_{ik} \in E \qquad (11.26)$$

where: v_i is node i, N_i is the neighborhood of the node i, e_{ik} is the link between node i and node k, and k_i is the degree of the node i.

In [25] it also introduces a trust evaluation algorithm to establish and update the trust relationship as follows: Assume that node i is a newcomer of a network. We can use the algorithm shown below to compute node i's trust of node j in the network (O_j^i):

Get all opinions about node j. $k = \{k_1, k_2, ..., k_n\}$ is a set of all the nodes that have opinion about node j.

$$O_{k_i}^{net} = (b_{net,k_i}, d_{net,k_i}, u_{net,k_i}) \qquad 11.27)$$

$O_{k_i}^{net}$ represents the position of node k_i in the whole network.

$$b_{net,k_i} = CENTRALITY \qquad (11.28)$$

$$d_{net,k_i} = 1 - b_{k_i,j} - u_{k_i,j} \qquad (11,29)$$

$$u_{net,k_i} = \min(1 - CENTRALITY, CLIQUE) \qquad (11.30)$$

CLIQUE and *CENTRALITY* are the normalized clustering coefficient and centrality, respectively.

$$O_j^{'k_i} = O_{k_i}^{net} \otimes O_j^{k_i} \qquad (11.31)$$

$O_j^{'k_i}$ and $O_j^{k_i}$ are the modified opinion and original opinion of node k_i about node j, respectively.

$$4 \ O_j^i = O_j^{'k_1} \oplus O_j^{'k_2} \oplus ... \oplus O_j^{'k_n} \qquad (11.32)$$

Algorithm of updating trust relationship [25]: Assume that node i and node j have existed in the network for a long time so that they can update their trust relationship based on certain experiences. The algorithm below illustrates the updating process.

Find all links from node i to node j in the network. $L = \{L_1, L_2, ..., L_n\}$ is a set of all links where $L_i = \langle i, p_1, p_2, ..., p_m, j \rangle$. $p = \{p_1, p_2, ..., p_m\}$ is a set of all nodes in the link.

$k = \{k_1, k_2, ..., k_l\}$ is a set of all nodes that have opinion about node j and are not included in the set P. We can then measure the network context in the algorithm of establishing trust relationship. And we can determine:

$$O_j^{'L_i} = O_{p_1}^i \otimes O_{p_2}^{p_1} \otimes O_{p_3}^{p_2} ... \otimes O_j^{p_m} \qquad 11.33)$$

where $O_j^{'L_i}$ represents the opinion passing along the link.

$$O_j^i = O_j^{'k_1} \oplus O_j^{'k_2} \oplus ... \oplus O_j^{'k_l} \oplus O_j^{'L_1} \oplus O_j^{'L_2} \oplus ... \oplus O_j^{'L_n} \qquad (11.34)$$

The model presented in [25] also has some shortcomings. The subjective logics are not appropriate enough to model uncertain probabilities. Besides, the model assumes that the recommendation sources are equally reliable. Thus, more complex operators are required in the trust model, which will lead to increasing time complexity.

11.4.9 Trusted Gossip Protocol

In Reference 27 is proposed a trusted gossip protocol that is used to maximize the spread of acceptable stories while simultaneously minimizing the spread of unacceptable stories by a story filtering process. It is very useful in the rating feedback system. Message level filtering can be used as supplementary for node level recommendation.

A story can be classified as fact, rumor, or questionable.

$$
story \begin{cases} fact(Trust_{sender} \geq (1 + \varphi)Trust_{rcvr}) \\ rumor(Trust_{sender} \leq (1 - \varphi)Trust_{rcvr}) \\ questionable(else) \end{cases} \tag{11.35}
$$

where $\varphi \leq 1$ is a threshold value set by the receiver, $Trust_{sender}$ and $Trust_{rcvr}$ are the trust of the story sender and receiver, respectively.

If a story is a fact, it will be accepted by the local node, included in the local aggregate, and disseminated to the neighboring nodes. The story classified as a rumor will be discarded. For the questionable story the receiver will ask for the additional information by sending a review request to a random set of nodes [27]. There is a rating process after acceptance called *postreviewing of stories* where an augmented Bayesian trust estimation [28] process can be used to compute the trust values which will be associated with the story senders according to the rating obtained from the post review.

11.4.10 TrustDavis

In Reference 26 it proposes a trust model called TrustDavis based on the insurance mechanism against malicious behaviors in the transaction. The main contributions of TrustDavis are [26]:

■ Honest nodes can limit the damage caused by collusion of malicious nodes.
■ The multiple identities of malicious nodes can be limited in the system.
■ The nodes incline to rate other nodes accurately.
■ TrustDavis is distributed.

In TrustDavis, nodes initially publish references, which is an acceptance of limited liability. Then the social relationships among the nodes are established. To join in the network the newcomer must provide the security deposits to a trustworthy node for the reference. This rule facilitates to limit the multiple identities of malicious nodes. Based on the insurance concept, the payment for reference and the payback in case the transaction fails can be easily calculated. Besides, TrustDavis adopts the strategy for the false claim scenario.

11.5 Future Research

The trust models we mentioned above are mostly originated from the social networks that constitute the top layer in the STNs. Although generally these trust models may adapt to the environment of the top layer of the STNs, some problems may emerge in case they extend to the lower layer of STNs such as the communication and physical layers. There is no clear definition of trust in the STNs. Thus, it is even more difficult to attach the concept of trust to a physical device. Moreover, the metrics of trust include some subjective elements in its social layer while in its device layer the trust should be more objective by eliminating some subjective part. For example, the device trust value can be associated with the reliability of the device. There must be some kind of interfaces between the layers to translate the trust upwards or downwards. These interfaces are very important, just like the protocol stack, to ensure the trust model in each layer works independently and cooperatively. Besides, although these trust models have provided some strategies for resilience to social attacks, these strategies cannot extend well to the device layer. We must consider the requirements of the device layer to detect device failures and physical attacks.

According to the characteristics of centralized and distributed trust models we can suggest a mixed system that makes use of the advantages of centralized systems to counterbalance the shortcomings of distributed systems and vice versa. For example, an STN can be separated into several cliques. In a clique there is a leader managing to compute the trust of each member and communicate to other leaders of different cliques. Besides, the calculation of trust among cliques is distributed. This scheme may be effective if the network is divided appropriately according to sociotechnical relationships. This topology is also easy to scale and maintain.

None of the trust models we mentioned above considers all the factors affecting the computation of trust. There should be a general trust computation model, especially in a distributed environment. Although it is very hard to achieve this goal, we can emphasize several factors at the expense of others, according to the requirements in a specific STN environment. As for the topology mentioned above, we can adopt different trust computation schemes in each clique based on their characteristics. A simplified model may be used in a more trustworthy environment while we should exploit a complex trust model with strategies limiting the malicious behaviors of nodes.

Because trust computation is an iterative process, converge time plays an important role in trust modeling. It is meaningless for the trust model if the calculation cannot follow the interaction of the nodes. However, most of the trust models above do not take time complexity into account. It is a challenge to balance the effectiveness and complexity.

According to the strategies we mentioned in the trust models, they can limit the malicious behaviors to some extent. However, some shortcomings which can be exploited by malicious nodes still exist in these strategies. We should enhance the strategies after future research. Based on the characteristics of STN there must be some nodes with high centrality, which means that the nodes have many links. The trust and the security of such nodes should be investigated. In the common sense, the node that has the highest trust value should be popular in the transactions among nodes. Other nodes should be prone to interact with it and make efforts to protect it from attacks due to its importance. We may refer the idea of the many-to-one attack and apply it to the group protection. This method helps to ensure the security of the central point in the network. The feedback mechanism has two sides that can facilitate trust computation and also may be a "gate" for malicious behaviors. The malicious nodes easily make use of their right of voting to spoil the target. Besides, there might be some incomplete data during feedback. Thus, we should pay attention to the message integrity. Because most of the trust models are based on the small world theory where the clique is the core concept, the formation of the clique may lead to the gathering of malicious nodes, which jeopardizes the whole network. A strategy is needed to determine the structure of cliques.

11.6 Conclusion

In this chapter, we have presented some trust models that are based on social networks and can also extend to the applications of STNs. We have defined the main factors that can influence the trust computation and provided the algorithms and processes of each trust model. Further, we have analyzed the advantages and disadvantages of the trust models. In future research, the trust model in STN needs to be enhanced due to the limitations of current models.

Reference

1. Zhai Dongsheng and Pan Hong. A social network-based trust model for E-commerce. *Wireless Communications, Networking and Mobile Computing, 2008. 4th International Conference on WiCOM '08.* October 12–14, 2008, pp. 1–5.
2. I-Hsien Ting. Web mining techniques for on-line social networks analysis. *International Conference on Service Systems and Service Management,* June 30–July 2, 2008, pp. 1–5.
3. Jamali, M. and Abolhassani, H. Different aspects of social network analysis. *Web Intelligence, 2006. IEEE/WIC/ACM International Conference on WI 2006.* December 18–22, 2006, pp. 66–72.
4. Callon, Michel (1991). Techno-economic networks and irreversibility. In John Law (Ed.), *A Sociology of Monsters: Essays on Power, Technology and Domination,* London: Routledge.
5. Lamb, R. and Davidson, E. Social scientists: Managing identity in STNs. *System sciences, 2002. Proceedings of the 35th Annual Hawaii International Conference on HICSS.* January 7–10, 2002, pp. 1132–1141.
6. Baker, D. Fortresses built upon sand. *Proceedings of the New Security Paradigms Workshop 1996.*
7. Brostoff, S. and Sasse, M. A. Safe and sound: A safety-critical approach to security design. *New Security Paradigms Workshop 2001.*
8. Ivan Flechais, Jens Riegelsberger, and M. Angela Sasse. Divide and conquer: The role of trust and assurance in the design of secure socio-technical systems. September 2005, *NSPW '05: Proceedings of the 2005 Workshop on New Security Paradigms.*
9. Bacharach, M. and Garnbetta, D. Trust as Type Detection. C. Castelfranchi and Y. Tan (Eds.), *Trust and Deception in Virtual Societies,* 2001. pp. 1–26. Dordrecht: Kluwer.

10. Riegelsberger, J., Sasse, M. A., and McCarthy, J. The mechanics of trust: A framework for research and design. *International Journal of Human Computer Studies,* 2004. 62(3), pp. 381–422.
11. Anderson, R. *Security Engineering: A Guide to Building Dependable Distributed Systems,* 2001. John Wiley & Sons, New York.
12. Riegelsberger, J., Sasse, M. A., and McCarthy, J. The mechanics of trust: A framework for research and design. *International Journal of Human Computer Studies* 2004. 62(3), pp. 381–422.
13. Winsborough, W. and Li, N. Towards practical automated trust negotiation. In *IEEE 3rd International Workshop on Policies for Distributed Systems and Networks,* 2002. pp. 92–103.
14 Fengming Liu and Yongsheng Ding. Social network-based trust computing in P2P environments intelligent control and automation, 2008. *7th World Congress on WCICA 2008.* June 25–27, 2008, pp. 2130–2135.
15. James Caverlee, Ling Liu, and Steve Webb. SocialTrust: Tamper-resilient trust establishment in online communities, June 2008. *JCDL '08: Proceedings of the 8th ACM/IEEE-CS Joint Conference on Digital Libraries.*
16. Xuan Wang and Lei Wang. P2P recommendation trust model. *Intelligent Systems Design and Applications,* 2008. *Eighth International Conference on ISDA '08.* Volume 2, November 26–28, 2008, pp. 591–595.
17. Taherian, M., Amini, M., and Jalili, R. Trust inference in web-based social networks using resistive networks. *Internet and Web Applications and Services, 2008. Third International Conference on ICIW '08.* June 8–13, 2008, pp. 233–238.
18. Maheswaran, M., Hon Cheong Tang, and Ghunaim, A. Towards a gravity-based trust model for social networking systems. *Distributed Computing Systems Workshops,* 2007. *27th International Conference on ICDCSW '07.* June 22–29, 2007, pp. 24–24.
19. Javed I. Khan and Sajid S. Shaikh. A phenotype reputation estimation function and its study of resilience to social attacks. *Journal of Network and Computer Applications,* 2009. Published by Elsevier Ltd. Vol 32, Issue 4, July 2009, Pages: 913–924.
20. Dabek, F., Cox, R., Kaashoek, F., and Morris, R. Vivaldi. A decentralized network coordinate system, *Proc. of the ACM SIGCOMM'04 Conference,* December 2004.
21. Ng, T. S. E. and Zhang, H. Predicting internet network distance with coordinate-based approaches, *IEEE Infocom,* June 2002.
22. Cohen, B. Incentives build robustness in bittorrent. In *Proceedings of the Workshop on Economics of Peer-To-Peer Systems,* 2003.
23. Colombo, G., Whitaker, R.M., and Allen, S.M. Cooperation in social networks of trust. *Self-Adaptive and Self-Organizing Systems Workshops, 2008. Second IEEE International Conference on SASOW 2008.* October 20–24, 2008, pp. 78–83.
24. Feldman, M. and Chuang, J. Overcoming free-riding behavior in peer-to-peer systems. *ACM SIGecom Exchanges,* 5: 41–50, 2005.
25. Kolaczek, G. Trust modeling in virtual communities using social network metrics. *Intelligent System and Knowledge Engineering,* 2008. *3rd International Conference on ISKE 2008.* Volume 1, November 17–19, 2008, pp. 1421–1426.
26. DeFigueiredo, Dd. B. and Barr, E.T. TrustDavis: A non-exploitable.online reputation system, *E-commerce technology,* 2005. *Seventh IEEE International Conference on CEC 2005.* July 19–22, 2005, pp. 274–283.
27. Mitra, A. and Maheswaran, M. Trusted gossip: A rumor resistant dissemination mechanism for peer-to-peer information sharing. *Advanced Information Networking and Applications,* 2007. *21st International Conference on AINA '07.* May 21–23, 2007, pp. 702–707.

28. Mitra, A. and Maheswaran, M. Benefits of targeting in trusted gossiping for peer-to-peer information sharing. In *IPDPS*, May 2007.
29. Fengming Liu and Yongsheng Ding. Dynamics analysis of trust computing evolution in P2P networks. *Signal-Image Technologies and Internet-Based System*, 2007. *Third International IEEE Conference on SITIS '07*. December 16–18, 2007, pp. 200–205.
30. Sun, Y. L., Yu, W., Han, Z., K.J., and Liu, R. Information theoretic framework of trust modeling and evaluation for ad hoc networks. *IEEE Journal on Selected Areas in Communications*, 24 (2): 305–317, 2006.
31. Pai, S., Roosta, T., Wicker, S., and Sastry, S. Using social network theory towards development of wireless ad hoc network trust. *Advanced Information Networking and Applications Workshops*, 2007, *21st International Conference on AINAW '07*. Volume 1, May 21–23, 2007, pp. 443–450.
32. S. Buchegger. Coping with misbehavior in mobile ad-hoc networks. Thesis, February 2004.

Chapter 12

Networking Protocols in Sociotechnical Networks

Dong Zhang and Fei Hu

Contents

12.1 Introduction

Currently, many researchers have proposed many ideas on the sociotechnical network protocol designs in different aspects. Some researchers have analyzed the Internet routing protocol, a new kind of communication architecture that has been invented with the aim to increase security. Davis Social Links is based on relationship (trust level) to establish the route between different nodes, eliminating many kinds of attacks or SPAM. Nowadays, many researchers worldwide want to model terrorist networks, because the terrorist activities in some regions are intense. The key issue for destabilizing the terrorist networks is how to find the important nodes or the high degree nodes. Some researchers have argued that if we can find the high degree nodes in the networks and remove them, the entire network will not work anymore.

For link prediction, people use mathematic ways to estimate the possibility of two nodes' communication. So they just calculate the common neighbors, which play very important roles such as a bridge that can make two nodes communicate with each other.

For disconnected social networks analysis, some researchers have proposed the design of clusters that do not connect with each other. They can use another cluster as a bridge for intercluster communication.

People also want to understand how messages or information propagate in the social network. The researchers try to model the spread of ideas in the online social networks. The propagation latency in these networks is a vital issue. Researchers can analyze the network backbone and use vector clock to measure the network latency. Furthermore, they can also find the reason why different nodes have different latencies.

12.2 Davis Social Links: Integrating Social Networks with Internet Routing [1]

12.2.1 The DSl (Davis Social Links) Architecture

To achieve the network security, a novel communication architecture called Davis Social Links (DSL) has been proposed in [1]. The links between nodes in the social network indicate the relationship between nodes. Generally, DSL demonstrates that communication between two networks through one path between them. When the links are established in the network, upon the trust ranking, the receiver can easily filter the messages, which means that the receiver can discard the SPAM from attackers.

In some cases, the communications between the nodes do not need the assistance of DSL. If two nodes have a strong relationship and they can establish a path between them directly, the nodes that use the direct link or preestablished link do not need DSL. In other cases, most of the nodes need to forward the data via the intermediate nodes. The nodes that want to send data need to execute the route discovery process. The sender and the receiver first need to exchange the commands. After that the receiver side will determine whether or not it allows the routing requirement.

12.2.2 Route Discovery

The first step of the route discovery is the RDM (route discovery message) sending phrase. In this phrase the sender will send the RDM which contains the name of receiver and the receiver's keywords. A middle node will check the keywords from the nodes that it directly connects to it. When the RDM has been delivered to the destination, the receiver will send an acknowledge message (ACK) to the sender which contains the path that the sender can use for the data transmission.

12.2.3 DSL Keyword-Based Route

DSL's keyword-based route is very similar to the Google case. For Google, the user provides some keywords and the Google search engine will execute several processes to match the webpages to the keywords. A major difference between the Google and DSL is that all the processes of the webpage searching and keyword matching are controlled by the administrator's domain. The other difference is that all the search information can be interpreted by Google; while for DSL, the content or message can determine whether or not it should announce the keywords.

12.2.4 Recipient's Controllability

In DSL, the receiver can control the routing path, in order to automatically discard the bad messages. It is a useful way to defend against the messages from the attackers.

12.2.5 Global Connectivity without Global Identities

Unlike the Internet, which assigns the global identities for each node such as IP address, DSL does not use the global address. Its RDM includes the path information and also does the routing loop detection.

12.2.6 Algorithm Notations

Let G(V,E) denote the undirected graph, in which V represents the set of nodes and E represents the set of edges in the network between each node. When e(u,v) denotes the link between the nodes u and v, if e(u,v) = 1, it means that the nodes u and v can directly connect to each other; otherwise e(u,v) = 0 means that nodes u and v cannot directly connect. Furthermore, if e(u,v) = 1, node v can be seen as the neighbor of node u.

In the network, each node has a number of neighbors. So by using N(u,i) it means the ith neighbor of the node u. For instance, if e(u,v) = 1, then N(u,i) = v. We use a neighbor list to represent the identities of the neighbors of each node. For example, if IN(u,v) = i, it means the index of the node v in the neighbor list is i. The number of neighbors of a node u, which doesn't include the node u, can be represented as $\#(u) = \Sigma_{v \in V, v \neq u} \; e(u,v)$. R(u,v) denotes whether or not the message can be forwarded from node u to v. For example, if e(u,v) = 1, then R(u,v) = R(v,u) = 1. Let KDes denote all the keywords for the destination or the receiver. KInt denotes the keywords for the intermediate nodes. KRDM denotes the intersection of KDes and KInt.

12.2.7 Keyword-Based Filtering

The keyword can represent the property of the message. Matching process is to find that whether or not the message contains the right or meaningful keyword. For example, a phone call can be seen as a message, and the keyword may be inferred as the caller's ID.

12.2.8 DSL Trust Model

In DSL trust model we can find out whether a neighbor is a trustworthy node. Suppose KACK denotes the set of keywords used by each node. The route discovery message can be matched from the node's neighbors.

Not only the sender and receiver can do the filtering process, each DSL node can also do such processes for others. For example, if e(u,v) = 1, then the nodes u and v will exchange the keywords. KAnn(u,i) denotes all the keywords which have been announced for exchanging function. The KACK can be different from the KAnn. For example, if v is the third neighbor u, which can receive the KAnn(u,3). In this case, it cannot determine the KACK(u). Each node can determine the KAnn or do the process on it. According to the local function, the KAnn for different nodes can be chosen differently. For instance, if Ii ≠ j, then K(u,i) ≠ K(v,j) and KAnn(u,i) ≠ KAnn(u,j).

For example, if two nodes in the social network can connect to each other, first, they need to exchange the keywords in order to do the route discovery on this link. Suppose that the node A uses "apple" as its keyword and the node B uses "banana." When node A sends an RDM to node B, the RDM must include the keyword of node B—"banana." Similarly, when node B does the same process to try to send an RDM to node A, the RDM from node B must include the keyword of node A—"apple." Otherwise, the RDM will be discarded by the receipts. For security purposes, all the contents in the message except the keywords will be encrypted.

12.2.9 Route Discovery

When a node A wants to establish a link to node B, node A needs to send an RDM in which it includes two kind of keywords: KInt and KDes. KRDM(A) = KInt $\cup$ KDes represents all the keywords in A's RDM. In the RDM, it also has some special space Af for recording the forwarding link of the RDM in order to make node B send an ACK message to node A.

For the node who receives the RDM, the major process for the route discovery is as follows:

■ *Acceptance:* A node u accepts an RDM from its *i*-th neighbor node only if KAnn(u,i) is the subset of KRDM(A). If the RDM does not correspond to u's i-th neighbor, this node will simply discard the RDM.
■ *Loop Detection:* In DSL, if a sender sends its message (RDM) to another node, in this message (RDM), the sender side must design a message ID. When a node receives the RDM, the message ID will be checked; if it is a duplicated one, the receiver will drop it.

If an RDM can survive in the loop detection, the receiver node v will do the following three optional processes:

■ Try to forward the RDM to the next node
■ Make an acknowledgment to the RDM
■ Discard the RDM

The receiver node v will first try to forward and acknowledge the RDM. If both of them do not happen, node v will discard the RDM.

12.3 Destabilization of Terrorist Networks through Argument-Driven Hypothesis Model [2]

The basic idea for network destabilization is to remove the key path in the network in order to destabilize the communication between nodes. It utilizes the following characteristics of the nodes:

■ How fast a node propagates the information
■ The followers of a given node

- The path between the nodes
- High degree nodes in the network
- The relative power of a node

Centrality (degree): Degree can be considered as the relative significance of a node in the network. The nodes can be characterized by the different degrees as the header, follower, border, etc. In general, if a node is in the middle of some nodes' communication route, it can be defined as the central node. The centrality of a node can be measured by the following ways: One method is to measure the distance or hops away from the nodes in the network. The other is to calculate the number of a node's immediate neighbors that are one hop away from it.

In Figure 12.1 there are eight nodes and nine edges in the graph. The degree of a given node is the number of nodes that directly connect to this node. For instance, node 2 connects to both node 1 and node 3, so the degree of node 3 is 2. In Figure 12.1 every node can reach every other node. The distance or path between two nodes is equal to the number of edges in the path. The shortest path for a given node to reach other node is the *geodesic distance*. For instance, the shortest path for node 1 to reach node 5 is through the node 4 (two hops), that is, it is the geodesic distance.

Betweenness: Betweenness denotes that a node is in the middle of the communication paths of the other nodes. For instance, many nodes do not communicate with each other by the geodesic distance or shortest path. In this situation, two measures are proposed that are based on all the paths between the nodes and any random selected paths.

Closeness: Closeness can be explained as a method which assumes the node propagates the information to other nodes by using the shortest route or geodesic distance. A function of measuring the closeness is to estimate the time for a node to spread information to other nodes in the network.

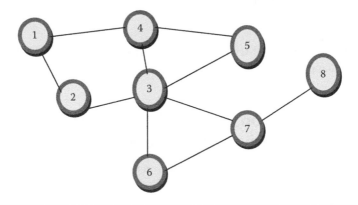

Figure 12.1 A graph example. (From Hussain, D. M. 2007. *Proceedings of the Second International Conference on Availability, Reliability and Security* [April 10–13, 2007]. ARES. IEEE Computer Society, Washington, DC, 480–492.)

12.4 The Link Prediction Problem for Social Networks [3]

12.4.1 Model of the Link Prediction

Let G = <V,E> represent a graph of a social network model. V denotes the all the nodes in the social network and E denotes all the edges between each nodes. For the e ∈ E, it is one edge between two nodes at a specific time t. In different time periods, we can record all the interactions among edges. For a given time period t < t', G[t, t'] represents a subset or a subgraph of G in which all the communication between nodes must happen in a given time period [t, t']. The training interval [t_0, t_0'] is a time period [t_1, t_1'] in which we know all the edges and t_1 > t_0. Correspondingly, the test interval is a time period in which the edges are unknown. For the G[t_0, t_0'], it must generate some possible edges that are not included in the G[t0, t0']. They are the outcome of the network prediction.

In the experiments explained in [3], we may select some authors, and each of them has a number of papers. A given set Core represents Jtrain edges in the training interval and Jtest edges in the test interval. Enews is the set of edges <a,b> in which authors a and b collaborate during the test interval instead of the set Eold, which is the set of edges in which the two authors have no collaboration in the training interval. Gcollab: = <V,Eold>.

12.4.2 Methods for Link Prediction

Score(x,y) denotes the connection weight score. We can calculate the proximity or similarity between nodes x and y, which are related to the geographical position. The basic method to find the shortest path between nodes is to use the small-world network theory. Small-world network can be explained as a type of social network in which most nodes are not directly connected to each other. However, they can reach other nodes by a several hops or steps.

Let φ(x) denote the set of neighbors of a given node x. We can infer that if the sets φ(x) and φ(y) have a large number of intersection sets, the two nodes x and y have more possibility to contact with each other.

12.4.3 Common Neighbors

Following this idea, we can measure *score* as follows: score(x,y) = φ(x) ∩ φ(y), which is the number of the common neighbors of x and y. It has been proved that the number of common neighbors of nodes *a* and *b* at time t has a relationship with the possibility of their collaborations in the future.

Jaccard's coefficient: The Jaccard coefficient was widely applied in the message retrieval. The weighted score can be measured as the number of the intersection between x and y, which was compared to the union set of x and y. The formulation was given as: score(x, y) = |φ(x) ∩ φ(y)|.

Adamic and Adar: These can be used to decide whether or not two Web pages are strongly related. Through this method they can calculate the similarity between two pages as: $\Sigma z: 1/\log(\text{frequency}(z))$. The score(x,y) is calculated as: $\Sigma z \in \varphi(x) \cap \varphi(y) 1/\log|\varphi(z)|$.

Preferential attachment: This theory is based on an assumption that the future edge that involves node x must belong to the set $\varphi(x)$. So the probability of the collaboration between node x and y can be measured as: $\text{score}(x,y) = |\varphi(x)| \cdot |\varphi(y)|$.

12.4.4 Mathematics of Centralities

In the social network, a node that directly connects with many nodes can be considered as a high degree node. In other words, the lower degree nodes need the high degree nodes to serve as a bridge in order to connect with other lower degree nodes. The high degree nodes can also be regarded as the information sources. Generally, the degree or centrality Dc(aj) can be measured by:

$$Dc(aj) = \Sigma_{i=1}^{n} d(ai, aj)$$

where
$$d(ai, aj) = \begin{cases} 1 \text{ } ai \text{ and } aj \text{ directly connected} \\ 0 \text{ } ai \text{ and } aj \text{ not connected} \end{cases}$$

This equation is useful for the subgraph of the whole network or a limited-size network for centrality calculation. However, in most cases, we need to measure the relative centrality for different high degree nodes which are independent of each other. For example, a maximum number of connected nodes for a certain graph is n–1. So we need to introduce a new formula to calculate the centrality of the node by using the proportion of the number of adjacent nodes to the maximum number (n–1).

$$D'c(aj) = \frac{\Sigma_{i=1}^{n} d(ai, aj)}{n - 1}$$

Betweenness is one method to measure the centrality of a node in the network. If a node is located in the middle of many shortest paths (geodesics) as an intermediate between other nodes, this node has a higher betweenness than others. Typically, in a network, G = <A,E>, where A denotes the nodes, and E denotes all the edges between the nodes. The betweenness Bc(m) for a node m can be measured by:

$$Bc(m) = \sum_{i \neq j \neq m \neq v} \frac{aij(m)}{aij}$$

where aij denotes the number of all the shortest paths between node i and j, and aij(m) represents the number of all the shortest paths from i to j coming through the node m.

Freeman has introduced another method to calculate the relative centrality of any node in the network.

$$B'c(m) = \frac{Bc(m)}{(n^2 - 3n + 2)/2}$$

This formula is tentative to calculate the relative betweenness of a node in the network. In fact, this method is a way to normalize Bc(m) by dividing the maximum number ((n-1)(n-2)) of nodes it connected to.

In Figure 12.2, node 1 can reach every node in the graph except node 5, so it has the higher closeness than other nodes; in other words, we can say node 1 is closer to all the nodes in the network.

The simplest way to measure the closeness centrality is to calculate the sum of the geodesics distance from one node to all other nodes in the network and then take its inverse. With the increase of the distance from node m to other nodes, the closeness will increase as well. The formula can be given by:

$$Cc(m) = [\Sigma_{i=1}^{n} \ d(m,j)]^{-1}$$

where d is the shortest path between nodes m and j. The relative closeness can be measure by:

$$Cc(m)' = \frac{n-1}{[\Sigma_{i=1}^{n} \ d(m,j)]^{-1}}$$

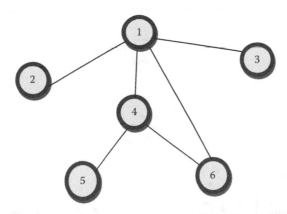

Figure 12.2 A graph example. (From Kossinets, G., Kleinberg, J., and Watts, D. 2008. *Proceeding of the 14th ACM SIGKDD International Conference on Knowledge Discovery and Data Mining* [Las Vegas, Nevada, August 24–27, 2008]. KDD '08. ACM, New York, 435–443.)

12.5 Routing in Disconnected Social Networks [4]

The clusters of some networks sometimes may not directly connect with each other. They have to select a suitable bridge tie to deliver a message to the destination. Using Figure 12.3 as an example, we assume that cluster 1 does not directly link to cluster 3. Thus, if the source node is in the cluster 1, it is very difficult to send a message to the destination node which is in the cluster 3. But it does not mean that there is no forward link for the source node to propagate its information. In Figure 12.3, node a1 that belongs to cluster 1 can directly connect to a2 (that belongs to cluster 2). Likewise, a3 (belongs to cluster 2) can directly connect with a4 (that belongs to cluster 3). Moreover, a2 and a3 are involved in the same cluster. The dark line illustrates the bridges which are established by a1 and a2, a3 and a4, respectively. Through this path the source node can forward its message to the destination node.

In fact, by indentifying the centrality of a node, we can explore the bridges between different clusters. Typically, the centrality of a node is the degree in the frame of a network. Centrality can demonstrate the ability of a central node to communicate with other nodes in the network. Nowadays, there are three popular centrality measures: the Freemans' degree, closeness, and betweenness measures.

"Degree centrality" is an efficient way to find the amount of directly connected ties, which includes a selected node. For instance, a high degree centrality node can keep connection with a huge number of other network nodes. During the information propagation this kind of node can play the role of bride for communications between different clusters. In contrast, other surrounding nodes may be not as important as the high degree node in maintaining the connectivity with other clusters. The degree calculation for a selected node ai as follow:

$$Cdegree(ai) \sum_{i=1}^{n} P(ai, ak)$$

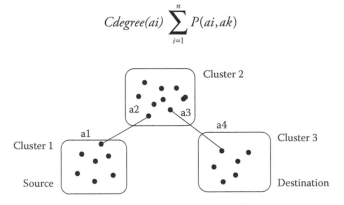

Figure 12.3 Bridge ties with disconnected clusters. (From Liben-Nowell, D. and Kleinberg, J. 2003. The link prediction problem for social networks. In *Proceedings of the Twelfth International Conference on Information and Knowledge Management* (New Orleans, LA [November 03–08, 2003]. CIKM '03. ACM, New York, 556–559.)

If P (ai,ak) = 1, the direct link between the two nodes exists, otherwise it does not exist.

"Closeness centrality" depends on the geographic distance $d(ai,ak)$. It means the shortest path between a node (ai) and other nodes connecting directly with it. By calculating the node's closeness, we can estimate the time delay for information propagation. The formula is as follows:

$$Closeness(ai) \frac{N-1}{\sum_{i=1}^{n} P(ai, ak)}$$

where N is the number of nodes in the network.

"Betweenness centrality" aims to find the node which is involved in the linking path of other nodes' communications. A node with high betweenness centrality can have a strong ability to interact with other nodes in the network.

So the calculation of betweenness centrality is as follows:

$$Betweeness(ai) = \sum_{j=1}^{N} \sum_{k=1}^{j-1} \frac{gik(ai)}{gjk}$$

gjk is the number of geographic paths connecting aj and ak, and $gjk(ai)$ means that the number of geographic paths include ai.

Ego networks consist of a bunch of nodes that must directly connect to one node ("ego"), and include all the edges among the alters.

It is difficult to measure the centrality of a large-scale network. Then we begin to analyze the "ego" network, which does not need the understanding of the complete network. Because of the limited number of links in the ego network, the degree centrality can be easily measured. However, closeness centrality in some degree is not significant, since ego can directly connect to all the alters in the network. Thus, the distance between the alter and ego is only one hop. Moreover, the betweenness centrality value means the ability of a node that connects the nodes that are not directly linked to each other.

In the social networks, a high transitivity degree means a high probability of two acquaintances if they have more common acquaintances. In other words, if two nodes share a common neighbor, the probability of being connected by one link is much higher.

Separation degree is the proportion of common neighbors among the nodes in the networks. For information spreading, the separation degree is crucial. For example, for two given nodes which have a higher separation degree (i.e., having several neighbors which do not connect to each other), the information propagation becomes more difficult and has more delay than the nodes having a lower separation degree. Therefore, for information dissemination, a node that enjoys a lower separation degree from a given node tends to have a good performance of information dissemination.

Newman's study of scientific collaborations shows that if two authors have more mutual co-authors before, then we can predict the probability of their collaborations is higher. For instance, we assume that two scientists have six previous common collaborators, then the possibility of their collaboration is about three times higher than the pair who only has two collaborators, and more than 200 times higher than the pair who has none. Newman deems that the probability of two scientists' collaborations increases when the number of their previous common collaborators rises.

In this way, Liben-Nowell and Keinberg use the neighbor metric to predict future collaborations. P(a,b) is the probability of collaboration of two assigned scientists a and b in the future. The formula is as follows:

$$P(a,b) = |N(a) \cap N(b)|$$

Where N(a) and N(b) are the total number of neighbors of scientists a and b individually. From this formula, the common set of neighbors of scientists a and b depends on the network layout. By using neighbor metrics we can predict the probability of the two scientists' collaborations in the future.

12.6 Modeling Spread of Ideas in Online Social Networks [5]

IM means an instant message network, which is a type of dynamic online social network. The major difference between the IM networks and traditional networks is that we cannot presume that a random node is active. A node may be offline (i.e., disconnected from all links with other neighbors) at a time when it is inactive. For instance, in our real world, a person with a communicable disease who avoids contact with others will prevent its spread.

12.6.1 Susceptibility

The susceptibility δ denotes the possibility of a node that can accept the content of a message, thus becoming a message carrier. In reality, one decides whether or not to accept content depending on its personal appeal or professional relevance. Hence, people tend to accept a message if its contents have something in common with their own interests. A high susceptibility indicates that the message is similar the person's other interests. A random value 1 and 0 can reflect a node's susceptibility.

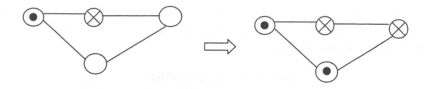

Figure 12.4 **In the message propagation in the IM network, the nodes with black dots represent the message carriers, and the nodes with crossing signal represent the nodes are offline. (From Mislove, A. et al. 2007. Measurement and analysis of online social networks. In** *Proceedings of the 7th ACM SIGCOMM Conference on Internet Measurement* **[San Diego, California, October 24–26, 2007]. IMC '07. ACM, New York, 29–42.)**

12.6.2 Transmissibility

Transmissibility γ denotes that the possibility that nodes x and y can contact each other. If x is a carrier of the message, the message will be sent to y. In the ideal model, transmissibility is assuming that all the nodes can always maintain contact. However, realistically the transmissibility of the network depends on the status of each node, which is online or offline.

Status: The status Pt denotes that one IM user at a given time in the set {Ponline, Poffline}. The status of a given node (active or inactive) can be assigned to either {1,0}or {0,1}.

Origin: The origin is the message's source in the network.

Active Node: Active node is a user who is online at a given time t.

12.6.3 A graph of IM Network

The set V denotes all the IM network users or nodes. The set E represents the edges between all the nodes. In the beginning, a selected node Vb is assumed as the message carrier. Vb is referred to the origin of the IM network. A neighbor node Vc is in the set A. The possibility of the joint between the node Vb and Vc, p(c∩b), denotes that the message is transmitted from the origin Vb to Vc. The probability of the joint for nodes b and c is: p(c∩b) = p(b).p(c). Figure 4 illustrates an IM evolution procedure.

12.6.4 The General Information Dissemination Model

To better calculate the number of nodes to which the message can be delivered at a given time t, we may define the term reachability to measure it as the set R. In the ideal case, we presume that the transmissibility and susceptibility are equal to one. The paths for the message transmission in the IM network are equal to the radius of the network. At time t, the set R is equal to set A because the possibility of the message transmission is equal to 1. After t iterations, the set At denotes all the neighbors that can be reached from the origin node V0 at the time t. $d(Vt,V0)$ represents the number of t iterations.

$$At = \{Vt: Vt \in V, d(Vt,V0) \le t\}$$

ηi denotes the set of Vi's neighbors, $Vi \in At$. $\eta i = \{x, d(x,Vi) = 1\}$. Then At can be given as:

$$At = At-1U \; (\cap_{i-1}^{k} \eta i)$$

For two selected nodes Vi and Vj, the possibility of being affected by the message or information can be decided by the subset of all the paths among the two nodes. For the given nodes Vi , $\alpha 1t$ represents all the nodes which are in the At, at a given time t. In the simplest case, we assume V2 is the neighbor node of V1. At the time t, the probability for the node V2 can be affected, which can be calculated as:

$$P1t = max (\alpha 1t, a1t, a2t)$$

Consider a two-path case where the message can be delivered from V1 origin to V3. Assume nodes V2 and V4 are the intermediate carrier nodes. The formulation can be given as:

$$P2t = max(\alpha 2t, a3t, a2t, a1t, a3t, a4t, a1t)$$

In the general case, for *n* paths from any given nodes to others, the possibility $\kappa(A,B)$ denotes all the paths between the nodes A and B:

$$Pnt = max\{ant, \; \prod_{i=1}^{n} kit \; \prod_{i=1}^{n} k2t, \; ...., \; \prod_{i=1}^{n} k(n=1), \; \prod_{i=1}^{n} knt\}$$

12.7 Conclusions

This chapter discussed some popular issues in social network protocol designs, such as security, link prediction issue, terrorist network issue, and disconnected cluster communication issue. There are still many challenging problems to be solved in order to build a robust social network.

References

1. Banks, L., Ye, S., Huang, Y., and Wu, S. F. 2007. Davis social links: integrating social networks with internet routing. In *Proceedings of the 2007 Workshop on Large Scale Attack Defense* (Kyoto, Japan, August 27–27, 2007). LSAD' 07. ACM, New York, NY, 121–128.

2. Hussain, D. M. 2007. Terrorist networks analysis through argument driven hypotheses model. In *Proceedings of the Second International Conference on Availability, Reliability and Security* (April 10–13, 2007). ARES. IEEE Computer Society, Washington, DC, 480–492.
3. Kossinets, G., Kleinberg, J., and Watts, D. 2008. The structure of information pathways in a social communication network. In *Proceeding of the 14th ACM SIGKDD International Conference on Knowledge Discovery and Data Mining* (Las Vegas, Nevada, August 24–27, 2008). KDD '08. ACM, New York, 435–443.
4. Liben-Nowell, D. and Kleinberg, J. 2003. The link prediction problem for social networks. In *Proceedings of the Twelfth International Conference on Information and Knowledge Management* (New Orleans, LA, November 03–08, 2003). CIKM '03. ACM, New York, 556–559.
5. Mislove, A., Marcon, M., Gummadi, K. P., Druschel, P., and Bhattacharjee, B. 2007. Measurement and analysis of online social networks. In *Proceedings of the 7th ACM SIGCOMM Conference on Internet Measurement* (San Diego, California, October 24–26, 2007). IMC '07. ACM, New York, 29–42.

Chapter 13

Design Tools of Sociotechnical Networks

Ling Xu and Fei Hu

Contents

13.1 Introduction

This chapter introduces some design tools of practical sociotechnical systems. As we know, sociotechnical systems theory is an approach to recognize the interactions between people and technologies in complex organizational societies in real human world. In this chapter, first, the analysis of sociotechnical systems is introduced, which includes seven innovative methods proposed in Reference 1. Robustness is a critical factor for sociotechnical systems that affects the stability of the systems. How to investigate the robustness of a sociotechnical system is then included. Finally, some design procedures of sociotechnical systems are discussed.

13.2 Analysis of Sociotechnical Systems [1]

How do we analyze sociotechnical systems? In this chapter, seven novel tools to analyze the sociotechnical activities are introduced, which are based on ICT (information and communication technologies) [1]. Sociotechnical systems are closely connected with dynamic and creative activities. All human activities are conducted by tools, and the ICT-based tools are interesting if they are used in sociotechnical systems. Seven novel ICT-based tools are introduced briefly and support the complex decision-making processes. New tools can also be added into the suite of the seven ICT-based tools.

13.2.1 Zing: A Facilitated Group Decision Support System [2]

Zing is a groupware system that allows a group of people to communicate, discuss, and solve problems together. The system permits multiple PC or laptop keyboards to control the cursors, and creates individual screens for each group member. It is convenient for group discussion. The screen displays a topic in the window, which notifies all the group members of what the problem is. Twelve private windows are given at the bottom, which allows the group members to type their own opinions, ideas, and comments in the private windows. When they feel ready, they can fire up the messages to the public window, and then all the other group members can see the speakers' ideas. Figure 13.1 illustrates such basic ideas. The talk progress can be stored for further reference. It is clear that this tool is suitable for group discussion and decision making. It can be used in school and small groups easily over the Web.

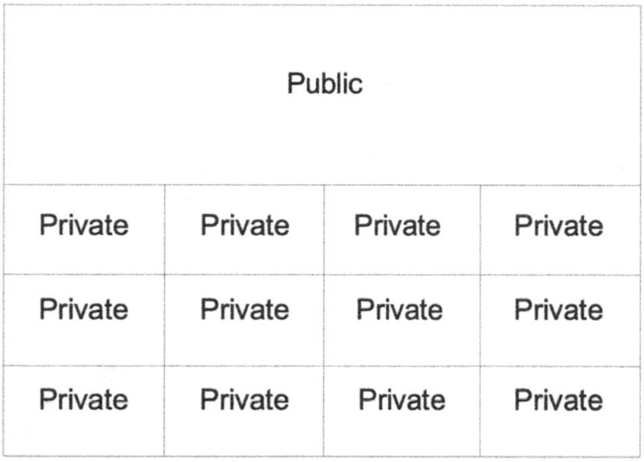

Public
Private
Private
Private
Private
Private
Private
Private
Private
Private
Private
Private
Private

Figure 13.1 Brief structure of Zing. (From Zing: A Facilitated Group Decision Support System. Available at http://www.anyzing.com.)

Views and Ideas Collection
Make Choice
Factor Analysis

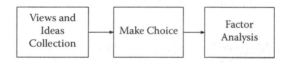

Figure 13.2 Steps of Q-Method. (From Q-Method: Capture of Subjective Perceptions and Factor Analysis. Available: http://www.qmethod.org.)

13.2.2 Q-Method: Capture of Subjective Perceptions and Factor Analysis [3]

Q-methodology provides a standard set of processing steps for analyzing numerical data by eliciting the subjective understandings held by participants. The data source in this case is the participants' own understanding of some particular topic or problem.

First, the process collects all the ideas of the participants and publishes those ideas together. This process allows the participant to access others' ideas. This is important and advantageous since many new ideas may come out through this process.

Second, participants make choices. This process will distribute a sort sheet to every participant and ask them to make choices among the statements of ideas presented. Once this process is completed, the Q-Method software can analyze the data provided by the participants and run the factor analysis to get the respective factor number, which indicates the views of the participants.

Figure 13.3 illustrates such a procedure.

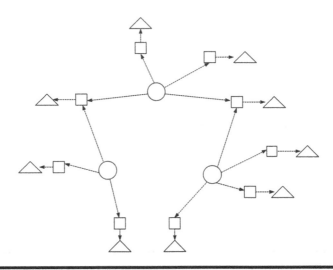

Figure 13.3 Network with associations (circles), businesses (squares), and people (triangles). (From Hasan, H. and Crawford. K. 2006. International Conference on Creativity and Innovation in Decision Making and Decision Support [CIDMDS 2006], London, June 28–July 1, 256–276.)

13.2.3 Social Network Analysis: Relationship Capture and Visualization

Social Network Analysis (SNA) (Figure 13.3) is used to identify, analyze, and represent the relationship between individuals and groups in an organization or community. The outcome of this tool is the structure and dynamics of an organization or community.

Netdraw (http://www.netdraw.com) is a typical SNA software example.

13.2.4 Leximancer: Concept Mapping from Content Analysis [4]

Content analysis is used to extract the insight concepts of the collections of text documents. It divides the documents into many pieces of parts and relations, which can be quantified and analyzed. This process can point out what are the most frequently use words or concepts contained in the text documents. The analysis results are highly reliable.

Leximancer [4] is a computer-based tool for content analysis. It can be used to analyze any form of verbal communication. This tool can also be used to extract insights from the historical text documents, which may have existed for a long time. The results may show the historical, social, and culture insights when the text documents were produced.

13.2.5 Stella Systems Modeling: Systems Thinking and Dynamic Simulations [5]

Dynamic Systems Modeling is a technique used to investigate the behaviors of a social system based on computer simulations. The system can model the structure and behavior of a specific social system and record the response data to estimate the situation of the real world. It is useful before new policies are applied to the real world since operating procedures, social response, and other important information can be collected from the simulation model without disrupting the real world. By changing the simulation period, it can easily investigate the behaviors and impacts of the social system for a long time or a short time. Simulating extreme conditions for the social system and investigating the results can improve the safety of the real system.

13.2.6 Go*Team-Gaming, Team Building, and Cooperative Profiling

Go*Team is a computer team version of the ancient strategy game of Go in China. The game is not turn-by-turn, but the next turn is specified by the server as a "relaxation time." All the team members are shown with a partial board on their individual screen, and all the team members are equal. The team members need to communicate with each other to express their own views and the ideas of the board, which is required to win the game. So the interaction between team members is important. [1]

13.2.7 Eviva: A Web-Based Groupware System for Communities

Web-based groupware system applications are used to support online activities of communities. The Web-based groupware system application can be customized by the users to adapt to their own situations. Different privileges and different work can be assigned to different level users. The users can work individually or work as a team with other users in the community [6].

13.3 Robustness Modeling of Sociotechnical Systems

Sociotechnical systems are always complex and not easy to be analyzed. However, the robustness is an important factor to evaluate the designed sociotechnical systems. If the designed sociotechnical system is not robust, it can be affected by other factors easily, such as environmental change or abnormal conditions. As a result, evaluating the robustness of a designed sociotechnical system is critical for designing a robust and well-organized sociotechnical system.

In [7] a theoretical background is proposed in order to model the robustness of complex sociotechnical systems. Classic, structural, and emergent and self-organized regulations are three categories of regulation proposed in this paper. The emergent and self-organized regulation plays an important role in a robust sociotechnical system. For the technical devices, they may face some emergent situations and malfunctions which have been considered before. If the device systems can respond effectively and correctly, they can be called robust systems [7, 8].

However, robustness has different definitions in different contexts. Obviously, a robust system should respond effectively and correctly no matter how the external environment changes, how an unpredictable situation occurs, or how an internal malfunction happens. Actually, a resilient system has similar characteristics as previous mentioned. The difference between robust and resilient systems is that the internal structure of a robust system may be modified under certain conditions.

The modifications are controlled by a structure that determines the organizational changes. Three main categories of regulation are considered: (1) classical, (2) self-adaptation, and (3) emergence and self-organization. The first two cases help to build a resilient system, which has an explicit border between a system and external environment, and the last case helps to build a robust system that does not have an explicit border between a system and external environment.

The case of Hurricane Katrina is an example of self-organization and emergence. When Hurricane Katrina attacked the city, the fact is that there were no immediate official actions by the government to rebuild the destroyed communication infrastructure system. At the same time, some actors started to rebuild the communication system using some new technologies such as WIFI and WIMAX. These actions were done immediately after the arrival of the hurricane, whereas no official actions were taken at the same time. These actions happened in spite of attempts by official organizations to limit the involvements of volunteers. This case is a typical self-organization mechanism that cannot be predicted.

"Classical" and "self-adaptation" are no longer suitable to analyze these cases since these two regulations assume the function of the system is constant. As seen in the hurricane example, with self-organization, the crisis situations can lead to the modifications of values, of the actors' interests, and of their interaction with the environment. Therefore, the border between the system and the external environment is no longer clear. The system and the environment may interfere with each other.

Figure 13.4 shows the stages and efficiency performance of the system in the example of Hurricane Katrina. The red curve indicates the actions of the volunteers who started to reestablish the communication system immediately after the arrival of the disaster. The black curve depicts the evolution process of the formal organization.

As a result, the ergonomics of the complex system requires different types of engineering: (1) classical engineering, (2) resilience engineering, and (3) robustness engineering. The first type is based on a functional approach and controls the simple and structural regulation mechanisms. The second type deals with borderline and incidental

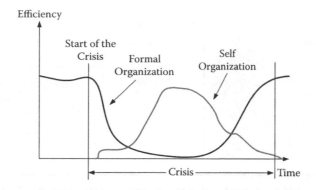

Figure 13.4 **The dynamics of self-organization and institutional mechanism in a crisis situation. (From Associated Press story by Mathew Fordhahl in *Mercury News* [http://radioresponse.org/wordpress/?page_id=46], October 4, 2005.)**

situations, but the framework is still constant. The third type deals with complex systems that contain nondeterministic processes such as in the crisis example.

13.4 Design of Sociotechnical Systems

The design process of a sociotechnical system is complex and time consuming. In Reference 10 it explained a way of participatory design using sociotechnical walkthrough. Documents are important in participatory design since they are shared with the participants, and affect the decision making of each participant. The documents should be accurate and up to date. How can these documents to be produced? The sociotechnical walkthrough (STWT) can help to achieve this. Also, to create such documents, a mix of abstract diagrams can be used. The practice shows that the STWT can support the participatory design process [10–12].

The participatory design is similar to groupware, which supports or modifies the cooperation between different roles or persons. Due to the large number of roles or persons, a lot of interactions, dependencies, and interference may occur between them. These may make the system much more complicated and not easy to analyze.

13.4.1 STWT Concepts

The core idea of STWT is to build a diagrammatic model to represent a sociotechnical system. The model may be developed from scratch or derived from an existing model. The model should be examined carefully step by step and be modified if necessary. Finally, the model should become the agreement of most of the participants.

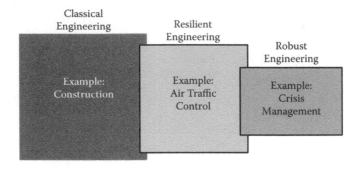

Figure 13.5 Different types of engineering. (From Pavard, B., Dugdale, J., Saoud, N. B.-B., Darcy, S., and Salembier, P. (2006), Paper presented at Resilience Engineering, Juan les Pins, France. 8–10 Nov, 2006. Paper available from http://www. resilience engineering. org/)

Table 13.1 Differences Between STWT and Cognitive Walkthrough

	STWT	*Cognitive walkthrough*
Evaluator	Whole group of participants	Single
Questions	Open questions	Not open questions

Source: Thomas Herrmann et al. Sociotechnical walkthrough: Designing technology along work processes. *Proc. Participatory Design Conference 2004,* Toronto, Canada, July 27–31.

Obviously, there are many similarities between STWT and cognitive walkthrough [13]. However, there are also some main differences between them: The cognitive walkthrough is a method for usability inspection of interactive systems. The evaluator acts as a user and walks through all the possible steps, then gives the feedback. At each step, the evaluator should answer a set of prepared questions, such as: "Have I achieved the desired result?" and "What are the next possible steps of dialogue?" The answers of the evaluator for those questions can help to improve the interactive system. The similarity happens in STWT, which inspects the model of a sociotechnical system step by step. At each step, there is also a set of prepared questions to be answered. However, the difference from cognitive walkthrough is the evaluator is not a single person, but the whole group of participants. The prepared questions in STWT are open ones, such as: "What is the next sensible activity?" and "Which information is needed to support this activity?" "How will this activity be changed?" and "Which questions have yet to be answered and when?" Table 13.1 shows the differences between STWT and cognitive walkthrough.

The product of the STWT is a series of diagrams, which can describe the structure of a sociotechnical system. These diagrams can be used as the basis of documentation. However, the main function of these diagrams is to support the communication processes of participators. Every sociotechnical system usually needs more than one model to be represented, and in each model, usually more than one walkthrough needs to be used. If many changes come out after one walkthrough, it means that the diagram needs to be improved before the next walkthrough. At this time, a break needs to be added for the participants to improve the diagram. Figure 13.6 shows the procedure between two walkthroughs.

After conducting the necessary number of walkthroughs, the whole group of participants should make an agreement on the final diagram.

13.4.2 Applicability of STWT

In this section, three selected techniques which share similar purposes with STWT will be discussed and compared. For example, JAD is very similar to STWT. Contextual Design is suitable for requirements elicitation and is based on ethnography and feedback of models.

13.4.2.1 JAD

Joint application design (JAD) is a concept developed by IBM in the 1980s [14]. A workbook is continuously updated in a series of facilitated workshops. As a result, the workbook in JAD is similar to the diagram in STWT. JAD takes more focus on the whole scale of system development, while STWT takes more focus on the detailed discussion of the cooperative work processes.

13.4.2.2 Scenario-Based Techniques

Scenario-based techniques are also used for similar purposes as the STWT. They focus on the instances of a process based on text. The interrelationship between a series of scenarios is not so easy to understand; as a result, some more techniques are introduced, For example, a technique called CARD was developed to improve the scenario-based techniques. The cards in the CARD technique are laid out and related to each other on a table. However, the STWT takes a much deeper look into organizational processes with strong relation to software systems.

Figure 13.6   Procedure between two walkthroughs. (From Thomas Herrmann, Gabriele Kunau, Kai-Uwe Loser, and Natalja Menold (2004). *Proc. Participatory Design Conference 2004,* **Toronto, Canada, July 27–31.)**

13.4.2.3 Contextual Design

Contextual design is a good design method for requirements elicitation. The analysis begins with a detailed ethnography, and then several types of diagrams are derived by the developer in CD. The learning process of organizations plays a less important role in CD, while it is important in the STWT. With the STWT, the users can discuss and make necessary organizational changes after each walkthrough, and the organizational development is also important as the requirements for software products. Table 13.2 shows the similarity and difference between STWT and the other three methods.

13.5 Conclusion

This chapter introduced some basic analysis and design methods of sociotechnical systems, robustness modeling, and design process. The seven innovative analysis methods proposed by References 1–6 are used to analyze the interactions between people and modern technology. However, each method has its own emphasized point. For example, Zing focuses on the group decision, Stella systems emphasize

Table 13.2   Similarity and Difference between STWT and Other Three Methods

	Similarity	Difference
JAD	1. Utilized workbook, similar to diagrams in STWT.	1. JAD takes broad view on system development, while STWT focuses on the details. 2. JAD relies on a leader, while STWT relies on all participants.
Scenario-based techniques	1. Used for similar purposes as the STWT.	1. Interrelationship between a series of scenarios is hard to understand. 2. STWT takes a deeper look into organizational processes.
Contextual design	1. Diagrams are also used in CD.	1. Learning process of the analyzed organizations plays a less important role. 2. Organizational development has the same importance as the development of requirements.

dynamic simulations, and Eviva is a Web-based groupware system. Robustness is an important factor for sociotechnical systems. This chapter explained how to evaluate the robustness of a sociotechnical system and how to rebuild the system through a disaster example of Hurricane Katrina. Finally, some basic and simplified design processes of sociotechnical systems are discussed. The similarities and differences are compared between STWT, JAD, and Scenario-Based Techniques and Contextual Design. STWT is a good approach for design purposes, utilizing diagrammatic models to represent sociotechnical systems. With these the system can be examined carefully step by step through walkthrough. Then, the system can be developed and modified through these processes, which improves the current design of the sociotechnical systems.

References

1. Hasan, H. and Crawford, K., (2006). Innovative Sociotechnical Systems for Complex Decision-making. International Conference on Creativity and Innovation in Decision Making and Decision Support (CIDMDS 2006), London, June 28–July 1, 256–276.
2. Zing: A Facilitated Group Decision Support System. Available: http://www.anyzing.com.
3. Q-Method: Capture of Subjective Perceptions and Factor Analysis. Available: http://www.qmethod.org.
4. Leximancer-Concept Mapping from Content Analysis. Available: http://www.leximance.com.
5. Stella Systems Modelling-Systems Thinking and Dynamic Simulations. Available: http://www.iseesystems.com.
6. Eviva—A Web based Groupware System for Communities. Available: http://www.eviva.com.au.
7. Pavard, B., Dugdale, J., Saoud, N. B.-B., Darcy, S., and Salembier, P. (2006). Design of robust sociotechnical systems, Paper presented at the *Resilience Engineering*, Juan les Pins, France.
8. Rizzo, A., Pozzi, S., Save, L., and Sujan, M. (2005). Designing complex sociotechnical systems: A heuristic schema based on cultural-historical psychology. Paper presented at the *Proc. 2005 Annual Conference on European Association of Cognitive Ergonomics*.
9. From "Associated Press" (http://radioresponse.org/wordpress/?page_id=46) Mercury news. October 4, 2005 Mathew Fordhahl.
10. Thomas Herrmann, Gabriele Kunau, Kai-Uwe Loser, and Natalja Menold (2004). Sociotechnical walkthrough: Designing technology along work processes, *Proc. Participatory Design Conference 2004*, Toronto, Canada, July 27–31.
11. Herrmann, Th., Hoffmann, M., Kunau, G., and Loser, K.-U. (2002). Modeling cooperative work: Chances and risks of structuring. In *Cooperative Systems Design, A Challenge of the Mobility Age (Coop 2002)*, IOS Press. pp. 53–70.
12. Herrmann, Th., Loser, K.-U., and Moysich, K. (2000). Intertwining training and participatory design for the development of groupware applications. In Cherkasky, T., Greenbaum, J., Mambrey, P., Pors, J. K. (Eds.), *Proc. of PDC 2000*. Palo Alto, CA. pp. 106–115.

13. Polson, P. G., Lewis, C., Rieman, J., and Wharton, C. (1992). Cognitive walkthrough: A method for theory-based evaluation of user interfaces. *Int. J. Man-Machines Studies*, 36. pp. 741–773.
14. Crawford, A. (1994). *Advancing Business Concepts in a JAD Workshop Setting*. Englewood Cliffs, NJ: Yourdon Press.

Chapter 14

Sociotechnical Networks for Healthcare Applications

Joshua Davenport, Gabriel Hillard, and Fei Hu

Contents

14.1 Introduction

Healthcare is a vital part of modern life and is the subject of massive attention due to its life-or-death implications for every person of every age, race, and gender. It is an ever-evolving entity that is constantly the topic of national and international debates, and tremendous sums of money are often spent to try to make the healthcare system more accessible and effective.

The tracking of patient illness, mapping of disease spread, and communication avenues for different parts of the healthcare community are typical healthcare research examples. Healthcare involves patients, individual medical staff, and large medical groups, all acting in a complex social network to achieve the best possible care for each patient. The social network that healthcare forms connects all these different entities together as well as acting as a discrete tool for each participant.

A sociotechnical network can be formed to integrate the various complex relationships in the current healthcare system. This network ranges from an individual tool that allows a doctor to make a particular diagnosis, to large-scale data-gathering systems that connect various large healthcare providers to a government body for oversight.

One way to analyze this model is to start at the smallest individual component and work toward the larger interconnecting parts. Each smaller piece of the network builds on other pieces to form a larger system that relates all the users and the technical tools, and by examining the steps that go from the small to the large, one may slowly arrive at an understanding of how the sociotechnical network is formed.

14.2 EpiSims Disease Model [1]

One example of small-scale technical analysis in the medical field is infectious disease spread. By using a network modeling system, it is possible to predict vectors of disease transmission to provide crisis plans and give estimations on how quickly and how far a disease may spread. The Modeling Infectious Disease Agent Study (MIDAS) is being conducted by the National Institute of Health to examine different methodologies toward these systems. One approach in particular, the Epidemiological Simulation System (EpiSims) [1], was created to model disease vectors particularly in computer environments.

One of the first tasks that must be accomplished in order to provide the functional basis for such a network is the accumulation of the necessary background data to form an environment in which to function. If one considers such simulation to be created to be a probability universe, then that universe must be populated by different entities and factors that approximate the real world. In the case of infectious disease spread, this would be actual places, census data, distances, transportation networks, and information regarding the activities that take place. All of these are necessary to create a simulation that outputs data that are meaningful in any real-world situation.

The EpiSims model uses a "person–activity" approach toward calculating vectors of disease transmission. Individual people are created to represent entities within the network. These people have different characteristics, be it race, gender, age, social status, etc. For every person, an appropriate set of activities is constructed to create a working timeline that places a given person in different places for different instances of time. The model also considers the travel from location to location as another potential vector of disease spread, which is particularly important in the case of mass transit. With this individual entity created, it then becomes possible to place that entity into the working universe to establish a working model, but the method of establishing and evaluating that data is yet to be determined.

The modeling method that EpiSims uses is based on repeating days with the same people performing various sets of activities. Running in a loop, a person may randomly visit various commercial outlets each day while always traveling to work, and may attend a different social event at night. Then a contact network can be established to show how disease is spread over time between the different people present at a given location. This creates a large sum of data that then need to be analyzed.

The analysis of the data is done using a vertex and edge approach. A given vertex represents a particular individual, while an edge represents the disease transmission between one vertex to another. The graphical representation used is in the form of concentric circles where vertices with interconnecting lines are the edges (Figure 14.1).

There are several different attributes that can be drawn from this analysis. The first is diameter, or the minimum length along the longest chain formed. This shows both the spread of a given disease as well as the efficiency of that spread. The graph can also show the time it takes for a given person to infect multiple people. Another interesting characteristic that can be drawn is the saturation of disease spread over time. Because certain people will be infected after a given time interval, it is likely that transmissions will begin to cluster within certain groups that infect each other, which will diminish in terms of infection speed as viable candidates diminish. However, that cluster only needs a single individual to pass infection on to another cluster. The concept of clusters of people is known as assortativity, and it can have a strong impact on disease spread depending on how efficiently groups of people mix.

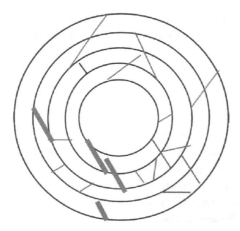

Figure 14.1   Vertex diagram [1].

Such a technical approach to a particular field presents a power tool for medical professionals, but it is still only a tool. Only when it is used by physicians in a particular case or applied by administrators in a larger sense does it really become helpful [1].

14.3 Transportation for the Disabled [2]

Cognition is defined as the process of thought. Therefore, a cognitive disability would be the inability to accurately process individual thoughts and ideas. A cognitive disabled person is one who is "significantly limited in at least two of the following areas: self-care, communication, home living, social/interpersonal skills, self-direction, and use of community resources, functional academic skills, work, leisure, health and safety" [2]. Some of the causes of cognitive disabilities include Down's syndrome, cerebral palsy, autism, and certain genetic disorders. This section addresses the need for "sociotechnical environments" to assist individuals with cognitive handicaps using public transit.

In large urban cities, public transportation is a necessity. The citizens of these cities depend on buses, subway trains, and trolleys to get to work, to shop, and to travel to distant destinations. Because of the large congestion, many people in these larger cities opt not to purchase personal vehicles, and depend solely on the city transit system. The same is true of people with disabilities who choose to live independently.

In 1990, the Americans with Disabilities Act (ADA) was signed to eliminate discrimination in, among other matters, transportation. Because of the complexity of some transportation routes and difficulty in access for disabled citizens, supplement vehicles have been integrated into most public transit systems to accommodate disabled travelers. These vehicles are necessary for both the physically handicapped and people with cognitive disabilities who cannot understand the more complicated transit systems. Although these vehicles make the public transportation more inclusive, the need for advanced reservations and lengthy wait time can be a hindrance.

Mentally handicapped travelers who would prefer to use nonspecialized transit are limited by their disability. Cognitively disabled individuals have trouble navigating some systems because of the difficulty in reading and understanding maps, as well as the confusion of following schedules. Certain improvements were identified to help these individuals in their attempts to use public transportation.

In 2001, a survey was conducted in 19 major cities around the United States. During this survey, various transportation operators were asked to categorize the communication practices of the transportation system for travelers with disabilities. The Transportation Research Board (TRB) survey helped to identify where the transit systems fell short in their communication with their cognitively disabled customers. The most common problems can be found in Figure 14.2.

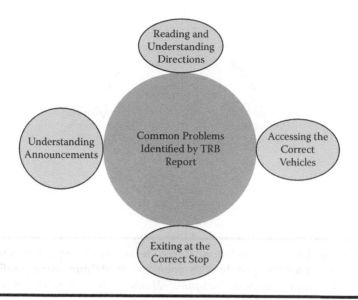

Figure 14.2 Transportation shortfalls. (From Stefan Carmien et al. Socio-technical environments supporting people with cognitive disabilities using public transportation. *ACM Transactions on Computer–Human Interaction (TOCHI).* **Vol. 12, No. 2. pp. 233–262, June 2005.)**

The design methodology clarifies the obstacles that stand in the way of the mentally handicapped. Pilot studies were performed to observe how these disabled individuals learned and how they used the transit systems. Beginning at the "How Things Are" box, the system continues to rotate through the four stages, creating a better system each time it reaches the "Sociotechnical Solutions" block (Figure 14.3).

The pilot studies were conducted in six cities: Denver, Milwaukee, Chicago, Washington, D.C., Tokyo, and Vail, Colorado. The studies focused on how the cognitively handicapped individuals used bus, light rail, subway, and transportation information technologies. They have summarized the needs for making public transportation systems easier for people with disabilities [2]: (1) Reduce the complexities of the current systems with the powerful role of technology as a social medium for socialization, independence, and self-worth. (2) Support both users with cognitive disabilities and their support communities. (3) Exploit the emergence of ubiquitous, location-aware, mobile technologies to deliver personalized information tailored to individual needs and abilities.

They also concentrated on the problems that could be addressed by sociotechnical systems. By completing this study, certain "navigation artifacts" were observed, which are shown in Table 14.1. These pilot studies also determined that there are two main classes for public transportation travelers: (1) those who routinely, and (2) those who occasionally, travel by the transit system. The less frequent travelers were considered to engage in higher cognitive actions because of the extra planning

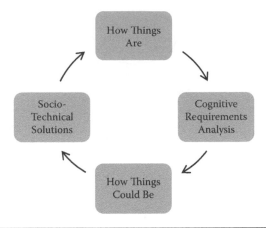

Figure 14.3 Sociotechnical solutions. (From Stefan Carmien et al. Socio-technical environments supporting people with cognitive disabilities using public transportation. *ACM Transactions on Computer–Human Interaction (TOCHI)*. Vol. 12, No. 2. pp. 233–262, June 2005.)

Table 14.1   Artifacts

Maps—Show physical representation, one's current location, and destination; help identify routing options.
Schedules—Transportation arrival and departure time.
Landmarks—Specific events or locations to identify positioning.
Signs—Written notifications to explain location, rules, upcoming events, etc.
Clocks—Schedule synchronization.

Source: Stefan Carmien et al. Socio-technical environments supporting people with cognitive disabilities using public transportation. *ACM Transactions on Computer–Human Interaction (TOCHI)*. Vol. 12, No. 2. pp. 233–262, June 2005.

and preparation necessary. Each class encountered errors in the form of misdirection during the study. Each error was quickly corrected by referring to one of the previously mentioned artifacts.

After the data were gathered from "normal" individuals using the transit systems, cognitively disabled students were observed while they learned how to travel using public transportation. A group of 13 mentally handicapped students were followed as they learned to use a local bus system. The study revealed that 45–75% of students learned to ride the bus unsupervised in at least one route. It is estimated that it takes an average of one year to teach a cognitively disabled person to travel using public transit. The length of the instruction is the reason many mentally handicapped people never learn.

For an individual with a cognitive disorder, learning to travel using public transportation can be essential to living independently. A Swedish research initiative called the Isaac project proposed a PDA/cell phone/camera in the mid-1990s, to help mentally handicapped people become more independent. Before these devices became commonplace among American citizens, it was proposed as a prompting system to assist in travel.

A tool called The Visions System is a technology that was also developed to help the disabled live a more independent life. This home-based product used a computer to prompt an individual to do simple household tasks. This idea was later expanded to PDA technology so that the prompting system would be mobile. Adding audio and visual prompts allowed individuals to learn and relearn certain task from the palm of their hand.

Through the pilot studies, an architecture was developed to allow cognitively impaired travelers to navigate transit systems without fully comprehending a complex, artifact-laden technique. The goal of this architectural design is to help the user effectively communicate with transit personnel as well as provide real-time support for "selecting a destination, locating the right bus, preparing to board, boarding the bus, signaling the driver where to get off, and disembarking." [2] The architecture can be contained in a small mobile device, PDA, or cellular phone, allowing each user easy access. Table 14.2 explores some of the different functions prototype models would include.

The different prototype functions were developed to assist users in several ways. The Personal Travel Assistant (PTA) gives the traveler a real-time map location of the different transit vehicles and the user himself. This allows the user to estimate wait time and to determine if they are traveling in the correct direction. This device also provides "just-in-time prompts and detects breakdowns by using real-time telemetry data (i.e., location, speed, and direction) from buses and travelers." [2] From the hand-held device, the user can select a presaved destination, and the device will provide step-by-step directions to their destination to include which transit vehicles to take.

Table 14.2 Prototype Function and Description

Personal Training Assistant—Attached GPS components on transit vehicles will provide real-time locations for users. This will allow easier navigation and estimated wait times.
Memory-Aiding Prompting System (MAPS)–Allows users and caregivers the opportunity to program and personalize the Personal Training Assistant.
Lifeline–Provides the real-time location and task status of the user. Allows caregivers or emergency organizations the ability to support the user remotely.

Source: Stefan Carmien et al. Socio-technical environments supporting people with cognitive disabilities using public transportation. *ACM Transactions on Computer–Human Interaction (TOCHI)*. Vol. 12, No. 2. pp. 233–262, June 2005.

The Memory-Aiding Prompting System (MAPS) allows users to develop and redesign alerts and the prompting system used in the PTA. This helps personalize the architecture and allows a more focused learning tool to help condition the traveler on routine routes. MAPS allows changes to audio and visual prompts and allows users to create more detailed instructions on how to complete a task. The technology gives caregivers the ability to tailor each PTA to a specific cognitively impaired traveler.

The final function allows caregivers the opportunity to monitor the location and progression of a PTA user. This technology, coupled with a communication link, would allow the caregiver to provide assistance to the user from a remote location. It would also be a helpful tool in locating a lost individual.

Implementation of the MAPS technology is a concern because of the cost to place GPS tracking in thousands of transit vehicles across the United States. This financial burden becomes even less appealing to cities because the technology is considered useful to only 5–7% of their citizens. Convincing these cities that it could be a stepping stone to more inclusive technologies and ideas will go a long way in getting this project off the ground [2].

14.4 The Integrated Healthcare Network [3]

Health information technology (HIT) has impacted the healthcare industry in a significant way. Having an available network with up-to-date patient data helps both the patient and medical personnel. It shortens the amount of patient wait time, and it allows medical facilities to reduce their overhead costs by preventing the duplication of unnecessary tests. HIT also has a large potential to prevent unfavorable incidents in the medical profession.

It has been found through different studies that unfavorable medical incidents are caused in large part by the exclusion of pertinent medical data. Such incidents, which occur often, could be avoided by using HIT. The HIT would contain patient data, including medicine prescriptions, intake, family history, and previous illnesses, which are all necessary to properly diagnose a patient. The omission of this information could be detrimental to the patient's health.

Not only would the HIT systems include all necessary medical data, they could also be designed as an alert system for medical personnel. Certain cues, prompts, and alarms could be included to assist the user in the process. Sequential checklists and organized data entry could also be used to decrease potential problems. This would help correct the issues associated with user interface to current systems already in place.

It is believed that a comprehensive IT framework can be created and can become a vital component in healthcare practice. For this to happen, certain inherent problems need to be considered while developing this framework. Any system that is created must have an open design that can easily integrate current systems being used by medical facilities. It must also be flexible enough to adapt to different work areas with different criteria. Finally, the system must be able to encompass sociotechnical aspects.

In order to obtain the necessary information, the University Medical Center (at Philipps University, Marburg, Germany) doctors were interviewed and data were collected from the center's own files. It was found that patients who were supplied with discharge summaries were less likely to be readmitted to the medical center. It was also found that discharge summaries for patients were often incomplete or missing completely. This not only caused increased readmittance but also led to missed follow-up tests and discontinuity in prescription information.

The root of these issues comes from both sides of the aisle. The practitioners blame the hospitals for not providing sufficient paperwork, including discharge summaries, and hospitals blame the physicians for not properly completing "preparatory" paperwork before a patient is discharged. The lack of an IT system only compounds the issue. Physicians also complain about the difficulty in scheduling hospital appointments for their patients because of the long wait time.

Through interviews with the medical center doctors and practitioners, it was determined that IT support was necessary in certain areas. Those areas are shown in the following chart (Table 14.3).

Though these issues are of immediate concern, they are not the only issues that a new IT system would alleviate. There are three main concepts that IT should

Table 14.3   Necessary IT Support

Scheduling	IT support for scheduling is necessary for medical center physicians and practitioners. It would also be helpful for patients to have access.
Generation and communication of discharge letters	IT support is necessary to create discharge letters and other reports. Access to reusable data is also necessary.
Order entry	IT support for supply ordering would be helpful to all physicians. Prep paperwork would also be important.
Access to knowledge bases	Knowledge bases are already available for medical center personnel, but IT support would make it available to practitioners and patients.
Access to databases for physicians and patients	Databases are necessary for medical personnel, and limited access would be granted to patients. Privacy could be a concern.

Source: Mario Beyer, Klaus A. Kuhn, Christian Meiler, Stefan Jablonski, Richard Lenz. Towards a flexible, process-oriented IT architecture for an integrated healthcare network, *Proceedings of the 2004 ACM Symposium on Applied Computing.* Nicosia, Cyprus, March 14–17, 2004.

be designed around. First, integration should be a priority of the new system. The system should be able to support and involve different individuals in the medical network. Next, the system should be highly adaptable to different procedures and applications. Finally, the network needs to be extensive. Adding new functions to the network should be done easily and without disruption.

A total of 17 different "use cases" were developed with specific "communication patterns." These are instructions for common tasks that might occur regularly. Each use case accompanies a description of how it is used, as well as a graphical representation. Figure 14.4 illustrates the process of placing an order from a hospital. Order placement is the fourth use case and a common task utilized by medical practitioners.

After determining the needs of the IT network, it was necessary to concentrate on how the system would be configured. During the design process, five different perspectives were considered. Those perspectives are given in Table 14.4, along with

Figure 14.4   Communication process. (From Mario Beyer, Klaus A. Kuhn, Christian Meiler, Stefan Jablonski, Richard Lenz. Towards a flexible, process-oriented IT architecture for an integrated healthcare network, *Proceedings of the 2004 ACM symposium on Applied computing*. Nicosia, Cyprus, March 14–17, 2004.)

Table 14.4   Perspective-oriented Model

Functionality perspective	How well the system works when performing processes and other activities.
Behavior perspective	The steps that the system performs when it performs a task. This perspective shows how different processes are linked together.
Informational perspective	This perspective controls the flow of information within the system. It provides the data for each process.
Organizational perspective	The organizational perspective controls which groups are involved in a process, as well as the roles they play.
Operational perspective	This perspective controls the distribution of packets from system to system.

Source: Mario Beyer, Klaus A. Kuhn, Christian Meiler, Stefan Jablonski, Richard Lenz. Towards a flexible, process-oriented IT architecture for an integrated healthcare network, *Proceedings of the 2004 ACM Symposium on Applied Computing*. Nicosia, Cyprus, March 14–17, 2004.

descriptions of each. The perspectives allow the IT system to be flexible to control data flow.

To achieve a general IT system that will work in any medical center, the system needs to be able to integrate data from current systems. Since different hospitals are using different systems, using one procedure to extract and transform the data would be difficult. Different systems would use different encoding schemes to represent their data. An XML is used for internal data management, transformation, and conversion.

In summary, Mario Beyer et al. [3] offer a solution to the many issues medical facilities are having with their current data control procedures. In it a detailed description of a new system is given and how it can be implemented is discussed, and a process is introduced in implementing a health IT network that has a large potential to prevent unfavorable incidents in the medical profession.

14.5 Telemedicine [4]

Telemedicine is another example of a tool in the medical industry used to create a point of interaction between the doctor and patient, and serves as a way to provide access to individual care without physically connecting the patient and the doctor. Of course, this presents a unique set of technical and social networking problems, but it must also satisfy the same purpose as a physical encounter. That is to say, the results for the patient should not largely change whether the patient was seen either in person or through technical proxy.

In one analysis, high-bandwidth visual conferencing was examined to determine the various factors that play a role in its success and to identify discreet components of the visual interaction model that work together to create the functional network. One way to analyze the model presented is an interconnected triangle between the medical facility, the medical professionals who provide analysis, and the patients who are involved. The connecting structure between each of these three parts is the underlying technology, and the pathways between them are all bidirectional (Figure 14.5).

Interestingly, in this approach, the information that should travel across these pathways is largely not for the purpose of the actual technical network. Rather, the technical network exists as an underlying entity that is mostly self-supporting and exists to facilitate the medical information, its analysis, and various forms of feedback between the various members of the network.

Within this framework, two particular forms of quality are reached. First is the functional quality of the network, which deals with the ability of the network to handle and process information. Included here are the functionality of the technology involved (Is there a clear connection between the various clients?) as well as the ability of the individuals to interact (Does the patient provide quality information into the system, and are all members capable of handling the technical aspects of

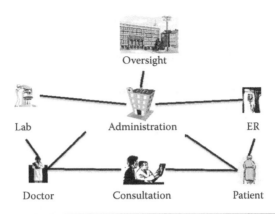

Figure 14.5 Basic telemedical network model. (From Cynthia LeRouge, Alan Hevner, Rosann Collins, Monica Garfield, David Law. Telemedicine encounter quality: comparing patient and provider perspectives of a socio-technical system. *Proceedings of the 37th Annual Hawaii International Conference on System Sciences (HICSS'04),* **Track 6, HICSS, Vol. 6, pp. 60149a. 2004.)**

videoconferencing?). The second form of quality is based on the actual clinical encounter results. Good examples of this form would be the accuracy of any diagnoses reached, and the satisfaction of the patients and staff with the system.

While there are standards governing the quality of those two forms independently, there has only recently been a push to develop standards encompassing all aspects of the problem. Healthcare standards such as the Joint Accreditation of Healthcare Organizations, and information systems standards such as the International Multimedia Telecommunications Consortium, provide very different ideas on how quality should be reached. In each case, one side largely ignores the other and fails to address important issues, such as the amount of information that can be relayed electronically effectively or the ability of the patient to feel like an active and important participant in the medical discussions taking place.

Any analysis of a sociotechnical system must be approached from multiple perspectives. For instance, colloquial speech of the medical staff might be jargon to the patients, and the opposite could very well be true. So, instead, a model is created wherein the analysis approaches the system from a provider and a patient point of view. The system must be functional for the provider to provide quality service while being worthwhile and friendly to the patient in order to be a successful product in a business sense.

The methods used to properly examine such a system must likewise be quite varied. It must examine a structure where the quality of individual elements contributes to the interactions of the more functional perceived components (Figure 14.6). A mixture of examining evidence of the effective history of telemedicine, real

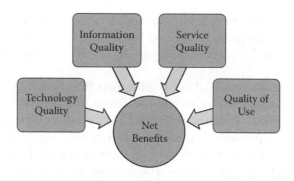

Figure 14.6 Telemedicine quality factors. (From Cynthia LeRouge, Alan Hevner, Rosann Collins, Monica Garfield, David Law. Telemedicine encounter quality: comparing patient and provider perspectives of a socio-technical system. *Proceedings of the 37th Annual Hawaii International Conference on System Sciences (HICSS'04)***, Track 6, HICSS, Vol. 6, pp. 60149a. 2004.)**

observation of current telemedicine encounters and their functionality, and opinions of patients and researchers working in the field must all be used in order to begin to gain an understanding of how the larger system works as a whole.

Analysis framework centers around four different factors that greatly contribute to the net functionality of the system. First, the technology quality is examined. The ability of the various components within the technical system to handle, relay, and process information within encounters is accounted for here, and it generally represents the quality of the backbone network. The second aspect is information quality. This is specifically how capable the information being passed is to allow for proper actions of the parties involved. Whether the input systems are limited, the patient fails to provide quality information to the doctor, or the information is hard to read once it is gathered, it all affects the information quality factor. The third factor is service quality. In this context, service quality refers to the way in which the organization running the telemedicine system supports infrastructure and creates an environment that is comfortable for the parties involved in order to facilitate proper and effective use. The last factor is the quality of use. Here, this is defined as the ability of the individual parties to effectively deploy and interact with the system in place in order to provide good outcomes. After all, a given system for social interaction may only be as effective as the individuals using the system allow it to be. Further, this encompasses the effectiveness of any diagnosis or advice given to the patient through the telemedicine encounter.

Technology quality was found to primarily focus on usability, as might be expected, though there were more demands being put on the system by the provider than the patients. Providers were concerned not only with the ability of the system to function once in use but also that it be secure and available for whomever wanted to use it. Reliability was the largest concern of all factors for providers, while being substantially lower for patients. It could be inferred here that the providers are very concerned with the ability of the system to be more efficient rather than more convenient.

Information quality outlined major differences in perspectives from both parties, as well as notable needs for an effective system. It was found that a clear and private connection was necessary, with good clarity and a quiet space to interact from. However, the providers were more concerned with aspects dealing with the comfort of the interaction, such as space or room layout, while the patients were very concerned with the ability of the system to provide feedback to an individual patient. Thus, the system needs to facilitate individuals using it both as a necessity because of a job and as a necessity to gain information.

Service quality was the most agreed-upon factor determining the effectiveness of the telemedicine system, and focused on both the ability of supporting staff to provide proper teaching for usage and the proper infrastructure such that the system may have comfortable and available terminals for interaction. The only singly noted item was in coordinator support, which was a noted aspect by providers. This highlights the fact that, while the patient is an entity in the system operating for itself, the providing medical professionals are likely working under the umbrella of a manager or medical facility providing service to other individuals. In other words, the system must be built with the realization that a certain level of oversight and support must be possible at the provider's end.

The quality of use was the primary focus of patients in the study. While common themes included trained staff and a focus on patient care, patients wanted to see more from the system. They wanted to see that the system was coordinated with in-person medical professionals both in later exams as well as being physically with the patient while the telemedicine encounter with a separate provider was being conducted. They also wanted the system to be able to convey patient records and provide future directives. This provides a common theme that telemedicine encounters are expected to be more convenient than in-person encounters while not having any trade-off in the quality of care to the individual.

The study shows that a telemedicine system has to be able to provide a service that is sound in both social and technical aspects. Patients expect to be given information that will provide quality care and advice that is not diminished by the distances involved. Providers expect to provide this service reliably to a broad audience over distance. In both cases, primary sub factors are a mix of social and technical aspects, and both groups rank environmental aspects (such as the comfort of terminals or their décor) notably lower than aspects which directly affect the communication of information. This is evidence for the fact that any telemedicine system must always be primarily focused on meeting its functional goals. It must provide effective information in a reliable way between both parties. The system can only be as good as the service it provides.

14.6 Emergency Medical Services [5]

In Schooley et al. [5] the authors have highlighted the importance of analyzing interorganizational procedures. By implementing an examination process, improvements can be made within the organization that would lead to more efficient multiorganizational information exchange.

A framework for understanding time-reliant data systems was researched through focus groups, field studies, and employee interviews. The purpose of this research was to understand the limitations in accessing significant end-to-end emergency medical services and how it affects EMS patients. By focusing on what information was being shared and who needed or had access to that data, problems in the system could be found and fixed.

To gather research data for the case study, a large EMS system was necessary. Such a facility was found in San Mateo County, California. The San Mateo County EMS Agency includes such organizations as the County Health Services Department, a fire services organization known as the Joint Powers Authority, the County Public Safety Communications Center (dispatch), and the American Medical Response ambulance service.

There are 11 different healthcare facilities in San Mateo County, none of which are included in the EMS system but which collaborate with different entities within the system. There is only one dispatch service for the ambulatory and fire-related emergencies. This dispatch service is also used by the local Sheriff's department and other law enforcement agencies. Figure 14.7 shows a loose interpretation of the EMS structure.

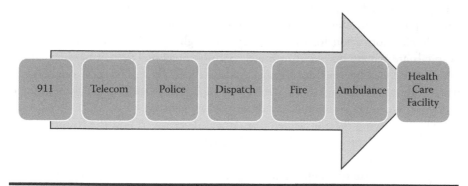

Figure 14.7   EMS structure. (From Benjamin Schooley, Michael Marich, Thomas Horan. Devising an architecture for time-critical information services: inter-organizational performance data components for emergency medical service (EMS). *Proceedings of the 8th Annual International Conference on Digital Government Research: Bridging Disciplines and Domains.* May 20–23, 2007. Philadelphia, PA.)

Three phases were defined to scrutinize the information-sharing procedures of EMS units. The first phase included visiting different facilities and interviewing their personnel. Ambulance drivers, firemen, and even dispatch personnel were questioned on their end-to-end operations from the time they received word of the emergency until they completed their particular assignments. The researchers traveled on real-world missions as well as simulations and witnessed what data are transferred between EMS entities.

The second phase also included interviews with EMS personnel and management; however, the questions were related to why each agency had, or did not have, access to the information being exchanged. Once it was determined what information was essential to each EMS organization, the deficiencies in the system could be found and corrected. The third and final stage evaluated the previous two stages in order to create a system that would eliminate foreseeable problems for a large emergency medical service system.

The San Mateo County EMS Agency uses a computer-aided dispatch (CAD) system to record patient information, such as caller information, location data, and initial health problem data. This CAD system is controlled by the dispatch's County Communication Center. The time stamp data from ambulances and fire stations are also recorded in the CAD system. The county also employs an electronic patient care record (PCR), which is controlled by the EMS Agency. The EMS crews enter information into the PCRs through wireless laptops. Patient health and treatment are recorded in the PCRs. The hospitals also have their own computer-based system; however, it has limited access to both the CAD and PCRs.

The many systems that rarely transfer information between each other hinder the ability of medical personnel to gather all the information necessary to treat a patient properly. Ideally, the county would like to employ only a PCR that would include all information for every agency. Through interviews, it was found that hospitals are a main deterrent to having a fully integrated system because, along with other concerns, they must respect patients' privacy and they do not want to pay the high cost of integration. San Mateo has begun pursuing legislation to force more data exchange between hospitals and other agencies.

After reviewing the San Mateo case, it was determined that the county might benefit from adopting the National Intelligent Transportation System (ITS) architecture. This ITS "provides a common structure for the design of intelligent transportation systems and prescribes a general framework that supports the development of many different designs." Table 14.5 shows how the San Mateo system would be mapped in the national architecture.

In Schooley et al. [5], a case study was explained as an examination of the particular EMS Agency in San Mateo through the TCIS framework. The issues concerning shared information between various medical organizations were discussed, as well as the end-to-end evaluation of the system [5].

Table 14.5   San Mateo Architecture

National ITS architecture	San Mateo County's system
Emergency telecommunications system	Telecom service provider
Emergency management	County Communications Center—PSAP
	Law Enforcement
	Fire Department
	Ambulance & fire crews
Emergency vehicle subsystem	Ambulance & fire vehicles
Care facility	Healthcare facilities

Source: Benjamin Schooley, Michael Marich, Thomas Horan. Devising an architecture for time-critical information services: inter-organizational performance data components for emergency medical service (EMS). *Proceedings of the 8th Annual International Conference on Digital Government Research: Bridging Disciplines and Domains.* May 20–23, 2007. Philadelphia, PA.

14.7 Conclusions

The growth of technology presents both major advantages and major hurdles that the healthcare industry must overcome. The ability to gather information, communicate it over distances, and analyze that information on a large scale presents an incredible opportunity for progress if that information can be handled correctly. However, large amounts of unprocessed and unfiltered information can tend to have an overwhelming effect on those who try to study it. It is only through the continued development of both tools and analysis techniques that technology can truly play an integral part in the workings of the healthcare world today. The studies outlined in this chapter show how the greater community is striving to make these developments, and with time, a seamless connection between technology and healthcare may be reached.

References

1. Eubank, S. Network based models of infectious disease spread. *Japanese Journal of Infectious Diseases*, 58, S9–S13. 2005.
2. Stefan Carmien, Melissa Dawe, Gerhard Fischer, Andrew Gorman, Anja Kintsch, James F. Sullivan, Jr. Socio-technical environments supporting people with cognitive disabilities using public transportation. *ACM Transactions on Computer–Human Interaction (TOCHI)*. Vol. 12, No. 2. pp. 233–262, June 2005.

3. Mario Beyer, Klaus A. Kuhn, Christian Meiler, Stefan Jablonski, Richard Lenz. Towards a flexible, process-oriented IT architecture for an integrated healthcare network, *Proceedings of the 2004 ACM Symposium on Applied Computing.* Nicosia, Cyprus, March 14–17, 2004.

4. Cynthia LeRouge, Alan Hevner, Rosann Collins, Monica Garfield, David Law. Telemedicine encounter quality: comparing patient and provider perspectives of a socio-technical system. *Proceedings of the 37th Annual Hawaii International Conference on System Sciences (HICSS'04)*, Track 6, HICSS, Vol. 6, pp. 60149a. 2004.

5. Benjamin Schooley, Michael Marich, Thomas Horan. Devising an architecture for time-critical information services: inter-organizational performance data components for emergency medical service (EMS). *Proceedings of the 8th Annual International Conference on Digital Government Research: Bridging Disciplines and Domains.* May 20–23, 2007. Philadelphia, PA.

Chapter 15

Collaborative Software Development Based on Socialtechnical Networks

Ryan Andrew Taylor and Fei Hu

Contents

15.1 Introduction

It has been said that wherever there are good products, there are less successful prototypes somewhere close by. This old saying has proved true time and time again throughout history. In the realm of engineering, for every accepted design, there are many crumpled-up sheets of design notes. And in the world of software design and development, for every design process that works well in practice, there are predecessors that were not quite up to par.

The world of software development has changed considerably since the first few lines of code were ever written. It has evolved from a single programmer in a room to many programmers, far and near, who all collaborate on the same design idea. Not only is the management of information in these projects important, but also vital is the management of the inherent knowledge of the programmers who may have experience in this area [1]. As we will discuss in the next few pages, this idea of different "groups" of programmers can lead to many problems if not handled in an efficient way.

Often, a good way to start solving the problems that collaborative software development brings about is to try and decide which tasks are interrelated somehow, and which ones will require a data connection of some sort. On the same train of thought, this same algorithm can be extended to work with different sets of programmers and how they are interconnected based on their current set of projects and workloads. A good theory has been set out in the research world by many different people in many different ways. This generalized theory says that in order to fully minimize the need for collaborative software development inside of projects, we need to find the total number of interconnections in the web of data, functions, and programmers [2]. If these connections are minimized, then less work between different "groups" of analysts, programmers, and actual function will be required, meaning the throughput of work will almost certainly rise. This is a reward that is desired at great cost.

This chapter focuses on two main implementations that have come on the scene to try and work at this angle, reducing interconnections and making the connections that do exist less prominent. The stand-alone STeP_IN framework [3] and the Ariadne framework built for the Eclipse environment [4] are both very successful solutions to the problem at hand. Not only do these frameworks help to smooth the transition of knowledge transfer and data interconnection collaborative development, but they also keep the programmers' social ecosystem in mind.

Finally, we will discuss the positive and negative impacts of both commercial off-the-shelf based systems software and customized software development against each other in order to determine the best way for a system to be designed. Obviously, different settings and needs will have to be weighed, and this chapter will attempt to decide which route is the best for certain groups and situations to call for.

15.2 The Need for Managing Information [1]

The software development industry has changed considerably since the first few lines of code were written. Initially, many different designs and systems were programmed by an equal number of designers and programmers. People who worked on these systems worked mainly alone, and in a commonly solitary environment. This led to monolithic system design patterns, or systems that were not modular and capable of being broken into different pieces or functions very easily. This, in turn, made turning a project over to someone else quite difficult, as following the structure of the code in a monolithic system is very tedious. A change needed to take place, and a change in the way of thinking was imminent if the software development industry was going to grow at any sort of fast pace.

Much research has been conducted around the subject of knowledge management. Knowledge management is known in the academic and engineering worlds as the stable controlling of information, both written-down and inherent programmer knowledge, that can be managed to provide programmers and programming teams the ability to access tools and ideas that they might not have otherwise. The first thing that must be done to begin working toward managing knowledge is to realize that a working environment, when dealing with software development, is not only a technical idea. The thought process should be centered on a sociotechnical idea. This is true whether the programming is part of collaborative software development or a single programmer writing a program. This line of thought introduces the idea that not only are programmers tied to their own hardware, software, and technology, but they are also tied to their social connections that keep them "in the know." Technical and social interworking all contribute to the overall success of the software development process, and knowing this is the first hurdle that must be jumped past present ideals.

Much of the research pertaining to the papers in question deal with the fact that there are many different types of resources that are available and used for programmers when they are working on a collaborative project of some sort in software development. Programmers have access to their past experiences, their past work, code that has been shared among many users and teams, and also other programmers themselves. To make any sort of collaboration of ideas work, an infrastructure must be in place to standardize the interface. If there are too many ways to access different information, then the workload to actually find the information is not worth the information to start with. Protocols and working practices must be in place to conform information and knowledge as described earlier to each other.

In most cases, the most productive types of assistance that programmers can receive when needed is interpersonal communication. Whether it be through face-to-face communication, electronic communication, or communication through production documents and other artifacts, interpersonal communication gives software teams and individual programmers alike access to codified information, but also to inherent knowledge from the situational expert in question that could not be obtained otherwise [1].

Face-to-face communication is among the most common types of information flow in the field of software design and development. Often, the communication that takes place in a face-to-face manner is between colleagues on a certain project or co-workers of a certain development group. Even throughout society, not confining oneself to the world of computer programming and software design, face-to-face communication is the most effective tool for understanding one another. It is sometimes forgotten that there is more to interpersonal communication than just words.

There are gestures, tones, and even facial expressions that influence a conversation and help move it in one direction or another. The meaning of words can easily be changed by moving one's hands in a certain way, or raising one's voice (or lowering it) an octave, or by smiling (or frowning) when saying the actual words. Face-to-face communication is so important to interpersonal information transfer because the bandwidth of data is so large, much larger than any other type of communication used frequently.

Electronic communication refers to any sort of interpersonal communication that takes places through electronic media. This refers to mainly e-mail and short message service (SMS) message usage in the software design and development world. The great thing about electronic communication as opposed to face-to-face communication is that it is time-independent. An e-mail or an SMS message can be sent to another person and stored until that person is able to receive it. This is a great advantage, in that it does not interrupt as face-to-face communication would. Electronic communication also has a leg up on face-to-face communication in that it can be stored and viewed again later in its entirety. If the advice of the communication needs to be taken, but the communication happened several days ago, the message can be retrieved and viewed as if for the first time. The message in this case will carry the same weight as the one that was viewed immediately. In face-to-face communication, however, a conversation can only be fully remembered in a person's memory. Communication through production documents and other artifacts is often combined with the two main forms of communication between programmers that have already been discussed. A scratch piece of code or an edited diagram can accompany both face-to-face communication and electronic communication (as an attachment) and add to the value of the data transfer.

To try and perform at a higher level, many computer scientists and software developers have tried to develop a system of patterns that could be used over and over again based on knowledge inherent in other programmers' minds [5]. For example, these patterns would consist of a situation similar to the one that the programmer has found in his or her assignment, and a bundle of solutions that have been used to solve this problem over time by various programmers. If the programmer so desires, he or she could choose one of these solutions and edit it to his or her desire, making it an acceptable solution to the problem at hand. If the solution becomes unique, it can be stored in the pattern and held for other programmers to possibly look at over time.

Whether patterns can be used or only interpersonal communication, the main problem in software development is clear from the research observed: knowledge management causes other programmers to lose time. Any type of interpersonal communication that takes place between programmers who need assistance is going to take the assister away from his or her work, and thus decrease his or her throughput, though increasing the throughput of the questioner. A solution must be found that can help manage knowledge in collaborative software design and development while minimizing the role that other "experts" must play in interpersonal communication, away from their own work.

15.3 Identifying How Social and Technical Dependencies Can Relate Tasks [2]

As discussed earlier, it is widely accepted that there are two parts to any software development project: a technical component and a social component. It is said that in order for any software development project to be successful, the technical and social elements must be aligned [2]. The way to connect these two dimensions is the first step in taking action toward reducing the experts' time away from their own work. Connecting the technical and social dependencies is the idea to focus on.

Any software engineer is familiar with the larger aspect of technical dependencies inside a development project. These kinds of dependencies can refer to functional dependencies, data dependencies, or any other kind of dependencies that may hinge on actual data transfer inside the software algorithm. Social dependencies are the connections between different people working on the projects themselves. If two programmers' workloads never intersect, then, theoretically, they should never have to deal with each other. This is only in theory, and the true process for finding technical and social dependencies is much more technical than simply what the programmer is working on currently.

Some research done at Carnegie Mellon University has been conducted to try and coordinate which dependencies lead to which assumptions about the software itself [2]. The researchers at Carnegie Mellon University in the Institute for Software Research have come up with a mathematical formula for realizing which engineers should be coordinating their activities, thus keeping people out of the loop who should not be there to begin with. The mathematical formula revolves around finding two sets of data to start with.

The first set of data that needs to be found is called Task Assignments, or T_A [2]. This value is whether or not an individual is working on a task. It is represented in the form of a matrix with m rows and n columns, where m is the number of workers in the development project and n is the number of tasks that need to be completed. A 1 in a cell (i,j) means that worker i has been assigned to task j. A sample T_A matrix is shown below in Figure 15.1.

In Figure 15.1, the matrix means that worker A has been assigned to task 2, worker B has been assigned to tasks 2 and 3, and worker C has been assigned to tasks 1 and 2. The other set of data that needs to be found to complete the mathematical formula found is called a Task Dependencies, or T_D, matrix. A sample is shown in Figure 15.2. The data in this figure means that task 1 is dependent on tasks 1 and 2, task 2 is dependent on all other tasks, and task 3 is dependent on task 2 and 3.

If the two sets of data (in their matrix form) were multiplied, a matrix would be obtained that would be in the form of "workers by tasks." This matrix would show which workers need to know and be in the loop regarding certain tasks. Every "1" in the row of a worker would be connected with a task that the worker needs to be involved in the completion of, according to the assignments and dependencies. To complete the mathematical formula, this matrix is multiplied by the transpose

Task

	1	2	3
A	0	1	0
B	0	1	1
C	1	1	0

Worker

Figure 15.1 Sample Task Assignments matrix. (From Cataldo, Marcelo et al. Socio-Technical Congruence: A Framework for Assessing the Impact of Technical and Work Dependencies on Software Development. Institute for Software Research (2008). Technical Report, see: http://reports-archive.adm.cs.cmu.edu/anon/isr2008/CMU-ISR-08-104.pdf.)

Task

	1	2	3
1	1	1	0
2	1	1	1
3	0	1	1

Task

Figure 15.2 Sample Task Dependencies matrix. (From Cataldo, Marcelo et al. Socio-Technical Congruence: A Framework for Assessing the Impact of Technical and Work Dependencies on Software Development. Institute for Software Research (2008). Technical Report, see: http://reports-archive.adm.cs.cmu.edu/anon/isr2008/CMU-ISR-08-104.pdf.)

of T_A, or the Task Assignments matrix, to compute a matrix that is called the Coordination Requirements, or C_R, matrix. This final C_R matrix represents the extent to which programmers should work together [2]. The complete mathematical formula is

$$C_R = T_A * T_D * T_A^T \tag{15.1}$$

Using the example matrices in Figures 15.1 and 15.2, the final C_R matrix is shown in Figure 15.3. In this final C_R matrix, the diagonal entries should be ignored because they have little relevance to the situation under consideration. For example, there is no need to know that worker B should be working with worker B to the 4th degree. But it is important to know, from the bottom row of the matrix, that worker C should spend a little more time with worker B than he or she does with worker C.

Congruence, or the relation between two numbers, of the coordination requirements can be found by using not only the C_R matrix that we have computed, but also the Actual Coordinating Requirements matrix, C_A. The C_A matrix represents

Worker

		A	B	C
Worker	**A**	1	2	2
	B	2	4	3
	C	2	3	4

Figure 15.3 Sample Coordination Requirements matrix. (From Cataldo, Marcelo et al. Socio-Technical Congruence: A Framework for Assessing the Impact of Technical and Work Dependencies on Software Development. Institute for Software Research (2008). Technical Report, see: http://reports-archive.adm. cs.cmu.edu/anon/isr2008/CMU-ISR-08-104.pdf.)

the actual interactions that took place between the workers listed in the C_R matrix. The equation for coordination congruence that was given by the Carnegie Mellon University researchers is

$$Congruence(C_R, C_A) = \frac{C_R - C_A}{|C_R|} \tag{15.2}$$

The methods discussed in this section so far have been methods used to discover social dependencies in the software development process. In order to find technical dependencies in the software system, different methods must be used. Technical dependencies can be divided into two main groups: data dependencies and functional dependencies. Data dependencies occur when one component of the software package edits data and passes it to another component. Without either component, the data will not get taken care of in the way that the total software package requires it to. Functional dependencies occur when a function calls another function. Without the subfunction, the higher-level function cannot work properly, and possibly, without the higher-level function, there is never any need for the subfunction, though this is not always the case.

The researchers at Carnegie Mellon University have proposed a call-graph [2]. This graph has not been expounded upon as heavily as the C_R matrix and its computations, but it would be a good avenue to pursue. The call-graph proposal has the idea of producing matrices similar to the C_R matrix and its associated matrices. This would be a good way to standardize finding dependencies in not just the social requirements field, but also among the technical requirements. This call-graph matrix functionality would basically be aimed at finding functional dependencies inside software packages. This could be an easy avenue to look at to find a way to group programmers together on things that are tied together, so as to make the communication between different programming groups minimal.

The mathematical work that has been explained in this section is very useful in the field of collaborative software development. As will be explained in the following sections, many concrete efforts are being made to put together a technical software system that will make use of the mathematical equations and relations that have been discussed here. Much good can come from grouping and organizing communication between different groups of programmers and engineers in the correct way, instead of just leaving them to group themselves, or worse, grouping them in some sort of random fashion.

However, technical systems are not completely necessary to make use of the ideas of congruence, technical coordination requirements, and call-graphs. The matrix for the technical coordination requirements, C_R, shows us some very important information regarding the level of coordination and working together that needs to take place between certain people. Taking the matrix in Figure 15.3 as our example, we can see the level of coordination that needs to be present between the workers that are a part of the matrix's data set. For example, worker B has a coordination requirements value of 2 when paired with worker A, but a value of 3 when paired with worker C. This tells us that worker B, though he or she does need to communicate with worker A, needs a strong communication link between him or her and worker C. Now, whether or not this "stronger link" represents more face time, a different type of communication, or a technical "grouping" is up to the implementation of the current situation, but the matrix tells us that workers B and C will need to work together more than workers B and A, and this information is very valuable.

The mathematical function for congruence is also very useful in the world of collaborative software engineering. The function for congruence is seen in Equation 15.1. In words, this equation for congruence is the technical coordination requirements matrix subtracted by the actual coordination requirements matrix, which is found by grading the level of coordination requirements that took place throughout the collaborative software development project, and then dividing the difference by the determinant of the technical coordination requirements matrix. This final value, a matrix termed the congruence matrix, shows the level of congruence that took place during the software development process, or the level to which coordination actually took place when it should have, and did not take place when it should not have. This value is invaluable for self-grading and self-evaluation of your own collaborative software development process. If the absolute value of a congruence value for a pair of workers is high to some degree, then the communication and grouping of a pair of workers should be evaluated to deem if it is needed or unnecessary.

The call-graph that can be produced is possibly the most important value that can be found between a software development system's components themselves. The ability to trace data through a software package and know which functions and components will be affecting that data is very important. Knowing the certain functions that will be affecting these data sets at any given time and what order they will be called is also very useful.

For example, assume the software package has only six functions and is not very complex; let the functional dependencies be fully represented by Figure 15.4. At the time of software execution, functions A and B are called. In time, function A calls functions C and D, and function B calls functions E and F. This means that C and D will never get called without function A; likewise, functions E and F will never get called without function B. This means that functions C, D, E, and F are functionally dependent on functions A and B, respectively. This is invaluable information, because the workers on function F should never have to talk with the workers on function A, theoretically. This would be proper division of communication if the only resource available were the call-graph information.

As can be easily seen in this section, there is ample data to be compiled to tell how much communication and coordination should take place among programmers and engineers in a collaborative software development package. The real question that we are faced with is this: how do we successfully and optimally manage the data in question to compile teams among workers that are beneficial and lead toward effective and distributed communication? The next two sections attempt to describe two separate software implementations that have striven to meet this need and answer this question in the best possible way.

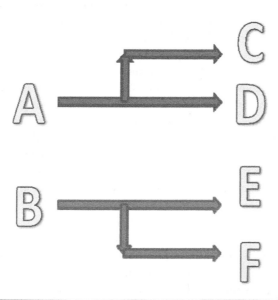

Figure 15.4 Functional dependency of a software package. (From Cataldo, Marcelo et al. Socio-Technical Congruence: A Framework for Assessing the Impact of Technical and Work Dependencies on Software Development. Institute for Software Research (2008). Technical Report, see: http://reports-archive.adm. cs.cmu.edu/anon/isr2008/CMU-ISR-08-104.pdf.)

15.4 STeP_IN Framework [3]

In the popular opinion, the most important avenues of information and assistance to the programmer who needs a little "boost" in their way of thinking about a certain programming situation are code, documentation, and various kinds of information repositories (including, but not limited to, reuse repositories, discussion archives, frequently asked question pages, etc.). However, possibly the most important way to receive assistance is through the advice of another programmer. This avenue is known as a peer programmer. Other programmers are often the most useful way to get a fresh look at a problem or a situation in the collaborative software development environment.

The problem with going to peer programmers for advice comes when the other programmers have their own issues that they are dealing with, which is almost always the case. If the "expert" programmers, as we will call them in this example, are working on their own problems that have extensive environments of their own, then they are most certainly engrossed in their work at that moment. The "amateur" programmer, as we will call him in this example, gets stumped on his own assignment and walks to the expert programmer's workspace. Once the interruption is initiated by the amateur programmer for the question, the expert programmer's concentration has been broken, and whether or not he answers the question, the time will have to be taken to regain focus on the problem that he was working on in the first place. This is inefficient for the expert programmer, and could possibly have social consequences for the amateur programmer if hard feelings result because of this setback.

A framework called the STeP_IN framework has been researched and created to try and alleviate some of the problems that were described in the previous paragraph. "It takes into consideration the social factor of treating peer programmers as information resources, and employs mechanisms that ensure communications between programmers that are not disruptive to the overall productivity as well as social atmosphere of the team as a whole" [3]. It is a desperately needed design that is attempted to be created in the STeP_IN framework. Imagine how much time is wasted in collaborative software development teams just by interruptions and having to get refocused on the task at hand. It has been estimated that 41% of a programmer's time is taken up by communication that has to do with other people's assignments and that have nothing to do with the original programmer's own tasks [3]. This type of communication happens in an ad hoc fashion. It is largely unscheduled, intense, and involves more people than it should. The STeP_IN framework tries to alleviate this problem with certain design principles.

In order to successfully build a framework that addresses all the issues that have been discussed so far, some basic principles had to be followed by the designers and programmers themselves. For the design of the STeP_IN framework, the builders had five design principles that were used to guide them as they worked. The next few paragraphs will discuss these five principles and their use in the STeP_IN framework.

The first design principle that was used states that when a programmer is looking for information and help, it is a highly individualized act. In other words, when a programmer is stuck and looking for outside advice, he tends to be working on highly specific problems and projects that require quite a bit of overhead to even begin to understand. In order for the programmer to not lose considerable time by having to set up the problem again, the information-seeking time should be as low as possible. If possible, the information that the programmer finds should also be presented in such a way that the programmer understands quickly and does not waste time wading through useless knowledge.

The second design principle that was used when designing the STeP_IN framework states that if it is ever left up to the programmer, the amount of peer advice he seeks should be limited. When a programmer seeks advice or help from a fellow programmer, both are losing time. Although the information seeker is looking for advice for a problem that is in his current workload, he is being inefficient by being required to set up the problem to the expert programmer. The information seeker in this case is not losing much more time than he or she would otherwise, on the other hand. However, the expert programmer, in this case, is being interrupted by the information seeker and is being completely taken away from his or her current workload and also his or her time-expensive concentration. The expert programmer is losing much more time relative to the information seeker, and this could have negative social impacts for both people involved.

The third design principle that was used states that when peer programmers are used as knowledge sources, the information seeker should be able to get the desired information relatively quickly and should not have to overly exert himself or herself to do so. A big problem in peer programming information seeking is knowledge of who knows what about certain topics. The STeP_IN framework is built to alleviate the stress of not knowing who is an expert on what topics. The information seeker should not have to have this seek this information as well. Also, major amounts of time are wasted if the information that is given to the seeker is not important or not helpful in some way. The information that the seeker receives should be as close to what the information seeker is looking for as possible, because otherwise everyone's time has been wasted with the likelihood of more time being wasted getting the right information.

The fourth design principle that was used in the design of the STeP_IN framework states that the interruption of expert programmers should be as brief as possible. This is a fairly simple statement that has been discussed before. Because of the extremely large cost of interrupting expert programmers, the time spent with them should be as small as possible.

The fifth and final major design principle that was used states that no programmer should be forced into sharing information or helping another programmer if he or she is not willing to. There are many reasons that programmers would need to make themselves unavailable for information seekers. For example, the expert programmer might have a deadline to meet, the programmer might be engrossed in a very technical and specific section of code, or the expert programmer might have personal reasons for not wanting to fulfill that particular request. Whatever the reason, the expert programmer should not be forced into fulfilling any information seeker's request if he or she does not so desire.

The type of thinking that the designers of the STeP_IN framework have for building this interface is an outside-the-box type of thinking. It uses a very abstract type of thought process to try and fully cover all bases of the information seeking that the interface and framework is built for. To conceptualize the way a collaborative software development project is completed, the designers speak of a software project as a "socio-technical information space" [3]. Figure 15.5 shows the information space, which includes three main components: code, documents, and programmers.

The above figure is a good representation of the tools the programmer has available. It was important to the designers of the STeP_IN framework to visualize the information space that a programmer had readily available to him or her. The next hurdle to cross was the explanation of all the relationships between the three individual components.

A code–code relationship means that the code is connected in some way. This idea has been addressed somewhat in earlier sections of this document. Two sections of code can be either functionally dependent, data dependent, or both if they are said to be connected. A code–document relationship means one of two things: either the code implements an idea that is described in the document, or

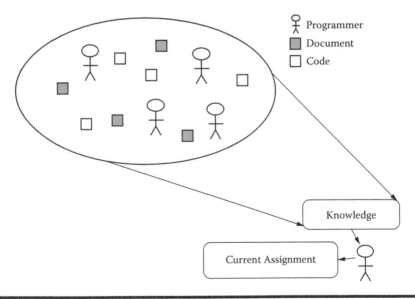

Figure 15.5 Sociotechnical information space for a programmer. (From Ye, Yunwen et al. A Socio-Technical Framework for Supporting Programmers. *6th Joint Meeting of the European Software Engineering Conference and the Symposium on the Foundations of Software Engineering (2007)*: Pages 351–360.)

the document describes in detail certain or all aspects of the code in question. A document–document relationship means that the two documents deal with the same concepts in some loose way. A programmer–code relationship means that the particular programmer has altered or created the said code in some fashion. A programmer–document relationship means that the programmer had some part in building the document or the discussion that it deals with. The last relationship in the information space, a programmer–programmer relationship, means that there is some sort of social interaction between the two programmers. At some point, they have collaborated on a project or they have helped each other and advised one another about some unknown or known topic.

The features that the instantiation of the STeP_IN framework held aimed to fully hold up the five design principles that were mentioned earlier. There are likewise five encompassing features that the instantiation attempts to incorporate into the implementation. The next few paragraphs will make an effort to describe these features in as much detail as possible.

The STeP_IN framework aims to have a tight integration with the programmer's home working environment. This is a very important feature because it allows the programmer to slide information seeking straight into the workspace that he or she is using. If there were such a large cognitive curve that the programmer must switch context each time he or she wanted to look up some knowledge, the disadvantages of the framework would possibly outweigh the benefits. Also, if the framework is integrated into the system, it has informative access to the code that the programmer would currently be working on, allowing background processes to "prepare" possible solutions for common issues that arise.

The framework also aims to present task-relevant information. More than likely, when a programmer is frustrated enough to go looking for outside help on an assignment, he or she is not interested in learning a great deal about the topic itself. Usually, the programmer in question is only interested in completing the assignment that is giving him trouble. There are two facets of the STeP_IN framework that help the programmer to this end. The information delivery facet leads the programmer preemptively to information that may be relevant to the current work that the programmer is outputting. The information access facet of the STeP_IN framework provides a mechanism for the programmers to actually query a certain topic that he or she may be thinking about prior to actually beginning the coding process. Both of these components allow the programmer ready access to task-relevant information.

The STeP_IN framework allows the programmer ready access to contextual information in incremental form. If the immediate relevant information brought about by methods discussed in the previous paragraph are not enough to spark new work in the assignment at hand, then information beyond the "first-cut" results are shown to the programmer. Thus, the initial burst of information that the programmer receives is only enough to possibly spark his or her own train of thought. Not so much information is given to him to overload him and possibly slow down the design process.

The framework also provides ways to identify another programmer as a resource without actually pulling that programmer away from his or her work. The information about the knowledge of each programmer is found in what is called the technical profile of a programmer. There is also a social profile of every programmer that pertains to whom the particular programmer is comfortable assisting and receiving assistance from. Both of these profiles are used to successfully show the programmer in question who may be able to help or advise them on their current situation. The most important concept to remember in this situation is that only people who are willing to help should be asked to assist someone. This is related to one of the five design principles of the STeP_IN framework.

The last main facet of the STeP_IN framework that is provided for the programmer is the creation of a socially aware communication channel. Similar to what was discussed in the previous paragraph, the main idea behind this mechanism is to allow an expert programmer to decline giving assistance without having any blatantly obvious social consequences that could lead to larger problems in the workplace. This concept is implemented with something that is quite similar to an electronic mailing list. Once an information seeker poses a question via the information access mechanism, all expert programmers that are deemed relevant by their technical and social profiles are notified. If one answers, then the information seeker will be able to communicate with him or her as needed. If an expert programmer chooses not to answer, then the information seeker would never know that he or she was denied assistance by that particular programmer and there would, theoretically, not be any extreme social consequences.

The basic layout for the STeP_IN framework is very loose, based on the fact that it needs to be incorporated into whatever environment the programming company is using at any given time. Therefore, there are only a few select screenshots that can be made.

15.5 Ariadne Framework [4]

In addition to the STeP_IN framework, a popular implementation of the thoughts and ideas mentioned in these papers is the Ariadne framework. Ariadne is a plug-in extension that is tailored and built for the Java-based Eclipse environment. The framework searches the currently loaded software project for software dependencies, as discussed in earlier sections, and also searches the authorship information that is inherently stored in the network repositories of Eclipse. Ariadne takes this information and translates technical dependency information into social dependency information. From these social and technical dependencies, Ariadne creates visualizations that are used to increase productivity and efficiency throughout the collaborative software development project.

In a paper introducing the Ariadne framework [4], four main situations from two companies are brought to the reader's attention. These four particular scenarios were chosen because they highlighted not only the software managers' awareness of the connection between dependencies and collaboration, but also tough issues that arise when these dependencies are not known and collaboration is not thought through intelligently. The four scenarios come from two companies that are discussed in further detail in the paper [4], and a visualization solution is given for each.

These visualization solutions hinge on the fact that the biggest hurdle to cross when solving a problem is understanding fully what is actually going on. One way to facilitate coordination activities is to make everyone completely aware of other workers' activities and current workloads, so as to make the environment more conducive to noninterrupting assistance-giving. However, when this information is obtained, it is important to decide a way to convey this information that does not confuse or impede the thought process in any way. Ariadne uses visualization to convey this information in a sociogram network much like the one shown in Figure 15.6 [4].

In the first scenario, a company has a software project manager who is in charge of eight sub-programmers who are working on a client–server application. Also working on this project is another team of programmers who are working on the server side of the application. The project managers of both teams are in close communication with each other at all times, for obvious reasons. In this scenario, the client-side software manager calls a meeting of the developers on her team so that she can be prepared for a software package meeting later in the day. Each programmer on the manager's team reports what he or she believes will be ready and prepared by the next scheduled deadline. It is at this meeting that the manager discovers that, with the deadline fast approaching, one of her programmers has not begun to integrate his code with two other developers, a step that is absolutely necessary to make scheduled deadline. The client-side software manager here determines that the programmer's deadline is not feasible because he will not have enough time to finish his workload on schedule. To work on this implementation in Ariadne, the plug-in provides a "Manager Awareness View" that lets managers know when team members have begun the integration process in their workload. The Manager Awareness View of Ariadne is shown in Figure 15.7. The nodes inside this view are the workers themselves, and recent connections between two programmers are shown as an edge in this graph. More information can be found about the connection by hovering over the edge itself.

In the second scenario, a programmer is working on a particular component of the software package in question that heavily interfaces with the user-interface application layer of the package. A second programmer is working on a component of the package that resides in the user-interface application layer itself, and regularly requests information from the component that the first programmer is working on. In this particular situation, the first programmer has finished the application programming interface that it required for the component in question. The second programmer, however, has not notified anyone of whether or not his component is finished. The first programmer is worried because there may not be

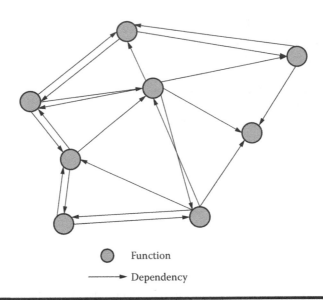

Function

Dependency

Figure 15.6 Visualization sociogram network from Ariadne. (From de Souza, C. R. et al. 2007. Supporting collaborative software development through the visualization of socio-technical dependencies. In *Proceedings of the 2007 International ACM Conference on Supporting Group Work* (Sanibel Island, Florida, USA, November 04–07, 2007). GROUP '07. ACM, New York, 147–156.)

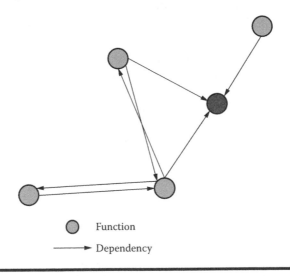

Function

Dependency

Figure 15.7 Manager Awareness View of Ariadne. (From de Souza, C. R. et al. 2007. Supporting collaborative software development through the visualization of socio-technical dependencies. In *Proceedings of the 2007 International ACM Conference on Supporting Group Work* (Sanibel Island, Florida, USA, November 04–07, 2007). GROUP '07. ACM, New York, 147–156.)

much time to alter the API for her component if integration does not begin soon. There should be a way for the first programmer to tell if the second programmer has begun the integration phase of his workload. Ariadne has a visualization view built in called the "Establishing Dependencies View," which is shown in Figure 15.8. This view allows individual programmers to see their own code and whether or not it is being used. There is a central node for the developer in question with outlying nodes representing the code that he or she has authored. This code is then connected to those other individuals that have used this code or component in some way, explicitly.

In the third scenario, a programmer is working on a component for the client side of the software package. This component is based around the fact that it requests a lot of information from the server side of the software package. The particular component on the server side that is affected is being written and coded by a second programmer. There exists a software component between the client and server sides of the software project that is being implemented by the second programmer while the first programmer uses this interface heavily. The first programmer, however, is not completely knowledgeable about how to use this interface. The problem arises when we find out that the first programmer has no idea who the

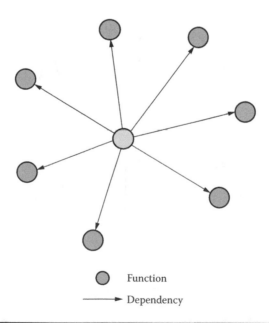

Figure 15.8 Establishing Dependencies View of Ariadne. (From de Souza, C. R. et al. 2007. Supporting collaborative software development through the visualization of socio-technical dependencies. In *Proceedings of the 2007 International ACM Conference on Supporting Group Work* (Sanibel Island, Florida, USA, November 04–07, 2007). GROUP '07. ACM, New York, 147–156.)

second programmer is or how to contact him. The second programmer, likewise, does not know how to contact the person who wrote the framework for the interface to shed some light on some of its issues. The problem gets even worse when we find out that the first programmer has been forced to use a dummy implementation of this interface to this point, so we do not even know if the first programmer's work is compatible with the second programmer's true interface. In Figure 15.9, we have the next visualization view from Ariadne, called the "Hierarchal Static Ordering." In this view, we find a tree of sorts that shows not only the hierarchy of code and components in the software package, but also the authors of such work in its own hierarchal tree. This is extremely beneficial to the users of a multilocation geographical software company.

In the fourth scenario, a programmer is trying to write a particular component for the client side of the software package. In order to fully implement his software component, he needs access to a particular service inside the software package. In this particular situation, the programmer who is responsible for writing the service needed

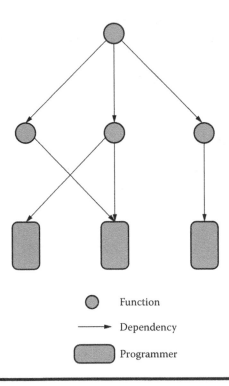

Figure 15.9 Hierarchal Static Ordering View of Ariadne. (From de Souza, C. R. et al. 2007. Supporting collaborative software development through the visualization of socio-technical dependencies. In *Proceedings of the 2007 International ACM Conference on Supporting Group Work* (Sanibel Island, Florida, USA, November 04–07, 2007). GROUP '07. ACM, New York, 147–156.)

is a part of a different design team and has an earlier deadline that does not involve this particular component. Because of this deadline, the service programmer is not being very responsive to the requests from the first programmer. Also, other programmers from multiple teams have been in need of this particular service for a while, and have been making many requests to the responsible programmer, to no avail. The programmers who all need this service and cannot get access to it somehow find each other and realize that they are all in the same predicament. The visualization given for this situation by the Ariadne plug-in is shown in Figure 15.10. It is one of the main design principles of the application that software developers should be able to easily find other developers and programmers who are in similar situations as themselves. This capability gives the software development team as a whole a greater probability of high throughput. An easy way for Ariadne, or any other sociotechnical framework, to make this capability available to programmers is to offer a database system of some kind that offers a simple interface to the sociotechnical dependencies of the entire collaborative software development package. The visualization provided by Ariadne that offers this view, the view shown in Figure 15.10, is called the "Finding Similar Developers view." This view is similar to the Establishing Dependencies View that was built for the second scenario of the paper in question. However, instead of associating programmers with the code that they have a dependency with, the Finding Similar Developers View associates programmers with other developers that they may need to associate with based on the sociotechnical dependencies of the software development

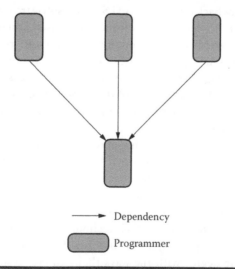

Figure 15.10 Finding Similar Developers View of Ariadne. (From de Souza, C. R. et al. 2007. Supporting collaborative software development through the visualization of socio-technical dependencies. In *Proceedings of the 2007 International ACM Conference on Supporting Group Work* (Sanibel Island, Florida, USA, November 04–07, 2007). GROUP '07. ACM, New York, 147–156.)

project. Information about each dependency is stored in the edge between any two programmers listed in the view.

As evidenced throughout the description and visualization of the Ariadne plug-in for the Eclipse development environment, the design process is centered on the idea of visually seeing the social dependencies as well as the technical dependencies for the programmer or developer in question to process the information in a more concise manner. In contrast to the STeP_IN framework, discussed earlier, Ariadne focuses more on compacting the dependency information into one screen so that the programmers and developers involved are not forced to search for this data to make timely decisions.

15.6 COTS-Based Systems or Customized Software [5,6]

In the case of both the STeP_IN framework as well as the framework for the Ariadne plug-in for the Eclipse development environment, the design goal is to assist programmers who are working on software from the ground up. These types of programmers work in a collaborative software development atmosphere to create customized software. Customized software consists of programs and code that is specially designed for a client or group of clients to perform one task or group of tasks only. Another method of designing software that is much less expensive but does have its drawbacks is called COTS-based software design. COTS-based software design refers to commercial-off-the-shelf based systems. These types of systems lean more toward software component reuse and recycling rather than a completely new "ground-up" implementation. There are pros and cons to both types of software package design, and many different occasions in the software development world call for either type of development process. However, for certain situations and certain groups of programmers, there are clear-cut decisions on which process should be used.

Many developing countries have chosen to have their software and technological needs filled by commercial-off-the-shelf based software development. A developing country is defined as a country that is poor and whose citizens are mainly agricultural workers but has the desire to become more advanced socially, economically, and technologically. Thus, a developing country has extremely limited resources that can be pushed toward their technological infrastructure. Because of their lack of resources, in-place systems, and qualified manpower, these countries are restricted to some degree with the ways they can create software systems and packages. Commercial-off-the-shelf based software systems involve picking out certain smaller components of the desired system that have been coded before for other projects, or simply for resale, and are available for a decreased price on the commercial market. These purchased components may be exactly what the buyer is looking for, or they may only qualify halfway, but regardless, the component is able to fit in and work in the new system. Reducing development time and resources and lowering maintenance costs are just a few ways that commercial-off-the-shelf based software development can drastically help a developing country today. The information technology support for such a country is able to be jump-started by this kind of development process very easily and quickly.

To this end, some research has been done on a framework called STACE that is described as a "generic sociotechnical framework for COTS software evaluation and selection" [6]. This research is aimed at helping potential programmers and developers who participate in collaborative software design truly examine the relationships between separate elements and components of the overall design. This packaged framework also helps the users to see the impact that their decisions in the commercial-off-the-shelf selection process will have on the final software evaluation. This framework helps users to successfully implement and plan their commercial-off-the-shelf based software systems.

Commercial-off-the-shelf based software development, also referred to as component-based software engineering, might be better defined as the methodical selection and integration of reusable software into a larger software package. To truly understand how this type of system could work and be beneficial to engineers, programmers, and developers worldwide, one must be able to see that many parts of software systems are redundant or appear commonly throughout the collaborative software development world. These components that appear over and over again throughout software components should be able to be written and composed only once, and then used over and over again, effectively recycling the code in an extremely efficient way.

Though there are many similarities between commercial-off-the-shelf based software development and component-based software engineering, there are many differences as well. In Figure 15.11, we have a table that can show the major differences between the two types of collaborative software development. As can be seen in Figure 15.11, the main differences in CBSE design and CBS design all come back to the fact that CBS design must at least partially comprise COTS components, where CBSE design does not have that requirement.

From Figure 15.11, a number of similarities, as well as differences, in Component-Based Software Engineering (CBSE) and Commercial-off-the-shelf Based System Design (CBS) can be seen. The first difference that can be seen is in the first column of the table. When dealing with the number of components in a software system, CBSE and CBS differ, but only slightly. Both of these design theories use the idea that multiple components can be a part of a larger software system. This means that any given software package should be able to be broken down into smaller subsections, or components, that perform smaller tasks inside the larger functioning of the system. However, CBS design promotes the idea that if the function of the overall system as a whole is on a small enough scale, then the software system can be scaled down to only include one component. In other words, it is unnecessary for a software system to be designed to be more complex than it needs to be.

	Number of components	Use of COTS software	Maintenance requirements
CBSE	Integrates many different components	Can contain all in-house components	Must maintain components that are used in-house
CBS	Can contain many components, but can also contain one component that solves the problem	Must contain at least one commercial-off-the-shelf component	May not be responsible for maintenance if components are COTS

Figure 15.11   Differences in CBSE design and CBS design. (From Kunda, Douglas. A socio-technical approach to selecting software supporting COTS-based systems. University of York (2001). Available from http://www.cs.york.ac.uk/ftpdir/reports/2002/YCST/01/YCST-2002-01.pdf.)

The idea of breaking a software package down is shown in Figure 15.12. As can be seen, a large component, such as the one on top, could be broken down into several different components. Also, a smaller-scale component such as the one on the bottom in Figure 15.12 could be only broken into one small component because of the limited functionality of the system itself.

The biggest difference that can be seen between CBSE and CBS methodologies is seen in the second column of the table in Figure 15.11. In the CBSE model of designing software packages, it is likely, and actually quite common, that a software package will comprise only components that are built in-house. The main guidelines behind the CBSE methodology simply coordinate the breaking down of a larger software package system into smaller subsystems, or components, as previously discussed. It is common for all components that make up a software package to be designed and built in-house. It is not against regulation or methodology to purchase outside components, but this is done very infrequently. On the other hand, for a software design process to be deemed a CBS design process, the final software package must contain at least one commercial-off-the-shelf component. This component can be all-encompassing, meaning the entire software package is only broken down into one component, or the components can be limited to only a few pieces of the system as a whole. Regardless of the type of component breakdown, in order for a software design process to be a CBS process, the final software package must contain at least one commercial-off-the-shelf component.

15.7 Conclusion

The world of software development has changed considerably since the first few lines of code were written. It has evolved from a single programmer in a room to

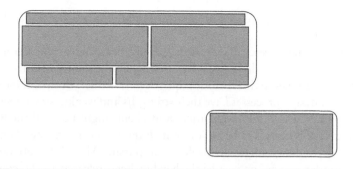

Figure 15.12   Component breakdown of a larger system. (From Kunda, Douglas. A socio-technical approach to selecting software supporting COTS-based systems. University of York (2001). Available from http://www.cs.york.ac.uk/ftpdir/reports/2002/YCST/01/YCST-2002-01.pdf.)

many programmers, young and old, far and near, who all collaborate on the same design idea. One of the most important aspects of these projects is the management of the inherent knowledge of programmers who have experience in certain areas. This chapter has shown that different groups of programmers can be handled in many different ways, some more efficient than others.

The first way that one can begin to solve these problems regarding groups of programmers and their throughput is to come up with a concrete way of determining which tasks are interrelated and which tasks have a data dependency of some degree. Similar to interrelated tasks, programmers who have connections regarding the functionality of their assigned workloads should be managed in great detail to increase throughput throughout the software package design process. The total matrix of data, function, and programmer interconnections should be found in order to have a definitive idea of what direction to begin grouping programmers and engineers and their respective workload assignments. The less the interaction between different groups of analysts and programmers, the more the time available for a particular group or bundle of groups to work together on their interrelated assignments. This is the goal we are striving for at most any cost.

This chapter has focused on two main implementations, reducing interconnections and making the connections that do exist less prominent. The stand-alone STeP_IN framework and the Ariadne framework built for the Eclipse environment are both very successful solutions to the problem at hand. Not only do these frameworks help to smooth the transition of knowledge transfer and data interconnection collaborative development, but they also keep the programmers' social ecosystem in mind. The idea of allowing the programmer to help at will is prevalent in both frameworks. Both of these systems allow the programmer to get help in synchronization with his or her normal programming style because of the environmental integrations and the visual aids that accompany them.

Also, this chapter covered the great debate over whether or not a commercial-off-the-shelf based system design is better than a simple component-based system design. The final answer to this rhetorical question is: neither. Both of these software package system design processes have their strengths and weaknesses, depending on the current situation that the programmer and client might be in. If the final software package that is needed to be built is quite large and cumbersome, then component-based system design might be the design to pursue. Also, if the software design package is similar to one, on any level, that has been released in the commercial market before, then it could possibly be wise to purchase the commercial-off-the-shelf software, in some quantity, and merge it with some level of in-house software for the final software package. There are many different situations that could bring a client or firm to use one or both of these methodologies; there are many correct uses of any combination of the two.

In conclusion, many efforts have been made, in the academic world and elsewhere, that make it much easier to group programmers and engineers together in ways that can possibly increase the overall throughput of the group. This increase in productivity can be due to a mathematical speedup from data and functional dependencies or a certain framework that is tailored to the current work environment that is used to produce the software package.

References

1. Björkstrand, R.V. and J.A. Lallimo. Socio-technical knowledge management—Connecting 3D-CAD design tools and designers' social environment. *18th International Conference on Production Research*. Available from: http://www.isv.hut.fi/files/Socio-technical%20knowledge%20management.pdf 2005.
2. Cataldo, Marcelo et al. Socio-Technical Congruence: A Framework for Assessing the Impact of Technical and Work Dependencies on Software Development. Institute for Software Research (2008). Technical Report, see: http://reports-archive.adm.cs.cmu.edu/anon/isr2008/CMU-ISR-08-104.pdf.
3. Ye, Yunwen et al. A Socio-Technical Framework for Supporting Programmers. *6th Joint Meeting of the European Software Engineering Conference and the Symposium on the Foundations of Software Engineering (2007)*: Pages 351–360.
4. de Souza, C. R., Quirk, S., Trainer, E., and Redmiles, D. F. 2007. Supporting collaborative software development through the visualization of socio-technical dependencies. In *Proceedings of the 2007 International ACM Conference on Supporting Group Work* (Sanibel Island, Florida, USA, November 04–07, 2007). GROUP '07. ACM, New York, 147–156.

5. Herrmann, T., Hoffmann, M., Jahnke, I., Kienle, A., Kunau, G., Loser, K., and Menold, N. 2003. Concepts for usable patterns of groupware applications. In *Proceedings of the 2003 International ACM SIGGROUP Conference on Supporting Group Work* (Sanibel Island, Florida, USA, November 09–12, 2003). GROUP '03. ACM, New York, 349–358.

6. Kunda, Douglas. A socio-technical approach to selecting software supporting COTS-based systems. University of York (2001). Available from http://www.cs.york.ac.uk/ftpdir/reports/2002/YCST/01/YCST-2002-01.pdf.

Chapter 16

Virtual Communities Based on Sociotechnical Systems

Keli Kohoue, Sadith Osseni, and Fei Hu

Contents

16.1 Introduction [2,6]

We might want to call the world we currently live an ensemble of "virtual communities." Computers have enabled the fast creation of diverse communities. Message boards, chat rooms, user groups, and blogs are currently the most active Internet communities.

Virtual communities are originally intended for a variety of needs, varying from communities of interest (intellectual Web sites), communities of relationship (Twitter, MySpace, etc.), gaming communities (e.g., in World of Warcraft, Second Life), or communities of transaction to peer-to-peer communities (eBay, Amazon, etc.). Web 2.0 mechanisms are also boosting the development of virtual communities (used for cell phones or PDAs) and the role of user-generated content within virtual communities.

The benefit of these communities is made obvious by the impact they have on the creation of information and its diffusion. As an example, these days, blogs are rapidly turning into a major source of information on a diversity of topics. These online gatherings are very appealing for members and operators. A side benefit of many of these online communities is their ability to sustain socialization and enable the participants to stand out.

It is also important to note that virtual communities are not standardized or uniform; they diverge extensively depending on the topic, purpose, and benefits. As far as the nature of the information mechanism is concerned, scientists are examining the interaction arrangements and methods, social structures, transaction plans, organization of features, business models, and design characteristics of information mechanisms and services for virtual communities. Community members cooperate by means of digital media and add value via feedback, analysis, and suggestions. Other important matters are expectation, network outcome, operation fees, and the design of applications as well as the generation of alterations or improvements. *Wisdom of crowds*, *collective intelligence*, and *crowdsourcing* are important concepts or buzzwords describing mechanisms around user-generated content in virtual communities. But how did it all start? Is there a powerful organization underlying the management of virtual communities? Could it be the government? In this chapter, we will attempt to answer those questions.

16.2 Managing Virtual Knowledge Networks [5]

To formulate the theory of knowledge creation, it is important to realize that the discursive formation of "self" employing mediational means is a source of knowledge creation. We need to understand the relationship between such a source and self-understanding and understanding of others, as well as the specific characteristics of virtuality [5].

The intriguing question that arises is, "How is knowledge created in a virtual context?" Knowledge generation in the real world as well as in an implicit context should be understood from the standpoint of public interaction. Social interaction in an implicit perspective as an ingredient of knowledge generation is referred by ICTs (information and communication technologies) such as cell phones, laptops, PDAs, etc. Language develops into something in the form of information symbolically coded. It is not unusual to see written language turning into, for lack of better words, a texting method of communication. The text in turn, gets transmitted by media deprived of context, and when the message is received, it goes into the same cycle where it gets recontextualized, reshuffled, or restructured based on already-gained information.

Self-understanding and acceptance of others, illustrated in theories of knowledge generation, are influenced by the type and amount of theoretical media-like characters that can be used as tools to internalize unfamiliar knowledge. Some

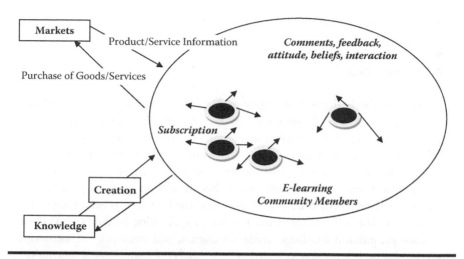

Figure 16.1 E-learning communities, virtual markets, and knowledge creation. (From Schrott, G. and Beimborn, D. 2003. Managing virtual knowledge networks: Topology and performance. In *Proceedings of the 2003 International ACM SIGGROUP Conference on Supporting Group Work* (Sanibel Island, Florida, November 09–12, 2003). GROUP '03. ACM, New York, 198–204.)

people would argue that in an implicit case self-understanding is fashioned, as an element of knowledge generation, through a tapering range of nonverbal figurative prompts that can be passed on. Others would suggest that self-understanding and acceptance of others are in the mind's eye as the person grows to be able to build personas in the language used while profiting from the lack of other visual prompts. The significance of verbal communication is noted in implicit surroundings in spite of the greater vagueness created concerning its sense.

Figure 16.1 illustrates the basic idea of knowledge creation [5].

16.3 Social Network Analysis [4]

Social network analysis is founded on the meaning of relations among cooperating members. The social network standpoint covers hypotheses, representations, and functions that are articulated in terms of relational perceptions or procedures. Besides, with rising attention, social network analysis has turned into an agreement about the central ideologies essential to the network point of view. Network analysis is the study of social relations among a set of actors. It is a field of study, a set of phenomena or data that we seek to understand. In order to work in this field, network scientists have come up with a set of distinctive hypothetical perspectives. Some of the main features of these perspectives are

- Greater attention on interactions between users rather than each individual's characteristics
- Wisdom of dependence
- Evolving effects

Network hypothesis depends on systems hypothesis and difficulty hypothesis. Social networks are also distinguished by a typical methodology involving techniques for gathering data, arithmetical analysis, illustrated representation, etc.

The important characteristic of social network analysis is its focus on the organization of interactions, varying from informal acquaintances to close liaisons, or in layman's term, from friends to best friends. Social network analysis presumes that connections between people are crucial. Social network analysis is becoming increasingly useful in the social sciences and has found application in domains as diverse as psychology, physical condition, trade association, and electronic infrastructures. Moreover, lately, interest has centered on the study of management networks to strengthen relationships inside and outside groups, associations, and similar systems.

The field of network analysis is typically criticized for its practical and less theoretical nature. Typically, social network analysis relies on surveys and discussions to collect information about the relations within a distinct group. The responses gathered are then analyzed. The information-gathering and examination procedures offer an initial base for the understanding of advance knowledge flows, which may involve recasting social relationships.

Social network analysis requires sifting through a surplus of knowledge with capable social network analysis computer programs. It needs participative and interpretative methods to the explanation and examination of social networks, with a focus on the easiest and most practical fundamentals. Key phases of the essential procedure will naturally require experienced personnel to recognize the network of people, organizations, and entities to be investigated. Such tasks could be accomplished by gathering background information, for example, by meeting and discussing with senior executives and important staff, to comprehend detailed requirements and matters. Concretely to say, we could describe the purpose, elucidate the range of the investigation, plan the questionnaire, keep queries short, direct, and to the point (both unrestricted and restricted questions can be used), investigate the persons, groups, and members in the network to recognize the relationships and information flows between them, employ a social network analysis tool to clearly work out the network, analyze the charts and difficulties and opportunities pointed out earlier using dialogues and workshops, propose and implement actions to bring about desired changes, and recreate a map of the network once more after an appropriate interval.

A practical difficulty with network analysis in history has been the inability to test theories in a more precise and accurate manner, because the information acquired is by its very nature "autocorrelated," which, of course, violates the supposition of independence (arbitrary sampling) built into the majority of traditional statistical surveys. However, with the advent of combination tests, this is much less of a predicament at the moment. An ongoing problem is the shortage of enough computing resources to deal with large datasets. It is frequently a challenge to constrict a social network. If we are looking at needle-sharing among drug users, we can artificially compress the network at some arbitrary border line, such as an urban center or district, but this would misrepresent the information. Yet we should not let the network get so large that it becomes unmanageable.

16.4 Mining Hidden Communities in Heterogeneous Social Networks [1]

It is essential to understand and explore the concept of community mining in more complex and diverse social networks. On account of its rapid growth, the social network becomes a center of interest for most people, especially researchers who want to know what leads people to join a social network and what makes a social network active and worldwide in reach. In fact, community mining is an important tool that will help us to understand those parameters. Obviously, assuming that the social network is unirelational and "mining results are independent of the user's needs or preferences" will leave out precious hidden community information.

Nowadays, there are a huge number of social networks, and it is certain that each network provides users some features that others do not have; moreover, a client **A** may have a distinct relationship with clients **B** and client **C**, and user **C** may also have a different relationship with user **D** and the same relationship with **A** or **F**. This means that each user creates a small network inside the colossal social network, depending on his or her interests, desires, and favorites. Therefore, the new approach to analyzing social network should include all those factors since, as stated earlier, the social network itself is becoming a multirelational social network.

As stated earlier, one of the main focuses here is to determine some criteria (maybe formulas) that will allow us to know whether a social network is strong or not. Because there are different relations between users in the social network, it might be wise to check the strength and importance of those relations. This leads researchers to recommend a mathematical model for relation extraction and selection. The main idea of this algorithm is to model the problem as an optimization problem, which means that once the algorithm is built, it can be applied to any social network to know how influential it is.

For this approach, each relation will be represented by a graph with a weight matrix, and each element of the matrix illustrates its relation strength between the two corresponding objects. In order to make the algorithm more efficient, researchers added the feature extraction problem to the relation extraction problem. In fact, the feature extraction problem is a way of reducing the dimensions of our data. Sometimes, we may have much data, but a lack of information; hence, the original data will be reduced to a representative set of vectors (only relevant information from the input data will be considered for performing the task). The relation extraction will be used whenever there is a clear relationship between clients or users.

In this section, we will discuss the procedure for relation extraction, present some experimental outcomes, explain how to solve the problem and, finally, propose some ideas and hints for potential work in that area.

The goal of social network analysis is to measure the relationship and information flows between individuals, groups, and people inside the network. We have to keep in mind that one of our important objectives is to discover a linear combination of relations that best describes movements or actions taking place between users in the social network.

It is undeniable that there are many relations in a social network. The way those relations are set or established will tell us what kind of social network we are dealing with. Furthermore, they will help us know whether or not the social network is dynamic. To understand the relation extraction problem, we will consider two examples.

In the first example (Figure 16.2), let us consider a network that consists of four objects, with assume that any users linked to those four objects are part of the community. Suppose that in that social network, we have eight other nodes surrounding the four objects. Network A has two nodes connected to the four objects, with the remaining nodes are linked together. Also, let a network B be designed as one node connected to two objects, another node linked to two objects, and the last six nodes connected to one another. Finally, let us assume a network C with two nodes connected to each object. Obviously, we can see that network A best represents the community structure. In design A, the four objects are grouped together with some nodes, creating a strong relation between users. Designs B and C, on the other hand, do not have their four objects assembled

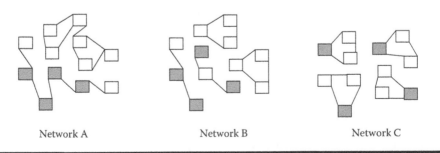

Network A   Network B   Network C

Figure 16.2   Relationships in networks. (From Cai, D. et al. 2005. Mining hidden community in heterogeneous social networks. In *Proceedings of the 3rd International Workshop on Link Discovery* (Chicago, Illinois, August 21–25, 2005). LinkKDD '05. ACM, New York, 58–65.)

together, so they cannot be used to determine the community configuration. It might be necessary to point out that design C is the worst one, since all the four objects are spread out in the network. In Figure 16.2, the shaded nodes represent the four objects.

Now, let us consider another situation with a more complex query (see Figure 16.3). Suppose we have two yellow objects (in circles), two red objects (in squares), and eight nodes in the social network. The two yellow objects and the two red objects belong to different communities. Let us consider a network A with the two red and two yellow objects connected together with two nodes and the remaining six nodes linked together. Let us design a network B with each of the four objects spread out, but with each of them linked to two regular nodes. Lastly, let us have a network C with two yellow objects connected to one node, the two red objects linked to two other nodes, and the leftover nodes linked to one another. In this situation, we can say that design C is the suitable one to discover the community structure. However, designs A and B have either both yellow and red objects linked together with some nodes or spread out, so they will be ineffective for our studies. The following diagram is actually the representation of the three networks A, B, and C discussed earlier.

Network A   Network B   Network C

The two foregoing examples show that community mining depends on what kind of relations users have between objects; also, we observe that a user's query may be very flexible, which supports our new idea that community mining methods need to concentrate on the multirelational network.

Since one of our main aims is to determine a linear combination that best describes the community structure, we might find some formulas for the relation extraction problem. Let V be a set of nodes and E_i a set of edges. From that, we can define a set of graphs $G_i = (V, E_i)$, where $i = 1, ..., n$. In addition, let M_i represents

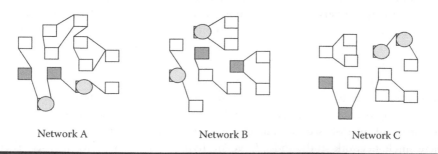

Network A   Network B   Network C

Figure 16.3 Networks with more complex query. (From Cai, D. et al. 2005. Mining hidden community in heterogeneous social networks. In *Proceedings of the 3rd International Workshop on Link Discovery* (Chicago, Illinois, August 21–25, 2005). LinkKDD '05. ACM, New York, 58–65.)

the weights matrix associated with G_i. M_i is defined according to the relation strength of two nodes. Similarly, the hidden relation can be represented by **G'** (**V, E'**) and its weight **M'**. There are two major constraints:

■ The bond between intracommunity nodes needs to be strong and more important as well.
■ Simultaneously, the connection between intercommunity nodes has to be as weak as possible.

If the weight on the edge is set to be **1** whenever a relation is made between nodes, the relation between the labeled nodes can be defined by the following:

$M_{ij} = 1$, when nodes **i** and **j** have an identical label and **0** otherwise.

When it is uncertain whether or not two objects belong to the similar community, an alternative M_{ij} formula is provided, and it is defined by $M_{ij} = $ **Prob** (**x_i** and **x_j** *belong to the same community*). Finally, after a series of mathematical computations, the extracted relation formula was found and can be identified as

$$M_{ext} = \sum A_i M_{ii}$$

where **i** can be any value between **1** and **4** and $A = [a_1, a_2, ..., an]^T$.

We all know that multiple social networks are composed of complicated, interconnected, and multiple graphs, which means that a huge amount of data need to be gathered. It is a very tough task since the social network is dynamic, and a user in such a network has a multiple relations with others. However, this network represents the life we are living (reality), so developing multinetwork mining algorithms based on users' example queries is a suitable approach to solving the problem.

From the network analysis, a weighted matrix was derived, which is a grouping of various existing networks. It is important to figure out that derivation, since it allows one to understand the hidden network even though the ideas behind it are complex.

It is important to realize that there are multiple and various social networks, and the blend of such multirelational network may create significant new relationships, which may be useful for users. Moreover, it is important to emphasize that the new approach to social network and community mining was based on multinetwork and query-based analysis in contrast to the long-established and incomplete single-network study. Indeed, we are living in a social network where there are several relations between users and objects, so the new approach needs to match this reality. One can say that the query-based relation extraction and community mining will be a tool applied to many network issues and will definitely lead to new applications in social network analysis.

16.5 Macroscopic Study of Social Networks [3]

Since the 1990s many researchers have been studying social network theory due to its rapid growth. In the earlier phase, researchers focused on small networks in various computer-supported collaborative learning (CSCL) environments. Their network investigations were exhaustive and based on assumptions of seeing the social network as a unirelational network. Unfortunately, their study results are incomplete since their analyses were based on short-range networks. Several important characteristics of social networks (Internet, phone call networks, World Wide Web, country road maps, electricity transmission network, etc.) are left out of such networks, such as detection of the network type, formation of giant clusters, and network properties.

It is unquestionable that the CSCL environments offer many applications to the user. Web-based/online discussion forum, e-mail, chat room, NetMeeting, video calls, etc., are some of the tools that are accessible to any member of the network. However, the actual study focuses on Web-based discussion forums because all participants' communication information can be recorded and messages can be recovered easily without "additional efforts for hardware or software modification."

Suppose that N is a set of nodes and R the set of relations between the nodes or objects. From this assumption, we can come up with another set called $G(N,R)$, which is basically a mathematical model of a network. If P represents a set of participants and M a set of messages posted in a discussion forum, we can build another network called $N = \{P,M\}$, which is the network for the discussion forum. We assume that the discussion is engaged by one participant (a single node), and this is what usually occurs in real life. Hence, let us call S the relationship set that means "who submits/posts that message." Moreover, the member who starts the conversation may post many messages or topics, but we do not assume that many participants post starting discussion messages since forum discussions do not work that way. According to the article [3], it is a one-to-many mapping from P to M. Let us consider the basic network $G_b(\{P,M\}, S)$, where there is no intrarelation between elements inside the set P or the set M. Then the question is, what is the right way to allow communication within elements in set P and what are the implications of studying those linkages in order to understand CSCL?

For a better understanding of the questions raised above, we used an idea of Newman, a researcher who works on several large-scale networks (up to 1.5 million nodes). In fact, he stated that two researchers are socially linked if they have published at least one paper together. In our online discussion forum case, there is a always a member who starts the conversation or posts an issue, and the other participants give their points of view. From that point, it can be said that the topic starter and the repliers are socially linked since they have been reciprocally exchanging ideas. Then, we can introduce another type of network called the collaborative learning network $G_c(P,M_t)$, where M_t is the relationship set representing all the submissions of messages in order to show the existing co-discussion of a specific topic by various members.

For building the basic network G_b and the collaborative learning network G_e, the following procedures were followed:

- Recover all the names of the participants from every message, and for each topic put them in the same line. The "HAS Centre Browser" is a Windows-based program that will routinely help us to accomplish this task.
- All the members' names are sorted, put in an Excel file, and tagged with unique sequence numbers.
- All the names of the participants are now changed into the unique number labels, and this is done by programming. The idea here is to put the names in an appropriate input format that can be used in any social network programs.
- Using the UCINET programs, diverse network statistics can be pulled out, and network graphs can be drawn.

An experiment was conducted from November 1, 2004, to November 14, 2004, to better understand the online discussion forum. Indeed, with the HAS Centre Browser, they pulled out messages from 36 forums, and we found 24,384 topics with 51,724 replies and 53,070 counts of members. The highest number of replies in a specific topic was 128. The idea here is to provide some formulas and graphs that best describe the distribution of replies and the distribution of views in all forums.

The following graph (Figure 16.4) shows the relationship between the frequency distribution and the number of replies for individual topics submitted in all the 36 forums.

The Y-axis for this graph is chosen to be logarithmic because the frequency numbers are a combination of both higher and lower numbers; moreover, selecting a logarithmic Y-axis will allow a better interpretation of their results. Also, they used an exponential trendline, and it is represented by a straight line in our figure. Note from this graph that most data fall along a straight line; hence, they folllow the exponential distribution, whose probability density function $P(k) = \lambda * e^{(-\lambda * k)}$, where $\lambda = 0.266$ represents the best-fitted straight line we can get from the figure. This implies that in an online discussion forum, the probability of having ignored (unreplied) messages is very low, and the average messages answered is close to $1/\lambda = 3.76$.

Now, we investigate the relationship between the number of topic viewers and the messages submitted in a Web-based discussion environment. This relationship will help us understand conversations going on inside the forum. Figure 16.5 shows the graph of the distribution of views in all forums.

After some studies, researchers discovered that the data followed an unsual kind of network distribution called the lognormal distribution. It can be represented by

$$P(k) = \frac{1}{k * s * \sqrt{(2 * \pi)}} * e^{\frac{\ln(k-m)^2}{2S^2}}$$

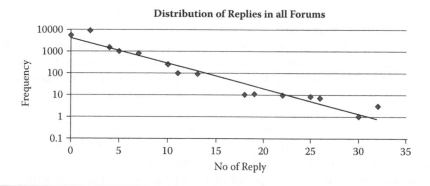

Figure 16.4 Distribution of replies in forums. (From Yeung, Y. 2005. Macroscopic study of the social networks formed in web-based discussion forums. In *Proceedings of the 2005 Conference on Computer Support for Collaborative Learning: Learning 2005: The Next 10 Years!* (Taipei, Taiwan, May 30–June 04, 2005). Computer Support for Collaborative Learning. International Society of the Learning Sciences, 727–731.)

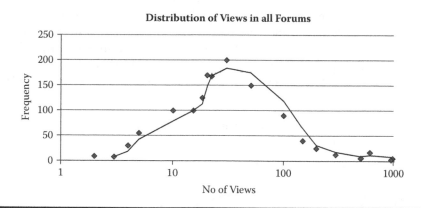

Figure 16.5 Distribution of views in forums. (From Yeung, Y. 2005. Macroscopic study of the social networks formed in web-based discussion forums. In *Proceedings of the 2005 Conference on Computer Support for Collaborative Learning: Learning 2005: The Next 10 Years!* (Taipei, Taiwan, May 30–June 04, 2005). Computer Support for Collaborative Learning. International Society of the Learning Sciences, 727–731.)

where $M = 4.3$ and $S = 0.92$. This implies that for each set of messages submitted around a certain topic, there will be most likely $e^{(m-s^2/2)} = 113$ viewers, or an average of $e^{(m-s^2/2)} = 32$ viewers. It is inportant to emphasize that the number of viewers will increase as long as the Web-based discussion exists.

Finally, for studying the relationship between the forum participants, a smaller collaborative learning network was constructed using the UCINET and PAJEk software. The network itself had 4 forums and contained 9327 topics with 3214 participants in total. The goal here was to determine what kind of network distribution can be generated from participants who posted at least one message from a specific topic. This will help us to understand the cluster formation in our social network. Figure 16.6 is the graph of distribution of co-discussants in our experiment. Both X- and Y-axis are logarithmic scales, and we realized that the power trendline was the best fit for these data.

It is clear from the graph that almost all the data converged to a straight line. It can then be said that these data follow a power-law form distribution $p(k)$ close to $1/k^n$, where $n = 1.20$ for the best fit of the straight line.

In summary, this section explored and examined social networks structured in online discussion forums. Among numerous key channels such as NetMeeting, phone calls, e-mail, and others, online discussion was selected for the study because it is easier to gather participants' information and messages without making hardware and software changes. A platform of analyzing online discussion forums was outlined, and some results were obtained. For instance, it is found that the number of responses on a specific topic follows a power distribution, while the number of views follows a lognormal distribution. Moreover, the study proves that the number of co-discussants follows a power-law distribution. Even though some interesting results have been found, more research needs to be done for a complete understanding of CSCL networks. More importantly, software needs to be developed for allowing efficient extraction of network attributes on a large-scale network. Finally, it will also be beneficial to study forums in other Web

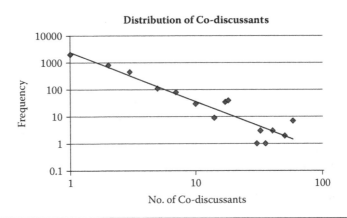

Figure 16.6 Distribution of co-discussants. (From Yeung, Y. 2005. Macroscopic study of the social networks formed in web-based discussion forums. In *Proceedings of the 2005 Conference on Computer Support for Collaborative Learning: Learning 2005: The Next 10 Years!* **(Taipei, Taiwan, May 30–June 04, 2005). Computer Support for Collaborative Learning. International Society of the Learning Sciences, 727–731.)**

sites different from CSCL environments to establish the global dimension of our network characteristics.

16.6 Conclusion

The perceptions of network analysis and communally semitransparent systems are significant for the formation of real practical knowledge, wealth, and online societies. The stones of modernism are lying everywhere around us, from Google's Backward Links to AOL's Buddy Lists to Amazon's Purchase Circles to the incestuous source links of Blogdex. Social networks offer an influential generalization of the arrangement and dynamics of assorted types of group or group-to-technology interaction. Web 2.0 has facilitated Web-based societies and social networks (such as Facebook, MySpace, and Hi5) facilitate collaboration among different communities.

References

1. Cai, D., Shao, Z., He, X., Yan, X., and Han, J. 2005. Mining hidden community in heterogeneous social networks. In *Proceedings of the 3rd International Workshop on Link Discovery* (Chicago, Illinois, August 21–25, 2005). LinkKDD '05. ACM, New York, 58–65.
2. Backstrom, L., Huttenlocher, D., Kleinberg, J., and Lan, X. 2006. Group formation in large social networks: Membership, growth, and evolution. In *Proceedings of the 12th ACM SIGKDD International Conference on Knowledge Discovery and Data Mining* (Philadelphia, PA, USA, August 20–23, 2006). KDD '06. ACM, New York, 44–54.
3. Yeung, Y. 2005. Macroscopic study of the social networks formed in web-based discussion forums. In *Proceedings of the 2005 Conference on Computer Support for Collaborative Learning: Learning 2005: The Next 10 Years!* (Taipei, Taiwan, May 30–June 04, 2005). Computer Support for Collaborative Learning. International Society of the Learning Sciences, 727–731.
4. Wellman, B. 1996. For a social network analysis of computer networks: A sociological perspective on collaborative work and virtual community. In *Proceedings of the 1996 ACM SIGCPR/SIGMIS Conference on Computer Personnel Research* (Denver, Colorado, United States, April 11–13, 1996). SIGCPR '96. ACM, New York, 1–11.
5. Schrott, G. and Beimborn, D. 2003. Managing virtual knowledge networks: Topology and performance. In *Proceedings of the 2003 International ACM SIGGROUP Conference on Supporting Group Work* (Sanibel Island, Florida, November 09–12, 2003). GROUP '03. ACM, New York, 198–204.
6. Gurzick, D. and Lutters, W. G. 2009. Towards a design theory for online communities. In *Proceedings of the 4th International Conference on Design Science Research in Information Systems and Technology* (Philadelphia, Pennsylvania, May 07–08, 2009). DESRIST' 09. ACM, New York, 1–20.

Index